EN FRANÇAIS

EN FRANÇAIS

French for Communication

Third Edition

Dana Carton

Anthony Caprio
The American University

Heinle & Heinle Publishers, Inc.
Boston, Massachusetts 02210 U.S.A.

Editor-in-chief: Stanley Galek
Production Manager: Erek Smith
Developmental Editor: Carlyle Carter
Production Editor: Elinor Y. Chamas
Copyeditor: Jane Wall-Meinike

Cover and text design: Carol H. Rose
Cover photograph: Lawrence Gartel/Photo Researchers, Inc.

Manufactured in the United States of America.

ISBN 0-8384-1285-8

10 9 8 7

TABLE DES MATIÈRES

————— ENTRACTE 12 —————

PREFACE

EN FRANÇAIS: French for Communication, Third Edition presents a complete program of study for mastering the essential elements of French. Originally designed for beginning courses, it has also proven successful in intermediate level courses that emphasize communicative skills. By using everyday situations of immediate practical interest, *EN FRANÇAIS* enables students to understand, speak, read and write French in context from the very beginning.

This new edition retains those features of the earlier editions that have proven effective in encouraging a rapid and thorough acquisition of contemporary spoken French. *EN FRANÇAIS* now provides materials for development of *all four skills* in a greatly revised and expanded context. The new subtitle, *French for Communication* (earlier editions were subtitled *Practical Conversational French*), reflects the more inclusive nature of this program.

What is new about the Third Edition?

Streamlined and Rebalanced Text   *EN FRANÇAIS* has been reorganized and streamlined into twelve Chapters and twelve Entractes that satisfy more effectively the needs of the contemporary language course. This reorganization provides a better balance of grammatical and lexical components for language programs proceeding sequentially through the text. Shortened **Dialogues** permit students to assimilate more fully the linguistic information presented.

New Entractes   Reoriented and expanded, the Entractes of the Third Edition have become a vital, integral element of the total language program. They provide a wealth of functional vocabulary, integrated into lively, communicative activities that focus on personalized responses.

New Exercises   *EN FRANÇAIS* has been enriched throughout with a variety of new communicative and situational exercises. Each segment of the text includes oral and written exercises. This new presentation allows immediate application of each informational module. On-page explanations regarding classroom implementation of the communicative exercises facilitate in-class utilization of these unique conversational activities.

Improved Illustration Program   Photographs and realia now serve two major functions. Some provide the basis for engaging pedagogical exercises. Others enhance a range of cultural and linguistic points in a manner directly related to the thematic content of each lesson.

Linguistic and Cultural Notes   This new feature, related thematically to each Chapter and Entracte, provides illustrated information on a variety of cultural and linguistic topics.

NEW ANCILLARY MATERIALS have been created to supplement the text and support the goals of this expanded program:

Tape program   A totally revised and expanded tape program offers exercises for oral practice and aural comprehension.

Laboratory Manual, Workbook and Readings   The Laboratory Manual that accompanies the new tape program features innovative oral exercises that allow personalized responses. Aural comprehension exercises with unique self-checking devices, structure highlights, *dictées*, and pronunciation drills are also included. The Workbook and Readings provide further reinforcement of materials presented in the text through a variety of written exercises, activities, and contemporary readings.

Instructor's Manual   This manual includes specific suggestions for using the text materials in a variety of course situations, as well as guidelines for testing and an answer key.

Tapescript   A printed version of the tape program is available to instructors.

Organization of the Text

EN FRANÇAIS: French for Communication, consists of twelve Chapters and twelve Entractes, in alternating sequence. Each of these units is a separate entity. This textual organization facilitates independent study and permits each student to assimilate all materials fully. A summary of the components of each Chapter and Entracte follows, with features new to this Third Edition indicated by an asterisk.

Chapter Contents
Each Chapter of *EN FRANÇAIS* centers on a specific real-life situation and contains the following closely interrelated materials:

Proverbe   A French proverb, related to the content of the Chapter, opens each Chapter.

*Lesson Statement   Each Dialogue is now preceded by a lesson statement outlining the practical value of the vocabulary and structures to be presented. By revealing the potential uses of these materials, such introductory statements provide additional motivation.

Dialogue   Unique to this language program, the Dialogue format consists of a main speaker ("Vous"), representing the individual student, and a French-speaking person, interacting in a typical real-life encounter. The use of "Vous" as the main speaker throughout the text enables students to picture themselves in the everyday experiences presented.

Each Dialogue consists of a set of core sentences that are the most common and useful in the given situations. Also provided are "vocabulary blocks" that contain options for varying the basic sentences. This format has the advantage of allowing students to express a wide variety of ideas by mastering only one basic grammatical structure. It also permits a high degree of meaningful personalization of materials through easy substitution of vocabulary items presented on the page.

*Phrases à retenir   This new feature presents selected sentences from the Dialogue recommended for memorization. Mastery of these phrases will assure spontaneous functioning in real-life situations.

*Dialogue Exercises   Following each Dialogue, these new exercises provide oral and written practice with the vocabulary and sentence patterns of the Dialogue. Using only the vocabulary and structures of the Dialogues, these exercises require no familiarity with other portions of the Chapter. They include personalized conversations, improvisations, and review. Dialogue Exercises relate the materials of the Dialogue directly to the individual student and to his or her daily life.

*À Propos: Language and Culture   New to the Third Edition, these richly illustrated sections contain insights into French language and culture. Each item is related to the thematic elements of the given chapter. Aspects of life in France and in francophone countries are highlighted. These sections also contain a popular feature entitled "Borrowed Words," presenting a variety of French terms and expressions directly borrowed by contemporary English.

Verbes Irréguliers   Each chapter presents one or more irregular verbs in a clear, straightforward fashion. The chosen verbs are related to the themes and vocabulary of the given chapter. Accompanying notes explain conjugation peculiarities, orthographic changes and idiomatic uses of the verbs. *Each *verbe irrégulier* is now followed directly by related oral and written exercises that permit students to apply immediately what they have just learned.

Structures   These sections provide a thorough grounding in the fundamentals of French grammar. Illustrations of each grammatical point are drawn from the preceding sections of the chapter. Such modular organization allows students to master the individual structures without having to learn new vocabulary. Succinct, straightforward explanations in English facilitate self-study and individualized instruction. *Each **structure** is now immediately followed by related exercises.

*Synthèse   These new exercises encourage students to strengthen language skills by using all the grammar and vocabulary of the chapter in a creative manner.

Prononciation   These sections cover the basics of contemporary French pronunciation. In keeping with the modular orientation of *EN FRANÇAIS*, examples and practice phrases are drawn entirely from the given chapter. Such capsulized organization allows students to concentrate on the individual sounds, without having to master new vocabulary or grammar.

Projets   Students respond with enthusiasm to these personalized projects, which encourage creative application of the vocabulary and structures of the given lesson. The *Projets* lend themselves to use both as in-class activities or as out-of-class assigned preparations. Many new projects have been added to the Third Edition.

*Activités: Learning by Doing   Students employ highly practical vocabulary in classroom simulations of real-life situations. These exercises are not at all the traditional classroom skit; rather, they have *all* class members participating *simultaneously* in lively classroom activities, such as: going shopping, dining out, asking directions, making a date, and so on. These innovative learning devices build student confidence by encouraging immediate and creative application of language skills in a realistic atmosphere.

Entracte Contents

The sections entitled *Entracte* are briefer, change-of-pace lessons inserted between the longer main chapters. Each Entracte centers on a specific topic, such as numbers, the weather, or the Family. Entracte components include:

Lead-in Question, Response Format, *Sample Response   Each Entracte begins with a lead-in question that relates directly to the student or to his or her daily life. These lead-in questions are grammatically simple, constructed to evoke brief responses in which a variety of substitutions are possible. These lead questions, furthermore, allow a wide range of different reactions, and consequently, for substantial vocabulary acquisition. The lead-in question is used for introduction and practice of the basic Entracte vocabulary. The response format that follows the lead-in question provides students with a straight-forward, conversationally correct sentence structure in which to place their selected replies. A sample response for each lead-in question shows students exactly what is expected in terms of conversational reply.

***Vocabulaire à retenir**   The newly streamlined **Vocabulaire à retenir** lists (alphabetized to facilitate student access) now contain only the most important vocabulary needed for self-expression in the communicative exercises. Vocabulary included in these initial lists has been based on student request frequency. Some Entractes include additional vocabulary presented in comprehensive Resource Lists. The resource lists, when used in conjunction with the initial vocabulary lists, provide an unusual opportunity for all students to express themselves in a truly personalized fashion.

***Springboards for Conversation**   These are personalized questions, answerable by simple, direct substitution of vocabulary from the vocabulary lists into supplied response formats. This special format allows even beginners to express themselves fully and accurately in a personally meaningful fashion.

***Récapitulation**   Vocabulary accumulation by all class members is assured when students use this section to recall what they have learned about classmates and instructor.

***Remarques**   Clarification of related points of grammatical usage is a new feature that frees the instructor from the necessity of referring students to various chapters in the text for explanations of grammar.

***Expansion**   These new exercises develop the Entracte theme vocabulary through a series of personalized conversational questions.

***Vocabulaire utile**   These colloquial phrases and interjections can be used spontaneously by students responding to the Entracte questions.

Each Entracte also includes the following components: **Proverbe**, Lesson Statement, **À Propos:** Language and Culture, **Synthèse, Projets,** and **Activités:** Learning by Doing.

End Matter
EN FRANÇAIS: *French for Communication*, includes four appendices. Appendix A: School Subjects serves as a reference for a number of communicative exercises. Complete verb paradigms are given in Appendix B: Compound Tenses **(Les Temps composés)** and Appendix C: **Conjugaison des verbes.**

The French folksongs in Appendix D: **Chansons** provide an effective means of vocabulary expansion and pronunciation drill as well as an enjoyable change of pace in class. These songs are recorded on a separate cassette as part of the tape program accompanying EN FRANÇAIS.

The Grammatical Index provides an alphabetically arranged guide, in English and French, to grammatical points. The Subject Index, expanded from earlier editions, provides a guide to the variety of situational contexts and conversational topics treated in the textbook.

Acknowledgments

We would like to thank reviewers of the earlier editions of EN FRANÇAIS for their enthusiastic response, particularly concerning the unique qualities of the program. We are also grateful to the many actual users of EN FRANÇAIS for their productive feedback over the years. Such input has been an important factor in the on-going development of new materials for this program. Special thanks to Stanley Galek, Editor-in chief, Elinor Chamas, Project Editor, and Roberta Lenner, Product Manager, of Heinle & Heinle Publishers, Inc.

Dana Carton
Anthony Caprio

*   *   *

The publisher wishes to thank the following professors for their helpful responses to the survey of users of EN FRANÇAIS: Michael Gould (Portland State University), Mary E. LeFriant (San Diego Mesa College), Gregory Sorrell (Shenandoah College & Conservatory of Music), Sister Perpetua Deane (St. Thomas Aquinas College), Amie Tannenbaum (Gettysburg College), Joseph Johnson (College of Lake County), Linda Skaife (Mission College), Mary Lou Wolsey (College of St. Thomas).

HOW TO USE THIS LANGUAGE PROGRAM

To Students and Instructors

Since many of the materials contained in *EN FRANÇAIS: French for Communication* are unique to this particular language program, students as well as instructors should be provided with insights into the many possibilities offered by these activities. We have found that incorporating students into the learning/teaching process in this fashion can have very positive results. When students clearly understand exactly what is expected of them, they learn with greater enthusiasm and progress with greater rapidity. This procedure, furthermore, will assure maximal student participation in the many unique activities offered by this innovative program of study. Instructors may wish to skim this section for an overview of the program. These materials may be perused more closely, and used in conjunction with the Instructor's Manual, when a specific course of study is actually being prepared.

Formulating a curriculum

Flexibility is the essence of *EN FRANÇAIS: French for Communication,* Third Edition. This element should be capitalized upon at every opportunity. The wide variety of materials presented in the text and their essentially modular format allows for great freedom in the selection of materials best suited to the needs of the individual classroom and its students. This freedom applies not only to the order in which these materials may be presented, but also to the individual portions of each Chapter and Entracte to be used.

With beginning students, an initial sequential chapter by chapter approach may be best until a firm grounding in the basics has been achieved (usually by Chapter 4 or 5). Later in the course, Chapters, Entractes and even Chapter/Entracte subdivisions, such as **Activités, Structures, Dialogues** and **Projets,** may be selected as desired in order to formulate a program of instruction geared to the specific needs and interests of the students. When using *EN FRANÇAIS* in intermediate level courses, or conversation and composition courses, chapters, entractes and various subdivisions of either of these may be chosen as desired, facilitating the creation of a program of language instruction tailored to the particular needs of these special student groups.

Suggestions for Using the Chapters

Each chapter component of *EN FRANÇAIS* lends itself to a variety of classroom uses.

Dialogues   Once the on-page English equivalents have served their initial purpose of enabling students to know what they are saying in French, the page should be folded back, length-wise, leaving only the French portion of the text visible. In this way, students can appraise their individual progress in mastering the new vocabulary and structures. Students should be urged to visualize themselves in real-life situations that will call for the use of those sentences in the **Dialogues**. Personalization can be encouraged by requesting word substitutions based on the vocabulary choices offered in the vocabulary blocks that accompany the multifunctional dialogue sentences.

Phrases à retenir   Assigning these sentences for memorization will assure student spontaneity in a variety of real-life situations. If a weekly quiz is to be part of the language program, these memory phrases can be used.

Dialogue Exercises   These exercises offer practice, both oral and written, in using the vocabulary and basic sentence patterns of the chapter **Dialogue**. For those instructors who choose to work exclusively with the **Dialogues** and accompanying exercises, these exercises have been designed to require mastery only of vocabulary and structures presented in the given **Dialogue**. Dialogue Exercises consist of the following components:

• **Exercices d'application**   These exercises provide practice with the vocabulary and basic sentences of the Dialogue. They may be used orally in class or assigned for outside written preparation.

• **Improvisation à deux: Exercice oral.**   Students work with assigned partners to create personalized oral interactions. A time limit of fifteen minutes is suggested for improvisation preparation. As students prepare improvisations, instructors may wish to circulate around the classroom, correcting pronunciation and grammar, while encouraging creativity. Students may be asked to present their improvisational dialogues in front of the class. Four to five minutes should be allowed for each presentation.

• **À Vous le choix: Exercises écrits.**   Students write six-to-eight line dialogues for each of a series of suggested situations by selecting appropriate phrases from the initial **Dialogue** of the chapter. Creativity is called into play as students select personalized options from the vocabulary blocks. Students should be encouraged to restrict their creations to the vocabulary and structures of the chapter **Dialogue** to assure total assimilation of the given materials. These written exercises may be done in class by students working together or assigned for at-home preparation.

• **Conversations**   provide students with an opportunity to respond orally to a series of personalized questions of direct interest. Answer formats are provided to assure rapid and accurate replies. Students should be advised to select vocabulary and structures directly from the Chapter **Dialogue**. No grammatical manipulation is necessary. These questions can be used effectively as a basis for individualized conversation in the classroom, either instructor-directed with the class functioning as a whole, or student-initiated in a small group or partners framework. The *Review* sections concluding each **Conversations** encourage students to recall what they have just learned about their classmates. Such review is best accomplished with the class functioning as a unit, with instructor acting as moderator directing the conversational flow. **Conversations**, although geared for oral communicative interaction, may also be assigned for written preparation.

A Propos: Language and Culture   These sections may be assigned for outside reading or used in class as a basis for discussion. Students who may have lived or traveled in francophone areas should be invited to share their experiences related to the topic at hand with the class at this time.

Verbes Irréguliers/Exercices   The verb exercises require only vocabulary used in immediately preceding textual elements. This modular orientation allows the selection of any or all of the verb exercises for independent use either as oral classroom drill or for written assignment. Many of these verb exercises consist of personalized questions. These inquiries may be used orally in class, with students assigned partners for periods of individualized classroom conversation.

Structures/Exercices   Grammatical presentations are intentionally straightforward and succinct. Each structure is directly followed by its own specific exercises. This format allows instructors to select any or all structures from a given chapter to use as desired, either for oral classroom drill or for outside written assignment. Many personalized structural exercises lend themselves to lively classroom conversation. The class can function as a unit, or students may be divided into small groups or assigned partners. Recapitulation may be incorporated by having students recall what they have just learned about one another.

Synthèse   These illustrated exercises may be used orally in class. The class may function as a unit or students may work with assigned partners. These exercises also lend themselves to out-of-class, written preparation.

Prononciation   Discussions of various phonetic points may be treated in order, as they appear in the chapters. Or, they may be introduced at any time during the language program, whenever interest and receptivity is highest. Treatments of individual sounds or of other phenomena, such as liaison, elision, intonation or syllabification may be incorporated whenever the issues spontaneously arise in class. The modularized presentation of the pronunciation sections in each chapter has been developed to assure such flexibility. Students should be taught as early as possible to break French words into syllables (See Chapter 2), and to pronounce each syllable in a clear, confident fashion. Class members should be urged to concentrate on mastering each individual sound in a slow, careful manner; speed, associated with fluency, will follow spontaneously.

Projets   Project preparation may take place in class, out of class, or started in class with instructor supervision and subsequently completed at home. Although any project can be done independently, many lend themselves to profitable collaboration between two or more students. Once completed, projects can be used in class as effective springboards for conversation. Many projects lend themselves to incorporation into the new learning-by-doing **activités**. For example, the menu may be used in the restaurant activity, the greeting cards in the gift exchange or post office activities, the postcard in the postal activity, and so on. Projects are also a natural item for colorful, pedagogically profitable classroom displays.

Activités: Learning by Doing   Calling for active group participation, these unique activities allow for immediate utilization of selected vocabulary and structures of each chapter in meaningful contexts. They require only a brief period of instructor-directed presentation of vocabulary and structures. These units provide in-class opportunities for students to learn to deal effectively with a variety of real-life situations, such as dining out, shopping, mailing letters, getting acquainted, and so on. They are a lively means of building student confidence in using French.

These activities may be used successfully with classes of any size, of from five to fifty students. In larger classes, they provide an unusual opportunity for every student to participate orally at the same time.

In keeping with the modular orientation of the text, each learning-by-doing activity uses only selected vocabulary and structures from the given chapter. In consequence, these activities can be used in a number of ways. They may be employed in synthesized form as a motivational introduction to the given chapter. Or, they may be utilized in expanded form as a review of a chapter's materials. In fact, they may be effectively incorporated independently, at *any* time during the language program, to provide a stimulating and productive change of pace.

Each learning-by-doing activity can benefit from the incorporation of some form of realia, props or tangible visual aids. For example, play money can be used in the shopping unit, postcards in the postal unit, and so. When encouraged, class members will volunteer to bring such items from home. The French terms for these objects will be retained with noticeable rapidity and ease, while the lessons themselves will be rendered that much more authentic as a result.

Whatever flexibility the physical classroom permits should be manipulated to pedagogical advantage. Tables, desks, chairs and even wastebaskets may be mobilized as props. Such productive use of physical elements and classroom space will facilitate and encourage maximum interaction among students.

During these activities, the instructor's role becomes one of general supervision and encouragement. Individual students may also be helped with specific questions or problems that may arise regarding vocabulary or pronunciation at this time.

Suggestions for Using the Entractes

The Entractes are truly modular in construction. In consequence, they may be used in any of a wide variety of pedagogically effective manners:

● Totally independent of the Chapters, and in any order. They may easily be treated as separate entities, since each one is fully liberated from the necessity of using previously accumulated knowledge.

● Coordinated with the Chapters they accompany, to enhance and develop the vocabulary and structures presented therein.

● At different points throughout the language program to introduce new materials.

● As "warm-up" exercises during the first ten or fifteen minutes of class time. After an initial period of instructor-directed interrogation, students may take over by asking the same questions of each other. Such warm-ups serve to establish a steady and vigorous class rhythm, in which active student involvement is the keynote.

- As group conversations for the entire class with instructor as moderator.
- As a basis for individualized small-group or partners conversations.
- To provide an effective change of pace at any point during the language program.

The initial vocabulary list of each Entracte, frequently entitled **Vocabulaire à retenir**, contains those responses that experience has shown to recur with the greatest frequency in the typical language class. If memorization is desired, students should be asked to learn by heart only the vocabulary in these initial lists. When additional vocabulary is needed for classroom conversation, students may select from the Resource Lists which appear at the end of many of the Entractes. The chosen terms will then relate directly to the individual students involved, and will allow for complete and meaningful self-expression in a truly personalized context.

Frequent recapitulation of information given out by class members will provide some spontaneous review and drill of vocabulary in an interesting and personalized fashion. The new **Récapitulation** sections offer an opportunity for such practice.

The new **Expansion** sections may be used orally in class for group or partners conversation, or they may be assigned for outside written preparation. When used in class for group conversation, recapitulation may be incorporated by having students recall what they have just learned about classmates during these conversations. Encouraging students to use the conversational interjections supplied in the **Vocabulaire utile** reference listings will increase conversational spontaneity.

Guidelines for Classroom Conversational Periods

Encouraging Recapitulation: When using any of the many personalized questions contained in the Chapters and Entractes for classroom conversation, total class participation can be assured by the frequent request that students recapitulate information given out by their fellow classmates. If a student cannot recall what a classmate has said, he or she should be encouraged to re-ask the given question. At this time, students should be assured that such repetition is good practice for all concerned, a procedure that will generate good group spirit.

An effective phrase to incorporate into such classroom discussion is **C'est tout?**, an inquiry that will prod students into making their answers as complete as possible, thereby enhancing the overall usefulness of the session. Similarly, during periods of recapitulation, this phrase will increase vocabulary accumulation as students recall what they have learned about their classmates.

Personalized Exercises: There are many new personalized exercises in this edition of *EN FRANÇAIS*. When using these exercises, it should be kept in mind that no one is obligated to divulge the entire personal truth. The point should consistently be made in class that these exercises are for linguistic purposes only, and, if the contents of a given question are deemed too personal, an answer may be fabricated. In such a manner, students will still be building language skills while keeping their privacy intact. During the course of any of these personalized exercises, instructors may choose to let students guess about themselves. This is often a good way to initiate the exercise, as it sets a lively and open tone for the exercise to follow.

Information Verification for Reinforcement: Incorporating the question **C'est vrai?** into these conversational periods will often render the given exercise more meaningful on a personal level. This procedure will assure that students actually apply the questions to themselves, and that they do not simply select the easiest response or the sample option for their replies.

Individualized Guided Conversation: As classes become more proficient in French, ten minutes of individualized conversation at regular intervals may well be integrated advantageously into the curriculum. Students may be assigned partners, basing their conversations upon any of the personalized questions to be found in the text. A variety of verbal experiences for individual students is achieved by varying student partner assignments for each conversation period.

Informal or Formal: In many classes, especially those with younger class members, students may prefer to use the informal **tu** form when conversing with one another. Other classes may prefer the more formal **vous** form. It is up to the individual instructor faced with a particular student group to determine what form of address best suits the needs of the given classroom. This text has been designed to allow for flexibility in this matter. Exercises requiring interpersonal communication between students offer options for both the **tu** and **vous** forms. Again concerning the matter of classroom formality, some students may prefer being called by their first names, others by French versions of these same names, and still others by Monsieur... Madame... or Mademoiselle... For this reason, response options presented in those exercises requiring interaction between students consistently offer both Monsieur/Madame/Mademoiselle... as well as typical English and French first names as possible options.

*   *   *

Details regarding classroom implementation of specific Chapter and Entracte components are given in the Instructor's Manual. For instructors intending to use *EN FRANÇAIS: French For Communication* in specialized programs for adult learners or in intensive language programs, the Instructor's Manual provides a section devoted to the utilization of these materials in such courses.

«Comment ça va'?»

Bonjour

C'est simple comme bonjour.

Getting Acquainted

It's as easy as A B C.

DIALOGUE

This **Dialogue** presents vocabulary for greeting people, making introductions, inquiring about matters of health, and leave-taking. Vocabulary blocks within this **Dialogue** offer options for personalization regarding your own health. They also provide possibilities for modification to suit a wide variety of classroom and real-life situations.

Bonjour	Getting Acquainted
VOUS: Bonjour, Monsieur / Madame / Mademoiselle.	YOU: Hello, (Sir / Madam / Miss).
UN MONSIEUR / UNE DAME: Bonjour, Monsieur / Madame / Mademoiselle.	A GENTLEMAN / A LADY: Hello.
VOUS: Je suis _votre nom_. Et vous?	YOU: I'm _your name_. And you?
LE MONSIEUR / DAME: Je suis _____.	GENTLEMAN / LADY: I'm _____.
VOUS: Pardon?	YOU: Pardon?
LE MONSIEUR / LA DAME: Je m'appelle _____.	GENTLEMAN / LADY: My name is _____.
VOUS: Enchanté(e), Monsieur / Madame / Mademoiselle.	YOU: Delighted (to know you).
LE MONSIEUR / LA DAME: Moi de même.	GENTLEMAN / LADY: Likewise (I am too).
VOUS: Je vous présente **mon ami...** M	YOU: Allow me to present my **friend....**

mon amie F	friend (feminine)
mes enfants	children
ma femme	wife
mon frère	brother
mon mari	husband
ma mère	mother
mes parents	parents
mon père	father
mon professeur	professor / teacher
ma sœur	sister
Monsieur ____	Mr. ____
Madame ____	Mrs. ____
Mademoiselle ____	Miss ____

LE MONSIEUR / LA DAME: Bonjour, Monsieur / Madame / Mademoiselle.	GENTLEMAN / LADY: Hello.
VOUS: Comment allez-vous, Monsieur / Madame / Mademoiselle?	YOU: How are you?
LE MONSIEUR / LA DAME: Très bien, merci. Et vous?	GENTLEMAN / LADY: Very well, thanks. And you?
VOUS: **Très bien,** merci.	YOU: **Very well,** thanks.

Bien	Well
Assez bien	Rather well
Comme ci, comme ça	So-so
Pas mal	Not bad
Pas très bien	Not very well

LE MONSIEUR / LA DAME: **Au revoir,**	GENTLEMAN / LADY: **Good-bye.**
À bientôt	See you soon
Bonsoir	Good evening
Bonne nuit	Good night
À demain	See you tomorrow
À tout à l'heure	See you later
À plus tard	See you later

Bun newè (handwritten)

Monsieur / Madame / Mademoiselle.

VOUS: **Au revoir,** Monsieur / Madame /	YOU: **Good-bye.**
À lundi	See you Monday (*Literally:* Until Monday)
À mardi	See you Tuesday
À mercredi	See you Wednesday
À jeudi	See you Thursday
À vendredi	See you Friday
À samedi	See you Saturday
À dimanche	See you Sunday

Mademoiselle.

Phrases à retenir

Memorizing these few simple phrases from the **Dialogue** will help assure fluency in a variety of real-life getting-acquainted situations.

1. Bonjour, Monsieur/Madame/Mademoiselle.
2. Je m'appelle ___votre nom___.
3. Enchanté(e). (*Note:* **Enchanté** is masculine. **Enchantée** is feminine. Both forms, however, are pronounced alike.)
4. Moi de même.
5. Je vous présente mon ami...
6. Comment allez-vous?
7. Au revoir, Monsieur/Madame/Mademoiselle.

DIALOGUE EXERCISES

The following exercises provide oral and written practice in using the vocabulary and basic sentence patterns of the **Dialogue: Bonjour**. These exercises use *only* vocabulary and structures presented in the getting-acquainted **Dialogue**. They do not require familiarity with any other portions of this chapter.

Exercices d'application

A.   **Greeting in French: Bonjour, Madame.**   When addressing someone in French, do not use the family name after **Monsieur, Madame,** or **Mademoiselle.** For example, when greeting Madame La France, you would simply say, **Bonjour, Madame**. Now greet each of the following people:

1. Mademoiselle La France
2. Madame Martin
3. Monsieur Martin
4. Monsieur La France
5. votre professeur

B. **Leave-taking: Au revoir, Monsieur.** Apply the same rule as in the preceding exercise when saying good-bye. For example: **Au revoir, Monsieur.** Say good-bye to the following people:

1. Mademoiselle Martin
2. Madame La France
3. Monsieur Martin
4. Monsieur La France
5. votre professeur

C. **Making introductions: Je vous présente...** Introduce the following people:

MODÈLE: Madame La France
   Je vous présente Madame la France.

1. Madame Dubois
2. Monsieur Dupont
3. Mademoiselle La France
4. your mother (ma mère)
5. your father (mon père)
6. your parents (mes parents)

D. **Dialogue responses.** Give an appropriate response to each of the following sentences from the **Dialogue**.

1. Bonjour, Monsieur.
2. Bonjour, Madame.
3. Je suis Monsieur La France.
4. Enchanté.
5. Je vous présente mon père.
6. Comment allez-vous?
7. Au revoir, Monsieur.
8. À bientôt!

E. **Review.** What do you say . . .

1. to greet someone?
2. to introduce yourself?
3. to someone after he or she has been introduced to you?
4. to introduce your friend to someone? to introduce your spouse? your parents? your brother or sister? your children? your teacher?
5. to ask about someone's health?
6. to tell someone that you are feeling very well? rather well? not very well?
7. when you are leaving?
8. to let someone know that you will be seeing him or her again soon?
9. to let someone know that you will see him or her on Monday? on Tuesday? on Wednesday? on Thursday? on Friday? on Saturday? on Sunday?

Improvisation à deux *(Exercice oral)*

F. Use the vocabulary block options and the basic sentence structures of the **Dialogue** to become acquainted with a classmate. Say hello. Introduce yourself. What is your classmate's name? How is he or she feeling today? Introduce your classmate to another class member sitting nearby. Use **Pardon?** whenever you cannot hear or clearly understand your partner.

À Vous le choix *(Exercices écrits)*

G. Write a six- to eight-line dialogue for each of the following situations, selecting appropriate phrases from the initial **Dialogue** of this chapter.

1. You are traveling with your best friend and meet a French person.
2. You are traveling by yourself and meet a French person.
3. You are traveling alone, by train, in a French-speaking country. You strike up a conversation with a couple sitting near you.

Conversations

H. Ask your classmates these personalized questions. Answer formats are provided. Do not limit your responses simply to those suggestions offered in these questions. Use the inclusive vocabulary options provided in the **Dialogue.**

1. Quel est votre nom?
   • Je suis _____. Je m'appelle _____.
2. Comment allez-vous?
   • Bien./Mal./Très bien./Assez bien./ Comme ci, comme ça./Pas mal./Pas très bien.
3. Comment va votre mère? votre père? votre ami? etc.
   • Bien./Mal./etc.
4. Comment va votre professeur de français?
   • Bien./Mal. etc.
5. Comment s'appelle votre mère? votre sœur? votre amie? votre femme?
   • Elle s'appelle _____. (*Her name is* _____.)
6. Comment s'appelle votre père? votre frère? votre ami?
   • Il s'appelle _____. (*His name is* _____.)
7. Comment s'appelle votre professeur de français?
   • Il/Elle s'appelle _____.

I. **Review.** What have you learned about your classmates from the preceding **Conversations**?

EXEMPLES: *Marc va bien. / Anne va très bien. / Madame Smith va très bien aussi* (too).

À PROPOS

Borrowed words. Many French words and expressions are used in English. À Propos, the title of this section, is a typical example. It means "pertinent to," "with reference to," or "relevant to." Each **Chapitre** and **Entracte** of this book has an À Propos section containing interesting insights into French language and culture, insights "pertinent to" the topic or vocabulary of the lesson.

Informal versus formal. The French use the **vous** (formal) form of address on first meetings and in situations where politeness or reserve is required. The **tu** (informal) form of address is commonly used among family members, between close friends or colleagues, among children, and when adults speak to children. Here are some informal greetings, health inquiries, responses, and introductions:

Salut!	Hi!
Comment ça va?/Ça va?	How's it going?
Ça va! Ça va bien!	Well!
Ça ne va pas du tout!	Not well at all!
Je te présente...	Here's. . . (Literally: I introduce. . .)
Voici mon ami(e)...	Here's my friend. . .

These close friends use the **tu** form.

LANGUAGE AND CULTURE

Monsieur

Abbreviations. The written abbreviation for Monsieur is M.; for Madame, Mme; and for Mademoiselle, Mlle. (There is a period after the abbreviation for **Monsieur**, but not after the abbreviation for **Madame** or **Mademoiselle**.) Plurals: Mesdames (Mmes), Messieurs (MM.), and Mesdemoiselles (Mlles).

Word origins. Many words in French have the same word origin as English words. Looking for these relationships will often help you remember word meanings. Examples from this lesson include: **mari** (marriage), **tard** (tardy), **heure** (hour), **présenter** (to present), **professeur** (professor), **parents** (parents), and **à tout à l'heure** (toodle-oo)! See what others you can find.

VERBES IRRÉGULIERS: aller, être, s'appeler

There are a number of commonly used verbs in French that are considered irregular because they do not follow a set pattern. Since these verbs are so common, it is important to master them. The only way to do so is by memorization. Each chapter presents a few of these important verbs.

aller	to go
je **vais**	I go, I am going, I do go
tu **vas**	you go, you are going
il **va**	he goes, he is going
elle **va**	she goes, she is going
on **va**	one goes
nous **allons**	we go, we are going
vous **allez**	you go, you are going
ils **vont**	they (*masculine*) go, they are going
elles **vont**	they (*feminine*) go, they are going

[handwritten margin note: news allon / vouz - alle]

Note: **On** is used conversationally in a general sense to mean "one," "we," "you," "they," and "people." **Ils** is used to mean "they" when referring to a mixed group.

1. **Aller** is used to express motion toward a place.

   Où **allez-vous?**   Where are you going?
   Je vais à Paris.   I am going to Paris.

2. **Aller** is used with expressions of health. In English, the verb "to be" is used.

   Comment **allez-vous?**
   Comment **vas-tu?** (*informal*)   How are you?

   Je vais bien, merci.   I'm fine, thanks.
   Comment **va-t-il?**   How is he?
   Il va bien.   He is well.
   Comment **va-t-elle?**   How is she?
   Elle va bien.   She is well.
   Comment **ça va?/Ça va?**   How's it going? How are things going?

   Ça va. Ça va bien.   Fine.

Cart1

Exercices d'application: **aller**[1]

A. **Vous allez...** Ask someone if what you heard is correct.

MODÈLE: Je vais à Paris.
Vous allez à Paris?

1. Je vais à Paris.
2. Je vais à Londres.
3. Je vais à Chicago.
4. Je vais à Montréal.
5. Je vais à Washington.

B. **Comment va...?** Ask how the following people are feeling.

MODÈLE: votre professeur
Comment va votre professeur?

1. votre mère
2. votre ami
3. votre frère
4. votre sœur
5. votre père

C. **Comment va-t-il? Comment va-t-elle?** Would you ask: **Comment va-t-il?** or **Comment va-t-elle?**

MODÈLE: Elle va bien.
Comment va-t-elle?

1. Il va bien.
2. Elle ne va pas bien.
3. Mon père va assez bien.
4. Ma mère va bien.
5. Ma sœur va très bien.

D. **Comment vas-tu? Comment allez-vous?** Would you ask the following people **Comment vas-tu?** or **Comment allez-vous?**

MODÈLE: votre ami
Comment vas-tu?

1. votre sœur
2. votre frère
3. votre amie
4. votre mère
5. votre professeur
6. Madame La France
7. votre père
8. Monsieur La France
9. votre femme/votre mari

1. Unless otherwise indicated the **Exercices d'application** on the irregular verbs may be used for written individual assignment as well as for oral classroom exchange in a group or in a partners framework.

être	to be
je **suis**	I am
tu **es**	you are
il **est**	he is
elle **est**	she is
on **est**	one is
c'**est**	it is, this is, that is
nous **sommes**	we are
vous **êtes**	you are
ils **sont**	they (*masculine*) are
elles **sont**	they (*feminine*) are
ce **sont**	they are, these are, those are

1. **Être** is a commonly used verb that is irregular as is its English counterpart, "to be."

2. Note these uses of **être:**

Où **êtes-vous?**	Where are you?
D'où **êtes-vous?**	Where are you from?
Je suis de Paris.	I am from Paris.

3. **Ce** used with **être** has several different English equivalents.

Qui **est-ce?**	Who **is it?**
C'est mon ami.	**He/It/This is** my friend.
C'est mon amie.	**She/It/This is** my friend.
Ce sont mes parents.	**These/Those/They are** my parents.

Exercices d'application: être

E. **Je suis de... Et vous? D'où êtes-vous?**   Tell your classmates what city or town you are from. Ask them where they are from.

EXEMPLE: *Je suis de Washington. Et vous? D'où êtes-vous?* (Note: If you are unsure of a response, ask, **Pardon? D'où êtes-vous? Vous êtes de...?**)

F. **Il est de...**   Talk about your classmates. Where are they from? To make sure you are correct, ask the classmate in question, **C'est ça?**

EXEMPLES: *Peter est de Miami.*
Marie est de Québec.
Monsieur Smith est de Chicago.

G. **D'où est-il? D'où est-elle?**   Ask classmates what cities or towns other class members are from.

EXEMPLES: —*D'où est-il?*
  —*Il est de Chicago.*
  —*D'où est-elle?*
  —*Elle est de San Francisco.*

H. **Qui est-ce? C'est mon frère.** _{Brother} In each case tell who it is.

MODÈLE: mon ami   *Qui est-ce? C'est mon ami.*

1. mon amie
2. mon frère
3. ma mère

4. mon professeur
5. ma sœur
6. mon ami

I. **Qui est-ce? Ce sont mes parents.**   In each case tell who it is.

MODÈLE: mes amis   *Qui est-ce? Ce sont mes amis.*

1. mes parents
2. mes amis
3. mes professeurs

4. mes amies
5. mes sœurs

➤

s'appeler	to be named
je **m'appelle**	my name is
tu **t'appelles**	your name is
il **s'appelle**	his name is
elle **s'appelle**	her name is
nous **nous appelons**	our name is/our names are
vous **vous appelez**	your name is/your names are
ils **s'appellent**	their (*masculine*) names are
elles **s'appellent**	their (*feminine*) names are

1. The endings **-e, -es, -e, -ons, -ez, -ent** are actually the same as regular verb endings. It is the double "l" that makes the verb **s'appeler** irregular.
2. **Je m'appelle** literally means "I call myself," but it translates as "my name is."
3. The endings **-e, -es,** and **-ent** are not pronounced.
4. Note these frequently recurring conversational forms:

   Comment **vous appelez-vous?**   What is your name?
   Comment **s'appelle-t-il?**   What is his name?
   Comment **s'appelle-t-elle?**   What is her name?

Exercices d'application: **s'appeler**

J. **Comment s'appelle-t-il?** After a classmate completes one of the following sentences with a person's name, pretend that you have not heard the name correctly and ask for it to be repeated.

MODÈLE: —Elle s'appelle *Anne.*
—*Pardon? Comment s'appelle-t-elle?*

1. Elle s'appelle _____.
2. Il s'appelle _____.
3. Le professeur s'appelle _____.

4. Mon ami(e) s'appelle _____.
5. Mon frère s'appelle _____.
6. Ma mère s'appelle _____.

K. **Il s'appelle... Elle s'appelle...** What are the names of your family members?

EXEMPLES: *Ma mère s'appelle Anne.*
Mon père s'appelle Georges.

L. **Il/Elle s'appelle...** What are the names of your classmates?

EXEMPLES: *Il s'appelle John Smith.*
Elle s'appelle Madame Jones.

STRUCTURES

Structure 1: Questions

There are several ways of forming a question in French.

1. In conversational French, simply raise your voice at the end of the sentence.

C'est vrai.	It's true.
C'est vrai?	It's true?

2. If you are asking a question to which you expect a "yes" answer, simply add the expression **n'est-ce pas?** at the end of the sentence. Depending on the sentence, **n'est-ce pas?** has various English equivalents: *isn't that true?, no?, isn't that the case?, don't you?,* etc.

Vous allez bien, **n'est-ce pas?**	You are well, aren't you?
Il va à Paris, **n'est-ce pas?**	He is going to Paris, isn't he?

3. A sentence may be turned into a question by placing **est-ce que** at the beginning.

Vous allez à Paris.	You are going to Paris.
Est-ce que vous allez à Paris?	Are you going to Paris?

Est-ce que becomes **est-ce qu'** when the following word begins with a vowel or mute **h.**

Il s'appelle Pierre.   His name is Pierre.
Est-ce qu'il s'appelle Pierre? Is his name Pierre?

4. A sentence with a pronoun subject can be made interrogative by placing the
   subject pronoun after the verb, linking the verb and subject with a hyphen.
   This is called *inversion*.

   Vous allez à Paris.   You are going to Paris.
   Allez-vous à Paris?   Are you going to Paris?

   When the third person singular **(il, elle, on)** form of the verb ends in a
   vowel, the letter **t** must be added in an inversion question.

   Il va à Paris.   He is going to Paris.
   Va-t-il à Paris?   Is he going to Paris?

   Elle va à Paris.   She is going to Paris.
   Va-t-elle à Paris?   Is she going to Paris?

5. Questions beginning with **comment** (*how*) and **où** (*where*) may invert a noun
   subject and verb, as in English.

   Comment va votre mère?   How is your mother?
   Où va votre père?   Where is your father going?

Exercices d'application: Questions

A.   **...n'est-ce pas?**   After introductions have taken place, say to your classmates:
Vous vous appelez _____, n'est-ce pas? Use their real names. If a name slips
your mind, introduce yourself and ask your classmate's name.

B.   **Il s'appelle Pierre, n'est-ce pas?**   Say to one classmate about another: **Il
s'appelle _____, n'est-ce pas?** or **Elle s'appelle _____, n'est-ce pas?**

C.   **Est-ce que...?**   Make each statement into a question by using **est-ce que**. Then
translate the question.

MODÈLE: Vous êtes de Paris.   *Est-ce que vous êtes de Paris?*
                                Are you from Paris?

1. Vous êtes de Rome.   5. Mes amis sont là (*there*).
2. Vous êtes touriste.   6. Vous allez bien.
3. Tu es à New York.   7. Nous allons à Paris.
4. Les enfants sont à Miami.

D.   **Êtes-vous de Paris?**   Make each statement into a question by using inversion.
Then translate the question.

MODÈLE: Vous êtes de Paris.   *Êtes-vous de Paris?*
                                Are you from Paris?

1. Vous êtes de Québec.
2. Vous êtes touriste.
3. Tu es à San Francisco.
4. Ils sont à Seattle.

5. Elles sont là *(there)*.
6. Il est à Paris.
7. Ils vont à Rome.

E. **Est-ce qu'...?** Make each statement into a question by using **est-ce qu'**. Then translate the question.

MODÈLE: **Il va à Paris.**   *Est-ce qu'il va à Paris?*
                                 Is he going to Paris?

1. Elle va bien.
2. Il s'appelle Pierre.
3. Elle s'appelle Marie.

4. Il va à Paris.
5. On va à Paris.
6. Elle va à New York.

«Où est-ce qu'on va?»

F. **Va-t-il à Paris?** Make each statement into a question by using inversion. The letter **t** must be added in each question. Then translate the question.

MODÈLE: Il va à Paris. *Va-t-il à Paris?*
Is he going to Paris?

1. Elle va bien.
2. Il s'appelle François.
3. Elle s'appelle Anne.
4. Il va à Montréal.
5. On va à Bruxelles.
6. Elle va à New York.

G. **Comment va...?** Ask about the health of these people.

MODÈLE: le professeur
Comment va le professeur?

1. Madame La France
2. Monsieur La France
3. le professeur
4. Mademoiselle Duval
5. Madame Duval

Structure 2: Possessive Adjectives **mon, ma, mes, votre, vos**

All French nouns are either masculine or feminine. Possessive adjectives agree in gender (masculine/feminine) and in number (singular/plural) with the nouns they modify.

Possessive Adjectives			
mon	before masculine singular[2] nouns:	**mon** père	(*my father*)
ma	before feminine singular nouns:	**ma** mère	(*my mother*)
mes	before all plural nouns:	**mes** parents	(*my parents*)
votre	before masculine or feminine singular nouns:	**votre** père **votre** mère	(*your father*) (*your mother*)
vos	before all plural nouns:	**vos** parents	(*your parents*)

Exercices d'application: Possessive Adjectives

H. **Mon/Ma/Mes.** Introduce the following people. Use **mon, ma,** or **mes.**

MODÈLE: your mother (*mère*)
Je vous présente ma mère.

2. **Mon** is also used before a feminine singular noun beginning with a vowel: **mon amie.**

1. your father (*père*)
2. your sister (*sœur*)
3. your wife or husband (*femme/mari*)
4. your friend (*ami*)
5. your friend (*amie*)
6. your professor (*professeur*)
7. your parents (*parents*)
8. your children (*enfants*)

I. **Oh là là! C'est ma mère!** Express surprise at seeing each of these people. Use **mon, ma,** or **mes.**

MODÈLE: votre mère   *Oh là, là! C'est ma mère!*

1. votre père
2. votre professeur
3. votre sœur
4. votre ami
5. votre amie
6. votre mari/votre femme

J. **Où est votre...?** Ask a classmate where these people are. Answers may include a simple shoulder shrug, a pointed finger, or a wave of the hand, accompanied by **là-bas** (*over there*).

MODÈLE: mère   *Où est votre mère?*

1. sœur
2. ami
3. amie
4. frère
5. père
6. professeur
7. mari/femme

K. **Mes/Vos.** Have you heard correctly? Seek verification.

MODÈLE: Mes enfants sont à Paris.
        Pardon? Vos enfants sont à Paris?

1. Mes parents sont à Paris.
2. Mes amis sont à Washington.
3. Mes professeurs sont là (*there*).
4. Mes enfants sont à Québec.
5. Mes amies sont à Montréal.
6. Mes frères sont à Rome.

Structure 3: Negation

To make a sentence negative, place **ne** before the conjugated verb and **pas** after it.

Je vais à Paris.	I am going to Paris.
Je **ne** vais **pas** à Paris.	I am not going to Paris.

1. **Ne** becomes **n'** before a verb beginning with a vowel or a mute **h.**

Nous allons à Paris.	We are going to Paris.
Nous **n'**allons **pas** à Paris.	We are not going to Paris.

2. **C'est** becomes **ce n'est pas.**

C'est mon père.	That's my father.
Ce n'est pas mon père.	That's not my father.

3. **Pas** is used alone when there is no verb.

Pas aujourd'hui!	Not today!
Pas moi!	Not I!
Pas vrai!	Not true!

Exercices d'application: Negation

L.   **Je ne _____ pas.**   Using only the vocabulary of this chapter, make at least four statements in the negative about yourself.

     EXEMPLES: *Je ne suis pas de Washington.*
                   Je ne m'appelle pas Tootsie.
                   Je ne suis pas à Paris.
                   Je ne vais pas bien.

M.   **Ne...pas.**   Using only the vocabulary of this chapter, make at least four statements in the negative about people you know.

     EXEMPLES: *Ma mère n'est pas de Paris.*
                   Mon père ne s'appelle pas Xavier.
                   Mon professeur ne va pas à Paris.
                   Mon ami n'est pas à Paris.

N.   **C'est/Ce n'est pas.**   Use the dialogue words **père, mère, frère, sœur, ami, amie, mari, femme,** and **professeur.** Look around the classroom. Make statements about each person you see. Employ **c'est** or **ce n'est pas** as appropriate.

     EXEMPLES: *C'est mon professeur.*
                   Ce n'est pas ma femme.
                   C'est mon ami.
                   Ce n'est pas mon frère.

O.   **Votre frère/Mon frère.**   Using the same vocabulary as in the preceding exercise, ask your classmates questions. Listen for their responses. Questions will all use the possessive adjective **votre.** Responses will use either **mon** or **ma.**

     EXEMPLES: —*C'est votre frère?*
                   —*Non, ce n'est pas mon frère.*

                   —*C'est votre ami?*
                   —*Oui, c'est mon ami.*

Synthèse

Je vous présente Madame La France.   Here is a photograph of Madame La France. Answer the following questions about her. Use complete sentences.

1. Qui est-ce?
2. Comment s'appelle-t-elle?
3. Comment va-t-elle?

4. C'est votre mère?
5. C'est votre sœur?
6. C'est votre professeur de français?

PRONONCIATION

1. Sound (Phonetic Symbol): [ɔ̃]

SPELLING:	**on om**
ENGLISH SOUND RESEMBLED:	Vowel sound in words *bone* and *home*

PRONUNCIATION:	To pronounce the nasal sound [$\tilde{ɔ}$], round and protrude lips tensely. Constrict throat slightly. Do not pronounce the final **n** or **m** as in English. Mouth remains open throughout entire sound.

EXAMPLES FROM THIS CHAPTER:

b<u>on</u>jour	<u>on</u> va
m<u>on</u> frère	nous all<u>ons</u>
b<u>on</u>soir	ils v<u>ont</u>
n<u>on</u>	elles s<u>ont</u>
n<u>om</u>	pard<u>on</u>

Notes:

1. The spellings **on** and **om** lose their nasal quality when followed by a vowel or by another n or m. Examples from this chapter: c<u>omme</u>   c<u>omme</u>nt nous s<u>omme</u>s   Quel d<u>omm</u>age!   b<u>onne</u> nuit

2. The possessive adjective **mon** and the personal pronoun **on** retain the nasal sound when they are followed by a vowel, with the second syllable picking up the sound [n]. Examples from this chapter: m<u>on a</u>mi (e) [m ɔ̃ -na-mi]   <u>on</u> est [ɔ̃ -ne]

3. The sound [ˈɔ̃] is dropped completely from m<u>on</u>sieur: B<u>on</u>jour, M<u>on</u>sieur.

2. Sound (Phonetic Symbol) [ã]

SPELLING:	**an, en, am, em**
ENGLISH SOUND RESEMBLED:	Vowel sound in words *T<u>om</u>* and *J<u>oh</u>n*
PRONUNCIATION:	To pronounce the nasal sound [ã], slightly round the lips. Constrict throat slightly. Do not pronounce the final **n** or **m** as in English. Mouth remains open throughout entire sound.

EXAMPLES FROM THIS CHAPTER:

<u>en</u>chanté	dim<u>an</u>che
prés<u>en</u>te	comm<u>en</u>t
<u>en</u>fant	<u>en</u> français
par<u>en</u>ts	v<u>en</u>dredi

Notes:

1. The spellings **en**, **em**, **am**, and **an**, when followed by a vowel or by another n or m, lose their nasal quality. Examples from this chapter: mad<u>ame</u>   d<u>ame</u>   <u>ami</u>   <u>amie</u>   f<u>emme</u>   s<u>ame</u>di

2. The spellings **en** and **em**, preceded by the letter i, are pronounced [ɛ̃]. (See **Chapitre 2.**) Examples from this chapter: b<u>ien</u>   très b<u>ien</u>

3. Sound (Phonetic Symbol): [R]

SPELLING:	**r, rr, rh**

PRONUNCIATION: [R] has various pronunciations depending upon
                                        the French-speaking region where it is used.
                                        The Parisian [R] may be obtained by letting the
                                        vocal cords vibrate while slightly constricting
                                        the back of the throat, as if gargling. In some
                                        French-speaking areas the [R] sound is
                                        produced by trilling the tongue against the
                                        front teeth. Notice that when the [R] sound
                                        appears in the middle or at the end of a word,
                                        it is pronounced very softly.

EXAMPLES FROM THIS CHAPTER: mère   merci   frère   sœur
                              père   pardon   mari   très

4. Silent Letters

Final consonants are generally not pronounced in French, except for the letters
c, r, f, and l. The English word careful contains these four consonants and will
help you remember this grouping.

EXAMPLES FROM THIS CHAPTER: Silent Final Consonants

                              nous   nuit   allons   vont
                              vous   à plus tard enfants   sont
                              parents   assez bien   pas
                              très   tu vas   bientôt

                              Pronounced Final Consonants

                              bonjour   sœur   il   oral
                              bonsoir   professeur   mal   au revoir

Notes: 1. The final consonant r is not pronounced in the infinitive verb ending -er or
                 in the word monsieur. Examples from this chapter: aller   s'appeler
                 monsieur

              2. The third person plural verb ending -ent is not pronounced. Example from
                 this chapter: ils s'appellent

              3. In conversational French, the /l/ sound in il and ils is often dropped before
                 a verb beginning with a consonant. Examples from this chapter: il va
                 ils vont

              4. The final vowel e is not pronounced in French, but it does cause the
                 preceding consonant to be pronounced. Examples from this chapter:
                 madame   dame   je vous présente

              5. The sound represented by the letter e is often dropped when it appears in
                 the middle of a long word or common expression. Examples from this
                 chapter: mademoiselle   moi de même   au revoir

6. Sometimes sounds are dropped from a word simply because the word is used so frequently in the language that usage has shortened its pronunciation. For example, in English, the expression "good-bye" is often simply pronounced "g'by" or even "'bye." An example in French from this chapter: m**o̸**nsieu**r̸**

Projet

Names (*Exercice oral ou écrit*). Use the family members vocabulary given in the **Dialogue (ma mère, mon père,** etc.), along with **mon ami, mon amie,** and **mon professeur de français.** Make a listing of names. You may wish to show photos.

EXEMPLES: *Mon père s'appelle Peter.*
Mon frère s'appelle John.
Ma mère s'appelle Anne.

Activités: Learning by Doing

A. **Getting Acquainted.** Say hello to the person sitting on your right. Introduce yourself. Find out that person's name. Introduce the person sitting on your right to the person sitting on your left.

Ask the person sitting on your right if he or she remembers the name of the person on your left. **Comment s'appelle-t-il? Comment s'appelle-t-elle?** To verify this information, ask the classmate in question, **C'est ça?** (*Is that so?*)

When a name is forgotten, say, **Excusez-moi! Je suis désolé(e)! Mais j'ai oublié votre nom.** (*Excuse me! I'm so sorry! But I have forgotten your name.*)

B. **How are you feeling today?** Ask the person sitting on your right how he or she is feeling today. Use the formal **(Comment allez-vous?)** or the informal **(Comment vas-tu?)** form of address. If the answer is **Pas très bien,** you may wish to ask **Qu'est-ce qui ne va pas?** (*What's wrong?*) Answers may include:

Je suis fatigué(e). I am tired.
Je suis très fatigué(e) aujourd'hui. I am very tired today.

Ça va mal. Things are going badly.
Ça va très mal aujourd'hui. Things are going very badly today.

To offer sympathy, say, **Dommage!** or **Quel dommage!** (*What a pity!*) Tell your classmate how you are feeling today.

Now ask the person on your left how he or she is feeling today. Listen to the response. Tell him or her how you are feeling today.

Tell the person on your right about the person on your left and vice versa: **Il/Elle va bien,** etc. To verify this information, ask your classmates **C'est ça?** *(Is that so?)* If you forget how someone is feeling, apologize and ask again: **Pardon! J'ai oublié... Comment allez-vous?** Other useful words and phrases for this activity include:

Comment ça va?   How are things going?
Ça va.   Things are going fine.
Ça ne va pas du tout!   Things are not going well at all!

Oui   Yes
Non   No
Merci   Thank you
C'est la vie!   That's life!

Quel est votre nom?

The Alphabet

Il n'y a que le premier pas qui coûte.

The first step is the hardest.

Knowing the French alphabet is important for spelling your own name, as when being introduced, making reservations, or leaving telephone messages. Spelling also helps to clarify addresses, place names, and other proper names during normal conversation.

Quel est votre nom? Pouvez-vous épeler, s'il vous plaît?

Réponse: • Je suis ___votre nom___ .[1]

EXEMPLE: *Je suis John Smith. J.O.H.N. S.M.I.T.H.*

A	[a] *ah*	H	[aʃ] *ash*	O	[o]	V	[ve]	
B	[be]	I	[i] *ee*	P	[pe] *pey*	W	[dublǝve]	
C	[se]	J	[ʒi] *Gee*	Q	[ky]	X	[iks]	
D	[de]	K	[kɑ] *kar*	R	[ɛR]	Y	[igRɛk]	
E	[ǝ] *err*	L	[ɛl]	S	[ɛs]	Z	[zɛd]	
F	[ɛf]	M	[ɛm]	T	[te]			
G	[ʒe] *jee*	N	[ɛn]	U	[y] *euu*			

Springboards for Conversation

Ask your classmates these personalized questions. Answer formats are provided. • Réponses

1. Quel est votre nom? Pouvez-vous épeler, s'il vous plaît?
   • Je suis *or* Je m'appelle _____. *(Full name and spelling)*

2. Quel *(what)* est votre prénom *(first name)?*

   EXEMPLE: *C'est Mark. M.A.R.K.*

3. Quels sont vos prénoms *(first and middle names)?*

   EXEMPLE: *Je m'appelle Mark Anthony. M.A.R.K. A.N.T.H.O.N.Y.*

4. Quel est votre nom de famille *(last name)?*

   EXEMPLE: *C'est Smith. S.M.I.T.H.*

5. Êtes-vous mariée *(married)?* Quel est votre nom de jeune fille *(maiden name)?* Épelez-le.

   EXEMPLE: *C'est Johnson. J.O.H.N.S.O.N.*

6. Avez-vous un diminutif, un surnom ou un sobriquet *(nickname, alias)?* Épelez-le.

   EXEMPLES: *C'est Betsy. B.E.T.S.Y.*
   C'est Rocky. R.O.C.K.Y.

---

1. What is your name? Please spell it. I'm ___your name___ .

Récapitulation

Recall what you have learned about your classmates and instructor. Answer formats are provided.

1. Comment s'appelle le professeur? Épelez son nom.
   • Il/Elle s'appelle _____. (Name and spelling)

2. Comment s'appelle votre voisin ou voisine de gauche (person on your left side)?
   • Il/Elle s'appelle _____. (Name and spelling)

3. Comment s'appelle votre voisin ou voisine de droite (person on your right side)?
   • Il/Elle s'appelle _____. (Name and spelling)
   Note: If a name is forgotten, simply ask again.
   Pardon. J'ai oublié votre nom. (I've forgotten your name.) **Ah oui. C'est ça.** (That's right.)
   Merci.

Remarques: *Accent Marks*

1. When the letter e has an **accent aigu** (é), it is indicated orally as follows:
   étudiant   E accent aigu, T, U, D, I, A, N, T

2. When the letters e and a have an **accent grave** (è, à), they are indicated orally as follows: très   T, R, E accent grave, S

3. When the letters a, e, i, o, and u have an **accent circonflexe** (ô), they are spelled aloud as follows: hôtel   H, O accent circonflexe, T, E, L

4. An accent mark over the letters e, a, and o often indicates that the letter s used to follow the vowel. The s often remains in the related English word.
   épelez spell   étudiant student   hôtel hostel   forêt forest   château castle

5. When the letter c has a **cédille** appended to it (ç), it is called c cédille. C cédille appears only before the letters a, o, and u and is pronounced [s]. Without the addition of the cedilla, the letter c followed by a, o, or u would be pronounced [k]. The cedilla, by maintaining the [s] sound, often reveals a relationship in meaning between two words of the same family.   français French—**France** France
   ça that (colloquial)—**cela** that   commençons let's begin—**commencer** to begin

6. The letters e and i sometimes have a **tréma** (ë) when they are preceded by another vowel. The **tréma** indicates that each vowel is to be pronounced separately.
   Noël   N, O, E tréma, L

Other spelling customs

1. Double letters (indicated in English oral spelling as "double R" or "R, R," for example) are indicated in French by the word **deux**.   professeur   P,R,O,F,E, deux S,E,U,R

2. The word for apostrophe (apostrophe) is inserted in the spelled word as in English.
   l'eau   L, apostrophe, E, A, U

3. Capital letters are indicated by the word **majuscule**. Hyphens are indicated by the words trait d'union.
   Jean-Marc   J majuscule, E, A, N, trait d'union, M majuscule, A, R, C

Expansion

The **Expansion** can be used for partners or group conversation and for oral or written composition. When two or more responses are possible, alternate answer formats are provided.

1. Épelez le prénom de votre mère, de votre père, de votre sœur, de votre frère, de votre meilleur(e) ami(e) (*best friend*), de votre chien (*dog*), etc.
   • Il/Elle s'appelle _____. (*Name and spelling*)

2. Quel est le nom de jeune fille de votre mère? de votre grand-mère (*grandmother*) maternelle? de votre grand-mère paternelle?
   • C'est _____. (*Name and spelling*)
   • Je ne sais pas. (*I don't know.*)

3. Quel est le nom de la rue où vous habitez? (*What is the name of the street where you live?*) Épelez-le.

   EXEMPLE: *La rue s'appelle Broadway.*
              B.R.O.A.D.W.A.Y.

Vocabulaire utile   The following phrases are frequently requested by students using the conversations of this **Entracte** involving the spelling of names.

Parlez plus fort, s'il vous plaît. Speak up, please.
Plus fort, s'il vous plaît. Louder, please.
Plus lentement, s'il vous plaît. More slowly, please.
D'accord. OK.
Bien sûr. Certainly.
Je recommence... I'll begin again...
Quel joli nom! What a pretty name!

Merci. Thank you.
Mon nom s'écrit... My name is spelled...
Son nom s'écrit... His/Her name is spelled...
Répétez cette lettre, s'il vous plaît. Repeat that letter, please.
Oh là là! Oh dear!
C'est difficile à prononcer! It's hard to pronounce!

Spelling by analogy.

The following standard spelling code is commonly used in French to clarify the spelling of names or words. Dictate the spelling of your own name to a classmate using this code.

A	comme *(as in)* Adèle	N	comme Nicolas
B	comme Berthe	O	comme Oscar
C	comme Célestin	P	comme Pierre
D	comme Désiré	Q	comme Quentin ou Quintal
E	comme Eugène	R	comme Raoul
É	comme Émile	S	comme Suzanne
F	comme François	T	comme Thérèse
G	comme Gaston	U	comme Ursule
H	comme Henri	V	comme Victor
I	comme Irma	W	comme William
J	comme Joseph	X	comme Xavier
K	comme Kléber	Y	comme Yvonne
L	comme Louis	Z	comme Zoé
M	comme Marcel		

Borrowed Words.

A nom de guerre *(literally:* name of war) is a pseudonym or a performer's stage name. A nom de plume *(literally:* name of quill pen) is a pen name, a writer's pseudonym.

French names.

Most French-speaking people have from two to five first names (prénoms) and no middle names as such. These first names generally include names of parents, grandparents, godparents, and Catholic saints. People normally use one or two first names (For example, Marie or Anne-Marie, Jacques or Jean-Pierre). They do not use middle initials.

Entracte.

The word entracte (sometimes spelled entr'acte) literally means "between acts." It is a brief interlude, a performance between two larger works. The sections entitled Entracte in this textbook are briefer change-of-pace lessons inserted between the longer main chapters.

Jean-Marc

Marie-Laure

Jean-Claude

Jean-Pierre

Anne-Marie

Synthèse

A. **Abbreviations.** The following countries, corporations, institutions, and expressions are commonly referred to by their abbreviations in French. Say them aloud.

S.N.C.F. (*Railroads:* Société Nationale des Chemins de fer Français)

U.R.S.S. (*USSR:* Union des Républiques Socialistes Soviétiques)

P.T.T. (*Post Office:* Postes, Télégraphes, Téléphones)

S.O.S. (*Save our ship! Help!*)

IBM (*International Business Machines Corporation*)

U.S.A. (*United States*)

É.-U. (*USA:* États-Unis)

O.R.T.F. (*Television and radio:* Office de Radiodiffusion et Télévision Française)

P.D.G. (*Big Boss:* Président-Directeur Général)

P.C.V. (*Collect telephone call*)

O.N.U. (*U.N.:* Organisation des Nations Unies)

B. **Street signs.** Spell the names of these Paris streets.

Projet

Eye chart. Work with a partner to create an eye chart (**un tableau**) of the sort opticians use, with rows of letters of different sizes. As your partner dictates letters of the French alphabet in random order, write them down in diminishing sizes on a piece of paper. Use the chart below as a model.

E

B C D G

F G L I H M

Z V O Q R S Q G T N

O C L F I R M N R Q Z S P T L S

Activités: Learning by Doing

A. **Chez l'opticien.** (*At the optician's.*) Everyone will have an eye examination in class. Use the eye charts created in the **Projet**. Post these **tableaux** around the classroom. Working with a partner, first ask some pertinent questions.

Portez-vous des lunettes? Do you wear glasses?
Portez-vous des verres de contact? Do you wear contact lenses?
Êtes-vous myope? Are you nearsighted?
Très myope? Very nearsighted?
Un peu myope? Slightly nearsighted?

Êtes-vous presbyte? Are you farsighted?
Êtes-vous astigmate? Are you astigmatic?
Je suis... I am...
Je ne suis pas... I'm not...
Je vois bien sans lunettes. I see well without glasses.

Now test your partner's vision. You may wish to have your partner cover one eye at a time or read the chart twice, with and without glasses. Say:

Regardez ce tableau. Look at this eye chart.
Pouvez-vous lire la première ligne? Can you read the first line?
Lisez la deuxième ligne. Read the second line.

C'est un E ou un F? Is it an E or an F?
C'est un G ou un J?
C'est un M ou un N?

B.   **Tombola.** Have a **tombola** *(raffle)* in class. (Prizes are optional and may consist of anything.) Everyone has a partner who will dictate, letter by letter, his or her full name. As names are spelled out by one student, they are written down on a small piece of paper by another. These pieces of paper are then folded and placed in **la tombola.** Winning names are drawn from **la tombola** and again spelled out loud for all to hear.

«D'abord, continuez tout droit. Puis...»

Comment Demander Son Chemin

Asking Directions

Qui cherche, trouve.

He who seeks, finds.

DIALOGUE

Being able to ask and understand directions is vital for getting around in a French-speaking country. This lesson presents vocabulary and structures related to asking and giving directions, including typical inquiries and responses, a variety of places and possible destinations of interest to tourists, prepositions of location, and modes of transportation. Vocabulary blocks within this **Dialogue** offer options to suit a wide variety of real-life situations.

Comment Demander Son Chemin	Asking Directions
VOUS: Pardon, Monsieur / Madame / Mademoiselle. Pouvez-vous m'aider? Je cherche **la gare.**[1] (*may Day*)	YOU: Excuse me. Can you help me? I'm looking for the **train station.**
la banque la bibliothèque la cathédrale la poste la préfecture de police la rue... la sortie	bank library cathedral post office police station ... Street exit
UN PASSANT: Je suis désolé(e). Je ne sais pas. Je ne suis pas d'ici. VOUS: Excusez-moi, Monsieur / Madame. Je cherche la gare. UN AUTRE PASSANT: **Le parc?**[2]	A PASSERBY: I'm sorry. I don't know. I'm not from (around) here. YOU: Excuse me. I'm looking for the train station. ANOTHER PASSERBY: The **park?**
Le château? Le cinéma? Le métro? Le musée? Les jardins (*m*) publics? Les toilettes (*f*)?	castle movies subway museum public gardens restrooms
VOUS: Non, la gare. C'est loin? LE PASSANT: Oui, c'est **assez loin** d'ici.	YOU: No, the train station. Is it far? PASSERBY: Yes, it's **rather far** from here.
très loin tout près à deux pas à cinq minutes à un mille à un kilomètre tout à côté juste en face	very far very near (to) two steps five minutes one mile one kilometer right next (to) right across

1. This vocabulary block contains only feminine nouns preceded by **la** (*the*). Note that these all end with the letter **e**.

2. This vocabulary block contains masculine nouns preceded by **le** (*the*) and plural nouns (both masculine and feminine) preceded by **les**. Note that **le musée**, although masculine, ends with the letter **e**. See also in this **Dialogue: un mille, un kilomètre.**

VOUS: Comment puis-je y aller?
LE PASSANT: C'est facile. D'abord,
   continuez tout droit. Puis...
   | tournez à gauche
   | tournez à droite
   | allez tout droit
   | allez par là

   Et voilà, vous y êtes!
VOUS: Pardon? Je ne comprends pas.
LE PASSANT: Alors, prenez **le métro.** C'est
   | l'autobus (*m*)
   | le bus
   | un taxi

   plus simple.

VOUS: Où est **la station de métro,** s'il vous
   | la station de taxis
   | l'arrêt d'autobus (*m*)

   plaît?

LE PASSANT: C'est là-bas, à votre gauche.
   Juste devant / derrière **l'église (f).**[3]
   | l'aéroport (*m*)
   | l'ascenseur (*m*)
   | l'école (*f*)
   | l'entrée (*f*)
   | l'escalier (*m*)
   | l'hôpital (*m*)
   | l'hôtel (*m*)
   | l'université (*f*)

VOUS: Merci bien, Monsieur / Madame.
LE PASSANT: Je vous en prie, Monsieur /
   Madame. Et bonne chance!

YOU: How can I get there?
PASSERBY: It's easy. First,
   continue / go straight ahead. Then . . .
   | turn left
   | turn right
   | go straight ahead
   | go that way

   And there you are!
YOU: Excuse me? I don't understand.
PASSERBY: Well then, take the **subway.** It's
   | the bus
   | the bus
   | a taxi

   easier.

YOU: Where is the **subway station,** please?
   | taxi stand
   | bus stop

PASSERBY: It's over there, on your left. Just in
   front of / behind the **church.**
   | airport
   | elevator
   | school
   | entrance
   | stairway
   | hospital
   | hotel
   | university

YOU: Thank you.
PASSERBY: You're welcome. And good luck!

Phrases à retenir

Memorizing these few simple phrases from the **Dialogue** will help assure
fluency in a variety of real-life situations in which you may be asking or giving
directions.

1. Pouvez-vous m'aider?
2. Je cherche la gare.
3. Je ne sais pas.
4. Je ne suis pas d'ici.

3. This vocabulary block contains examples of "elision." **Le** and **la** become **l'** before a noun
beginning with a vowel or silent **h.** **La** + **école** becomes **l'école.** **Le** + **hôpital** becomes **l'hôpital.**
Since there is no way to determine if an elided noun is masculine or feminine without an adjective
present, this gender information is included here for your reference in parentheses.

5. C'est loin?   9. C'est là-bas.
6. Comment puis-je y aller?   10. C'est à gauche.
7. Je ne comprends pas.   11. C'est à droite.
8. Où est la gare, s'il vous plaît?   12. Continuez tout droit.

DIALOGUE EXERCISES

The following exercises provide oral and written practice in using the
vocabulary and basic sentence patterns of the **Dialogue: Comment demander
son chemin**. These exercises use *only* vocabulary and structures presented in the
asking directions **Dialogue**. They do not require familiarity with any other
portions of this chapter.

Exercices d'application

A. **Places vocabulary: Je cherche...**   Ask for help. You are looking for each of
these places.

MODÈLE: la gare   *Pouvez-vous m'aider? Je cherche la gare.*

1. la cathédrale   5. l'hôtel
2. le parc   6. l'aéroport
3. la banque   7. la poste
4. le cinéma   8. la bibliothèque

B. **Places vocabulary: Où est...?**   Ask where each of the following is located.

MODÈLE: la gare   *S'il vous plaît, où est la gare?*

1. la banque   5. le parc
2. la bibliothèque   6. l'église
3. le cinéma   7. la station de métro
4. l'hôpital   8. l'arrêt d'autobus

C. **Expressions related to location: C'est loin d'ici.**   Give the location of each of
the places indicated.

MODÈLE: la gare (loin d'ici)   *La gare? C'est loin d'ici.*

1. la cathédrale (très loin d'ici)
2. la gare (à gauche)
3. la poste (juste devant l'église)
4. l'église (là-bas, à gauche)
5. la banque (juste en face)

      6. la sortie (tout droit)
      7. l'arrêt d'autobus (derrière l'église)
      8. la station de taxis (tout près)

D.   **Dialogue responses.**   What could you respond to each of the following? Use sentences and phrases taken directly from the **Dialogue**.

      1. Pouvez-vous m'aider?
      2. Je cherche la gare.
      3. C'est loin.
      4. Comment puis-je y aller?
      5. Je suis désolé, mais je ne comprends pas.
      6. Où est la station de métro, s'il vous plaît?
      7. Merci bien!

E.   **Review.**   What do you say...

      1. to get someone's attention?
      2. to ask for help when you want to go to the train station?
      3. to ask if your destination is far away?
      4. to ask the best means of getting someplace?
      5. when someone is speaking French a little too quickly for you to understand?
      6. to ask where the subway station is?
      7. to thank someone for having helped you?
      8. when someone thanks you for something?

Improvisation à deux *(Exercice oral)*

F.   Use the vocabulary block options and the basic sentence structures of the **Dialogue** to improvise a dialogue with a classmate. Ask directions to the restrooms, the exit, the stairway, or to a nearby building. Begin with: **Pardon, Monsieur/Madame/Mademoiselle. Pouvez-vous m'aider? Je cherche...** Use **Pardon?** whenever you cannot hear or clearly understand your partner.

À Vous le choix *(Exercices écrits)*

G.   Write a six- to eight-line dialogue for each of the following situations, selecting appropriate phrases from the initial **Dialogue** of this chapter.

      1. You are looking for the library. It is very close by.
      2. You want to get to the Ritz Hotel (*L'Hôtel Ritz*). It is very far away. You may have to take a bus or subway.
      3. You want to get to the university. You will have to take a taxi.

Conversations

H. Ask your classmates these personalized questions. Answer formats are provided. Do not limit your responses simply to those suggestions offered in these questions. Use the inclusive vocabulary options provided in the **Dialogue.** (You may wish to use the **tu** form of address with your classmates.)

1. Où habitez-vous (habites-tu)? *(Where do you live?)* Loin d'ici? Tout près d'ici?À deux pas d'ici? À cinq minutes d'ici? À un mille d'ici? Tout à côté d'ici? Juste en face d'ici?
   • J'habite *(I live)* _____.

2. Ask a classmate whether specific places are nearby or far away from the building in which your French class is held.

   EXEMPLE: *La bibliothèque. C'est loin d'ici?*

I. **Review.** What have you learned about your classmates from these **Conversations?**

EXEMPLES: *Marc habite près d'ici.*
              Monsieur Smith habite juste en face d'ici.

French police. If you are lost, do not hesitate to ask directions from a police officer. In towns and cities, police are known as **les agents de police** or, more familiarly, as **les flics**. They are easily recognizable by their blue uniforms and special hats **(des képis)**. Generally on foot, they will be directing traffic and maintaining order. When addressing an officer, use a courteous **Pardon, Monsieur. La gare, s'il vous plaît?** In rural areas, **gendarmes** in tan uniforms replace the **agents**. On highways, blue-uniformed **motards** patrol on motorcycle.

Public transportation in Paris. The Paris subway system, conversationally referred to as **le métro** (short for **le métropolitain**), is a network of crisscrossing lines that connect with suburban train **(R.E.R.)** and bus lines. Many of the **métro** lines have rubber-wheel cars that are fast, quiet, and efficient. You can go to any point in Paris by changing lines at one of the many transfer points called **correspondances**.

Abbreviations.   The expression **s'il vous plaît** is often abbreviated in written French as **s.v.p.**

Les Toilettes.   To locate a restroom ask, **Les toilettes, s'il vous plaît?** You may wish to specify **pour dames** or **pour messieurs**, although frequently men and women share the same facilities in France.

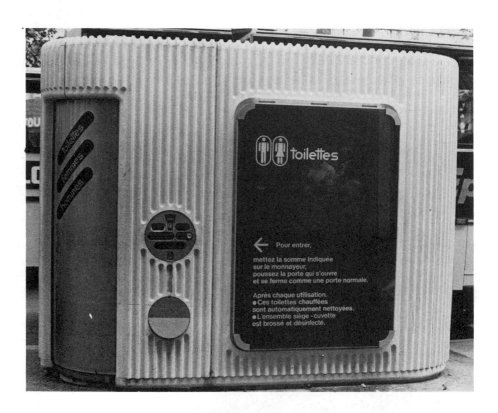

Entrée et sortie.   To locate the entrance, ask, **L'entrée, s'il vous plaît?** For the exit, **La sortie, s'il vous plaît?**

VERBES IRRÉGULIERS: pouvoir, prendre, savoir

➤

pouvoir	to be able, can
je **peux**	I can, I am able
tu **peux**	you can, you are able
il/elle **peut**	he/she can, he/she is able
nous **pouvons**	we can, we are able
vous **pouvez**	you can, you are able
ils/elles **peuvent**	they can, they are able

1. The question "Can I?" is often expressed by a special verb form: **Puis-je?**
2. The verb **pouvoir** is often followed by an infinitive.

   Vous **pouvez prendre** l'autobus.   You can take the bus.

Exercices d'application: **pouvoir**

A.   **Puis-je...?**   Ask if you can do the following things.

MODÈLE: prendre l'autobus   *Puis-je prendre l'autobus?*

1. tourner
2. continuer
3. aller tout droit

4. prendre le métro
5. tourner à gauche
6. continuer tout droit

B.   **Je peux...Je ne peux pas.**   Give the affirmative form. Then change your mind and give the negative form.

MODÈLE: je peux
   Oui, je peux. Non. À vrai dire, je ne peux pas!
   (Yes, I can. No. Actually, I cannot!)

1. tu peux
2. je peux
3. ils peuvent
4. elle peut

5. nous pouvons
6. vous pouvez
7. il peut

C.   **Tu ne peux pas...**   Tell a good friend that he or she cannot do the following things. Use the **tu** form.

MODÈLE: continuer   *Tu ne peux pas continuer!*

1. tourner
2. aller par là
3. demander

4. tourner à gauche
5. tourner à droite

prendre	to take
je **prends**	I take, I am taking
tu **prends**	you take, you are taking
il/elle **prend**	he/she takes, he/she is taking
nous **prenons**	we take, we are taking
vous **prenez**	you take, you are taking
ils/elles **prennent**	they take, they are taking

The verbs **apprendre** *(to learn)* and **comprendre** *(to understand)* are conjugated like **prendre**.

Exercices d'application: prendre

D. **Vous prenez... Je prends...**   Someone is giving you directions. Repeat what you plan to do as you are given the directions.

MODÈLE: D'abord *(first)* vous prenez la rue à gauche.
          Oui. Je prends la rue à gauche.

1. D'abord vous prenez la rue à gauche.
2. Et puis *(then)* vous prenez la rue à droite.
3. Puis vous prenez la rue juste en face.
4. Puis vous prenez l'avenue *(the avenue)* à gauche.
5. Puis vous prenez le métro juste devant la poste.

E. **Vous prenez...? Je ne prends pas...**   Answer in the negative, adding that you are going to go by foot instead.

MODÈLE: Vous prenez le métro?
          Non, je ne prends pas le métro. J'y vais à pied.

1. Vous prenez l'autobus?
2. Vous prenez le taxi?
3. Vous prenez le bus?
4. Vous prenez le métro?

F. **Il prend...? Il ne prend pas...**   Answer **non** to each question.

MODÈLE: Votre frère prend l'autobus?
          Non, il ne prend pas l'autobus.

1. Le professeur prend le métro?
2. Il prend l'escalier?
3. Elle prend l'autobus?
4. Ils prennent l'autobus?
5. Madame prend l'ascenseur?
6. On prend le métro?

➤

savoir	to know
je **sais** *Say*	I know
tu **sais**	you know
il/elle **sait**	he/she knows
nous **savons**	we know
vous **savez** *Savée*	you know
ils/elles **savent**	they know

1. **Savoir** means "to know" or "to have knowledge of" a fact.

   Je sais votre nom.   I know your name.
   Savez-vous la date?   Do you know the date?

2. **Savoir** followed by an infinitive means "to know how."

   Savez-vous parler français?   Do you know how to speak French?

3. Savoir may be followed by:

   comment how   **quand** when
   où where   **que** that
   pourquoi why   **si** if

   Savez-vous **où** il est?   Do you know where he is?
   Je sais **que** vous prenez le métro. I know that you take the subway.

Exercices d'application: **savoir**

G.   **Je sais...**   Say that you know the following.

MODÈLE: la réponse   *Je sais la réponse.*

1. la date   4. l'alphabet
2. le nom   5. la réponse
3. le numéro (*number; telephone
   number*)

H.   **Savez-vous où est...?**   Ask directions to the following places.

MODÈLE: la gare   *Savez-vous où est la gare?*

1. la cathédrale   4. la sortie
2. l'aéroport   5. l'ascenseur
3. l'église   6. l'entrée

I.   **Est-ce que vous savez où est...?**   Ask someone where the following places are.
You may wish to use the informal **tu** form of address with your classmates.

MODÈLE: la gare   *Est-ce que vous savez où est la gare?*
                       Est-ce que tu sais où est la gare?

1. l'entrée   4. l'église
2. la sortie   5. l'aéroport
3. l'ascenseur   6. la cathédrale

STRUCTURES

Structure 1: Definite Articles

All French nouns are either masculine or feminine. Most nouns are made plural
by adding **s** to the singular. **Le, la,** or **les** is used to mean "the," depending on
whether the noun that follows is masculine or feminine, singular or plural. **Le**
and **la** become **l'** before a noun that begins with a vowel or mute **h**.[4]

Definite Articles	
le	before masculine nouns beginning with a consonant: **le taxi, le musée**
la	before feminine nouns beginning with a consonant: **la banque, la gare**
l'	before masculine or feminine nouns beginning with a vowel or mute **h**: **l'ascenseur** *(m)*, **l'hôtel** *(m)*, **l'église** *(f)*
les	before all plural nouns: **les taxis** *(m)*, **les banques** *(f)* **les ascenseurs** *(m)*

Pronunciation note: The definite article **les** [le] is pronounced [lez] when it is
                           followed by a word that begins with a vowel or mute **h**:
                           les ascenseurs, les hôtels, les églises.
                               z   z   z

Exercices d'application: Definite Articles

A.   **Où est...?** Ask where the following places are located, using **le** or **la** before the
           noun as appropriate.

4. Regarding "mute **h**," see **Prononciation**, Chapter 4, page 120.

MODÈLE: the exit   *Où est la sortie?*

1. the cathedral
2. the museum
3. the library
4. the street

5. the subway sation
6. the exit
7. the park

B.   **Les taxis sont par là.**   When someone asks you where something is, point and
tell that person it is "over there." Use the plural definite article, **les.**

MODÈLE: Les taxis, s'il vous plaît?   *Les taxis sont par là.*

1. Les bus, s'il vous plaît?
2. Les jardins publics, s'il vous plaît?
3. Les musées, s'il vous plaît?
4. Les toilettes, s'il vous plaît?
5. Les taxis, s'il vous plaît?

Structure 2: Indefinite Articles

Un or **une** is used to mean "a (an)," depending on whether the noun that
follows is masculine or feminine. **Des** means "some" or "any."

Indefinite Articles	
un	before all masculine nouns: **un taxi, un ascenseur**
une	before all feminine nouns: **une banque, une église**
des	before all plural nouns: **des taxis** (*m*), **des banques** (*f*), **des ascenseurs** (*m*)

Pronunciation note: The indefinite article **des** [de] is pronounced [dez] when it is
followed by a word that begins with a vowel or mute **h.**
Examples from this lesson:
des ascenseurs   des hôtels   des églises

Exercices d'application: Indefinite Articles

C.   **Qu'est-ce que c'est? C'est un... C'est une...**   (*What is it? It's a. . .*) Working with
a classmate, take a piece of paper and make a rough sketch of any of the places
from the **Dialogue: une bibliothèque, une cathédrale, un aéroport,** etc. Ask
your partner what you have drawn.

EXEMPLE: —*Qu'est-ce que c'est?*
          —*C'est un parc?*
          —*Non! Ce n'est pas un parc.*
          —*C'est un taxi?*
          —*Oui! C'est ça!* (That's it!)
          —*C'est un taxi?*
          —*Non! C'est un aéroport!*
          —*Ah bon...*

D. **J'habite près d'un...près d'une...** (*I live near a . . .*) Using as many places from the **Dialogue** as possible, describe where you live. Use **un** or **une** as appropriate.

EXEMPLES: *J'habite près d'un musée / près d'une église / près d'une bibliothèque.*

Structure 3: Contractions with à and the Definite Article

The preposition **à** *(to, at)* contracts with **le** and **les**.

```
à + le → au
à + les → aux
à + la remains à la
à + l' remains à l'
```

EXEMPLES:

à + le parc → au parc   to or at the park
à + les jardins → aux jardins   to or at the gardens

à + la gare remains à la gare   to or at the train station
à + l'aéroport remains à   to or at the airport
   l'aéroport

Exercices d'application: Contractions with à and the Definite Article

E. **Pour aller à la gare, s'il vous plaît?** (Literally: *For going to the train station, please?* This is a conversational way of asking directions without using **Où est...?**) Ask how to get to the following locations taken from the **Dialogue**. Use **au, à la,** or **à l'** as appropriate.

MODÈLE: la gare   *Pour aller à la gare, s'il vous plaît?*

1. l'Hôtel Ritz
2. le cinéma
3. l'aéroport
4. la poste

5. le musée
6. la cathédrale
7. l'hôpital

F.   **Je vais au...à la...à l'...**   Where are you going today? Where are you going this week? Look through all the locations given in the **Dialogue**. Select those places where you really intend to go today **(aujourd'hui)** or this week **(cette semaine)**. Use **au, à la,** or **à l'** as appropriate.

EXEMPLES: *Je vais à la banque aujourd'hui.*
            Je vais à l'hôpital cette semaine.

Structure 4: Contractions with **de** and the Definite Article

The preposition **de** *(of, from, about)* contracts with **le** and **les**.

> **de** + **le** ⟶ **du**
> **de** + **les** ⟶ **des**
> **de** + **la** remains **de la**
> **de** + **l'** remains **de l'**

EXEMPLES:

de + **le parc** ⟶ **du parc**	**from** the park
de + **les jardins** ⟶ **des jardins**	**from** the gardens
de + **la gare** remains **de la gare**	**from** the train station
de + **l'aéroport** remains **de l'aéroport**	**from** the airport

De is used to express possession or relationship.

l'adresse **de Marie**	Marie's address *(literally:* the address of Marie)
l'ami(e) **de ma sœur**	my sister's friend *(literally:* the friend of my sister)

Exercices d'application: **de la, du, des**

G.   **Où êtes-vous?**   Which of the following locations describe your present situation? Select as many as applicable. Pay attention to prepositions of location contracting with the definite article.

EXEMPLES: *Je suis près de la porte.*
            Je suis loin des fenêtres.

1. à côté de la porte *(door)*
2. près de la porte
3. à côté de la fenêtre *(window)*
4. loin de la porte
5. loin des fenêtres
6. en face de la fenêtre
7. à deux pas de la porte
8. tout près de la porte
9. près du professeur
10. à côté du professeur

H. **C'est le livre de...**   Pass several textbooks belonging to different class members around the room. When you receive a book, state whose book it is and hand it to someone else.

EXEMPLE: —*Voilà le livre de Marc.*
           —*De qui?* (Whose?)
           —*C'est le livre de Marc.*

Structure 5: -er Verbs (Present Tense)

The infinitives of many French verbs end in **-er**. The infinitive is the form you will find when you look up a verb in the dictionary. The English equivalent is *to . . .* For example, **parler** means *"to speak."*

1. The present tense of **-er** verbs is formed by adding the appropriate endings to the base, or stem, of the verb. The base is found by dropping the **-er** ending from the infinitive. For example, the base of the verb **parler** is **parl-**.

je parl**e**	nous parl**ons**
tu parl**es**	vous parl**ez**
il parl**e**	ils parl**ent**
elle parl**e**	elles parl**ent**
on parl**e**	

[handwritten: Parler e ons / es ez / e ent]

2. There are often three possible English meanings for each form. **"je parle"** can mean *"I speak," "I am speaking,"* or *"I do speak."*
3. *Pronunciation note:* The verb endings **-e, -es,** and **ent** are silent.
4. The negative form of the present tense is as follows.

je **ne parle pas**	nous **ne parlons pas**
tu **ne parles pas**	vous **ne parlez pas**
il **ne parle pas**	ils **ne parlent pas**
elle **ne parle pas**	elles **ne parlent pas**
on **ne parle pas**	

5. **Je** becomes **j'** before verbs beginning with a vowel or mute **h.**
   J'aime voyager.
   J'habite Paris.

   Elle remains **elle.**
   Elle aime voyager.
   Elle habite Paris.

Merci de ne pas fumer.

6. Some common **-er** verbs used in everyday conversation:

adorer to adore	**étudier** to study	**regarder** to look (at)
aider to help	**fermer** to close	**téléphoner (à)** to
aimer to like, to love	**fumer** to smoke	telephone
chanter to sing	**habiter** to live (in)	**tourner** to turn
chercher to look for	**inviter** to invite	**travailler** to work
commencer to begin	**jouer** to play	**trouver** to find
continuer to continue	**manger** to eat	**visiter** to visit (a
danser to dance	**nager** to swim	place)
donner to give	**oublier** to forget	**voyager** to travel
écouter to listen (to)	**parler** to speak	

Exercices d'application: Present Tense of **-er** Verbs

I. **Aimez-vous…?**   What do you like to do? Ask classmates what they like to do. (You may wish to use the **tu** form of address with your classmates.)

MODÈLE: nager   —*Aimez-vous (Aimes-tu) nager?*
                        —*Oui, j'aime nager.*
            or: —*Non, je n'aime pas nager.*

1. danser
2. fumer
3. manger
4. voyager
5. jouer au tennis
6. étudier

7. chanter
8. parler au téléphone
9. travailler
10. regarder la télévision
11. écouter la radio
12. parler français

J. **Il aime chanter.**   If the preceding exercise has been used orally in class, review what you have learned about your classmates.

EXEMPLES: *Marie aime chanter.*
                 Marc n'aime pas regarder la télévision.
                 Monsieur Smith aime étudier.

K. **Savez-vous…?**   *(Personalized exercise)* What do you know how to do? Ask classmates whether they actually know how to do the following things or not. (You may wish to use the **tu** form of address with your classmates.)

MODÈLE: nager   —*Savez-vous (Sais-tu) nager?*
                        —*Oui, je sais nager.*
            or: —*Non, je ne sais pas nager.*

1. danser
2. parler français
3. étudier

4. fumer
5. jouer au tennis
6. nager

L.   **Oui, j'étudie le français.**   What do you actually do? Respond as applicable to yourself.

MODÈLE: habiter New York
Oui, j'habite New York.
or: *Non, je n'habite pas New York.*

1. étudier le français
2. jouer au tennis
3. parler français
4. parler espagnol *(Spanish)*
5. habiter Paris

6. voyager beaucoup *(a lot)*
7. manger beaucoup
8. travailler
9. habiter tout près d'ici
10. fumer

Structure 6: Imperatives

The imperative (a command or order) is formed in French by using the present tense of the verb without the subject pronoun.

Continuez tout droit!   Continue (going) straight ahead!
Tournez à gauche!   Turn left!

1. The **tu** (informal) form of the verb can be used for commands with close friends, relatives, or children.

   Prends le métro.   Take the subway.

   Exception: With **-er** verbs and the verb **aller**, the letter **s** of the second person singular is dropped.

   Mange!   Eat!
   Étudie!   Study!
   Va à l'école!   Go to school!

2. The imperative in the first person plural **(nous)** is translated as "let's," or "let us."

   Allons!   Let's go!
   Regardons la télévision!   Let's watch television!

3. A negative command is formed as follows.

   Ne tournez pas à gauche!   Don't turn left!
   Ne mange pas!   Don't eat!
   Ne regardons pas la télévision! Let's not watch television!

4. The verb **être** has an irregular imperative.

   Sois calme!   Be calm! (**Tu** form)
   Ne soyons pas ridicules!   Let's not be ridiculous! (**Nous** form)
   Soyez sage!   Be good! (**Vous** form)

Exercices d'application: Imperatives

M. **Écoutez bien en classe!**   What should you do in class? What shouldn't you do in class? Using the verbs studied so far, tell a classmate what he or she should or should not do in class.

EXEMPLES: *Ne parlez pas en classe!*
Ne fumez pas en classe!
Écoutez bien en classe!

What about **chanter, danser, étudier, jouer, manger, travailler,** and so on?

N. **Écoute bien en classe!**   Now tell a classmate what he or she should or should not do in class. This time use the **tu** (informal) form of command.

EXEMPLES: *Ne fume pas en classe!*
Ne mange pas en classe!

O. **Je cherche...**   Form a command in response to each statement given below.

MODÈLE: Je cherche l'Opéra.
          Eh bien. (Let's see/O.K.) Tournez à droite.

1. Je cherche la place de la Concorde.
2. Je cherche la place de l'Étoile.
3. Je cherche l'Opéra.
4. Je cherche les Invalides.

Structure 7: Future Tense with **Aller** + Infinitive

There is a simple way of expressing the future in French. It is called the **futur proche** *(near future)*. All you need to know is the verb **aller** in the present. By adding the infinitive form of any verb after the conjugated form of **aller**, you are expressing an idea in the near future. We have the same construction in English.

Je vais regarder la télévision.	I am going to watch television.
Elle va étudier.	She is going to study.

Exercices d'application: **Futur Proche**

P. **Je vais...**   What are you going to do later on today **(aujourd'hui)?** This evening **(ce soir)?** tomorrow **(demain)?** Use the verbs of Chapters 1 and 2 to tell about what you actually will be doing in the near future.

EXEMPLES: *Je vais manger.*
            Je vais étudier.
            Je vais prendre le métro.
            Je vais être fatigué(e).

Q. **Je ne vais pas...**   Use the verbs of Chapters 1 and 2 to describe some things that you will probably *not* be doing within the next day or so.

EXEMPLES: *Je ne vais pas regarder la télévision.*
            Je ne vais pas fumer.
            Je ne vais pas étudier.

Synthèse

A.   **What about you?**   Ask a classmate the following personalized questions. Tell your partner about yourself. (You may wish to use the **tu** form of address with your classmates.)

1. Fumez-vous (Fumes-tu) des cigarettes? des cigares? une pipe? beaucoup?
2. Étudiez-vous beaucoup?
3. À qui téléphonez-vous souvent *(often)*? de temps en temps *(from time to time)*? À vos parents? À des amis?
4. Habitez-vous loin d'ici? près d'ici?
5. Savez-vous nager? danser? jouer au tennis?
6. Aimez-vous parler français?
7. Voyagez-vous souvent? beaucoup? de temps en temps?
8. Regardez-vous la télévision souvent? beaucoup? de temps en temps?
9. Travaillez-vous?
10. Jouez-vous au tennis?
11. Habitez-vous près d'un parc? près d'un cinéma? près d'une église? près d'une gare? près d'une banque? etc.

B.   **Giving directions.**   Looking at this map, discuss how to get from **la gare** to (1) **la banque,** (2) **le cinéma,** (3) **l'Hôtel Ritz.** Use vocabulary from the **Dialogue.**

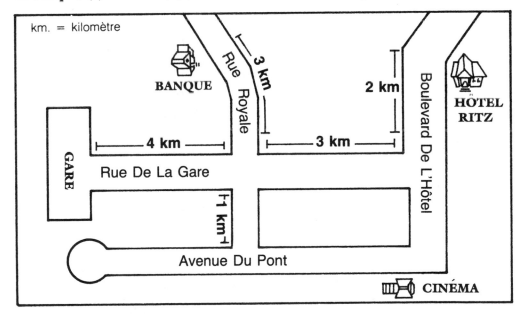

Other useful vocabulary:

Prenez/Suivez la rue/l'avenue/le boulevard...   Take/Follow the street/avenue/boulevard...

Prenez la première/deuxième/troisième rue à droite/gauche.   Take the first/second/third street on the (your) right/left.

Passez devant le/la...   Pass in front of
the...
Au carrefour...   At the intersection/
crossroads...

**Tournez à gauche/à droite dans la
rue...**   Turn left/right onto/on/at
...street.

PRONONCIATION

1. Sound (Phonetic Symbol): [ɛ̃]

SPELLING: **in, im, ain, aim, ein, eim, en** (after **i** or **é**)

ENGLISH SOUND RESEMBLED: Vowel sound in words *Anne* and *ham*

PRONUNCIATION: To pronounce the nasal sound [ɛ̃], open the lips. Constrict throat slightly. Do not pronounce the final **n** or **m** as in English. Mouth remains open throughout entire nasal sound.

EXAMPLES FROM THIS CHAPTER:

chemin	cinq	bien
jardin	maintenant	simple
loin		

Notes:
1. The spellings **in, im, ain, aim** change pronunciation and lose their nasal quality when followed by a vowel or by another n or m. Examples from this chapter: aimer   ai - mer; **cinéma**   ci - né - ma; **continuez**   con - ti - nuez; **minute**   mi - nute.
2. American speakers will have to pay particular attention to the fact that the spelling **in** is pronounced [ɛ̃], especially in such words as **vin** (*wine*), **vingt** (*twenty*), and **lingerie**.

2. Sound (Phonetic Symbol): [œ̃]

SPELLING: **un, um**

PRONUNCIATION: This nasal vowel sound [œ̃], similar to the nasal vowel sound [ɛ̃], is produced by rounding the lips a little more. The [œ̃] sound, however, is gradually disappearing from current usage. Many French-speaking people actually use only the one sound [ɛ̃] for both cases. For this reason, you will hear the word **un** pronounced either [œ̃] or [ɛ̃], **lundi** pronounced either [lœ̃di] or [lɛ̃di], and so forth.

Note: The spellings **un** and **um** lose their nasal quality when they are followed by a vowel or another n or m. Examples from this chapter: **une**; **université**   u-ni-ver-si-té.

3. Syllabification

Knowing how to break French words into syllables facilitates correct pronunciation. Once you can syllabify a word, you can pronounce it, no matter how long it is. Here are some general rules.

1. French syllables tend to end in vowel sounds. This is different from English syllables, which tend to end in consonant sounds. French syllables are generally "open." English syllables are generally "closed."

2. Single consonants between two vowels go with the following vowel: **ci - né - ma** (English often joins the single consonant to the preceding syllable.)

3. Double consonants between two vowels are generally treated as one and go with the following vowel sound: **co - mment** (English generally splits these double consonants.)

4. Two different consonants in a row are usually divided between syllables: **u-ni-ver-si-té**. *Exception:* the consonant groups **bl, br, cl, cr, dr, fl, fr, gl, gr, pl, tr, vr** remain intact and go with the following vowel sound: **bi-bli-o-thèque, é-glise, ca-thé-drale**

Breaking French words into syllables also promotes authentic-sounding stress patterns, with each French syllable receiving the same even stress. In the following list, consider why each word taken from this chapter has been broken into syllables as it has. Then practice each one for pronunciation and stress.

par-don	cher-che	es-ca-lier
pou-vez	sor-tie	u-ni-ver-si-té
ai-der	co-mment	bi-bli-o-thèque
toi-lettes	a-ller	tour-nez
jar-dins	pre-nez	con-ti-nu-ez
pu-blics	mé-tro	de-vant
ci-né-ma	ta-xi	é-glise
sa-vez	au-to-bus	en-trée

Note: The pronunciation shift discussed in item 1, page 52 is easier to understand when viewed as actually being a result of syllabification. *For example:* vin *(wine)* + aigre *(sour)* = vinaigre *(vinegar, soured wine).* The word vin is pronounced [v ɛ̃], *but* vinaigre is pronounced vi - nai - gre [vin ɛ gR].

Projet

Come visit me.   *(Exercice oral ou écrit)* You are giving a party. Give directions to your place (house, apartment, dormitory, etc.). Start from the location of your French class **(la salle de classe)**. You may wish to include a simple illustrative map with key landmarks such as churches, post offices, schools, hospitals, hotels, or other locations given in the **Dialogue** of this chapter.

Activité: Learning by Doing

Asking, giving, and taking directions in the classroom. Begin by asking a classmate:

Où est la fenêtre *(window)?*
Où est la porte *(door)?*
Où est le professeur *(professor)?*
Où est le tableau noir *(blackboard)?*

Où est la table *(table)?*
Où est le mur *(wall)?*
Où est le bureau du professeur
(professor's desk)?

Respond with one of the following expressions:

Là-bas! Over there!
Le voilà! There he/it (masc. noun) is!

La voilà! There she/it (fem. noun) is!

Now direct a classmate around the classroom, to the window, to the door, to the blackboard, and so on. Get up from your seat and *actually move* about the room. Use these expressions. Remember to say "please": **s'il vous plaît.**

Tournez à gauche. Turn left.
Tournez à droite. Turn right.
Allez tout droit. Go straight ahead.
Continuez tout droit. Continue (going) straight ahead.

Encore. Again.
Encore une fois. Once again.
Maintenant... Now...
Avancez un peu. Go forward a little.
Arrêtez!/Stop! Stop!

Variation: Make signs based on the vocabulary blocks of the **Dialogue** of this chapter: **la banque, la cathédrale, la gare,** etc. Post these signs around the classroom with tape. Ask classmates for directions to these places. Begin with: **Pour aller à la bibliothèque, s'il vous plaît?** or **Pardon, Monsieur/Madame/ Mademoiselle? Je cherche la bibliothèque. Pouvez-vous m'aider?**

Vocabulaire utile

The following phrases are frequently requested by students participating in this asking directions activity.

Levez-vous, s'il vous plaît. Get up, please.
Bien! Oui! C'est ça! Good. Fine. That's right.
Pardon? Excuse me?
Je ne comprends pas. I don't understand.
(Parlez) plus lentement, s'il vous plaît. (Speak) more slowly, please.
Parlez) plus fort, s'il vous plaît. (Speak) more loudly, please.
Retournez-vous. Turn around.
Attention! Watch out!
Eh! Doucement! Take it easy!
Vite! Vite! Quickly!
Dépêchez-vous! Hurry up!

Allons! Let's go.
Allez-y! Go to it!
Un moment. (Wait) a moment!
Pas si vite! Not so fast!
Oh là là! Oh dear!
Zut, alors! Darn it!
Flûte alors! *(milder expletive)* Darn it.
Merci. Thank you.
Je vous en prie. You're welcome.
Asseyez-vous, je vous prie. Sit down, please.
Et vous voilà! There you are!
Bravo! Great! Good job!

Quel âge avez-vous?

Numbers

| Deux avis valent mieux qu'un. | Two heads are better than one. |

Knowing numbers and how to count is essential for dealing effectively with situations arising in daily life, in travel, and in business—settling restaurant bills, tipping, dealing with salespeople, paying cashiers, placing phone calls, making travel arrangements, and so on. This lesson introduces numbers vocabulary formation and pronunciation.

Quel âge avez-vous?

Réponse: • J'ai _____ ans.[1]

EXEMPLE: *J'ai vingt-cinq ans.*

Direct substitution of the French numbers from this list into the given response formats will allow immediate and correct conversational self-expression. No grammatical manipulation is necessary.

0	zéro	20	vingt	80	quatre-vingts	
1	un	21	vingt et un	81	quatre-vingt-un	
2	deux	22	vingt-deux	82	quatre-vingt-deux	
3	trois	23	vingt-trois	90	quatre-vingt-dix	
4	quatre	30	trente	91	quatre-vingt-onze	
5	cinq	31	trente et un	92	quatre-vingt-douze	
6	six	32	trente-deux	100	cent	
7	sept	40	quarante	101	cent un	
8	huit	41	quarante et un	102	cent deux	
9	neuf	42	quarante-deux	200	deux cents	
10	dix	50	cinquante	201	deux cent un	
11	onze	51	cinquante et un	300	trois cents	
12	douze	52	cinquante-deux	1000	mille (*invariable*)	
13	treize	60	soixante	2000	deux mille	
14	quatorze	61	soixante et un	5000	cinq mille	
15	quinze	62	soixante-deux	10.000	dix mille	
16	seize	70	soixante-dix	100.000	cent mille	
17	dix-sept	71	soixante et onze	1.000.000	un million (de...)	
18	dix-huit	72	soixante-douze	1.000.000.000	un milliard (de...)	
19	dix-neuf					

1. How old are you? (*Literally:* What age have you?)
I'm _____. (*Literally:* I have _____ years.)
There is no need to be absolutely truthful in your response. You may prefer to answer with the age you would rather be (**seize ans**) or the age you actually feel at the moment (**cent ans**).

Springboards for Conversation

Ask your classmates these personalized questions. Answer formats are provided.

1. Quel âge avez-vous?
   - J'ai _____ ans.
2. Quel âge a le professeur? Devinez! *(Guess!)*
   - Il/Elle a peut-être *(perhaps)* _____ ans.
   - Il/Elle a environ *(around)* _____ ans.
   - Il/Elle a à peu près *(approximately)* _____ ans.
   - Je crois *(I believe)* qu'il/qu'elle a _____ ans.

er

par le

Récapitulation

Recall what you have learned about your classmates and instructor. Answer formats are provided.

1. Quel âge a Monsieur...? Madame...? Mademoiselle...? Et votre voisin(e) de gauche? Et votre voisin(e) de droite? Et le professeur?
   - Il/Elle a _____ ans.

   If you have forgotten, simply apologize and ask again: **Pardon! Je suis désolé(e)! J'ai oublié.** *(I have forgotten.)* **Quel âge avez-vous? Ah oui. C'est ça.** *(That's right.)* **Merci.**

   To verify, use **c'est ça** or **n'est-ce pas**:
   —**Vous avez** _____ **ans, n'est-ce pas** *(don't you)?* —**Oui. C'est ça.**

2. Qui dans la classe a _____ ans? Qui d'autre? *(Who else?)* C'est tout? *(Is that all?)*
   - Monsieur/Madame/Mademoiselle... a _____ ans.
   - Le professeur a _____ ans.
   - Moi, j'ai _____ ans.
   - Tout le monde *(everyone)* a _____ ans.
   - Personne *(No one).*

Remarques

1. The French idiom for talking about ages uses **avoir** *(to have)* rather than **être** *(to be).* In French, you "have" a certain age. The word **ans** *(years)* must, therefore, be included in the answer. Native speakers of English must be careful. Simply remembering to use the verb **avoir** is not enough. If you say **J'ai vingt-deux**, rather than saying **J'ai vingt-deux ans**, you will leave a French person wondering, "He (or she) has twenty-two of what?"

2. The verb **avoir** *(to have)* is needed for talking about age.

j'ai I have	nous **avons** we have
tu **as** you *(informal)* have	vous **avez** you *(formal or plural)* have
il/elle **a** he/she has	ils/elles **ont** they have

3. **Et** is used with the numbers 21, 31, 41, 51, 61, and 71. A hyphen is used in other compound numbers under 100.

4. **Il y a** (*there is, there are*) introduces a statement.
   Il y a des livres sur le bureau. **There are** books on the desk.
   The interogative forms are **est-ce qu'il y a?** and **y a-t-il?**
   Combien d'étudiants **y a-t-il?** How many students **are there?**

5. Some guidelines for the pronunciation of numbers:

   2 and 3. The final consonants of **deux** and **trois** are usually not pronounced. When followed by a word beginning with a vowel sound, however, the final **x** and **s** join up with the following vowel and are pronounced z; deux ans, trois ans.

   5 and 8. The final consonants of **cinq** and **huit** are pronounced except when followed by a word beginning with a consonant: cinq livres, huit livres.

   7. The final **t** of **sept** is always pronounced. The letter **p**, however, is silent: sept.

   6 and 10. Six and dix are pronounced [sis] and [dis] when they are the only or *final* words in a sentence. When followed by a word beginning with a consonant, they are pronounced [si] and [di]: six livres, dix livres. When followed by a word beginning with a vowel, the x is pronounced z and joins up with following vowel: six ans, dix ans.

   9. The f of **neuf** is pronounced. However, the f is pronounced as a v when followed by the words *ans (years)* and **heures** *(hours, o'clock)*. **Neuf ans** is pronounced [nœv͜ɑ̃]. **Neuf heures** is pronounced [nœvœR].

   Note these pronunciations: **17** [dissɛt]; **18** [dizɥit]; **19** [diznœf]; **20** [vɛ̃]; **21** [vɛ̃te͝œ] **Vingt et//un** (There is never liaison after **et**.)

Expansion

The **Expansion** can be used for partners or group conversation and for oral or written composition. Answer formats are provided.

1. Quel âge a votre mère? votre père? votre femme? votre mari? votre frère? votre sœur? votre chien *(dog)?* votre meilleur(e) *(best)* ami(e)?
   • Il/Elle a _____ ans.

2. Combien d'étudiants y a-t-il aujourd'hui dans la classe? *(How many students are in class today?)* Comptez... Combien de personnes *(people)* en tout *(altogether)?*
   • Il y a _____ étudiants.
   • Il y a _____ professeur(s).
   • Il y a _____ personnes en tout.

3. Combien de frères avez-vous? Combien de sœurs avez-vous? Combien d'enfants avez-vous?
   • J'ai _____ sœurs.
   • J'ai _____ frères.
   • J'ai _____ enfants.
   • Je n'en ai pas. *(I don't have any.)*

4. Regardez dans vos poches, dans votre sac, etc. *(look in your pockets, handbag, etc.).* Avez-vous des bonbons *(any candy)?* des cigarettes? des Kleenex? des cartes de crédit *(credit cards)?* des clés *(keys)?* Combien? Comptez-les! *(Count them!)*
   • J'ai _____ cigarettes (cartes de crédit, clés, etc.).
   • Je n'en ai pas.

5. If the preceding **Expansion** questions have been used for group or partners conversation, review what you have learned about your classmates.

   EXEMPLES: *Marc a deux frères.*
   Monsieur Smith a trois cartes de crédit.
   Marie a trois sœurs.

Vocabulaire utile The following phrases are frequently requested by students using the various age-related conversations of this **Entracte**.

Quel âge a-t-il/elle? How old is he/she?
C'est difficile à dire. It's hard to say.
____ ans, je crois. ____ years, I believe.
Oh là là! Oh dear!
Ah non! No!
Il/Elle est plus jeune que ça. He/she's younger than that.

____ ans peut-être. ____ years old, maybe.
Impossible! Impossible!
Incroyable! Unbelievable!
Cela ne vous regarde pas. None of your business.

Combien d'étudiants y a-t-il dans la classe?

Handwritten numbers.

You will see handwritten numbers on bills, store prices, exchanged addresses, telephone numbers, etc. Pay special attention to 1, 4, 7, and 9. Note how an American might think a handwritten French one is a seven, or a French person might confuse an American's handwritten seven with a one.

zéro	0	quatre	4	huit	8
un	1	cinq	5	neuf	9
deux	2	six	6	dix	10
trois	3	sept	7		

Charlottes avec coulis

N° 1   85F
N° 2   70F
N° 3   105F
N° 4   140F

FRAISIER Génoise Kirsché Moulé beurre – Fraises –

N° 1   30F
N° 2   60F
N° 3   90F
N° 4   120F

Number variations.

In French-speaking Belgium and Switzerland you will hear these variations:

70 **septante**
80 **octante** (Belgium) or **huitante** (Switzerland)
90 **nonante**

Sixième Arrondissement

Ordinal numbers.

Ordinal numbers describe the order in which things occur—first, second, third, etc. *One, two, three . . .* are referred to as cardinal numbers. Ordinals are most often formed by adding the ending -ième to cardinal numbers. Final vowels are dropped (**quatrième, onzième**). Special cases: **premier, second, neuvième**.

premier, première first	**quatrième** fourth
second (*when referring to only two things*) second	**cinquième** fifth
	sixième sixth
	septième seventh
deuxième second	**vingtième** twentieth
troisième third	**vingt et unième** twenty-first

Ordinals can be abbreviated as shown here.

1er, 1°, 1ère	1st	3^{e}	3rd
2^{e}	2nd	4^{e}	4th

Number formation. Vingt and cent take s when a multiplying number precedes them and no other number follows them: quatre-vingt<u>s</u>, deux cent<u>s</u>, quatre-vingt-un, deux cent un.

Unlike in English, un is not used in front of cent and mille: cent = *one hundred/a hundred*.

From 1100–1900, mille may be used: mille cent = onze cents; mille deux cents = douze cents.

Beginning with 2,000, mille must be used: deux mille cent = *two thousand one hundred* or *twenty-one hundred*.

In the French system, periods or spaces are used instead of commas. (*Period* = point.) A comma is used instead of a period. (*Comma* = virgule.) 10,820.08 (*American*) = 10.820,08 or 10 820, 08 (dix mille huit cent vingt virgule zéro huit)

Synthèse

A. **Quel âge a-t-il (elle)?**   How old are the people in these photos? Use the following constructions in your answers.

Il/Elle a peut-être _____ ans.
Il/Elle a l'air *(seems)* d'avoir _____ ans.
Il/Elle doit *(must)* avoir entre *(between)* _____ et _____ ans.

Il/Elle a environ _____ ans.
Je crois qu'il/elle a _____ ans.
Plus de *(more than)* _____ ans.

Mademoiselle X

Monsieur X

Other useful expressions:

D'accord.   I agree.
Je ne suis pas d'accord.   I disagree.
Je ne (le) crois pas.   I don't think so.
Je crois qu'il/qu'elle est plus/moins âgé(e) *(older/younger)* **que ça.**

Il/Elle a l'air plus jeune/âgé(e) *(younger/ older)* **que ça.**
Il/Elle fait beaucoup plus jeune/âgé(e) *(appears younger/older).*

B. **Counting.**   Glance through this textbook. Select photographs or illustrations that show several items—houses, people, cars, trees, etc. How many items are pictured in the photograph? Count them in French. Indicate the page number aloud before you begin. For example, **À la page trois cent vingt-cinq…**

Projet

Bookmark. Copy or trace the bookmark below. Use it for EN FRANÇAIS: FRENCH FOR COMMUNICATION. Write the appropriate page number on it in pencil each time you use it: **trente-huit, quarante-deux,** etc.

Je suis à la page ____.

Activités: Learning by Doing

A. **Bingo.** Play "Bingo" in French.

B. **Go Fish.** Play "Go Fish," a simple card game. Vocabulary needed:

un	cinq	neuf	**roi** *m* king
deux	six	dix	**as** *m* ace
trois	sept	**valet** *m* jack	
quatre	huit	**dame** *f* queen	

Rules for "Go Fish"

The goal is to accumulate the greatest number of packs of four cards of the same denomination. There are three players per group. Each receives seven cards. The player on the dealer's left goes first. He asks any player in his group for a card to complete a pack of which he has at least one representative card in his hand. This continues until that player receives a negative answer, at which point he draws a card from the pack on the table. If he gets the card he had asked for, he goes again. If not, the turn passes to the player on his left. The winner is the player who has the greatest number of packs of four at the game's end. Players cannot ask for a card unless they have at least one card of that denomination in their hands.

Vocabulaire utile

The following phrases are frequently requested by students participating in this game-playing activity.

Avez-vous des...? Do you have any...?
J'ai... I have...
Voilà un... Here's a...
Pardon? Excuse me?
C'est tout? Is that all?
Merci. Thank you.

À qui le tour? Whose turn is it?
C'est à vous. It's yours.
C'est à moi. It's mine.
Quelle chance! What luck!
Zut alors! Darn it!
Tricheur! Tricheuse! Cheater!

«Vous avez choisi?»

Au Restaurant

At the Restaurant

L'Appétit vient en mangeant.

Appetite comes with eating.

DIALOGUE

Dining at a French restaurant, either near home or abroad, can be all the more pleasurable when you are able to discuss the menu and place your order in French. This **Dialogue** presents some essential restaurant vocabulary. It is divided into five segments to facilitate application of these useful phrases in real contexts: making reservations, being seated, ordering a meal, conversing during a meal, and asking for the check. Vocabulary blocks within this **Dialogue** offer options for personalization regarding food preference. They also provide possibilities for modification to suit a wide variety of real-life dining situations.

Au Restaurant

VOUS: Je voudrais réserver une table pour
  deux personnes .
  | trois
  | quatre
  | cinq
  | six

  pour **sept heures,** s'il vous plaît.
    | sept heures et demie
    | huit heures
    | neuf heures
    | dix heures

LE MAÎTRE D'HÔTEL: Votre nom, Monsieur /
Madame / Mademoiselle?
VOUS: C'est ___votre nom___ .
  ⌒

LE MAÎTRE D'HÔTEL: Vous êtes deux? Avez-
vous réservé?

VOUS: Oui, je suis Monsieur / Madame /
Mademoiselle ___votre nom___ . Je voudrais
une table **près de la fenêtre.**
    | dans le coin
    | dehors / à l'extérieur
    | sur la terrasse
    | dans le jardin
    | là-bas

LE MAÎTRE D'HÔTEL: Très bien, Monsieur /
Madame / Mademoiselle. Par ici, s'il vous
plaît.
  ⌒

At the Restaurant

(Making reservations)
YOU: I would like to reserve a table for
  two people
  | three
  | four
  | five
  | six

  for **seven o'clock,** please.
    | seven thirty
    | eight o'clock
    | nine o'clock
    | ten o'clock

THE HEADWAITER: Your name?

YOU: It's ___your name___ .
  ⌒

(Being seated)
HEADWAITER: A party of two? *(Literally:* You are two?) Do you have reservations? *(Literally:* Have you reserved?)
YOU: Yes. I'm ___your name___ . I'd like a table
near the window.

    | in the corner
    | outside
    | on the terrace
    | in the garden
    | over there

HEADWAITER: Very well. This way, please.
  ⌒

LE GARÇON / LA SERVEUSE: Voici la carte, Monsieur / Madame / Mademoiselle. Un apéritif?

VOUS: Merci, non…

LE GARÇON: Vous avez choisi?

VOUS: Qu'est-ce que vous recommandez?

LE GARÇON: Eh bien, **le coq au vin** est très

| l'agneau *(m)* |
| le jambon |
| le lapin |
| le poisson |
| le poulet |
| le rosbif |
| le veau |

bon. C'est la spécialité de la maison.

VOUS *[à votre ami(e)]*: Qu'est-ce que vous allez prendre?

VOTRE AMI(E): J'ai très faim. Pour commencer je prendrai *prandreve* **la soupe à l'oignon.**

| des artichauts *(m)* |
| des asperges *(f)* *des asperg* |
| du caviar |
| des crudités *(f)* *de cruditee* |
| des escargots *(m)* |
| des hors-d'œuvre *(m)* |
| du pâté |
| des radis *(m)* |

Puis un bifteck, des (pommes) frites et une salade.

LE GARÇON: Comment voulez-vous le bifteck?

VOTRE AMI(E): **Saignant.**

| Bleu |
| À point |
| Bien cuit |

LE GARÇON: Et pour Monsieur / Madame / Mademoiselle?

VOUS: Pour commencer, un demi-pamplemousse. Et puis **une omelette.**

| une omelette aux champignons |
| au fromage |
| aux fines herbes |
| au jambon |
| nature |
| des œufs *(m)* |

0 en_4

(Ordering the meal)

WAITER / WAITRESS: Here's the menu. (Would you like) a cocktail?

YOU: No, thanks.

WAITER: Are you ready to order? *(Literally:* You have chosen?*)*

YOU: What do you recommend?

WAITER: Well, the **chicken in wine** is very good.

| lamb |
| ham |
| rabbit |
| fish |
| chicken |
| roast beef |
| veal |

It's the specialty of the house.

YOU *(to your friend)*: What are you going to have?

YOUR FRIEND: I'm very hungry. To begin, I'll have the onion soup.

| artichokes |
| asparagus |
| caviar |
| raw vegetables |
| snails |
| appetizers |
| pâté |
| radishes |

Then a steak, French fried potatoes, and a salad.

WAITER: How do you want the steak?

YOUR FRIEND: **Rare** *(literally:* bloody*)*.

| Very rare |
| Medium |
| Well-done |

WAITER: And for (you)?

YOU: To begin, half a grapefruit. And then an **omelet.**

| mushroom omelet |
| cheese omelet |
| omelet with herbs |
| ham omelet |
| plain omelet |
| eggs |

[handwritten: Kes cur vou Avey com]

Qu'est-ce que vous avez comme légumes?

LE GARÇON: **Des carottes** *(f)*...
| **Du chou-fleur**
| **Du concombre**
| **Des épinards** *(m)*
| **Des haricots verts** *(m)*
| **Des petits pois** *(m)*
| **Du riz**
| **Des tomates** *(f)*

VOUS: Des petits pois, s'il vous plaît.

LE GARÇON: Et comme boisson?

VOTRE AMI(E): Je prendrai **du vin rouge**, s'il

[handwritten: do van Blah / do low]

| du vin blanc
| de l'eau minérale *(f)*
| une bière
| un Coca
| un Perrier

vous plaît.

VOUS: Pour moi, **un jus de fruits.** J'ai soif.

[handwritten: a ju]

| un jus d'orange
| un jus de pomme   *[handwritten: pum]*
| un jus de tomate
| un citron pressé
| du lait   *[handwritten: do la]*

LE GARÇON: Très bien. Merci, Monsieur / Madame / Mademoiselle, et bon appétit.

What sort of vegetables do you have?

WAITER: Carrots. . .
| Cauliflower
| Cucumber
| Spinach
| Green beans
| Green peas
| Rice
| Tomatoes

YOU: Green peas, please.

WAITER: And to drink?

YOUR FRIEND: I'll have **red wine**, please.
| white wine
| mineral water
| a beer
| a Coke
| a Perrier

[handwritten: blang]

YOU: For me, a **fruit juice.** I'm thirsty.
| orange juice
| apple juice
| tomato juice
| lemonade
| milk

WAITER: Very well. Thank you. Have a good meal. (*Literally:* Good appetite.)

(During the meal)

LE GARÇON: Voilà. Un Coca…

WAITER: Here (you are). A Coke…

VOUS: Ce n'est pas ce que j'ai commandé!

YOU: That's not what I ordered!

LE GARÇON: Excusez-moi, Monsieur /
  Madame / Mademoiselle…

WAITER: Excuse me.

VOTRE AMI(E): Le vin est **très bon.**

YOUR FRIEND: The wine is **very good.** (Proposing

délicieux	delicious
extraordinaire	extraordinary
magnifique	magnificent
excellent	excellent
affreux *affra*	terrible

(trinquant) À votre santé!

a toast) To your health!

VOUS: À la vôtre.

YOU: To yours!

VOTRE AMI(E): (Passez-moi) **le pain,** s'il

YOUR FRIEND: (Pass me) the **bread,** please.

le beurre	butter
la confiture	jam
les croissants (m)	croissants
la margarine	margarine
le miel	honey
la moutarde	mustard
les petits pains (m)	rolls
le poivre	pepper
le sel	salt
le sucre *suk*	sugar

vous plaît. Hmm… C'est bon.

Mmmmm… This is good.

VOUS: Voulez-vous encore du vin?

YOU: Do you want some more wine?

VOTRE AMI(E): Merci, non. Ça va.

YOUR FRIEND: No, thanks. I'm fine. (Literally: It
  goes.)

ↄ·ↄ

ↄ·ↄ

(Ordering dessert / Asking for the check)

LE GARÇON: Voulez-vous du fromage?

WAITER: Do you want some cheese?

VOUS: Non, pas ce soir. *alesace ca voule com desse*

YOU: No, not tonight.

VOTRE AMI(E): Qu'est-ce que vous avez
  comme dessert?

YOUR FRIEND: What do you have for dessert?

LE GARÇON: Nous avons **du gâteau au**

WAITER: We have **chocolate cake,** ice cream,

des crêpes (f)	thin pancakes
des gaufres (f) *got*	waffles
de la pâtisserie	pastry
des tartes (f)	tarts

chocolat, des glaces, des sorbets
et **des fruits.** *de kreez*

sherbet, and **fruit.**

des abricots (m)	apricots
des bananes (f)	bananas
des cerises (f)	cherries
des fraises (f)	strawberries
des framboises (f)	raspberries
du melon	melon
des pêches (f)	peaches
des poires (f)	pears
des pommes (f)	apples

VOTRE AMI(E): Je prendrai le gâteau. Ça sent bon. Faites mes compliments au chef!

VOUS: Pas de dessert pour moi. Je n'ai plus faim. Vous prenez du café?

VOTRE AMI(E): Oui.

VOUS: Alors, **deux cafés** et l'addition, s'il

> un café
> un décaféiné
> un digestif / un pousse-café
> un express
> un thé

vous plaît.

LE GARÇON: C'est tout?

VOUS: Oui, mais apportez-moi **une autre cuillère,** s'il vous plaît.

> une autre assiette
> un autre couteau
> une autre fourchette
> une autre nappe
> une autre serviette
> une autre tasse
> un autre verre

LE GARÇON: Tout de suite, Monsieur / Madame/Mademoiselle.

YOUR FRIEND: I'll have the cake. This smells good. My compliments to the chef!

YOU: No dessert for me. I'm full. (Literally: I have no more hunger.) Are you having coffee?

YOUR FRIEND: Yes.

YOU: And so, **two coffees** and the check,

> one coffee
> decaffeinated coffee
> after-dinner drink
> espresso
> tea

please.

WAITER: Is that all?

YOU: Yes, but bring me another **spoon**, please.

> plate
> knife
> fork
> tablecloth
> napkin
> cup
> glass

WAITER: Right away.

Phrases à retenir

Memorizing these sentences based on the **Dialogue** will help assure fluency in a variety of real-life dining-out situations.

1. Je voudrais une table là-bas.
2. La carte, s'il vous plaît.
3. Qu'est-ce que vous recommandez?
4. Quelle est (What is) la spécialité de la maison?
5. Qu'est-ce que vous avez comme dessert?
6. Bon appétit!
7. Ce n'est pas ce que j'ai commandé.
8. Hmmmm. Ça sent bon!
9. À votre santé! À la vôtre!
10. L'addition, s'il vous plaît.

DIALOGUE EXERCISES

The following exercises provide oral and written practice in using the vocabulary and basic sentence patterns of the **Dialogue: Au Restaurant.** These exercises use *only* vocabulary and structures presented in the restaurant **Dialogue.** They do not require familiarity with any other portions of this chapter.

Exercices d'application

A. **Making reservations: Je voudrais réserver...** You have invited some guests to a restaurant. Make reservations. Include yourself in the count.

MODÈLE: votre mère et votre père
Je voudrais réserver une table pour trois personnes.

Vous avez invité...
1. votre ami(e)
2. vos parents et votre professeur
3. cinq collègues *(colleagues)*
4. votre grand-mère et votre grand-père
5. votre ami(e) et les parents de votre ami(e)
6. tous les membres de la classe de français et le professeur de français

B. **Table selection: Je voudrais une table...** Express a table preference other than that suggested by the **maître d'hôtel.** You may use the alternative offered in parentheses or another of your own choosing.

MODÈLE: Voilà une table près de la fenêtre. (dans le coin)
Je voudrais une table dans le coin.

1. Voilà une table sur la terrasse. (dans le jardin)
2. Voilà une table près de la fenêtre. (dans le coin)
3. Voilà une table dans le coin. (à l'extérieur)
4. Voilà une table dans le jardin. (sur la terrasse)
5. Voilà une table dans le coin. (près de la fenêtre)

C. **Recommendations: Qu'est-ce que vous recommandez?** Say that each item below is good and that it is the house specialty.

MODÈLE: Et le jambon?   *Le jambon est très bon. C'est la spécialité de la maison.*

1. Et le lapin?   4. Et le rosbif?
2. Et le poisson?   5. Et le veau?
3. Et le poulet?

D. **Ordering: Pour commencer...** Order these items, using the basic sentence format of the model.

MODÈLE: du pâté, un bifteck
Pour commencer, je prendrai du pâté et puis un bifteck.

1. des hors-d'œuvre, un bifteck
2. un demi-pamplemousse, une omelette
3. du pâté, du rosbif
4. des crudités, un steak-frites (bifteck + pommes frites)
5. des escargots, du jambon

E.   **Dialogue responses.**   What could you respond to each of the following? Use sentences and phrases taken directly from the **Dialogue**.

1. Avez-vous réservé?
2. Voilà une table près de la fenêtre.
3. Un apéritif?
4. Vous avez choisi?
5. Qu'est-ce que vous recommandez?
6. Qu'est-ce que vous allez prendre?
7. Et comme boisson?
8. À votre santé!
9. Voulez-vous encore du vin?
10. Prenez-vous du café?

F.   **Review.**   What do you say?...

1. to reserve a table for two for seven o'clock?
2. to get a table in the corner?
3. to find out what the waiter recommends?
4. to comment on how good something is?
5. to ask what someone else is thinking of ordering?
6. to order an appetizer?
7. to find out what kind of vegetables there are?
8. when you want the waiter to bring you some red wine?
9. to tell someone to enjoy their meal?
10. to propose a toast?

Improvisation à deux *(Exercice oral)*

G.   Use the vocabulary block options and the basic sentence structures of the **Dialogue** to improvise a dialogue with a classmate. Express personal preferences concerning table choice, meal selection, etc. One of you may be a waiter or waitress while the other is a diner. Or both of you may choose to be diners at the same or at separate tables.

À Vous le choix *(Exercices écrits)*

H.   Write a six- to eight-line dialogue for each of the following situations, selecting appropriate phrases from the initial **Dialogue** of this chapter.

1. It is a hot summer evening. You and a friend stop at a sidewalk café. You are thirsty rather than hungry. Your friend is hungry.
2. You are dining out at a luxurious restaurant. You wish to impress your dining companion.
3. You are eating lunch at a simple family restaurant. You are very hungry.

Conversations

I. Ask your classmates these personalized questions. When two or more responses are possible, alternate answer formats are offered. Select the option that best applies to you personally. Do not limit your responses simply to those suggestions offered in these questions. Use the inclusive vocabulary options provided in the **Dialogue.** (You may wish to use the **tu** form of address with your classmates.)

1. Quand vous allez (tu vas) au restaurant, préférez-vous (préfères-tu) une table dans le coin? sur la terrasse? dans le jardin? près de la fenêtre? à l'extérieur?
   • Je préfère une table _____.

2. Allez-vous (Vas-tu) au restaurant ce soir *(tonight)*? Avez-vous (As-tu) réservé? Pour quelle heure? Pour combien de personnes?
   • Je vais (Je ne vais pas _____.) J'ai réservé une table pour _____ personnes pour _____ heures.

3. Avez-vous soif maintenant? Avez-vous faim?
   • Oui, j'ai _____.
   • Non, je n'ai pas _____.

4. Voulez-vous (Veux-tu) manger quelque chose *(something)*? une omelette? du rosbif? du poulet? du jambon? une glace? un sorbet? etc.
   • Oui, je voudrais (manger) _____.
   • Non, je n'ai pas faim.

5. Aimez-vous (Aimes-tu) le vin rouge? la bière? l'eau minérale? le café? le thé? le lait? etc.
   • Oui, j'aime _____.
   • Non, je n'aime pas _____.

6. Quelle est votre boisson préférée *(favorite)*? le café? l'eau? le thé? le lait? le jus d'orange? le jus de tomate? etc.
   • C'est _____.

7. Aimez-vous le poulet? le rosbif? le jambon? le veau? l'agneau? etc.
   • Oui, j'aime _____.
   • Non, je n'aime pas _____.

8. Qu'est-ce que vous détestez? les épinards? les carottes? les haricots verts? les oignons? les petits pois? etc.
   • Je déteste _____.

9. Qu'est-ce que vous avez mangé aujourd'hui? un sandwich? un bifteck? des légumes? des carottes? de la pâtisserie? etc.
   • J'ai mangé/J'ai pris *(I ate)* _____.

J. **Review:** What have you learned about your classmates from the preceding **Conversations?**

EXEMPLES: *Marie va au restaurant ce soir.*
Marc a soif.
Madame Smith aime le vin rouge.

À PROPOS

Accepting or refusing. Merci is often interpreted as merci, non *(no, thank you)*. Consequently, when offered something to eat or drink, you may refuse with: Merci, or merci, non. To accept, say, Oui, s'il vous plaît. Once you have been given an item, however, you may then say merci or merci beaucoup to express thanks.

Bow coo

French wine. Wine is a standard beverage at French meals. To ask for a restaurant's wine list, say, La carte des vins, s'il vous plaît. In many restaurants customers are required to order a whole bottle (une bouteille), a half-bottle (une demi-bouteille), or a carafe (une carafe) of wine rather than a single glass (un verre).

The waiter. French people signal the waiter (le garçon, le serveur), with Monsieur (or, Garçon), s'il vous plaît. They get their waitress's (la serveuse) attention with Mademoiselle (Madame), s'il vous plaît.

Rapid order. To place an order with a busy waiter, omit the expressions je voudrais..., je prendrai..., and apportez-moi.... Simply name the food or beverage item desired, adding s'il vous plaît. For example: Un Perrier, s'il vous plaît.

Au café. At French cafés, prices may seem rather high for a single drink. The reason is that you are paying for the privilege of sitting as long as you wish.

LANGUAGE AND CULTURE

Menu du jour. The menu du jour, menu à prix fixe, and menu touristique are complete meals with little or no choice allowed in item selection. They are less expensive than à la carte meals, where you may choose from a wide variety of items.

MENU
93F
AU CHOIX
4 ENTREES
5 PLATS GARNIS
5 DESSERTS Maison
33 cl de vin
PRIX NET

Service compris. Generally a fifteen-percent service charge is included in the bill. To find out, ask Est-ce que le service est compris? *(Is service included?)*

Tipping. The word for tip in French is le pourboire *(literally: for drinking)*. You may wish to leave a **pourboire** in addition to the service charge. This, theoretically, is to offer helpful restaurant personnel a drink at your expense in gratitude for services rendered.

Credit cards. To pay with a credit card, ask: Quelles cartes de crédit acceptez-vous? *(Which credit cards do you accept?)*.

Borrowed words. The English language has borrowed many words from French cuisine (including the word **cuisine** itself). For example, **cordon bleu** (top-notch cooking, a first-rate chef), **pièce de résistance** (crowning dish of a meal), **hors d'œuvres** (appetizers), **entrée** (a course during the meal), and **dessert**.

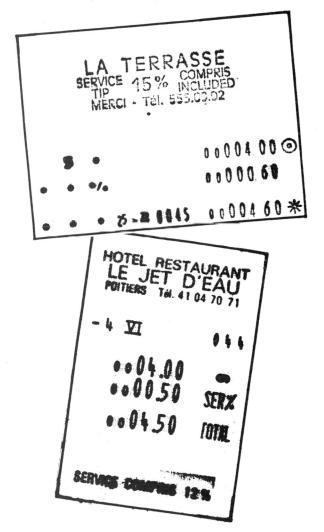

VERBES IRRÉGULIERS: avoir, boire, vouloir

➤

avoir	to have
j'**ai**	I have
tu **as**	you have
il/elle **a**	he/she has
nous **avons**	we have
vous **avez**	you have
ils/elles **ont**	they have

1. **Avoir** is used idiomatically in certain expressions.

   J'ai faim.   I'm hungry. (*Literally:* I have hunger.)
   J'ai soif.   I'm thirsty. (*Literally:* I have thirst.)

2. The verb **prendre** is used instead of **avoir** meaning "to have something to eat or drink."

   Qu'est-ce que tu prends?   What are you (will you be) having (to drink/to eat)?

3. **Avoir** means "to have" when indicating whether or not a food item is available.

   Avez-vous du poulet?   Do you have (any) chicken?
   Qu'est-ce que **vous avez** comme   What do you have (serve) for
      dessert?   dessert?

Exercices d'application: avoir

A. **J'ai soif! J'ai faim!** Place the orders suggested below. Then declare that you are thirsty or hungry or both.

MODÈLE: Je prendrai une omelette, un sandwich et des frites.   *J'ai faim!*

1. Je voudrais une bière tout de suite!
2. Apportez-moi trois Cocas.
3. Pour moi, un bifteck, des pommes frites, une salade, un Perrier et une glace.
4. De l'eau minérale—une bouteille, s'il vous plaît.
5. De la tarte aux fraises, s'il vous plaît, et de la glace à la vanille.

B. **Qu'est-ce que vous avez comme dessert?** Ask the waiter what he has. Use the expression **Qu'est-ce que vous avez comme...?**

MODÈLE: cheese   *Qu'est-ce que vous avez comme fromage?*

1. ice cream
2. dessert
3. sherbet
4. cheese
5. beverage
6. sandwiches
7. vegetables
8. fruit juice
9. meat **(viande)**

➤

boire	to drink
je **bois**	I drink, I am drinking, I do drink
tu **bois**	you drink
il/elle **boit**	he/she drinks
nous **buvons**	we drink
vous **buvez**	you drink
ils/elles **boivent**	they drink

The verb **prendre** is sometimes used meaning to have something to drink: **Je prends du lait avec mes repas** (*I have milk with my meals* or *I drink milk with my meals*).

Exercices d'application: boire

C. **Qu'est-ce que vous buvez?** *(What do you drink?)* Answer this question yourself. Then ask your classmates. (You may wish to use the informal **tu** form of address with your classmates: **Qu'est-ce que tu bois?**) Answers may include the following:

du café
du lait
du thé
du vin
du Coca
du Perrier

de l'eau
de l'eau minérale
du champagne
de la bière
du jus d'orange
du chocolat

du jus de tomate
du jus de
   pamplemousse
du jus de pomme
du jus de fruits

D.   **Il boit...Elle boit.**   If the preceding exercise has been used orally in class, review what you have learned about your classmates and instructor.

EXEMPLES: *Le professeur boit du lait.*
Marie boit du café.
Monsieur Smith boit de l'eau.

➤

vouloir	to want, to wish
je **veux**	I want, I wish
tu **veux**	you want
il/elle **veut**	he/she wants
nous **voulons**	we want
vous **voulez**	you want
ils/elles **veulent**	they want

1. As in English, the conditional form **je voudrais** (*I would like*) is considered more polite than **je veux** (*I want*).
2. **Vouloir** may be followed by the infinitive, as in English: **Voulez-vous manger quelque chose?** (*Do you want to eat something?*)
3. The expression **oui, je veux bien** means "yes, I'd like to": **Voulez-vous dîner au restaurant? Oui, je veux bien.**
4. **Voulez-vous bien** followed by an infinitive is used in polite commands or requests to mean "would you kindly" or "would you please": **Voulez-vous bien passer le sel, s'il vous plaît?** (*Would you please pass the salt?*)

Exercice d'application: **vouloir**

E.   **Voulez-vous...? Veux-tu...?**   Ask several classmates if they would like to go out to eat with you. **Voulez-vous dîner au restaurant avec moi? Veux-tu dîner au restaurant avec moi?** *Réponse:* **Oui, je veux bien.**

STRUCTURES

Structure 1: **Passé Composé** (-er Verbs)

The **passé composé** is composed of a conjugated form of **avoir,** which is called the auxiliary or "helping" verb, plus the past participle of the main verb.

1. Past participles of **-er** verbs end in **é**.

LE PASSÉ COMPOSÉ	INFINITIVE: réserv**er** PAST PARTICIPLE: réservé
j'**ai** réservé tu **as** réservé il **a** réservé elle **a** réservé on **a** réservé	nous **avons** réservé vous **avez** réservé ils **ont** réservé elles **ont** réservé

There are three possible English equivalents for the **passé composé**.

J'ai réservé une table.
{ I have reserved a table.
I reserved a table.
I did reserve a table.

2. In negative sentences, the auxiliary verb is made negative.

| je **n'ai pas** réservé
tu **n'as pas** réservé
il **n'a pas** réservé
elle **n'a pas** réservé
on **n'a pas** réservé | nous **n'avons pas** réservé
vous **n'avez pas** réservé
ils **n'ont pas** réservé
elles **n'ont pas** réservé |

3. In questions using inversion, the subject pronoun follows the auxiliary verb and is joined to it with a hyphen.

Vous avez réservé une table.   **Avez-vous réservé** une table?
   (Statement)   *(Inverted question)*
Il a mangé. *(Statement)*   **A-t-il mangé?** *(Inverted question)*

Exercices d'application: **Passé Composé** (-er Verbs)

A.   **J'ai déjà téléphoné au restaurant!**   Respond to each of these commands. Say that you have already done what you are being asked to do. Translate.

MODÈLE: Téléphonez au restaurant!
              J'ai déjà téléphoné au restaurant.
              I already called the restaurant.

1. Parlez avec le maître d'hôtel!
2. Invitez le professeur au restaurant!
3. Mangez!
4. Réservez une table!
5. Regardez la carte!
6. Commandez le vin!
7. Recommandez un dessert!
8. Téléphonez au restaurant!

B. **J'ai regardé la télévision.**   Review the **-er** verbs from Chapter 2 (Structure 5). Tell what you did yesterday **(hier).**

EXEMPLES: *J'ai regardé la télévision.*
J'ai étudié et j'ai nagé.

C. **Je n'ai pas regardé la télévision.**   What didn't you do yesterday?

EXEMPLES: *Je n'ai pas regardé la télévision.*
Je n'ai pas fumé et je n'ai pas dîné au restaurant.

D. **Il a regardé la télévision./Elle n'a pas étudié.**   If the preceding two exercises have been used orally in class, review what you have learned about your classmates.

EXEMPLES: *Paul a regardé la télévision.*
Il n'a pas étudié.
Madame Smith a dîné au restaurant.

E. **A-t-il étudié? A-t-elle regardé la télévision?**   Review what you have learned about your classmates in the preceding three exercises. Ask the person on your left about the person on your right, and so on.

EXEMPLE: *—A-t-il nagé?*
        —Oui, il a nagé.
   or: *—Non, il n'a pas nagé.*

Structure 2: **Passé Composé** (Irregular Verbs)

Irregular verbs often have irregular past participles. **Avoir** is the auxiliary verb for the following irregular verbs.

INFINITIVE		PAST PARTICIPLE
apprendre	to learn	appris
avoir	to have	eu
boire	to drink	bu
comprendre	to understand	compris
être	to be	été
pouvoir	to be able, can	pu
prendre	to take	pris
vouloir	to wish	voulu

Exercices d'application: **Passé Composé** (Irregular Verbs)

F.   **Qu'est-ce que vous avez bu?**   Answer these questions yourself. Then ask your classmates. See the **Dialogue** for beverage vocabulary. Responses will begin with **Ce matin, j'ai bu...** or **Hier soir, j'ai bu...**

   1. Qu'est-ce que vous avez bu ce matin au petit déjeuner *(this morning for breakfast)?*

   2. Qu'est-ce que vous avez bu hier soir au dîner *(last night for dinner)?*

G.   **Il a bu...Elle a bu...**   If the preceding exercise has been used orally in class, review what you have learned about your classmates.

   EXEMPLE: *Anne a bu du lait, du thé et du jus d'orange.*

H.   **Qu'est-ce que vous avez pris aujourd'hui?**   Answer this question yourself. Then ask your classmates what they have had to eat and drink today. Use the verb **prendre.** Responses will begin with **J'ai pris....** See the **Dialogue** for a selection of food and beverage items. (You may wish to use the informal **tu** form of address with your classmates. **Qu'est-ce que tu as pris aujourd'hui?)**

I.   **Il a pris...Elle a pris...**   If the preceding exercise has been used orally in class, review what you have learned about your classmates.

   EXEMPLES: *Marc a pris un bifteck, des frites et une salade.*
   Madame Smith a pris du café et des œufs.

Structure 3: **Passé Composé** (Verbs Conjugated with **être**)

Many verbs of motion form the **passé composé** with **être** as the helping verb. Commonly called "verbs of coming and going," their grammatical name is *intransitive verbs.* The past participle agrees with the subject in gender (masculine or feminine) and in number (singular or plural). That is, with verbs of "coming and going" you add the letter **e** to the past participle if the subject is feminine, the letter **s** to the past participle if the subject is plural, and the letters **es** to the past participle if the subject is both plural and feminine.

je **suis allé(e)**	nous **sommes allé(e)s**
tu **es allé(e)**	vous **êtes allé(e)s**
il **est allé**	ils **sont allés**
elle **est allée**	elles **sont allées**

The following **-er** verbs are conjugated with **être.**

arriver	to arrive
entrer	to enter
monter	to climb up, to go up, to come up
rentrer	to go home, to come back
retourner	to return, to go back
tomber	to fall

Note: **Rester** *(to remain, to stay)*, although not actually a verb of "motion," is also conjugated with **être.**

Exercices d'application: **Passé Composé** (Verbs Conjugated with **être**)

J.   **Je suis...Je ne suis pas...** *(Personalized Exercise)* Answer these questions yourself. Then ask your classmates. Answers will begin with **Oui, je suis...** or **Non, je ne suis pas...** (You may wish to use the **tu** form of address with your classmates.)

1. Êtes-vous (es-tu) allé(e) au restaurant cette semaine *(this week)?*
2. Êtes-vous arrivé(e) en classe à l'heure *(on time)?*
3. Êtes-vous rentré(e) tard hier soir *(late last night)?*
4. Êtes-vous tombé(e) récemment *(recently)?*
5. Êtes-vous allé(e) au restaurant hier *(yesterday)?*

K.   **Il est allé au restaurant.**   If the preceding exercise has been used orally in class, review what you have learned about your classmates.

EXEMPLES: *Marc est tombé récemment.*
            Anne est allée au restaurant hier soir.

Structure 4: The Partitive Construction

Although the words *some* and *any* are often omitted in English, they are rarely left out in French. To indicate *some* or *any*, use:

du before masculine singular nouns:	Je prendrai **du** rosbif.
de la before feminine singular nouns:	Nous avons **de la** glace à la vanille.
de l' before all singular nouns beginning with a vowel or mute **h:**	Apportez-moi **de l'**eau minérale, s'il vous plaît.
des before all plural nouns:	Je prendrai **des** asperges.

1. **Un, une, du, de la, de l',** and **des** all become **de (d')** after a negative.

J'ai **un** couteau.	I have a knife.
Je **n'**ai **pas de** couteau.	I don't have a knife.
J'ai **une** fourchette.	I have a fork.
Je **n'**ai **pas de** fourchette.	I don't have a fork.
Je prends **du** fromage.	I'm having (some) cheese.
Je **ne** prends **pas de** fromage.	I'm not having (any) cheese.
Nous avons **des** bananes.	We have (some) bananas.
Nous n'avons **pas de** bananes.	We don't have (any) bananas. We have no bananas.

Exception: With **être, un** and **une** remain **un** and **une** in the negative.

C'est **un** restaurant?	Is it a restaurant?
Non, ce **n'**est **pas un** restaurant.	No, it's not a restaurant.

2. The definite article **(le, la, l', les)** is used before nouns meant in a general sense. The definite article is often used after **aimer, adorer, détester,** and **préférer.**

J'aime **le** poisson.	I like fish (in general).
L'eau est bonne quand on a soif.	Water is good when you are thirsty.

Note that **le, la, l',** and **les** do not change to **de** after a negative verb.

J'aime **le** poisson.	I like fish.
Je **n'**aime **pas le** poisson.	I don't like fish (in general).

But:
Je veux **du** poisson.	I want (some) fish.
Je **ne** veux **pas de** poisson.	I don't want (any) fish.

Exercices d'application: The Partitive Construction

L. **Je voudrais du/de la/des...** Say that you would like the following foods.

MODÈLE: chicken   *Je voudrais du poulet.*

1. roast beef
2. ham
3. cake
4. ice cream
5. peas
6. milk

M. **Je voudrais...** Which food items in the **Dialogue** would you actually like right now? List as many as possible. Begin with **Je voudrais du/de la/de l'/des....**

N. **Qu'est-ce qu'il y a dans votre réfrigérateur?** What food items are usually found in your refrigerator? Use **du, de la, de l',** and **des.** Refer to the **Dialogue** for food and beverage items. List as many as possible.

EXEMPLE: *En général* (in general) *il y a* (there is, there are) *de l'eau, du lait, des œufs, du fromage, du jus d'orange et du beurre dans mon réfrigérateur.*

O. **Qu'est-ce que vous avez acheté cette semaine?** Which foods or beverages mentioned in this chapter have you actually purchased this week?

EXEMPLE: *J'ai acheté* (bought) *du café, du lait et des tomates.*

P. **Il a acheté du pain.** If the preceding exercise has been used orally in class, review what your classmates have bought this week.

EXEMPLE: *Marc a acheté du thé, du riz, des oranges et de la glace.*

Q. **Je ne bois jamais de thé.** Name at least five items you never eat or drink. You will be using the negative expression **ne...jamais** (*never*) followed by **de** (or **d'** before a noun beginning with a vowel or mute **h**). Use a complete sentence for each item.

EXEMPLES: *Je ne bois jamais de thé.*
Je ne mange jamais de poisson.
Je ne bois jamais d'eau.
Je ne mange jamais d'épinards.

R. **Qu'est-ce que vous n'avez jamais goûté?** What items of French cuisine mentioned in this chapter have you never tried? You will be using the negative expression **ne...jamais** followed by **de** (or **d'**). Suggestions: **crêpes, tartes, escargots, coq au vin, soupe à l'oignon, pâté, lapin, omelette aux fines herbes,** etc.

EXEMPLE: *Je n'ai jamais goûté de caviar.*

S. **Qu'est-ce que vous aimez?** Which food and beverage items presented in this chapter do you like? Which do you not like?

EXEMPLES: *J'aime le café.*
Je n'aime pas les épinards.

T. **Il aime...Il n'aime pas...** If the preceding exercise has been used orally in class, review what you have learned about your classmates' food preferences.

EXEMPLE: *Madame Smith n'aime pas les épinards, mais* (but) *elle aime le caviar.*

Structure 5: Expressions of Quantity

Expressions of quantity may be used alone or with a noun preceded by **de. De** becomes **d'** before a noun beginning with a vowel or mute **h**.

Expression of Quantity	Alone	Before a noun
assez enough	C'est **assez**, merci.	Je n'ai pas **assez de légumes.**
beaucoup many, a lot, much, very much	Elle aime le café? Oui, **beaucoup.**	J'ai acheté **beaucoup de lait.**
combien how much, how many	C'est **combien**, s'il vous plaît?	**Combien de café** voulez-vous? **Combien de pommes** voulez-vous?
peu little, few, not much, not many	Il mange très **peu.**	Il mange **peu de légumes.**
un peu a little	Mange **un peu!**	Encore **un peu de pain**, s'il vous plaît.
tant so much, so many	Tu voyages **tant!**	Tu manges **tant de chocolat!**
trop too much, too many	J'ai **trop** mangé.	J'ai mangé **trop de glace.**

Note that **beaucoup** can mean "much" or "*very* much." Consequently, the word **très** is never used with **beaucoup. Beaucoup**, however, can be used to modify **trop.**

> Je mange **beaucoup trop** de glace.   I eat **much too much** ice cream.

Other expressions of quantity include:

> **une bouteille (de)** a bottle (of)
> **un paquet (de)** a package (of)
> **une boîte (de)** a box (of), a can (of)

Exercices d'application: Expressions of Quantity

U. **Je mange beaucoup.** Describe yourself. Complete each sentence with **assez, beaucoup, trop, beaucoup trop, peu,** or **très peu.**[1]

1. Je mange…
2. Je voyage…
3. Je bois…
4. J'étudie…

5. Je travaille…
6. Je parle au téléphone…
7. Je marche…
8. Je parle…

---

1. For **-er** verbs not in Chapter 3, see Chapter 2, **Structure** 5.

V. **Oui, beaucoup!** Ask classmates if they like the various food items presented in this chapter. Refer to the chart of expressions of quantity to personalize your responses to each question. (You may wish to use the **tu** form of address with classmates.)

EXEMPLE: —*Aimez-vous (Aimes-tu) le café?*
            —*Oui, beaucoup.*
  or: —*Oui, un peu.*
  or: —*Non, pas du tout* (not at all).

W. **Je mange trop de glace.** Select several food and beverage items presented in this chapter. How much of them do you generally eat or drink? Use **trop de, beaucoup de, beaucoup trop de, assez de, un peu de, peu de,** or **très peu de,** followed by the item.

EXEMPLES: *Je mange beaucoup trop de frites.*
             Je bois trop de café.
             Je bois très peu d'eau.

Synthèse

A. **Votre restaurant préféré.** Answer these questions about your favorite restaurant. Then ask your classmates. (You may wish to use the **tu** form of address with classmates.)

1. Quel est votre (ton) restaurant préféré?
2. Dînez-vous (Dînes-tu) souvent dans ce *(this)* restaurant?
3. Y êtes-vous (es-tu) allé(e) récemment? *(Did you go there recently?)* Avec qui? *Réponse: J'y suis allé(e)...Je n'y suis pas allé(e)...*
4. Avez-vous (As-tu) réservé une table? Pour quelle heure? Pour combien de personnes?
5. Avez-vous pris un apéritif?
6. Qu'est-ce que vous avez commandé?
7. Qu'est-ce que vous avez bu?
8. Comment est le service? bon? mauvais *(bad)?* trop rapide? rapide? lent *(slow)?* trop lent?
9. Comment sont les prix *(prices)?* raisonnables? élevés *(high)?* bas *(low)?*
10. Combien avez-vous payé? Avez-vous laissé *(Did you leave)* un pourboire? Combien?

B. **Vos Repas.** Answer these questions about your own meals. Then ask your classmates. Do not limit your responses simply to those suggestions offered in these questions. Use the inclusive vocabulary options provided in the **Dialogue**. (You may wish to use the **tu** form of address with your classmates.)

1. Qu'est-ce que vous avez (tu as) pris au dîner hier soir? Au déjeuner *(lunch)* hier? Au déjeuner aujourd'hui?
2. Qu'est-ce que vous avez pris au petit déjeuner *(breakfast)* ce matin? des œufs? du pain grillé *(toast)*? du jus? etc.
3. Que prenez-vous (prends-tu) d'habitude *(usually)* au déjeuner? du yaourt? du café? un sandwich? un bifteck? etc.
4. Que prenez-vous d'habitude au casse-croûte *(snack)*? à la pause-café *(coffee break)*? du café? du thé? des fruits? de la glace?
5. D'habitude que prenez-vous au petit déjeuner en semaine? le dimanche? en voyage? en vacances?
6. Que prenez-vous après le dîner? un digestif? du café? du thé?

C. **Le Menu.** Order a light lunch at a French café. Select from these two menus. Note that the food items are illustrated to the left of each listing.

PRONONCIATION

1. Sound (Phonetic Symbol) [u]

SPELLING:	**ou, oû, où**
ENGLISH SOUND RESEMBLED:	Vowel sounds in words *you* and *who*
PRONUNCIATION:	Push lips forward into a little circle. Do not let the sound glide as in English. Keep it short and abrupt.
EXAMPLES FROM THIS CHAPTER:	

je v<u>ou</u>drais   bout<u>ei</u>lle *Doute*   p<u>ou</u>let
p<u>ou</u>r *pwr*   m<u>ou</u>tarde   v<u>ou</u>lu *new vulon vulu*
s<u>ou</u>pe   nous v<u>ou</u>lons   n<u>ou</u>s
pample<u>mou</u>sse *pamamoose*   v<u>ou</u>lez-v<u>ou</u>s   ret<u>ou</u>rner *retune*
ch<u>ou</u>-fleur *shoe flour*   c<u>ou</u>teau *cuto*   beauc<u>oup</u> *BUCUP*

2. The Sound (Phonetic Symbol): [y]

SPELLING:	**u, û** (also **eu** in past participle of **avoir**)
PRONUNCIATION:	Round and protrude the lips while attempting to say the sound [i].
EXAMPLES FROM THIS CHAPTER:	

<u>u</u>ne	v<u>ou</u>lu	confit<u>u</u>re
d<u>u</u>	lég<u>u</u>mes	b<u>u</u>vons *buvon*
t<u>u</u>	j<u>u</u>s	ét<u>u</u>dié
b<u>u</u>	exc<u>u</u>sez-moi	f<u>u</u>mer *fume*
p<u>u</u>	s<u>u</u>cre	men<u>u</u>

Contrast the vowel sound [u] with the vowel sound [y] using the following examples from this chapter:

[u]	[y]
n<u>ous</u> *new*	b<u>u</u>vons
v<u>ous</u>	b<u>u</u>vez
n<u>ous</u>	avons <u>eu</u>
v<u>ous</u>	avez b<u>u</u>
avez-v<u>ous</u>	p<u>u</u>
n<u>ous</u> avons	ét<u>u</u>dié
v<u>ous</u> avez	f<u>u</u>mé

Projets

A. **Le Menu** *(Exercice écrit)*. Design a menu for your own restaurant. Choose an appropriate name. Then list all the items you yourself would actually be willing or able to prepare for your clients. Include your specialties: **Bifteck, Hamburger avec de la sauce tomate** *(ketchup),* **Sandwich au beurre de cacahuètes** *(peanut butter),* **Salade de thon** *(tuna),* **Hot-dog,** etc. Price each item. Include as many of the following categories as possible: **Hors d'œuvre, Soupes/Potages, Entrées, Salades, Desserts, Boissons.**

B. **Liste d'achats** *(Shopping list).* Using the food and beverage items presented in this chapter, make a shopping list of things you really have to buy this week.

Liste d'achats

tomates — œufs *deser*
carottes — lait
oignons — fromage
oranges — yaourt *yoaser*
pommes — eau minérale
pêches — sel
jambon — poivre
pâté — sucre
poulet — olives *001N*

Activité: Learning by Doing

Au Restaurant. Have an in-class restaurant. Everyone should bring to class enough of a selected food or beverage item to allow every class member who orders that item actually to be served some. Suggestions: **du jus, du pain, du fromage, du gâteau, des pommes,** etc. Menus may be prepared. These would include only those food items actually to be served. A few class members will be chefs, maître d', and waiters or waitresses. Everyone else will be diners. Whatever role you play, be sure to use as many of the terms and phrases from the **Dialogue** and **Structures** sections of this chapter as possible. *(Note:* You will find the sentences in **Phrases à retenir** especially useful.)

Quelle heure est-il?

Telling Time

Le temps c'est de l'argent.

Time is money.

Being able to tell time correctly is essential for making appointments, reservations, dates, and travel plans. This **Entracte** presents commonly used vocabulary and structures related to time.

Quelle heure est-il?

Réponse: • Il est _____.[1]

EXEMPLE: *Il est cinq heures dix.*

Direct substitution of vocabulary items from these lists into the given response formats will allow immediate and correct conversational self-expression. No grammatical manipulation is necessary.

une heure	1 o'clock	huit heures	8 o'clock
deux heures	2 o'clock	neuf heures	9 o'clock
trois heures	3 o'clock	dix heures	10 o'clock
quatre heures	4 o'clock	onze heures	11 o'clock
cinq heures	5 o'clock	midi	noon
six heures	6 o'clock	minuit	midnight
sept heures	7 o'clock		

Minutes after: Add the number of minutes past the hour.
3:10 = trois heures dix

Minutes before: Use **moins** and measure back from the next hour.
2:50 = trois heures moins dix

1 un	7 sept	13 treize	19 dix-neuf	25 vingt-cinq
2 deux	8 huit	14 quatorze	20 vingt	26 vingt-six
3 trois	9 neuf	15 quinze	21 vingt et un	27 vingt-sept
4 quatre	10 dix	16 seize	22 vingt-deux	28 vingt-huit
5 cinq	11 onze	17 dix-sept	23 vingt-trois	29 vingt-neuf
6 six	12 douze	18 dix-huit	24 vingt-quatre	

Quarter past: Add **et quart.**   *Half past:* Add **et demie.**
3:15 = trois heures et quart   3:30 = trois heures et demie
                                          Exception: midi et demi, minuit et demi

Quarter to/of: Use **moins le quart** and measure back from the next hour.
2:45 = trois heures moins le quart

---

1. What time is it? It is _____.

Springboards for Conversation

Ask your classmates these personalized questions. Answer formats are provided.

1. Quelle heure est-il? À votre montre *(according to your watch)*? À la pendule *(according to the classroom clock)*?
   • Il est _____.
   Note: Use **à ma montre** to mean "according to my watch."

2. À quelle heure commence *(begins)* la classe de français?
   • Elle commence à _____.

3. À quelle heure finit *(ends)* la classe de français?
   • Elle finit à _____.

4. À quelle heure vous êtes-vous couché(e) hier soir?[2] *(What time did you go to bed last night?)*
   • À/Vers *(At/Around)* _____.

5. À quelle heure vous êtes-vous levé(e) ce matin? *(What time did you get up this morning?)*
   • À/Vers *(At/Around)* _____.

Récapitulation

Recall what you have learned about your classmates and instructor.[2] Answer formats are provided.

1. À quelle heure est-ce que le professeur s'est couché hier soir? Et votre voisin(e) de gauche? Et votre voisin(e) de droite? Et Monsieur...? Et Madame...? Et Mademoiselle...? etc.

   EXEMPLE: *Vers dix heures.*

2. À quelle heure est-ce que le professeur s'est levé ce matin? Et votre voisin(e) de gauche? Et votre voisin(e) de droite? Et Madame...? Et Monsieur...? Et Mademoiselle...? etc.
   • À/Vers _____.

3. Qui dans la classe s'est levé *(got up)* vers _____? Qui d'autre? C'est tout?
   • Monsieur/Madame/Mademoiselle... s'est levé(e) vers _____.
   • Le professeur s'est levé vers _____.
   • Moi, je me suis levé(e) vers _____.

   • Tout le monde s'est levé vers _____.
   • Personne. *(No one).*

4. Qui dans la classe s'est levé(e) très tôt *(very early)* ce matin? Et très tard *(very late)*?
   • Monsieur/Madame/Mademoiselle... s'est levé(e) très tôt/tard ce matin. Il/Elle s'est levé(e) à _____.
   • Le professeur s'est levé...
   • Moi, je me suis levé(e)...

5. Qui dans la classe s'est couché(e) très tôt hier soir? Et très tard?
   • Monsieur/Madame/Mademoiselle... s'est couché(e) très tôt/tard hier soir. Il/Elle s'est couché(e) à _____.
   • Le professeur s'est couché...
   • Moi, je me suis couché(e)...

2. No mastery of the past tense or of reflexive verbs is required. Simply use **à** or **vers** and the correct time in your responses.

Remarques

1. **Heure(s)**, which literally means "hours," is the equivalent of "o'clock."
2. The term **heure(s)** is never omitted in French. This is unlike English, where the word "o'clock" is often dropped.
3. With **une heure** (*one o'clock*), the word **heure** is singular. In all other cases, **heures** is plural: **deux heures, trois heures,** etc.
4. The following vocabulary is used with the twelve-hour clock: **du matin** = A.M. (in the morning); **de l'après-midi** = P.M. (in the afternoon); **du soir** = P.M. (in the evening). **Il est trois heures du matin.** It's 3:00 A.M.
5. *Pronunciation:* When followed by **heures**, the final x and s in **deux, trois, six,** and **dix** are pronounced [z]; the final q of **cinq** is pronounced [k]; the final t of **sept** and **huit** is pronounced [t]; and the final f of **neuf** is pronounced [v].

Expansion

The **Expansion** can be used for partners or group conversation and for oral or written composition. No mastery of the past tense or of reflexive verbs is required. Simply use **à** or **vers** plus the correct time in your responses.[3]

1. À quelle heure avez-vous dîné (*did you have dinner*) hier soir?
   • À/Vers _____.

2. À quelle heure avez-vous pris votre petit déjeuner (*did you have breakfast*) ce matin?
   • À/Vers _____.
   • Je n'ai pas pris de petit déjeuner ce matin.

3. À quelle heure êtes-vous rentré(e) (*did you get home*) hier soir?
   • À/Vers _____.

4. À quelle heure êtes-vous parti(e) de chez vous (*did you leave home*) aujourd'hui?
   • À/Vers _____.

5. À quelle heure commence la classe de français?
   • À _____.

6. À quelle heure êtes-vous arrivé(e) (*did you arrive*) en classe aujourd'hui?
   • À/Vers _____.
   • En avance (*early*)/en retard (*late*)/à l'heure (*on time*).

7. En général, à quelle heure...
   vous couchez-vous (*do you go to bed*)?
   vous levez-vous le matin (*do you get up*)?
   dînez-vous (*do you eat dinner*)?
   prenez-vous le petit déjeuner (*do you eat breakfast*)?
   rentrez-vous le soir (*do you get home*)?
   • À/Vers _____.
   Note: **en semaine** (*weekdays*), **le dimanche** (*on Sundays*), **je me couche** (*I go to bed*), **je me lève** (*I get up*), **je dîne** (*I eat dinner*), **je prends le petit déjeuner** (*I eat breakfast*), **je rentre** (*I get home*).

8. If the preceding **Expansion** questions have been used for group or partners conversation, review what you have learned about your classmates.

   EXEMPLES: *Marc a dîné à huit heures.*
   Suzanne a pris le petit déjeuner vers sept heures et demie.
   Monsieur Smith est rentré vers dix heures.

---

3. Answer formats are provided. Once you have mastered the past tense, you may wish to return to this **Expansion** exercise for practice with these forms.

Vocabulaire utile   The following phrases are frequently requested by students using the time-related conversations of this **Entracte**.

Pardon? Excuse me?

(Je suis) désolé(e), mais je ne sais pas. I'm sorry, but I don't know.

Je ne porte pas de montre aujourd'hui. I'm not wearing a watch today.

À ma montre, il est _____. On my watch it's _____.

Maintenant il est _____. Now it's _____.

En ce moment il est _____. Right now it's _____.

À quelle heure? When? What time?

À _____ heure(s). At _____ o'clock.

Vers _____ heure(s). Around _____ o'clock.

Entre _____ et _____ heures. Between _____ and _____ o'clock.

Avant _____ heure(s). Before _____ o'clock.

Après _____ heure(s). After _____ o'clock.

Ma montre avance (je crois). My watch is fast (I believe).

Ma montre retarde (je crois). My watch is slow (I think).

Ma montre s'est arrêtée. My watch has stopped.

Quelle heure avez-vous? What time do you have?

Il est _____ heure(s) précise(s). It's precisely _____.

Il est _____ heure(s) juste(s). It's exactly _____.

Comment!? What! How can that be!?

Déjà! Already!

Que le temps passe vite! How time flies!

The twenty-four hour clock.   In France, although the twelve-hour system is generally used in conversation, the twenty-four hour clock is used for offical purposes, such as transportation schedules, business hours, government work, theater schedules, performances, and announcements. It is also used for formal invitations and business appointments.

1 A.M. = **une heure (1 h.)**
1 P.M. = **treize heures (13 h.)**
8:30 A.M. = **huit heures trente (8 h. 30)**
8:30 P.M. = **vingt heures trente (20 h. 30)**

L'Horloge parlante.   In France, people telephone **l'horloge parlante** *(literally: the speaking clock)* for the correct time. A typical call: **Au troisième top** *(sound),* **il sera exactement treize heures, vingt minutes et trente secondes...top...top...top...**

O'clock.   The letter **h** (capital H or small h, with or without a period) is the standard abbreviation for **heures** *(o'clock).* **11 h** is **onze heures** *(eleven o'clock).*

LA CAFETERIA EST OUVERTE
du lundi au samedi de
11h30 à 14h30 et de 18h30 à 21h30

Digital clocks.   As digital watches gain in popularity, time is often expressed in minutes after the hour (from one to fifty-nine). For example, instead of the traditional **deux heures moins le quart,** we often hear **une heure quarante-cinq** *(one forty-five).*

la brasserie des tuileries

52F

SERVICE 15% ET
TVA 18,60% COMPRIS

AU CHOIX   AU CHOIX

6   6
ENTRÉES PLATS
         GARNIS

DONT
1 PLAT
Du JOUR

SERVICE PERMANENT
DE 11 H 30 A 22 H 30

Synthèse

A. **Quelle heure est-il?** Complete the caption underneath each photograph.

Il est _____.   Il est _____.

Il est _____.

B. **À quelle heure commence...?** What time do the movies listed below begin? Use both the twelve-hour and the twenty-four–hour systems in your responses.

10 CAPRI GRANDS BOULEVARDS 161 rue Mont-martre. 508.11.69. Mᵒ Rue Montmartre. Perm vers 13h30 à 24h. Ven, Sam Séance Suppl vers 24h. Pl : 25 F et 24 F. Lun, toute la journée, du Dim 20h au Mar 15h et du Mer au Ven de 14h à 15h., C.V. jusqu'à 18h en sem., tarif unique Pl : 16 et 17 F.
Gandhi v.f.
Séances :, 13h30 (film), 16h50, 20h20.
Kramer contre Kramer v.f.
Séances : 13h55, 15h55, 17h55, 19h55, 21h55.
Midnight express v.f. Int — 18 ans.
Séances : 13h30, 16h, 18h30, 21h.
11 GAITE BOULEVARDS 25 Bd Poissonnière. 233.67.06. Perm de 13h30 à 24h. Sam séance suppl à 24h. Pl : 16 F.
2 salles :
L'Exécuteur de Hong-Kong v.f. et *Un espion de trop*
La Vengeance de Liu v.f. et *Cette femme est un flic* v.f.

Projet

Photographs. Leaf through an illustrated magazine, assigning a time of day to each photograph. For example, a scene depicting people eating breakfast may be described as **Il est huit heures du matin.** The illustrations in this textbook may be used for the same purpose.

Activité: Learning by Doing

Asking and telling time. Circulate around the classroom, asking classmates for the exact time according to their watches or, if need be, according to the classroom clock. **Pardon, Monsieur/Madame/Mademoiselle. Avez-vous l'heure, s'il vous plaît? Il est trois heures précises. Il est deux heures justes. Merci, Monsieur/Madame/Mademoiselle.**

If you are not wearing a watch, use the classroom clock. If there is no classroom clock, when you are asked the time, ask a third classmate who is wearing a watch. **Pardon. Vous avez l'heure?** Then, relay this information to the person who had originally asked you for the time. (You may wish to review the **Vocabulaire utile,** page 95.)

«Je cherche un cadeau pour mon ami(e).»

Les Achats

Shopping

Les bons comptes font les bons amis.

Short reckonings make long friends.

DIALOGUE

This **Dialogue** presents vocabulary necessary for going shopping. It also introduces vocabulary for a variety of objects used in daily living along with selected adjectives for describing these items. Vocabulary blocks within this **Dialogue** offer possibilities for modification to suit a wide variety of real-life shopping situations.

Dans un Grand Magasin	In a Department Store
LE VENDEUR LA VENDEUSE: Vous désirez, Monsieur / Madame / Mademoiselle?	SALESMAN / SALESWOMAN: May I help you? *(Literally:* You desire?)
VOUS: Je cherche **un cadeau** pour mon	YOU: I'm looking for a **present**

un dictionnaire anglais-français
    un disque
    un journal
    un livre
    un souvenir
	English-French dictionary
	    record
	    newspaper
	    book
	    souvenir

ami(e).	for my friend.
LE VENDEUR: **Des mouchoirs,** peut-être?	SALESMAN: **Handkerchiefs,** perhaps?

Ceci
    Cela (ça)
    Des cartes postales
    Une montre
    Des bonbons
    Du papier à lettres
    Une revue / un magazine
	This
	    That
	    Postcards
	    A watch
	    Candy
	    Stationery
	    A magazine

VOUS: Euh… Vous n'avez pas autre chose?	YOU: Umm . . . Don't you have anything else?
LE VENDEUR: Mais bien sûr! Voilà **un portefeuille.**	SALESMAN: (But) of course! Here's a **wallet.**

un jeu
    un jouet
    un parapluie
    un porte-clés
    un porte-monnaie
    un stylo
	game
	    toy
	    umbrella
	    key chain
	    change purse
	    pen

Il est **joli,** n'est-ce pas?	It's **pretty,** isn't it?

adorable
    grand
    magnifique
    petit
    pratique
    solide
	adorable
	    big
	    magnificent
	    small
	    practical
	    solid

VOUS: C'est combien?	YOU: How much is it?

LE VENDEUR: **Cent** francs.
> **Trente**
> **Quarante**
> **Cinquante**
> **Soixante**
> **Soixante-dix**
> **Quatre-vingts**
> **Quatre-vingt-dix**

VOUS: C'est **trop cher**.
> **exorbitant**
> **une bonne affaire**
> **bon marché**
> **bien**

LE VENDEUR: Le parfum est en solde aujourd'hui.

VOUS: **Parfait**. Je le prends.
> **Bon. D'accord.**
> **Bonne idée!**
> **Formidable!**
> **Quel trésor!**

Acceptez-vous les chèques de voyage?
> **Acceptez-vous les cartes de crédit?**
> **Puis-je payer par chèque?**

LE VENDEUR: Certainement. Désirez-vous autre chose, Monsieur/Madame?

VOUS: Non, merci. C'est tout. C'est pour offrir. Pouvez-vous me faire un paquet-cadeau, s'il vous plaît?

LE VENDEUR: Oui, Monsieur / Madame. À votre service.

SALESMAN: **One hundred** francs.
> Thirty
> Forty
> Fifty
> Sixty
> Seventy
> Eighty
> Ninety

YOU: That's **too expensive**.
> exorbitant
> a bargain
> cheap
> fine

SALESMAN: The perfume is on sale today.

YOU: **Perfect**. I'll take it.
> Good. OK.
> Good idea.
> Terrific!
> What a treasure!

Do you accept traveler's checks?
> Do you accept credit cards?
> May I pay by check?

SALESMAN: Certainly. Do you want something else?

YOU: No, thanks. That's all. It's a gift. *(Literally:* It's for offering.) Can you giftwrap it, please? *(Literally:* Can you make me a gift package?)

SALESMAN: Yes. Glad to help you. *(Literally:* At your service.)

Phrases à retenir

Memorizing these phrases from the **Dialogue** will help assure fluency in real-life dealings with French-speaking sales personnel and shopkeepers.

1. Je cherche un cadeau pour mon ami(e).
2. Vous n'avez pas autre chose?
3. Ceci, peut-être.
4. C'est combien?
5. C'est trop cher.
6. C'est une bonne affaire.
7. Je le prends.
8. Acceptez-vous les chèques de voyage?
9. Acceptez-vous les cartes de crédit?
10. C'est tout.

DIALOGUE EXERCISES

The following exercises provide oral and written practice in using the vocabulary and basic sentence patterns of the **Dialogue: Les Achats**. These exercises use *only* vocabulary and structures presented in the shopping **Dialogue**. They do not require familiarity with any other portions of this chapter.

Exercices d'application

A. **Inquiries: Avez-vous des...?**   Ask a salesperson if he or she has any of the items you want. Use **des** and a plural noun.

MODÈLE: watches   *Avez-vous des montres?*

1. records
2. books
3. postcards
4. pens
5. magazines
6. perfumes
7. wallets
8. souvenirs
9. handkerchiefs

B. **Gift vocabulary: Vous n'avez pas autre chose?**   You are looking for a gift for a friend. When a classmate suggests a specific item selected from the **Dialogue**, ask if he or she has something else to show you. Continue until your partner runs out of suggestions.

EXEMPLE: —*Je cherche un cadeau pour mon ami(e).*
           —*Un disque, peut-être* (perhaps)?
           —*Vous n'avez pas autre chose?*
           —*Un portefeuille, peut-être?...*

C. **Requests: Je voudrais...**   Tell the salesperson what you want based on the circumstances described below. Use gift items selected from the **Dialogue**.

MODÈLE: C'est l'anniversaire (*birthday*) de votre mère. Elle aime le parfum.
          Je voudrais du parfum.

1. Vous cherchez un cadeau pour votre professeur de français. Il/Elle aime beaucoup la musique.
2. Vous êtes à Paris. Vous cherchez un souvenir pour un ami.
3. C'est l'anniversaire de votre femme ou de votre mari ou de votre ami(e).
4. Vous voulez acheter (*buy*) quelque chose (*something*) pour un ami qui aime la littérature.
5. Vous êtes à Paris. Vous voulez acheter un cadeau pour un ami qui étudie le français.
6. Vous cherchez quelque chose de typiquement (*typically*) français pour une amie.

7. Vous cherchez un cadeau pour vos enfants ou pour les enfants d'un(e) ami(e).

D.   **Dialogue responses.**   Respond to each of the following statements or questions. Use sentences and phrases taken directly from the **Dialogue**.

1. Vous désirez, Monsieur/Madame/Mademoiselle?
2. C'est pour offrir?
3. Un portefeuille, peut-être?
4. Il est joli, n'est-ce pas?
5. Cent francs.
6. Le parfum est en solde aujourd'hui.
7. Désirez-vous autre chose?
8. C'est tout?

E.   **Review.**   What do you say . . .

1. to indicate you are looking for a gift?
2. when you would like a souvenir?
3. when you do not really like what the salesperson has shown you?
4. to find out how much something costs?
5. when you find out that a little bottle of perfume costs over one thousand francs?
6. to indicate you'll take an item?
7. when you want to pay with traveler's checks?
8. to indicate that you wish the item you have just bought to be giftwrapped?

Improvisation à deux *(Exercice oral)*

F.   Use the vocabulary block options and the basic sentence structures of the **Dialogue** to improvise a dialogue with a classmate. Express personal preferences concerning gift selection. One of you may be a salesperson and the other a customer or both of you may choose to be customers shopping at the same store.

À Vous le choix *(Exercices écrits)*

G.   Write a six- to eight-line dialogue for each of the following situations, selecting appropriate phrases from the initial **Dialogue** of this chapter.

1. You are traveling in France. You wish to buy a few souvenirs for yourself.
2. You are shopping in a boutique where all the items seem overpriced.
3. You are selecting a gift for someone. Have in mind a real person for whom you would actually like to buy a gift.

Conversations

H. Ask your classmates these personalized questions. When two or more responses are possible, alternate answer formats are offered. Select the option that best applies to you personally. Do not limit your responses to those suggestions offered in these questions. Use the inclusive vocabulary options provided in the **Dialogue**. (You may wish to use the **tu** form of address with your classmates.)

1. Qu'est-ce que vous avez (tu as) acheté cette semaine? un livre? des livres? un stylo? etc. C'est tout? Quoi d'autre? *(What else?)*
   • J'ai acheté un/une/des _____.

2. Avez-vous (As-tu) acheté un livre? une montre? des cartes postales? etc.
   • Oui, j'ai acheté un/une/des _____.
   • Non, je n'ai pas acheté de _____.

3. À qui avez-vous offert *(did you give)* un cadeau récemment? Qu'est-ce que vous avez offert? des bonbons? du parfum? un livre? etc.
   • J'ai offert un/une/des _____ à mon ami(e) (ma mère/mon père/mes parents/mon mari/ma femme/ma fille/mon fils).

4. Allez-vous bientôt *(soon)* acheter un cadeau pour quelqu'un *(someone)*? Que pensez-vous acheter? *(What are you thinking of buying?)*
   • Je pense acheter un/une/des _____.

5. De quoi avez-vous besoin? *(What do you need?)* d'un dictionnaire? d'un portefeuille? d'un stylo? d'un parapluie? d'une montre? etc.
   • J'ai besoin d'un/d'une _____.

I. **Review.** What have you learned about your classmates from the preceding **Conversations**?

EXEMPLES: *Marc a acheté un livre cette semaine.*
Marie a offert un cadeau récemment à sa mère.
Madame Smith a besoin d'une montre.

Money. The French word for money is l'argent (which also means "silver"). Bills or bank notes are **des billets**, coins are **des pièces**, and the word for change is **la monnaie**. This latter term should not be confused with the English word "money." **La Monnaie** is also the name of the place where coins are made in France. **Billets** are printed at the **Banque de France**.

Monetary systems of Francophone countries. In France, the monetary system is based on the **franc**. One franc equals 100 **centimes**. In Belgium, Belgian francs (**des francs belges**) are used. In Switzerland, Swiss francs (**des francs suisses**) are the currency. The basis of the Canadian monetary system is the Canadian dollar (**des dollars canadiens**).

Old francs—new francs. In France, 7,60F or 7F60 means **sept francs soixante**, or seven francs and sixty centimes. The letters F or **NF** stand for **Nouveau Franc** (new franc). Some people still refer to the system of old francs (**anciens francs**) that dates from before 1960. One new franc equals 100 old francs. For example 2 000 **ancien francs (AF)** equals 20 NF. Many French people still refer to the former system in their conversation.

Du Fric. There are many slang expressions for money in French: for example, **du fric, du pognon, du pèse, de la galette, des sous**. *I'm broke* is **je n'ai pas de fric, je n'ai pas un rond,** or **je suis fauché(e)**. Someone who is cheap is **radin**: **Il est radin celui-là! Ne sois pas radin!**

Payez à la caisse. In many larger shops you will be told to pay at the cash register: **payez à la caisse**. Some shops offer discounts for traveler's checks or tax refunds for large purchases. Be sure to inquire as you pay.

Shops in France. Small shops in France usually open around 9:00 A.M. and close between 5:30 and 7:00 P.M. Some close for lunch. In southern France, the lunch break often includes a siesta break. Most French shops are closed on Sundays and public holidays. Many smaller shops are closed on Mondays as well.

CHANGE

PAYS	UNITE	DEVISE	ACHAT
AUTRICHE	100	SH.	40·55
BELGIQUE	100	F.B.	13,97
CANADA	1 $ CAN.		6·21
DANEMARK	100	KRD	77·60
ESPAGNE	100	PTA.	5·00
FINLANDE	100	MF	
GRANDE-BRETAGNE	1	£	11,40
ITALIE	1000	LIT.	4,66
NORVEGE	100	KRN	100·88
PAYS-BAS	100	FL.	249
PORTUGAL	100	ESC	5,92
R.F.A	1	DM	2,81
SUEDE	100	KRS	95,06
SUISSE	1	F.S.	3,50
U.S.A	1 $	US	7,71 7.c 7,84

Le Cours du change. Foreign currency can be converted into **francs** at a bank (**une banque**) or a money exchange (**un bureau de change**), where the rate of exchange (**le cours du change**) is posted daily. Since exchange rates are subject to constant fluctuation, check your newspaper or local bank for today's rate of exchange.

Soldes. French sales are announced by signs reading **soldes**.

Faire du lèche-vitrines. The French expression for window shopping is **faire du lèche-vitrines** (*literally:* to do some window licking).

LES ACHATS

VERBES IRRÉGULIERS: voir, croire, offrir, ouvrir

voir	to see
LE PRÉSENT	LE PASSÉ COMPOSÉ
je **vois**	j'**ai vu**
tu **vois**	tu **as vu**
il/elle **voit**	il/elle **a vu**
nous **voyons**	nous **avons vu**
vous **voyez**	vous **avez vu**
ils/elles **voient**	ils/elles **ont vu**

The irregular verb **croire** (*to believe*) is conjugated like **voir: je crois, tu crois, il/elle croit, nous croyons, vous croyez, ils/elles croient.** The past participle is **cru.**

Je crois.	I think so.
Je ne crois pas.	I don't think so.
Je crois que oui.	I think so.
Je crois que non.	I think not.

Exercices d'application: voir, croire

A. **Vous voyez...? Oui, je vois...**   What people or items in the classroom do you see? Ask your classmates. Use the verb **voir** in the questions and responses. (You may wish to use the informal **tu** form of address with your classmates.)

EXEMPLE: —*Vous voyez (tu vois) le professeur?*
—*Oui, je vois le professeur.*
or: —*Non, je ne vois pas le professeur.*

Some possibilities include: **Madame..., Monsieur..., Mademoiselle...,** your classmates, and, from the **Dialogue: le livre, le dictionnaire anglais-français, le livre du professeur, le journal, le parapluie, le portefeuille, ceci, cela,** etc.

B. **Avez-vous vu...?**   Answer these questions yourself. Then ask a classmate. (You may wish to use the **tu** form of address with your classmates.)

1. Avez-vous vu vos amis (As-tu vu tes amis) récemment?
2. Avez-vous vu un film français récemment? (*Note:* **Un** becomes **de** in the negative.)
3. Avez-vous vu le professeur de français hier?
4. Avez-vous vu le stylo du professeur?
5. Avez-vous vu le livre de français du professeur?

C. **Oui, je crois. Non, je ne crois pas.** Ask a classmate to verify another classmate's name.

EXEMPLE: —*C'est Monsieur Brown, n'est-ce pas?*
 —*Oui, je crois.*
 or: —*Non, je ne crois pas. Je crois qu'il s'appelle Monsieur Green.*

offrir	to offer
LE PRÉSENT	LE PASSÉ COMPOSÉ
j'**offre** tu **offres** il/elle **offre** nous **offrons** vous **offrez** ils/elles **offrent**	j'**ai offert** tu **as offert** il/elle **a offert** nous **avons offert** vous **avez offert** ils/elles **ont offert**

1. *Note:*

   offrir un cadeau   to give a gift
   C'est pour offrir?   Is it intended to be a gift?

2. The irregular verb **ouvrir** *(to open)* is conjugated like **offrir: j'ouvre, tu ouvres, il/elle ouvre, nous ouvrons, vous ouvrez, ils/elles ouvrent.** The past participle is **ouvert.**

3. Note that even though the infinitives of **offrir** and **ouvrir** look like **-ir** verbs (see **Structures**), their present tense actually uses **-er** verb endings.

Exercices d'application: offrir, ouvrir

D. **Qu'est-ce que vous avez offert comme cadeaux récemment?** What gift items from the **Dialogue** have you actually given recently as gifts? To whom did you give them?

EXEMPLES: *J'ai offert des bonbons à une amie.*
 J'ai offert un livre à un ami.
 J'ai offert une montre à ma mère.

E. **Ouvrez...tout de suite!** It's urgent. Tell someone to open the following things right away.

MODÈLE: la fenêtre   *Ouvrez la fenêtre tout de suite* (right away)!

You may wish to use the informal command form: **ouvre.**

1. le cadeau
2. le paquet
3. la porte
4. le parapluie
5. la bouteille *(bottle)*
6. le livre

STRUCTURES

Structure 1: -ir Verbs (Present Tense and **Passé Composé**)

The infinitives of some French verbs end in **-ir**. The present tense of these verbs is formed by adding the appropriate endings to the base of the verb. The base is formed by dropping the **-ir** of the infinitive. For example, the base of **finir** *(to finish)* is **fin-**.

LE PRÉSENT	
je fin**is**	nous fin**issons**
tu fin**is**	vous fin**issez**
il fin**it**	ils fin**issent**
elle fin**it**	elles fin**issent**
on fin**it**	

1. some common **-ir** verbs:

choisir	to choose	**obéir (à)**	to obey
finir	to finish	**remplir**	to fill (up); to fill out (a form)
grossir	to gain weight		
maigrir	to get thin	**rougir**	to blush

Note: Remember that **offrir** and **ouvrir** are irregular verbs. Even though their infinitives end in **-ir**, they are not conjugated like regular **-ir** verbs.

2. The past participle of **-ir** verbs ends in **-i**.

LE PASSÉ COMPOSÉ	INFINITIVE: **finir** PAST PARTICIPLE: **fini**
j'**ai fini**	nous **avons fini**
tu **as fini**	vous **avez fini**
il **a fini**	ils **ont fini**
elle **a fini**	elles **ont fini**
on **a fini**	

Negative: **Je n'ai pas fini, tu n'as pas fini,** etc.
Interrogative: **As-tu fini, a-t-il fini,** etc.

Exercices d'application: -ir Verbs

A. **Ah, c'est pourquoi il grossit.** Referring to the list of **-ir** verbs, comment on each of the following statements. Begin with: **Ah, c'est pourquoi** *(that's why)* **il/elle....** Then complete your sentence with an appropriate **-ir** verb.

MODÈLE: Il mange beaucoup.   *Ah, c'est pourquoi il grossit!*

1. Il mange très peu.
2. Elle est timide.
3. Il a peur *(is afraid).*

4. Elle n'aime pas manger.
5. Elle mange beaucoup.

B. **Avez-vous fini? As-tu fini?** Answer these questions yourself. Then ask a classmate. (You may wish to use the **tu** form of address with your classmates.)

1. Avez-vous (As-tu) rougi récemment?
2. Avez-vous maigri récemment?
3. Avez-vous fini la leçon?
4. Avez-vous obéi au professeur de français?
5. Avez-vous grossi récemment?

C. **Elle a fini la leçon. Il a maigri récemment.** If the preceding exercise has been used orally in class, review what you have learned about your classmates.

EXEMPLES: *Paul n'a pas grossi récemment.*
Marie a fini la leçon.
Monsieur Smith a maigri récemment.

Structure 2: -re Verbs (Present Tense and **Passé Composé**)

The present tense of **-re** verbs (verbs whose infinitives end with the letters **-re**) is formed by adding the appropriate endings to the base. The base is formed by dropping the **-re** of the infinitive. For example, the base of **attendre** *(to wait* or *to wait for)* is **attend-**:

LE PRÉSENT	
j'attends	nous attend**ons**
tu attends	vous attend**ez**
il attend	ils attend**ent**
elle attend	elles attend**ent**
on attend	

1. Some common **-re** verbs:

attendre   to wait (for)
entendre   to hear
perdre   to lose
vendre   to sell

rendre   to give back, to return;
     to exchange
répondre (à)   to answer

Note: Remember that the verbs **prendre** *(to take)*, **apprendre** *(to learn)*, and **comprendre** *(to understand)* are irregular verbs. (See Chapter 2.)

2. The past participle of **-re** verbs ends in **-u**.

LE PASSÉ COMPOSÉ	INFINITIVE: **attendre** PAST PARTICIPLE: **attendu**
j'ai attendu tu **as attendu** il **a attendu** elle **a attendu** on **a attendu**	nous **avons attendu** vous **avez attendu** ils **ont attendu** elles **ont attendu**

Exercices d'application: -re Verbs

D.   **Non, je ne veux pas...**   You are very sorry, but you simply do not want to do what you are being told to do.

MODÈLE: Attendez!   *Je suis désolé(e), mais je ne veux pas attendre.*

1. Répondez à la question.
2. Vendez cela.
3. Rendez le livre.
4. Attendez un peu.
5. Répondez en français.

E.   **Alors, n'attends pas!**   What do you hate to do? Select only those items from the following list that actually apply to you. Classmates will give you some friendly advice using the **tu** form of the imperative. You will do the same for them.

MODÈLE: Je n'aime pas attendre.   *Alors, n'attends pas!*

1. Je n'aime pas répondre en classe.
2. Je n'aime pas attendre longtemps *(for a long time)*.
3. Je n'aime pas perdre mon livre.
4. Je n'aime pas rendre mes livres à la bibliothèque *(library)*.
5. Je n'aime pas vendre mes livres à la fin du semestre *(at semester's end)*.

F. **Avez-vous attendu? As-tu attendu?** Answer these questions yourself. Then ask your classmates. Answer formats are provided. (You may choose to use the **tu** form of address with your classmates.)

1. Avez-vous (As-tu) attendu quelqu'un *(someone)* récemment? votre ami(e)? votre mère? votre professeur? etc.
   - Oui, _____.   • Non, personne *(no one)*.
2. Avez-vous perdu vos clés *(keys)* récemment?
3. Avez-vous perdu votre livre de français récemment?
4. Avez-vous perdu quelque chose récemment? votre portefeuille? votre porte-monnaie? votre porte-clés? etc.
   - Oui, _____.   • Non, rien *(nothing)*.

À la caisse

Structure 3: Adjective Agreement

French adjectives agree with the nouns they describe both in gender (masculine/feminine) and in number (singular/plural).

1. The letter **e** must be added to the masculine singular form of many adjectives to derive the feminine form. The letter **s** is added to make the adjective plural.

> MODÈLE: masculine singular: **petit**
> feminine singular: **petit<u>e</u>**
> masculine plural: **petit<u>s</u>**
> feminine plural: **petit<u>es</u>**

The adjectives below, which follow the **modèle,** are used in the exercises and activities of this chapter:

bleu blue	**fin** fine, thin
brun brown	**foncé** dark *(in color)*
bruyant noisy	**froid** cold
carré square	**grand** big
cassé broken	**intelligent** intelligent
charmant charming	**intéressant** interesting
chaud warm, hot	**joli** pretty
chiffonné wrinkled, rumpled, crumpled	**laid** ugly
clair light *(in color)*, bright	**lourd** heavy
content happy	**ouvert** opened
court short *(in length)*, brief	**parfait** perfect
déchiré torn	**petit** little, small
dur hard	**prêt** ready
étroit narrow	**rond** round
fatigué tired	**usé** worn-out
fermé closed, shut	**vert** green

When the adjective ends in **-é** (as in **fatigué**) another **e** must be added for the feminine form.

Some adjectives, like **anglais** *(English)*, **français** *(French)*, **gris** *(gray)*, and **mauvais** *(bad)*, already have an **s** in the masculine singular. Consequently, the masculine singular and masculine plural forms of the adjectives are identical.

2. The following adjectives already have the letter **e** in the masculine form. Consequently, the masculine singular and the feminine singular are

identical. The letter **s** is added to make the adjective plural.

> MODÈLE: masculine singular: **pratiqu<u>e</u>**
> feminine singular: **pratiqu<u>e</u>**
> masculine plural: **pratiqu<u>es</u>**
> feminine plural: **pratiqu<u>es</u>**

agréable pleasant	**moderne** modern
autre other	**orange** orange
beige beige	**ovale** oval
calme calm, peaceful	**pourpre** purple
chaque each	**pratique** practical
confortable comfortable	**propre** clean
énorme enormous	**rectangulaire** rectangular
étrange strange	**riche** rich
fragile fragile	**rose** pink
inutile useless	**rouge** red
jaune yellow	**sale** dirty
jeune young	**solide** solid, sturdy
large wide	**sombre** dark, gloomy
libre free	**tranquille** quiet, peaceful
magnifique magnificent	**utile** useful
mince thin, slim	**vide** empty

3. Adjectives with the masculine singular form ending in **-eux** have the feminine singular form ending in **-euse**.

> MODÈLE: masculine singular: **heur<u>eux</u>**
> feminine singular: **heur<u>euse</u>**
> masculine plural: **heur<u>eux</u>**
> feminine plural: **heur<u>euses</u>**

affreux horrible	**heureux** happy
curieux curious, strange	**joyeux** merry, joyous
dangereux dangerous	**malheureux** unhappy, unfortunate
délicieux delicious	**merveilleux** marvelous
fameux famous	**sérieux** serious

4. Adjectives with the masculine singular form ending in **-er** have the feminine singular form ending in **-ère**.

> MODÈLE: masculine singular: **premi<u>er</u>**
> feminine singular: **premi<u>ère</u>**
> masculine plural: **premi<u>ers</u>**
> feminine plural: **premi<u>ères</u>**

cher expensive, dear	**étranger** foreign
dernier last	**léger** light *(in weight)*
entier entire	**premier** first

5. Some irregular adjectives:

IRREGULAR ADJECTIVES				
SINGULAR		**PLURAL**		
Masculine	Feminine	Masculine	Feminine	
beau (bel)	**belle**	**beaux**	**belles**	pretty, beautiful
blanc	**blanche**	**blancs**	**blanches**	white
bon	**bonne**	**bons**	**bonnes**	good
épais	**épaisse**	**épais**	**épaisses**	thick
favori	**favorite**	**favoris**	**favorites**	favorite
frais	**fraîche**	**frais**	**fraîches**	fresh, cool
gentil	**gentille**	**gentils**	**gentilles**	nice, kind
gros	**grosse**	**gros**	**grosses**	big, fat
long	**longue**	**longs**	**longues**	long
nouveau (nouvel)	**nouvelle**	**nouveaux**	**nouvelles**	new
tout	**toute**	**tous**	**toutes**	all
vieux (vieil)	**vieille**	**vieux**	**vieilles**	old

Note: Beau, nouveau, and vieux become bel, nouvel, and vieil before masculine nouns beginning with a vowel or mute h: un nouvel hôtel.[1]

Exercices d'application: Adjective Agreement

G. **Il est cassé.**   What do you have with you in class today? Describe a few of these objects using as many adjectives from Structure 3 (part 1) as possible. Suggestions: **mon parapluie, mon livre de français, mon stylo, mon portefeuille, mon porte-monnaie, mon journal, mon dictionnaire, mon sac** (*purse*), **mon sac à dos** (*backpack*), **mon cahier** (*notebook*).

Note that these items are all masculine, requiring the masculine form of the adjectives selected.

EXEMPLE: *Mon parapluie est cassé. Il est déchiré et il est fermé.*

H. **Il n'est pas cassé.**   Now use some other adjectives selected from Structure 3 (part 1) to describe the items used in the preceding exercise. This time, however, indicate what the item is *not*. Use **il n'est pas.**

EXEMPLE: *Mon parapluie n'est pas cassé. Il n'est pas grand. Il n'est pas joli.*

---

1. Regarding mute **h**, see the **Prononciation** section of this chapter, p. 120.

I.   **Mon livre de français est pratique, utile et ouvert.**   Describe each of the following, using any adjectives presented in Structure 3. Be thorough in your descriptions. Do not limit yourself simply to one or two adjectives. Note that all of these items are masculine, requiring the masculine form of the adjectives selected.

1. Mon livre de français est...
2. Mon portefeuille est...
3. Paris est...
4. Mon restaurant préféré est...
5. Mon père (grand-père, fils, oncle, frère) est...
6. Mon mari (fiancé, meilleur ami) est...

J.   **Son livre est...**   If the preceding exercise has been used orally in class, review what you have learned about your classmates.

EXEMPLE: *Son père est intelligent, gentil, beau et vieux. (Note:* **son** *= his or* her.)
            Son portefeuille est rectangulaire, vieux, brun, usé, sale et vide.

K.   **Ma chambre est...**   Describe each of the following items, using adjectives from Structure 3. Describe each as thoroughly as possible. Do not limit yourself to only one or two adjectives. Note that these are all feminine nouns, so the feminine form of the adjective is required.

1. Ma chambre est...
2. Ma montre est...
3. Ma maison *(house)* est... (If you describe **mon appartement** *(m)* instead, use adjectives in the masculine form.)
4. Ma mère (grand-mère, fille, sœur, tante) est...
5. Ma femme (fiancée, meilleure amie) est...
6. Ma chaise est...

L.   **Sa chambre est...**   If the preceding exercise has been used orally in class, review what you have learned about your classmates.

EXEMPLE: *Sa chambre est propre, tranquille et claire. (Note:* **Sa** *= his or* her.)

M.   **Il est parfait. Elle est parfaite.**   Describe your French teacher. Use adjectives in the masculine or feminine as appropriate. Be thorough. (Be kind.)

N.   **Je suis parfait(e).**   Describe yourself. Use as many adjectives as possible. Use the masculine or feminine as appropriate, depending upon your own gender.

Structure 4: Position of Adjectives

French adjectives usually come after the noun they describe.

un livre pratique   **une revue intéressante**

The following adjectives, however, generally precede the noun they modify.

autre	jeune	mauvais	premier
beau	joli	nouveau	tout
bon	long	petit	vieux
chaque			

un beau cadeau   **une jolie carte postale**

Exercices d'application: Position of Adjectives

O. **Oui, c'est un bon professeur.**   Agree with each statement. Decide if the adjective belongs before or after the noun.

MODÈLE: Le professeur est bon, n'est-ce pas?
Oui, c'est un bon professeur.

1. Le cadeau est magnifique, n'est-ce pas?
2. Le dictionnaire est cher, n'est-ce pas?
3. La revue est intéressante, n'est-ce pas?
4. La montre est très jolie, n'est-ce pas?
5. Le jouet est adorable, n'est-ce pas?
6. Le paquet est petit, n'est-ce pas?
7. Le film est mauvais, n'est-ce pas?
8. Le monsieur est riche, n'est-ce pas?

P. **C'est un livre rouge.**   Place your hand quickly, without thinking, on an object near you. Describe it with an adjective in correct position.

EXEMPLE: *C'est un livre intéressant.*
C'est un joli sac.
C'est une chaise confortable.

Structure 5: Comparisons with Adjectives

The expressions **plus...que, moins...que**, and **aussi...que** are used in making comparisons with adjectives.

plus...que   more . . . than
Il est **plus grand que** moi.   He is taller than I (am).

moins...que	less . . . than
Le livre est **moins cher que** la revue.	The book is less expensive than the magazine.
aussi...que	as . . . as
Il est **aussi fatigué que** vous.	He is as tired as you.

The comparative of **bon/bonne** (*good*) is **meilleur/meilleure** (*better*).

| Le sac rouge est **meilleur que** l'autre. | The red bag is better than the other. |

The comparative of **mauvais/mauvaise** (*bad*)) is **pire/pire** or **plus mauvais/plus mauvaise** (*worse*).

| Le petit est **pire que** le grand. | The little one is worse than the big one. |

Exercice d'application: Comparison with Adjectives

Q.   **Je suis plus grand(e) que ma mère.**   *(Personalized Exercise)* Answer each of these questions in regard to yourself. Then ask your classmates.

1. Êtes-vous aussi grand(e) que votre mère?
2. Êtes-vous aussi grand(e) que votre père?
3. Êtes-vous aussi intelligent(e) que votre professeur de français?
4. Êtes-vous aussi fatigué(e) aujourd'hui que hier?
5. Êtes-vous aussi gentil(le) que le professeur?

Synthèse

A.   **Descriptions.**   Use as many adjectives as possible from this chapter to describe these two men. Use **Il est...** or **Il a l'air...**(*He seems . . .*). To refer to the man on the left, use **le monsieur à gauche**, the man on the right, **le monsieur à droite**.

B. **Comparisons.** Now make a few comparisons regarding these two men.

> EXEMPLE: *Le monsieur à gauche est plus (moins) âgé que le monsieur à droite. Il a l'air plus (moins) gentil. Il est plus (moins) beau*, etc.

PRONONCIATION

1. Liaison (Linking) and Enchaînement (Chaining)

Liaison and **enchaînement** both reflect the French tendency to have syllables end in a vowel sound. (See Chapter 2: Syllabification.) **Liaison** occurs when a normally silent final consonant is pronounced with the initial vowel sound of a following word. For example, the final consonant **t** in the verb form **ils ont** is not pronounced: however, when inverted, the final consonant **t** is pronounced with the following vowel: **ont-ils?** In **liaison** some final consonants change pronunciation:

s is pronounced [z]: **ils ont**

x is pronounced [z]: **deux ans**

d is pronounced [t]: **quand il parle**

There are certain times in conversational French when **liaison** must be made and others when it is prohibited. On still other occasions it is considered optional. The best guideline to keep in mind is that **liaison** occurs only between words that are naturally grouped together.

Obligatory Liaisons:
1. Between articles and following nouns: **les églises des affaires personnelles**
2. Between adjectives and following nouns: **mon hôtel ces affaires   quelques heures**
3. Between subject pronouns and verbs: **elles ont   ont-ils**

Prohibited Liaisons:
1. Between a proper name used as subject and the following verb: **Robert // a une valise.**
2. Before **oui**: **mais // oui**
3. After **et**: **et // elle a...**
4. Between **ils** or **elles** in the interrogative verbal form and the following word: **Ont-ils // une valise?**
5. Before an aspirate **h**: **les // héros**

Enchaînement occurs when the normally pronounced final consonant of one word is treated as if it were the initial sound of the following word beginning with a vowel sound. For example, from this chapter: **il a** = [i-la]

sac à dos = [sa-ka-mɛ̃]

il ouvre = [i-luvrə]

2. Mute and Aspirate h

In French words that start with the letter **h**, the **h** is never actually pronounced. These initial **h** letters, however, are divided into two categories: "mute" or "silent" **h** and "aspirate" **h**.

The "mute" **h** is treated as if it were not even there. For example: **l'hôtel, les hôtels l'homme, les hommes l'heure, les heures.**

On the other hand, the "aspirate" **h** is treated as if it were actually a silent consonant. As such, it has an effect on the pronunciation of the word it begins by preventing **liaison** (*linking*) with preceding words. For example: **les // héros, les // huit, des // haricots verts, des // hors-d'œuvre.**

The "aspirate" **h** also prevents elision (**l'**, **d'**) with preceding words. For example: **le héros, le huit, le haricot vert, le hors-d'œuvre.** Words that begin with the aspirate **h** are fairly rare. The only way for a non-native speaker to know for sure whether the letter **h** is aspirate or not is to look the word up in a dictionary or word glossary that gives this information.

Projet

Describing classroom objects *(Exercice écrit)*. Work alone or with a partner. Using as many adjectives as possible from this lesson, make descriptive labels for a variety of items actually present in your classroom. Here are some items you may wish to describe.

le bureau du professeur	teacher's desk	**la lumière**	light
le cahier	notebook	**le morceau de craie**	piece of chalk
la chaise	chair	**le mur**	wall
la corbeille à papier	wastebasket	**la porte**	door
le crayon	pencil	**le stylo**	pen
la fenêtre	window	**la table**	table
le livre	book	**le tableau noir**	blackboard

Indicate color, size, shape, condition, etc. Make sure adjectives agree in gender (masculine/feminine) and in number (singular/plural) with the objects described. Tape these labels to the respective items. It is interesting to see how many different adjectives are selected for each classroom object. Labels may be read aloud by instructor or students.

EXEMPLES: *Le tableau noir est rectangulaire et grand.*
Le bureau du professeur est brun, solide et laid.
Les fenêtres sont sales.

Activités: Learning by Doing

A.   **In-class flea market.**   Bring to class donations of four or five items (such as old magazines, books, postcards, records, pencils, stationery, etc.) to be sold to classmates for play money. Everyone will actually keep whatever he or she buys, so make sure you are willing to donate what you bring to class. With one or two other classmates, set up and name a "store." Price your items: **9F, 12F,** etc. Shopping then begins. One person must stay in each store at all times to tend shop. The others go out shopping. Once you have purchased something, return to your own shop to allow your partner or partners to go out shopping. This continues until nearly all items have been sold.

The purpose of this **Activité** is to practice the vocabulary and structures of this chapter. So keep buying whether you really want an item or not. (You can always give it to another classmate as a gift.) In addition to the phrases from the **Dialogue** of this chapter, you will find the following sentences useful for this activity:

Je voudrais cela.   I would like that.
Je ne fais que regarder.   I'm only looking.
Je vais réfléchir.   I'll think about it.

Pour vous, Monsieur/Madame/ Mademoiselle, quatre francs!   For you, four francs!

To dispose of any unsold items at the end of class, this session may conclude with an auction **(une vente aux enchères)**. The instructor or a class member may serve as auctioneer.

Une fois, deux fois, trois fois, adjugé!   Going, going, gone!
Vendu!   Sold!

C'est à vous!   It's yours!
Félicitations!   Congratulations.

If you do not want to keep what you have purchased, you may choose instead to give it as a gift to a classmate or to your instructor.

C'est pour vous!   It's for you!

Merci. C'est gentil à vous.   Thank you. That's nice of you.

B.   **Lost and found.**   This activity will provide some lively practice with the **passé composé** of **perdre** (to lose), as well as with the adjectives of this chapter. At least one possession belonging to each class member should be placed in a central area labeled **Bureau des objets trouvés** (Lost and Found). To reclaim these

possessions, tell the person in charge of this area (either a classmate or the instructor), **J'ai perdu mon/ma/mes...** *(I lost my. . .).* The person in charge will use such inquiries as:

De quelle couleur est votre...?   What color is your. . . ?
Comment est-il/elle?   Describe it. What does it look like?
C'est votre...?   Is this your. . . ?

When asked to describe your lost or missing possession(s), use as many adjectives as possible from this lesson. Be sure they agree in number and in gender with your possession(s).

• Il/Elle est _____.
• Ils/Elles sont _____.
• Oui, merci!
• C'est bien mon/ma _____. *(It's really my _____. That is my _____.)*
• Ce sont bien mes _____. *(Those are really my _____. Those are my _____.)*

Quelle est la date de votre anniversaire?

Dates

Mieux vaut tard que jamais. | Better late than never.

Knowing how to form and use dates correctly is essential for making plans and arrangements, including restaurant, hotel, and plane reservations. Dates are also used when relating information about yourself and others. This **Entracte** deals with the pronunciation and use of days, months, and years vocabulary in French.

Quelle est la date de votre anniversaire?

Réponse: • C'est le _____ _____ [1].
              (numéro)   (mois)

EXEMPLE: *C'est le vingt et un septembre.*

The following vocabulary items may be substituted directly into the response format: C'est le _____ _____. No grammatical manipulation is necessary.
(numéro)   (mois)

MONTHS OF THE YEAR

janvier January	mai May	septembre September
février February	juin June	octobre October
mars March	juillet July	novembre November
avril April	août August	décembre December

---

1 premier	9 neuf	17 dix-sept	25 vingt-cinq
2 deux	10 dix	18 dix-huit	26 vingt-six
3 trois	11 onze	19 dix-neuf	27 vingt-sept
4 quatre	12 douze	20 vingt	28 vingt-huit
5 cinq	13 treize	21 vingt et un	29 vingt-neuf
6 six	14 quatorze	22 vingt-deux	30 trente
7 sept	15 quinze	23 vingt-trois	31 trente et un
8 huit	16 seize	24 vingt-quatre	

Remarques

1. Months are not capitalized in French.
2. No preposition is used between the day and month: le deux janvier.
3. Dates are preceded by le: le cinq décembre.
4. In French, cardinal numbers (three, ten, twenty-one, etc.) are used with dates. (In English, ordinals are often used: second, fifth, twenty-first, etc.) *Exception:* le premier (*the first*): le premier novembre, le premier avril.
5. No elision occurs between le huit or le onze; that is, le does not become l': le huit avril, le onze septembre.

---

1. When is your birthday? (*Literally:* What is the date of your birthday?)
It's the _____ (number + month).

Springboard for Conversation

Ask each of your classmates the following personalized question. Try to memorize their responses. The answer format is provided.

Quelle est la date de votre anniversaire?

• C'est le _____ _____.

          (numéro)   *(mois)*

Récapitulation

Recall what you have learned about your classmates and instructor. Answer formats are provided.

1. Quelle est la date de l'anniversaire du professeur? de Monsieur...? de Madame...? de Mademoiselle...? Et votre voisin(e) de gauche? Et votre voisin(e) de droite? etc.
   • C'est le *(numéro)* *(mois)* .
   Note: If a date is forgotten, simply ask again. **Pardon. Je suis désolé(e), mais j'ai oublié la date de votre anniversaire. Quelle est la date de votre anniversaire? Ah oui. C'est ça. Merci bien.** To verify, ask **c'est ça?** or **n'est-ce pas?** For example: **Votre anniversaire, c'est le ____, n'est-ce pas? C'est ça? (Oui. C'est ça.** or **Non. C'est le ____.)**

2. Qui dans la classe est né *(was born)* en ___*(mois)*___? Qui d'autre? C'est tout?
   • Monsieur/Madame/Mademoiselle est né(e) en ____.
   • Le professeur est né(e) en ____.
   • Moi, je suis né(e) en ____.
   • Personne *(No one).*

Remarques

1. The verb **naître** *(to be born)* is conjugated with **être** in the past tense. **Je suis né(e)** translates as *I was born.* (The additional **e** for female speakers is not pronounced.)

2. **En** and **au mois de** are used to express "in" with months: **en septembre / au mois de septembre** *(in [the month of] September).*

3. Qui dans la classe est né le _(numéro)_ ? Qui d'autre? C'est tout?
   • Monsieur/Madame/Mademoiselle... est né(e) le ____.
   • Le professeur est né(e) le ____.
   • Moi, je suis né(e) le ____.
   • Personne.

Remarque

An equivalent for the English preposition "on" is not used with French dates:

Je suis né(e) le douze avril.   I was born (on) April twelfth.

Expansion

The **Expansion** can be used for partners or group conversation and for oral or written composition. Answer formats are provided.

1. Quel jour est-ce aujourd'hui? *(What day is [it] today?)*
   - C'est aujourd'hui _____. *(Today is _____.)*

lundi	Monday
mardi	Tuesday
mercredi	Wednesday
jeudi	Thursday
vendredi	Friday
samedi	Saturday
dimanche	Sunday

Remarques:
— Days of the week are not capitalized in French.
— Days are masculine in gender.

2. Quelle est la date aujourd'hui? *(What is today's date?)*
   - C'est aujourd'hui _____, le _____ _____.

   EXEMPLE: *C'est aujourd'hui lundi, le dix décembre.*

Remarque:
If the month is known, you may simply say: **C'est le dix** or **On est le dix.**

3. En quelle année êtes-vous né(e)? *(What year were you born?)*
   - En _____.

   EXEMPLE: *Je suis né(e) en dix-neuf cent quarante-cinq.*

Remarques:
— With years (**les années**), the word **cent** *(hundred)* must be used. In English it is optional.

— **En** is used to indicate *in*: **en 1986** = *in* 1986.
— **Mille** *(one thousand)* may be used:
   1985 = **mille neuf cent quatre-vingt-cinq**
       = **dix-neuf cent quatre-vingt-cinq.**

1890	dix-huit cent quatre-vingt-dix
1900	dix-neuf cents
1905	dix-neuf cent cinq
1910	dix-neuf cent dix
1920	dix-neuf cent vingt
1930	dix-neuf cent trente
1940	dix-neuf cent quarante
1950	dix-neuf cent cinquante
1960	dix-neuf cent soixante
1970	dix-neuf cent soixante-dix
1980	dix-neuf cent quatre-vingts
1986	dix-neuf cent quatre-vingt-six

4. En quel mois êtes-vous né(e)? *(What month were you born in?)* En février? En avril? etc.
   - En _____.

5. Quelle est la date de Noël *(Christmas)*? du Thanksgiving? du Nouvel An *(New Year's)*? de la fête nationale américaine? de la fête nationale française? de la Saint-Valentin?
   - C'est le _____ _____.

6. **Review.** If the preceding **Expansion** questions have been used for group or partners conversation, review what you have learned about your classmates.

EXEMPLES: *Monsieur Smith est né en avril.*
Marie est née en 1964.

en raison
des fêtes, notre
magasin sera fermé
le *lundi 15 Août*

Vocabulaire utile   The following phrases are frequently requested by students using the dates-related conversations of this **Entracte**.

Pardon? Excuse me?
Quelle coïncidence!   Mon anniversaire aussi c'est le _____ _____! What a coincidence!
Oui. C'est ça.   Yes. That's right./That's it.
C'est aujourd'hui mon anniversaire!   Today's my birthday!
Sans blague!?!   No kidding!?!

31 MAI
11 JUIN

22^{éme} BRADERIE DE PARIS

C.N.I.T. PARIS LA DÉFENSE
TOUS LES JOURS DE 11H A 22H
SAMEDIS DIMANCHES LUNDIS JUSQU'A 21H

Anniversaires. Anniversaire *(birthday)* is short for anniversaire de naissance *(anniversary of birth)*. A wedding anniversary is un anniversaire de mariage.

Abbreviating dates. The European system for indicating dates numerically is different from the American. The American abbreviation for December 5, 1985 is 12/5/85, or month/day/year. The French equivalent would be 5/12/85, or day/month/year. The French system is actually more logical, progressing from the smaller unit of measure (day) to the larger (the month/the year).

Saint's Days. In France, nearly everybody has a Saint's Day (Name Day or **fête**) in addition to his or her birthday. The following listing is taken from a calendar distributed by the French post office.

FÊTES À SOUHAITER

A

Achille	12 Mai
Adèle	24 Décembre
Adeline	20 Octobre
Adrien	8 Septembre
Agathe	5 Février
Agnès	21 Janvier
Ahmed	1 Juin
Aimé	13 Septembre
Alain	9 Septembre
Alban (e)	22 Juin
Albert	15 Novembre
Alexandre	22 Avril
Alexis	17 Février
Alfred	12 Octobre
Alice	16 Décembre
Aline	20 Octobre
Alphonse	1 Août
Amandine	9 Juillet
Amélie	19 Septembre
Anatole	3 Février
André(e)	30 Novembre

Angèle	27 Janvier
Angèlique	27 Janvier
Annabelle	26 Juillet
Anne	26 Juillet
Annick	26 Juillet
Anouck	26 Juillet
Anthony	17 Janvier
Antoine	17 Janvier
Ariane	17 Septembre
Armand	23 Décembre
Armelle	16 Août
Arnaud	10 Février
Arnold	18 Juillet
Arthur	15 Novembre
Aude	18 Novembre
Audrey	23 Juin
Auguste	29 Février
Aurélie	15 Octobre
Aymeric	4 Novembre

B

Barbara	4 Décembre
Bastien	20 Janvier
Baudouin	17 Octobre
Béatrice	13 Février
Bénédicte	16 Mars
Benjamin	31 Mars
Benoît	11 Juillet
Bernadette	18 Février
Bernard	20 Août
Berthe	2 Juillet
Bertrand	6 Septembre
Bettina	17 Novembre
Blanche	3 Octobre
Blandine	2 Juin
Boris	2 Mai
Brice	13 Novembre
Brigitte	23 Juillet
Bruno	6 Octobre

C

Camille	14 Juillet
Carine	7 Novembre
Carole	4 Novembre
Caroline	4 Novembre
Catherine	24 Mars
Cécile	22 Novembre
Cédric	7 Janvier
Céline	21 Octobre
Chantal	12 Décembre
Charles	4 Novembre
Charlotte	4 Novembre
Christel	24 Juillet
Christian	12 Novembre
Christine	24 Juillet
Christophe	25 Juillet
Claire	11 Août
Claude	6 Juin
Claudine	15 Février
Clément	23 Novembre
Clotilde	4 Juin
Colette	6 Mars
Coralie	18 Mai
Corinne	18 Mai
Cyrille	18 Mars

D

Damien	21 Février
Daniel	11 Décembre
David	29 Décembre
Deborah	21 Septembre
Delphine	26 Novembre
Denis	9 Octobre
Denise	15 Mai
Didier	23 Mai
Dominique	8 Août
Donald	15 Juillet
Dorothée	6 Février

E

Edgard	8 Juillet
Edith	16 Septembre
Edmond	20 Novembre
Edouard	5 Janvier
Edwige	16 Octobre
Eliane	7 Juillet
Elise	17 Novembre
Elisabeth	17 Novembre
Emeric	4 Novembre
Emile	22 Mai
Emma	19 Avril
Emmanuel	25 Décembre
Eric	18 Mai
Ernest	7 Novembre
Ernestine	7 Novembre
Estelle	11 Mai
Etienne	26 Décembre
Esther	1 Juillet
Eugène	8 Juillet
Eugénie	7 Février
Evelyne	6 Septembre
Eve	6 Septembre

F

Fabien	20 Janvier
Fabrice	22 Août
Fanny	26 Décembre
Félix	12 Février
Ferdinand	30 Mai
Fernand	27 Juin
Florence	1 Décembre
Florent	4 Juillet
France	9 Mars
Francine	9 Mars
Francis	4 Octobre
Franck	4 Octobre
François	4 Octobre
Françoise	9 Mars
Frédéric	18 Juillet

G

Gabriel	29 Septembre
Gael	16 Octobre
Gaston	6 Février
Geneviève	3 Janvier
Geoffroy	8 Novembre
Georges	23 Avril
Gerald	5 Décembre
Gérard	3 Octobre
Germaine	15 Juin
Gervaise	19 Juin
Ghislain	10 Octobre
Gilbert	4 Février

Gildas	29 Janvier	Léa	22 Mars	**O**		**T**	
Gilles	1 Septembre	Léon	10 Novembre				
Gisèle	7 Mai	Liliane	27 Juillet	Odette	20 Avril	Tania	12 Janvier
Guillaume	10 Janvier	Linda	28 Août	Odile	14 Décembre	Teddy	5 Janvier
Guy	12 Juin	Lionel	10 Novembre	Olivia	5 Mars	Tessa	17 Décembre
Gustave	28 Août	Loic	25 Août	Olivier	12 Juillet	Thibaut	8 Juillet
Gwendoline	14 Octobre	Lolita	25 Décembre	Oswald	5 Août	Thérèse	15 Octobre
		Louis	25 Août			Thierry	1 Juillet
H		Louise	15 Mars	**P**		Thomas	28 Janvier
		Luc	18 Octobre				
Harold	14 Mai	Lucie	13 Décembre	Paola	26 Janvier	**U**	
Hélène	18 Août	Lucien	8 Janvier	Pascal	17 Mai		
Henri	13 Juillet	Ludovic	25 Août	Patrice	17 Mars	Ursula	9 Juillet
Henriette	16 Mars	Lydie	3 Août	Patrick	17 Mars		
Herbert	20 Mars			Paul	29 Juin	**V**	
Hervé	17 Juin			Paule	26 Janvier		
Honoré	16 Mai	**M**		Pauline	26 Janvier	Valentin	14 Février
Hortense	11 Janvier			Perrine	31 Mai	Valérie	28 Avril
Hubert	3 Novembre	Madeleine	22 Juillet	Philippe	3 Mai	Vera	17 Septembre
Hugues	1 Avril	Magali	22 Juillet	Pierre	29 Juin	Véronique	4 Février
		Maggy	22 Juillet			Victor	21 Juillet
I		Maïté	7 Juin	**R**		Vincent	22 Janvier
		Manuel	25 Décembre			Violette	5 Octobre
Igor	5 Juin	Marc	25 Avril	Raoul	7 Juillet	Virginie	7 Janvier
Ingrid	2 Septembre	Marcel	16 Janvier	Raphaël	29 Septembre	Vivien	10 Mars
Isaac	20 Décembre	Marguerite	16 Novembre	Raymond	7 Janvier		
Isabelle	22 Février	Marianne	9 Juillet	Réginald	12 Février	**W**	
		Marie	15 Août	Régine	7 Septembre		
J		Marina	17 Juillet	Régis	16 Juin	Walter	23 Juin
		Marius	19 Janvier	Renaud	17 Septembre	Wilfried	12 Octobre
Jacob	20 Décembre	Marilyne	15 Août	Rémi	15 Janvier	William	10 Janvier
Jacques	3 Mai	Marjorie	15 Août	René	19 Octobre		
Jacqueline	8 Février	Marthe	29 Juillet	Richard	3 Avril	**X**	
Jean	27 Décembre	Martine	30 Janvier	Robert	30 Avril		
J.-Baptiste	24 Juin	Marylise	15 Août	Rodolphe	21 Juin	Xavier	3 Décembre
Jeanne	30 Mai	Mathias	14 Mai	Roger	30 Décembre		
Jeannine	12 Décembre	Mathieu	21 Septembre	Roland	15 Septembre	**Y**	
Jérôme	30 Septembre	Mathilde	14 Mars	Romain	28 Février		
Joël	13 Juillet	Maud	14 Mars	Romuald	19 Juin	Yan	27 Décembre
Josselin	13 Décembre	Maurice	22 Septembre	Roseline	17 Janvier	Yolande	15 Juin
Joseph	19 Mars	Maximilien	12 Mars			Yves	19 Mai
Josephine	19 Mars	Michel	29 Septembre			Yvonne	19 Mai
Josette	19 Mars	Micheline	19 Juin	**S**			
Jules	12 Avril	Mireille	15 Août				
Julien	2 Août	Monique	27 Août	Sabine	29 Août		
Juliette	30 Juillet	Muriel	15 Août	Sabrina	29 Août		
		Myriam	15 Août	Salomon	25 Juin		
K				Samuel	20 Août		
				Sandra	22 Avril		
Karen	7 Novembre	**N**		Sébastien	20 Janvier		
Karine	7 Novembre			Serge	7 Octobre		
Katia	29 Avril	Nadege	18 Septembre	Séverine	27 Novembre		
Katy	29 Avril	Nadine	18 Septembre	Sidonie	14 Novembre		
		Natacha	26 Août	Simone	28 Octobre		
L		Nathalie	27 Juillet	Solange	10 Mai		
		Nelly	18 Août	Sophie	25 Mai		
Laetitia	18 Août	Nicolas	6 Décembre	Stanislas	11 Avril		
Laure	10 Août	Nicole	6 Décembre	Stéphane	26 Décembre		
Laurence	10 Août	Noël (le)	25 Décembre	Suzanne	11 Août		
Laurent	10 Août	Norbert	6 Juin	Sylvain	4 Mai		
				Sylvie	5 Novembre		

Synthèse

A.   **Naissances** *(Birth Announcements).*   The birth announcements below were taken from a French newspaper. Answer the following questions based on these items.

1. Quand est-ce que Clément d'Halluin est né? et Adrien Visseaux? et Thibault de la Debutrie?
   • Il est né le _____ _____, _____.

2. Quand est-ce que Stéphanie Laffargue est née? et Hortense Willaume? et Anabelle Ubald-Bocquet?
   • Elle est née le _____ _____, _____.

---

naissances

Mme veuve Adrien **VISSEAUX**
M. et Mme Albert **VISSEAUX**
docteur et Mme Jean-Pierre **VISSEAUX**
ont la joie de vous faire part de la naissance
   d'Adrien
chez
Bertrand et Josiane VISSEAUX
Massy, le 13 août 1983.

M. Roland
UBALD-BOCQUET et Mme,
née Marie-Christine Bleynie,
Capucine et Sophie
ont la joie d'annoncer la naissance
   d'Anabelle
Paris, le 3 août.

M. Pierre **LAFFARGUE,**
Mme, née Monique Borgetto,
et Sophie
ont la joie d'annoncer la naissance de
   Stéphanie
le 6 août 1983.
Boulogne-sur-Seine,
Saint-Jean-de-Luz.

M. Thierry **d'HALLUIN**
et Mme, née Véronique Fellmann,
ont la joie de vous annoncer la naissance de leur fils
   Clément
le 8 août 1983.
36 bis, rue de Granville,
54000 Nancy.

M. Bernard **WILLAUME**
et Mme, née Nathalie Brisset,
et Xavier
ont la joie de vous faire part de la naissance d'
   Hortense
Neuilly, le 15 août 1983.

Le comte Bernard
de la **DEBUTRIE**
et la comtesse, née
Michèle Martin de Frémont
ont la joie de vous faire part de la naissance de
   Thibault
le 16 août.
10, rue de la Pommeraie,
37250 Montbazon.

B.   **Important Dates.**   Make a list of important dates. Use complete sentences.

   1. Quelle est la date de l'anniversaire de votre mère? de votre père? de votre sœur? de votre frère? (For additional family members, see **Entracte 9:** The Family).
   2. Quelle est la date de l'anniversaire de votre meilleur(e) ami(e)?
   3. Êtes-vous marié(e)? Quelle est la date de l'anniversaire de votre mari? de votre femme? Quelle est la date de votre anniversaire de mariage *(wedding anniversary)*?
   4. Quelle est la date de l'anniversaire de mariage de vos parents?

C.   **Les anniversaires de naissance.**   You may wish to make an official "birthday list" for your own records. Use the model below as a guide for your own list, which you can prepare on a larger sheet of paper.

Les Anniversaires de naissance	
janvier:	juillet:
février:	août:
mars:	septembre:
avril:	octobre:
mai:	novembre:
juin:	décembre:

Projets

A.   **Engagement calendar.**   Make an engagement calendar for whatever month and year it is now. Write out each day's date **(le premier, le deux, le trois,** etc.). Place **le premier** in the small block directly beneath whatever day of the week the first falls in the month, and then continue numbering consecutively. Note that French calendars generally start with **lundi.** Days and months are not capitalized.

_____ (mois)				_____ (année)		

lundi	mardi	mercredi	jeudi	vendredi	samedi	dimanche

B. **Year Calendar.** Using large sheets of paper, make a French calendar for the coming year. Use one sheet for each month. Each page should resemble the calendar format of **Projet A**. Check an official calendar to make sure you place the dates in the correct blocks. Punch two holes through the page tops and attach them with a loop of yarn. Hang your French calendar over your desk, near your refrigerator, or some place where you will notice it every day.

Note: Save these calendars. They can be used for several activities and exercises appearing elsewhere in this textbook.

Activité: Learning by Doing

Fêtes. Find your own Saint's Day next to your name on the list of **Fêtes** in the **À Propos** section. If your name does not appear on this list, select a name that resembles yours. Find out your classmates' Saint's Days by asking, **Quelle est la date de votre fête?** The answer is, **C'est le _____.** Wish anyone whose Name Day is near **Bonne Fête!**

«Le chasseur va monter vos bagages.»

À L'Hôtel (Arrivée)

Hotel Arrival

Tout est bien qui finit bien.

All's well that ends well.

DIALOGUE

This **Dialogue** provides the vocabulary necessary for reserving a hotel room. The vocabulary and structures presented here are also useful for describing places you have lived or live. Vocabulary blocks within this **Dialogue** offer options that will allow you to reserve a hotel room actually suited to your own personal needs and preferences.

À la Réception	At the Reception Area
L'EMPLOYÉ(E) À LA RÉCEPTION: Bonjour, Monsieur / Madame.	RECEPTIONIST AT THE FRONT DESK: Hello.
VOUS: Bonjour, Monsieur / Madame. J'ai réservé une chambre **pour une personne.**	YOU: Hello. I've reserved a **single** (literally: a room for one person).

à un lit
   pour deux personnes
   à deux lits
   avec un grand lit
	room with one bed / single
	room for two people / double
	room with two beds
	room with a large bed / double bed

L'EMPLOYÉ: C'est à quel nom, s'il vous plaît?	RECEPTIONIST: Under what name, please?
VOUS: ___votre nom___. Voici la confirmation. Et je voudrais une chambre avec vue sur **la mer.**	YOU: ___your name___. Here's the confirmation. And I'd like a room with an **ocean** view

le square
   le jardin
   le lac
   la piscine
   la plage
   la rue
	(town) square
	   garden
	   lake
	   swimming pool
	   beach
	   street
	(literally: with a view over the ocean).

L'EMPLOYÉ: C'est pour combien de temps?	RECEPTIONIST: (It's) for how long?
VOUS: **Juste pour la nuit.**	YOU: **Overnight.**

Deux nuits.
   Trois jours.
   Une semaine.
   Jusqu'à lundi.
   Jusqu'à mardi.
   Jusqu'à mercredi.
   Jusqu'au dix.
	Two nights.
	Three days.
	One week.
	Until Monday.
	Until Tuesday.
	Until Wednesday.
	Until the tenth.

L'EMPLOYÉ: Un instant, je vous prie... J'ai encore une chambre avec **salle de bains**	RECEPTIONIST: One moment, please . . . I still have a room with **bath**

balcon
   bidet
   climatisation
   téléphone
   douche
     seulement
   lavabo
	balcony
	   bidet
	   air conditioning
	   telephone
	   shower only
	
	   sink

au **premier** étage.[1]
| deuxième
| troisième
| quatrième
| cinquième
| sixième
| septième
| huitième
| neuvième

on the **second** floor.[1]
| third
| fourth
| fifth
| sixth
| seventh
| eighth
| ninth
| tenth

VOUS: Est-elle tranquille?
L'EMPLOYÉ: Oui. Elle donne sur la cour.

YOU: Is it quiet?
RECEPTIONIST: Yes. It faces (*literally:* gives on) the courtyard.

VOUS: Quel est le prix par nuit?
L'EMPLOYÉ: Deux cents francs, service et petit déjeuner compris.
VOUS: Est-ce que vous avez un garage?
L'EMPLOYÉ: Nous avons un parking à côté.

YOU: How much is it per night?
RECEPTIONIST: Two hundred francs, service (charge) and breakfast included.
YOU: Do you have a garage?
RECEPTIONIST: We have a parking lot nearby (adjacent).

VOUS: Parfait.
L'EMPLOYÉ: C'est la chambre trente. Voilà la clé. Le chasseur va monter vos bagages. Voulez-vous bien remplir cette fiche, s'il vous plaît?[2]
VOUS: Oui...Y a-t-il des messages ou du courrier pour moi?
L'EMPLOYÉ: Oui. Voilà... Voulez-vous me suivre? Par ici, s'il vous plaît.

YOU: That's good. (*Literally:* Perfect.)
RECEPTIONIST: It's room thirty. Here's the key. The bellboy (porter) will bring your luggage up. Will you kindly fill out this form?[2]
YOU: Yes . . . Are there any messages or mail for me?
RECEPTIONIST: Yes. Here (it is). . . Please follow me. This way, please.

Phrases à retenir

Memorizing these sentences from the **Dialogue** will help assure fluency in dealing with hotel personnel in a French-speaking country.

1. J'ai réservé une chambre pour une personne.
2. Voici la confirmation.
3. Je voudrais une chambre pour deux personnes.
4. Je voudrais une chambre avec salle de bains.
5. C'est pour une nuit.
6. Quel est le prix par nuit?
7. Y a-t-il des messages pour moi?

1. In Europe, the American first floor or ground floor is called **le rez-de-chaussée**. The American second floor is called **le premier étage**. The American third floor is **le deuxième étage**, etc.
2. **Voulez-vous bien** followed by the infinitive is used in polite commands. See Chapter 3, **Verbe irrégulier: vouloir.**

DIALOGUE EXERCISES

The following exercises provide oral and written practice in using the
vocabulary and basic sentence patterns of the **Dialogue: À L'Hôtel (Arrivée).**
These exercises use *only* vocabulary and structures presented in the hotel arrival
Dialogue. They do not require familiarity with any other portions of this
chapter.

Exercices d'application

A. **Room selection: Je voudrais une chambre...** What kind of room will you
want? Base your room selection on the circumstances presented below. Use
vocabulary from the **Dialogue.**

MODÈLE: Vous voyagez avec votre mère.
　　　　　Je voudrais une chambre pour deux personnes.
　　ou: *Je voudrais une chambre à deux lits.*
　　ou: *Je voudrais deux chambres à un lit.*

1. Vous voyagez seul(e) *(alone).*
2. Vous voyagez seul(e) mais vous n'aimez pas les lits à une place *(single beds).*
3. Vous voulez une chambre avec vue sur la plage.
4. Vous voulez une chambre tranquille.
5. Vous aimez regarder la télévision.
6. Vous voyagez avec un très bon ami.
7. Vous voyagez avec une très bonne amie.
8. Vous voyagez avec votre femme/votre mari ou avec votre mère/votre père.

B. **Dialogue responses.** What could you respond to each of the following? Use
sentences and phrases taken directly from the **Dialogue.**

1. Avez-vous une réservation?
2. C'est à quel nom?
3. Voulez-vous une chambre avec vue sur la mer?
4. C'est pour combien de temps?
5. Je n'ai pas de chambres avec salle de bains.
6. La chambre donne sur la rue.
7. Voulez-vous bien remplir cette fiche, s'il vous plaît?

C. **Review.** What do you say. . .

1. to ask for a hotel room for one person?
2. to ask for a room with a double bed?
3. to request a room with an ocean view?
4. to find out the cost of the room?

5. to request a room with a bath?
6. to request a room with a television?
7. when you don't know where to leave your car?
8. to find out if there were any messages left for you?

Improvisation à deux *(Exercice oral)*

D. Use the vocabulary block options and the basic sentence structures of the **Dialogue** to improvise a dialogue with a classmate. One of you may be a traveler with specific preferences arriving in a hotel while the other is a desk clerk. Or, you may choose to be friends traveling together, discussing your individual preferences and plans.

À Vous le choix *(Exercices écrits)*

E. Write a six- to eight-line dialogue for each of the following situations, selecting appropriate phrases from the initial **Dialogue** of this chapter.

1. You arrive at a hotel and find that there are only a few rooms left. You do not have a reservation.

2. You have just arrived at a new hotel that you know nothing about. You want to find out as much as possible about the hotel.

3. You had reserved a room, but upon arrival are told that the hotel has absolutely no record of your reservation.

Conversations

F. Ask your classmates these personalized questions. When two or more responses are possible, alternate answer formats are offered. Select the option that best applies to you personally. Do not limit your responses simply to those suggestions offered in these questions. Use the inclusive vocabulary options provided in the **Dialogue.**

1. Avez-vous un lit à une place ou un grand lit?
   • J'ai _____.
   • Cela ne vous regarde pas! *(It's none of your business!)*

2. Où donne votre chambre *(bedroom)*? sur la rue? sur un jardin? sur un parking? sur le campus?
   • Elle donne sur _____.

3. Avez-vous le téléphone dans votre chambre? la télévision?
   • Oui, j'ai _____ dans ma chambre.
   • Non, je n'ai pas _____ dans ma chambre.

4. À quel étage est votre chambre? au deuxième étage? au troisième étage?
   • Elle est au _____ étage.

5. Est-ce que votre chambre est tranquille?
   • Elle _____.
   • Elle n'est pas _____.

6. Combien de chambres *(bedrooms)* y a-t-il chez vous *(where you live)?* Combien de salles de bains? Combien de douches? Combien de téléphones? Combien de télévisions? Combien d'étages?

   EXEMPLES: *Nous avons une salle de bains.*
               Nous avons deux télévisions.

G.   **Review.**   What have you learned about your classmates from the preceding **Conversations?**

   EXEMPLES: *Marc a le téléphone dans sa chambre.*
               La chambre de Marie donne sur la rue.
               La chambre de Monsieur Smith est au troisième étage.

Hotels in France.   Hotels in France are rated according to the amenities they offer. This rating is done by the **Commissariat Général au Tourisme** (Government Tourist Board). Each hotel receives a rating of from one to four stars. One star, for example, means it is a small hotel with limited services and clean but simple rooms. Such hotels often do not have private baths. On the other hand, a four star hotel is a first-class hotel with all amenities. Luxury hotels are rated L or four stars plus L (* * * * L).

Le syndicat d'initiative.   A listing of recommended hotels and their room prices can be obtained from the **syndicat d'initiative** (tourist office) in most French towns. You may contact this office ahead of time or in person upon your arrival.

Bed and breakfast.   Many hotels in France and other French-speaking countries still observe the custom of including breakfast **(le petit déjeuner)** in the price of the room. To find out, inquire: **Est-ce que le petit déjeuner est compris? Petit déjeuner** will generally be a continental breakfast of juice, a hot beverage **(café, café au lait, thé),** and a roll or croissant with butter and jam.

LANGUAGE AND CULTURE

VERBES IRRÉGULIERS: dire, suivre, venir

> | **dire** to say, to tell | |
> |---|---|
> | LE PRÉSENT: | je **dis**   nous **disons** |
> | | tu **dis**   vous **dites** |
> | | il/elle **dit**   ils/elles **disent** |
> | | on **dit** |
> | LE PASSÉ COMPOSÉ: j'**ai dit,** tu **as dit,** etc. | |

1. **Vouloir dire** = "to mean."

Que **voulez-vous dire?**	What do you mean?
Qu'est-ce que **cela veut dire?**	What does that mean?
Que **veut dire** le mot "fiche"?	What does the word "fiche" mean?

2. **Comment dit-on ____ en français?**   How do you say ____ in French?

3. **Dire à quelqu'un de faire quelque chose** means "to tell someone to do something." (Note the use of à and **de.**)

Dites à Marc de réserver une chambre.	Tell Mark to reserve a room.

4. **Que (qu')** is obligatory after **dire,** whereas the word *that* is optional in English after the verb *to say.*

Il **a dit qu'il** est à l'hôtel.	He said (that) he is at the hotel.

Exercices d'application: **dire**

A. **Que veut dire le mot...?** Select nouns from the **Dialogue** of this chapter—**fiche, piscine, mer,** etc. Quiz your classmates on the meanings of these words, using the expression **Que veut dire...?**

   EXEMPLE: —*Que veut dire le mot "fiche"?*
             —*Le mot "fiche" veut dire* form.

B. **Comment dit-on ____ en français?** Select vocabulary items from the **Dialogue** of this chapter—*bed, swimming pool, luggage,* etc. Quiz your classmates on these vocabulary items using the phrase **Comment dit-on ____ en français?**

   EXEMPLE: *Comment dit-on* bed *en français?*

C. **Pardon? Qu'est-ce que vous avez dit?** Make a statement using phrases from the **Dialogue** of this chapter. Your classmates will pretend that they have not heard what you said. They will ask, **Pardon? Qu'est-ce que vous avez dit?** Repeat your original statement, beginning with **J'ai dit que....** (You may wish to use the **tu** form of address with your classmates.)

EXEMPLE: —*Ma chambre est au deuxième étage.*
—*Pardon? Qu'est-ce que vous avez (tu as) dit?*
—*J'ai dit que ma chambre est au deuxième étage.*

suivre to follow	
LE PRÉSENT: je **suis** tu **suis** il/elle **suit**	nous **suivons** vous **suivez** ils/elles **suivent**
LE PASSÉ COMPOSÉ: j'**ai suivi**, tu **as suivi**, etc.	

1. The only way to tell the difference between **je suis** meaning "I am" and **je suis** meaning "I am following" is by the context in which the expression appears.
2. The expression **suivre un cours** means "to take a course."

un cours de (d')...		a course in/on. . .	
art	français		mathématiques
chimie (*chemistry*)	espagnol		philosophie
biologie	gestion (*management*)		sciences économiques
commerce (*business*)	informatique (*computer*)		sciences politiques
éducation physique	littérature		anglais

Exercices d'application: suivre

D. **Quels cours suivez-vous maintenant?**   What courses are you taking now? Answer this question. Then ask your classmates. (You may wish to use the **tu** form of address with classmates: **Quels cours suis-tu?**)

EXEMPLE: *Je suis un cours de français et un cours de biologie.*

Now indicate what courses you have taken in the past.[3] Then ask your classmates. (You may wish to use the **tu** form of address: **Quels cours as-tu suivis?**)

EXEMPLE: *J'ai suivi un cours de chimie et un cours d'art.*

---

3. For more courses, see **Appendice:** School Subjects.

E.   Il suit un cours de français.   If the preceding exercise has been used orally in class, review what you have learned about your classmates. What courses are they taking? What courses have they taken? Use the present tense and then the **passé composé** of the verb **suivre.**

➤

venir to come	
LE PRÉSENT	LE PASSÉ COMPOSÉ
je **viens**	je **suis venu(e)**
tu **viens**	tu **es venu(e)**
il **vient**	il **est venu**
elle **vient**	elle **est venue**
nous **venons**	nous **sommes venu(e)s**
vous **venez**	vous **êtes venu(e)(s)**
ils **viennent**	ils **sont venus**
elles **viennent**	elles **sont venues**

1. **Venir** is a verb of "coming and going." It is conjugated with **être** in the **passé composé.** The past participle **venu** agrees in gender (masculine/feminine) and in number (singular/plural) with the subject.

2. The verb **venir** is used in the present tense followed by **de (d')** plus an infinitive to express an action in the recent past **(le passé récent).** The English equivalent is *(to have) just. . . .*

    Je viens d'arriver.   I (have) just arrived.
    Il vient d'arriver.   He (has) just arrived.

Exercices d'application: venir

F.   Qu'est-ce que vous venez de faire? (le passé récent)   What did you actually do within the past few minutes? Use **je viens de** in your answers. Possibilities include: **regarder le professeur, prendre des notes, parler, parler avec mon voisin, parler avec ma voisine, regarder ma montre, regarder mon livre, regarder par la fenêtre** *(look out the window)*, **lever la main** *(raise my hand)*, **mordiller** *(nibble on)* **mon stylo, fermer mon livre, ouvrir mon livre. (de + ouvrir = d'ouvrir)**

G.   Questions with *venir*.   Answer these questions yourself. Then ask your classmates. (You may wish to use the **tu** form of address with your classmates.)

1. De quelle ville *(city)* venez-vous (viens-tu)?

2. De quelle ville vient votre (ton) père? et votre (ta) mère? votre professeur? votre mari ou femme? et votre meilleur(e) ami(e)?

3. D'habitude, venez-vous en classe à pied *(by foot)*? en voiture *(by car)*? en métro? en autobus?

4. Comment êtes-vous (es-tu) venu(e) en classe aujourd'hui?

STRUCTURES

Structure 1: Future Tense (Regular Verbs)

To form the future tense of **-er** and **-ir** verbs, add the future endings to the infinitive. To form the future tense of **-re** verbs, drop the final **e** from the infinitive and add the future endings to this base. The future endings are **-ai, -as, -a, -ons, -ez, -ont.** The usual English equivalent of the future is *shall* or *will*.

Verbes en **-er**	Verbes en **-ir**	Verbes en **-re**
téléphoner	**finir**	**vendre**
je téléphoner**ai**	je finir**ai**	je vendr**ai**
tu téléphoner**as**	tu finir**as**	tu vendr**as**
il téléphoner**a**	il finir**a**	il vendr**a**
elle téléphoner**a**	elle finir**a**	elle vendr**a**
on téléphoner**a**	on finir**a**	on vendr**a**
nous téléphoner**ons**	nous finir**ons**	nous vendr**ons**
vous téléphoner**ez**	vous finir**ez**	vous vendr**ez**
ils téléphoner**ont**	ils finir**ont**	ils vendr**ont**
elles téléphoner**ont**	elles finir**ont**	elles vendr**ont**

Exercices d'application: Future Tense (Regular Verbs)

A. **Je mangerai quelque chose.** What will you do today or tomorrow? What will you not do? You may wish to review the **-er** verbs presented in Chapter 2 (Structure 5) as well as the **-ir** and **-re** verbs of Chapter 4 (Structures 1 and 2).

EXEMPLES: *Je mangerai quelque chose.*
Je téléphonerai à un ami.
Je ne finirai pas mon travail.

B. **Il mangera quelque chose.** If the preceding exercise has been used orally in class, review what you have learned about your classmates.

EXEMPLES: *Marie regardera la télévision.*
Paul téléphonera à un ami.
Madame Smith finira son travail.

Structure 2: Future Tense (Irregular Verbs)

Some irregular verbs have irregular future bases. These bases must be learned individually. The future endings, however, are the same as those of "regular" verbs.

L'INFINITIF	LA BASE DU FUTUR
aller to go	**ir-**
avoir to have	**aur-**
être to be	**ser-**
pouvoir to be able	**pourr-**
savoir to know	**saur-**
venir to come	**viendr-**
voir to see	**verr-**
vouloir to want	**voudr-**

Other irregular verbs follow the pattern of **-ir** and **-re** verbs.

L'INFINITIF	LA BASE DU FUTUR
apprendre to learn	**apprendr-**
boire to drink	**boir-**
comprendre to understand	**comprendr-**
croire to believe	**croir-**
dire to say, to tell	**dir-**
offrir to offer	**offrir-**
ouvrir to open	**ouvrir-**
prendre to take	**prendr-**
suivre to follow	**suivr-**

Exercices d'application: Future Tense (Irregular Verbs)

C. **J'irai demain.**   Respond to each of the following commands. Say that you will do whatever is being asked. You will, however, do it tomorrow.

MODÈLE: Allez à l'université.
J'irai à l'université demain.

1. Venez ce soir.
2. Allez à l'hôtel.
3. Buvez du café.
4. Ouvrez les fenêtres.

5. Prenez les valises *(suitcases)*.   7. Apprenez les verbes.
6. Dites au revoir au professeur.

D.   **Vous serez riche.**   Tell your classmates' fortunes. Use the future tense of the irregular verbs **être, avoir,** and **aller.** (You may choose to use the informal **tu** form of address with your classmates.)

EXEMPLE: *Je regarde dans ma boule de cristal. Vous serez (tu seras) riche. Vous serez heureux (heureuse). Vous serez célèbre. Vous aurez (tu auras) beaucoup d'enfants. Vous aurez un mari (une femme) riche. Vous irez (tu iras) en France.*

Structure 3: **Futur Proche** (Review)

By adding the infinitive form of any verb after the conjugated form of **aller,** you are expressing an idea in the near future.

Je **vais regarder** la télévision.   I am going to watch television.
Je **vais étudier.**   I am going to study.

Exercices d'application. **Futur Proche**

E.   **Allez-vous manger après la classe?**   Ask your classmates what they will be doing after class. Use **Allez-vous** or **Vas-tu** as appropriate. Use the verbs of this and preceding chapters in your questions. (You may wish to review the **-er** verbs presented in Chapter 2 and the **-ir** and **-re** verbs of Chapter 4.)

EXEMPLE: —*Allez-vous (Vas-tu) étudier après la classe?*
          —*Oui, je vais étudier après la classe.*
     ou: —*Non, je ne vais pas étudier après la classe.*

F.   **Après la classe il va manger.**   What have you just learned about your classmates?

EXEMPLES: *Marie va regarder la télévision après la classe.*
          Marc va écouter la radio après la classe.
          Monsieur Smith va fumer après la classe.

G.   **Je serai en retard.**   The following sentences are in the near future (**futur proche**). Change them all to the regular future tense.

MODÈLE: Je vais aller à l'hôtel.
          J'irai à l'hôtel.

1. Je vais être fatigué(e).   5. Elle va ouvrir la valise.
2. Tu vas venir, n'est-ce pas?   6. Vas-tu prendre la chambre?
3. Nous allons voir l'hôtel.   7. Je vais avoir une chambre avec
4. Vous allez boire quelque chose?   vue sur la mer.

Structure 4: Demonstrative Adjectives

Demonstrative adjectives agree in gender and number with the object pointed
out. The singular forms (ce, cet, cette) mean either *this* or *that*. The plural form
(ces) means either *these* or *those*.

Use **ce** before a masculine singular noun beginning with a consonant.

    ce téléphone   this telephone/that telephone

Use **cet** before a masculine singular noun beginning with a vowel or mute **h.**

    cet aéroport   this airport/that airport
    cet hôtel   this hotel/that hotel

Use **cette** before any feminine singular noun.

    cette valise   this suitcase/that suitcase

Use **ces** before any plural noun, masculine or feminine.

    ces téléphones   these telephones/those telephones
    ces aéroports   these airports/those airports
    ces hôtels   these hotels/those hotels
    ces valises   these suitcases/those suitcases

To emphasize the distinction between *this/these* and *that/those*, use **-ci** *(this/these)*
or **-là** *(that/those)* after the noun:

—**Ouvrez votre valise!** *(Open your suitcase!)*
—**Cette valise-ci** ou **cette valise-là?** (This *suitcase* or that *suitcase?*)

Exercices d'application: Demonstrative Adjectives

H. **Ce livre-ci ou ce livre-là?** You are being told to do something. Ask a related
question using **ce** or **cette**, depending upon the gender of the noun involved.

MODÈLE: Fermez la fenêtre!
           Cette fenêtre-ci ou cette fenêtre-là?

1. Prenez le livre!
2. Regardez le monsieur!
3. Remplissez la fiche!

4. Fermez la porte!
5. Ouvrez la fenêtre!
6. Prenez la clé!

I. **Que pensez-vous de ce/cet/ces...?** Use the following nouns in the sentence
format: **Que pensez-vous de...?** *(What do you think of. . .?)* Use **ce, cet, cette,** or

ces before each noun, depending upon its gender (masculine or feminine) and number (singular or plural).

MODÈLE: hôtel   *Que pensez-vous de cet hôtel?*

1. jardin   3. rue   5. parking   7. hôtels
2. piscine   4. message   6. livres   8. église

J.   **Que pensez-vous de ce stylo?**   Ask your classmates what they think of items you have with you in class. You may use the following: **livre** (m. *book*), **stylo** (m. *pen*), **crayon** (m. *pencil*), **cahier** (m. *notebook*), **gomme** (f. *eraser*). (You may wish to use the **tu** form of address with your classmates.)

EXEMPLE: —*Que pensez-vous (penses-tu) de ce livre?*
             —*Il est intéressant. J'aime beaucoup ce livre.*

K.   **À qui est ce (cette)...?**   Find out the owners of items you see in the classroom by asking, **À qui est ce (cette)...?** Use **ce** or **cette**, according to the gender of the item selected. Possible items: **ce livre, ce cahier** *(notebook)*, **ce sac, ce sac à dos** *(backpack)*, **ce stylo, ce paquet de cigarettes, ce parapluie** *(umbrella)*, **cette clé, cette montre, cette gomme** *(eraser)*.

EXEMPLE: —*À qui est ce stylo?*
             —*C'est le stylo de Monsieur Green.*

Synthèse

Je voudrais une chambre...   Request this hotel room using the vocabulary and sentence structures of this chapter. Be thorough. **Je voudrais une chambre...**

PRONONCIATION

Sound (Phonetic Symbol) [i]

SPELLING:	**i, î, y**
ENGLISH SOUND RESEMBLED:	Vowel sound in word _tea_
PRONUNCIATION:	Smile. Pull the corners of the mouth back tightly. Do not let the sound glide as in English. Keep it short and abrupt. Also, do not slip into the English short **i** sound, as in the word _hit_.

EXAMPLES FROM THIS CHAPTER:

il	service	y a-t-il
lit	petit	suivre
piscine	compris	ici
lundi	parking	confirmation
climatisation	remplir	dis
télévision	fiche	voici

Projets

A. **Hotel registration form** (_Exercice oral et écrit_). Fill out the guest information form shown on page 150 for a partner. Begin by saying **Voulez-vous bien remplir cette fiche?** To obtain the necessary information, ask your partner the following questions.[4] Verify what you have written by asking **C'est ça? C'est correct?** When you have completed the form, request your partner's signature in the appropriate space: **Signez ici, s'il vous plaît.**

1. **(Nom)** Quel est votre nom, s'il vous plaît? Épelez-le.
2. **(Prénoms)** Quels sont vos prénoms?
3. **(Nationalité)** Quelle est votre nationalité?
4. **(Domicile habituel)** Quelle est votre adresse? Où habitez-vous?
5. **(Profession)** Quelle est votre profession? Que faites-vous?
6. **(Nbre pers.)** Combien de personnes êtes-vous?
7. **(CH N°)** Quel est le numéro de votre chambre?
8. **(S^té ou Cie)** Pour quelle société ou compagnie travaillez-vous?

B. **Le Petit Déjeuner (_Breakfast_).**   What would you select for your room-service breakfast if you were a guest at the luxurious **Hôtel Plaza Athénée** in Paris?

---

4. In answering the questions you may wish to refer to the following **Entractes:** (1) The Alphabet, (2) Numbers, (12) Nationalities and Geographical Place Names.

Hôtel Plaza *Athénée - Paris*

POUR VOTRE PETIT DÉJEUNER
SI VOUS ETES PRESSE
VEUILLEZ NOTER VOTRE
COMMANDE CE SOIR
SUR VOTRE FICHE ET
L ACCROCHER AU
....
DE VOTRE PORTE
SINON APPELEZ LE
SERVICE D ETAGE
DEMAIN MATIN
COMME D HABITUDE
MERCI

SHOULD YOU BE IN A HURRY FOR
YOUR BREAKFAST KINDLY FILL
IN THIS FORM TONIGHT AND
HANG IT OUTSIDE YOUR
DOOR. IF NOT PLEASE
CALL ROOM SERVICE
AS USUAL
THANK YOU.

NOMBRE DE PERSONNES
NUMBER OF PERSONS

N° DE CHAMBRE
ROOM NUMBER

NOM *NAME*

SERVEZ ENTRE   H. ET   H.
TO BE SERVED BETWEEN

PARAGON 8

PETIT DÉJEUNER			CONTINENTAL BREAKFAST		
SIMPLE		COMPLET	SIMPLE		COMPLET
	CAFÉ			THÉ	
	NESCAFÉ			CHOCOLAT	
	AMÉRICAIN			LAIT CHAUD	
	SANKA			LAIT FROID	

SUPPLÉMENTS - *EXTRAS*

ŒUFS COQUE BOILED EGGS	2'	3'	4'	5'	6'

RICE CRISPIES		PORRIDGE		CORN FLAKES	

ŒUFS	AU PLAT FRIED	BROUILLÉS SCRAMBLED	POCHÉS POACHED	OMELETTE OMELET	EGGS
NATURE					PLAIN
JAMBON					HAM
FROMAGE					CHEESE
TOMATE					TOMATO
BACON					BACON
FINES HERBES					HERBS

JAMBON - COLD HAM		JAMBON GRILLÉ	
BACON GRILLÉ		PRUNE JUICE	
YOGOURTH		GRAPE FRUIT	
COMPOTES			
FRUIT SALAD			
FROMAGES - CHEESE			

JUS DE FRUITS FRAIS - *FRESH FRUIT JUICES*

ORANGE		*GRAPEFRUIT*	

EAUX MINÉRALES - *MINERAL WATER*

ÉVIAN	VITTEL	VICHY	BADOIT
PERRIER	JUS TOMATE	JUS ANANAS	COCA-COLA

N° DE CHAMBRE

S/TOTAL

SERVICE

TOTAL

DATE

Activité: Learning by Doing

Hotel registration.   Check into a hotel, using this guest information form. Students acting as desk clerks will supervise registration activities and answer all questions from students playing the roles of clients. Use as many phrases from this chapter as possible.

	Nbre pers.	CH N°

NOM : ....
(écrire en majuscules)
Name in capital letters
Name in Drückschrift

Prénoms : ....   NATIONALITÉ : ....
Christian names   Nationality
Vornamen   Nationalität

Domicile habituel : ....
Permanent address
Gewönhlicher Wohnort

                                                    ....

Signature :   Profession : ....
Unterschrift   Occupation
                                                    Beruf

                                                    Sté ou Cie :

Quel temps fait-il aujourd'hui?

Weather

| Après la pluie le beau temps. | After the rain (comes) nice weather. |

Knowing how to talk about the weather will enable you to make small talk on any occasion. This **Entracte** presents the basic expressions needed to describe the weather and to express your feelings about it. This vocabulary is also essential for understanding weather reports in the newspaper, on television, and on the radio.

Quel temps fait-il aujourd'hui?

Réponse: • Il _____. Quel(le) _____![1]

EXEMPLE: *Il fait beau. Quelle belle journée!*

Vocabulaire à retenir   The weather expressions given here have been selected from those most commonly heard in contemporary French conversation. Learning these useful expressions by heart will enable you to talk about a variety of possible weather conditions.

Il fait beau.   It's nice out.
Il fait (très) chaud.   It's (very) hot.
Il fait (très) froid.   It's (very) cold.
Il fait gris.   It's cloudy.
Il y a du soleil.   It's sunny.
Il y a du vent.   It's windy.

Il pleut.   It's raining.
Il fait humide.   It's humid.
Il fait mauvais.   It's terrible weather.
Il neige.   It's snowing.
Il va pleuvoir.   It's going to rain.
Il va neiger.   It's going to snow.

Quel beau temps!   What beautiful weather!
Quel mauvais temps!   What bad weather!
Quelle belle journée!   What a beautiful day!
Quel temps affreux!   What terrible weather!
Quelle chaleur!   What heat!
Quel froid aujourd'hui!   What cold today!

Quel climat!   What a climate!
Quel orage!   What a storm!
Quel sale temps!   What terrible weather!
Quel temps de chien!   What terrible weather!
Quelle humidité!   What humidity!

Springboard for Conversation

Ask your classmates about the weather. Find out how they feel about it.

Quel temps fait-il aujourd'hui?
• Il _____.
• Quel(le) _____!

---

1. What is the weather today? It is _____. What a _____!

Récapitulation

Recall your classmates' and instructor's opinions about today's weather. Answer formats are provided.

1. Quel temps fait-il aujourd'hui? Pleut-il? Fait-il beau? Neige-t-il? etc.
   • Il _____.

2. Et qu'en dit Monsieur/Madame/Mademoiselle...? (*What do [your classmates] say about it?*)
   • Quel(le) _____!

Remarque: French uses the impersonal il to refer to weather.
          Il **fait** + *adjective:* il **fait beau**, il **fait chaud**, etc.
          Il + *present tense of verb:* il **neige**, il **pleut**, etc.
          Il **y a** + *noun:* Il **y a du vent**, il **y a du soleil**, etc.

Expansion

The **Expansion** can be used for partners or group conversation and for oral or written composition. Answer formats are provided.

1. Fait-il chaud pour la saison (*for the season/ for this time of year*)? Fait-il plus chaud que l'année passée (*than last year*)?
   • Il fait chaud _____
   • Il ne fait pas chaud _____
   • Il fait plus (moins) chaud _____

2. Fait-il froid pour la saison? Fait-il plus froid que l'année passée?
   • Il fait froid _____
   • Il ne fait pas froid _____
   • Il fait plus (moins) froid _____

3. Quelle est votre saison (*season*) préférée? Pourquoi?
   • Je préfère l'hiver (*winter*)/le printemps (*spring*)/l'automne (*autumn*)/l'été (*summer*) parce qu'il fait beau (parce qu'il fait chaud, parce qu'il neige, etc.)

4. Quel temps fait-il dans votre région en automne (*in autumn*)? au printemps (*in spring*)? en hiver (*in winter*)? en été (*in summer*)?
   • En automne, il _____, etc.

5. Est-ce qu'il pleut beaucoup dans votre région? Est-ce qu'il neige beaucoup?

   • Oui. Il _____ beaucoup.
   • Non. Il ne _____ pas beaucoup.
   • Non. Il ne _____ pas du tout (*at all*).
   You may also wish to use these expressions:
   Ça dépend. It depends.
   Parfois. Sometimes.
   Rarement. Rarely.
   En général, il... Generally, it . . .
   Au printemps, seulement (*only*). etc.

6. Que dites-vous quand il fait beau? chaud? froid? gris? humide?
   • Quel(le) _____!

7. **Review.** If the preceding **Expansion** questions have been used for group or partners conversation, review what your classmates have said. **Êtes-vous d'accord (*Do you agree*)? Fait-il chaud pour la saison? Fait-il froid pour la saison? Pleut-il beaucoup dans votre région? Neige-t-il beaucoup? Fait-il trop chaud en été? Quelle est la saison préférée de Monsieur/Madame/Mademoiselle...** (your classmates)?

France's climate. Thanks to the warming influence of the Gulf Stream and of the Mediterranean, France has a milder climate than French-speaking Québec, Canada, which is at the same latitude. There are frequent showers in France, making it a green, fruitful country. In Paris, May and June are referred to as **la belle saison**. **Le Mistral** is a famous cold northwest wind that blows down the Rhône valley to the Mediterranean in spring and fall. (The bullet train **Le Mistral** is named for this strong wind because it travels the Rhône valley, too.)

La température. In many French-speaking countries, the centigrade (Celsius) scale is used for indicating temperature.

C	F
100°	212°
40	104
30	85
20	68
10	50
0	32
−10	14
−17,8	0
−20	−4

La météo. Here is a typical weather report for France taken from the French newspaper **Le Figaro**. Weather and temperatures (in centigrade) are given for cities in France, Europe, and the rest of the world (**reste du monde**). Weather reports are found in the newspaper under the headings **météo** or **la météo** (abbreviation for **Le Bureau météorologique**, the weather bureau).

Weather expressions used in this chart:
S: **soleil** sunny   **ciel clair** clear sky
N: **nuageux** cloudy   **peu nuageux** few clouds
C: **couvert** totally   **variable** variable
   cloudy   **très nuageux** very
P: **pluie** rain   cloudy
A: **averse** downpours   **bruines** drizzle
O: **orage** storm   **verglas** ice
B: **brouillard** fog   **brumeux** hazy
*: **neige** snow   **vents** winds

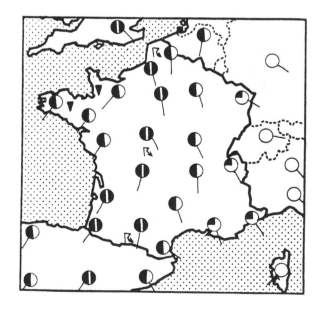

METEO

Chaud et orageux

FRANCE

Ajaccio	S	19	27
Biarritz	S	18	25
Bordeaux	O	18	24
Brest	P	18	19
Cherbourg	S	19	25
Clermont-F.	P	17	26
Dijon	S	16	27
Dinard	A	20	24
Embrun	N	16	26
Grenoble	S	16	28
La Rochelle	O	30	21
Lille	S	16	29
Limoges	P	18	19
Lorient	N	20	22
Lyon	N	17	28
Marseille	N	20	28
Nancy	S	15	30
Nantes	C	20	21
Nice	S	22	28
Paris	S	16	29
Pau	O	18	23
Perpignan	S	20	29
Rennes	N	19	26
Rouen	S	18	28
St-Étienne	S	17	28
Strasbourg	S	16	29
Toulouse	N	20	25
Tours	S	17	27

EUROPE

ANGLETERRE – IRLANDE

Brighton	B	18	29
Edimbourg	B	13	15
Londres	B	18	28
Cork	B	16	19
Dublin	B	14	21

ALLEMAGNE – AUTRICHE

Berlin	S	17	28
Bonn	S	15	30
Hambourg	S	15	28
Munich	S	15	26
Vienne	S	18	25

BELGIQUE – HOLLANDE

Bruxelles	S	15	29
Amsterdam	B	16	26

ESPAGNE – PORTUGAL

Barcelone	C	21	26
Las Palmas	S	22	25
Madrid	S	17	26
Marbella	S	18	29
Palma Maj.	N	18	29
Séville	S	17	27
Lisbonne	N	17	23
Madère	N	21	23
Porto	N	18	20

ITALIE

Florence	S	17	31
Milan	S	19	27
Naples	B	18	29
Olbia	B	23	30
Palerme	S	25	27
Reggio Cal.	B	23	30
Rimini	B	19	28
Rome	N	21	28

GRÈCE – TURQUIE

Athènes	C	24	28
Corfou	S	23	29
Patras	S	19	29
Rhodes	S	20	27
Salonique	S	18	26
Ankara	S	15	28
Istanbul	S	20	26

PAYS NORDIQUES

Copenhague	N	17	19
Helsinki	N	11	15
Oslo	S	11	21
Stockholm	S	15	22

SUISSE

Bâle	S	15	29
Berne	N	14	27
Genève	B	16	28

U.R.S.S.

Leningrad	C	15	16
Moscou	S	14	19
Odessa	S	21	28

YOUGOSLAVIE

Belgrade	S	18	25
Dubrovnik	S	23	28

RESTE DU MONDE

AFRIQUE DU NORD

Agadir	C	19	23
Alger	S	19	30
Casablanca	S	20	23
Djerba	S	27	29
Marrakech	S	20	24
Tunis	S	20	30

AFRIQUE

Abidjan	C	24	26
Dakar	C	26	29
Le Cap	—	—	—

PROCHE-ORIENT

Beyrouth	S	27	30
Eilat	S	29	37
Le Caire	S	28	32

U.S.A. – CANADA

Boston	S	20	21
Chicago	B	23	25
Houston	S	26	27
Los Angeles	N	21	21
Miami	P	21	26
New York	B	22	23
Nouv.-Orl	B	27	24
San Francis	N	25	23
Montréal	B	20	20

CARAIBES

Ft-d.-France (F)	O	27	27
Pte-à-Pitre (F)	P	27	29
San Juan (US)	N	27	29

EXTREME-ORIENT

Bangkok	P	30	24
Hongkong	A	27	27
Pékin	S	31	26
Singapour	N	28	26
Tokyo	C	36	28

AMÉR. CENTR. ET SUD

Acapulco	C	24	27
Buen. Aires	S	3	6
Cancun	C	25	24
Lima	N	19	18
Mexico	B	19	12
Rio de Jan	C	20	22
Santiago	B	5	0

PACIFIQUE

Papeete	S	23	22

TEMPS EN FRANCE AUJOURD'HUI A 13 HEURES

◯	CIEL CLAIR	●	COUVERT	✳	NEIGE
◖	PEU NUAGEUX	▨	PLUIES	∼	VERGLAS
◐	VARIABLE	❟	BRUINES	◿	ORAGES
◑	TRÈS NUAGEUX	▼	AVERSES	=	BRUMEUX

VENTS
FAIBLES   MODÉRÉS   FORTS   TEMPÊTE

CLIMATS POUR VOS VACANCES

● Première colonne : temps à 14 heures (heure de Paris), le 19 août.
  (S : soleil ; N : nuageux ; C : couvert ; P : pluie ; A : averse ; O : orage ;
  B : brouillard ; * : neige).
● Deuxième colonne : température à 8 heures (heure de Paris), le 19 août.
● Troisième colonne : température à 14 heures (heure de Paris), le 19 août.

Étant donné l'important décalage horaire entre Paris et certaines stations étrangères (celles d'Extrême-Orient, en particulier), les températures qui y sont relevées à 8 heures (heure de Paris) peuvent être parfois supérieures à celles relevées à 14 heures (heure de Paris).

Synthèse

A. **Weather forecast.** **Avez-vous écouté la météo aujourd'hui? Avez-vous regardé la météo dans le journal aujourd'hui?** Answer the following questions: **Quel temps va-t-il faire ce soir** (*tonight*)? **Et demain** (*tomorrow*)?
• Il va _____.
• Il va faire environ (*around*) _____ degrés. etc.[2]

B. **Quel temps fait-il?** Look at these photos. Describe the weather and season shown, using complete sentences.

Photo A

Photo B

2. The near future uses **il va** + the appropriate weather expression in the infinitive form: **il va faire beau, il va neiger,** etc.

Photo C

Photo D

C. **La Température.** Refer to the temperature chart in **À Propos** to respond to the following questions: **Quelle température fait-il dehors** *(outside)?* **Quelle température fait-il dans la salle de classe** *(in the classroom)?* **Quelle température fait-il chez vous** *(at your place)?*
• Il fait _____ degrés.

EXEMPLES: *Il fait zéro.*
           Il fait moins dix. (It's ten below.)

Projets

A. **Postcards.** Write a letter or postcard to a friend or relative. Discuss the weather at great length—what the weather has been this past week, what it is doing now, what they are predicting it will be, your opinions on the matter, and so on.

B. **Weather report.** Keep track of the weather for one week. Note changes, weather predictions, temperatures, etc.

C. **Photographs.** Look through some illustrated magazines. Discuss weather conditions visible in any outdoor scenes. For example: **Il neige. Il pleut. Le soleil brille. Il fait beau.** As an alternative, use the illustrations in this textbook for the same purpose.

Activité: Learning by Doing

Talk about the weather. Circulate around the classroom as you would at a party. Complain about the temperature in the room (**Quelle chaleur! Quel froid!** etc.). Complain about the weather outside (**Quel temps affreux!** etc.). Talk about the weather (**La météo dit que... Je crois que...** etc.). Other phrases you may wish to try out:

La chaleur est accablante! The heat is overwhelming!
Le froid est glacial! The cold is glacial!
Je meurs de froid/de chaleur! I'm dying of the cold/heat!
Le temps est détraqué. The weather is crazy.
Ça tape aujourd'hui. It's really hot today.
Il fait trop chaud/froid. It's too hot/cold.
Il fait trop humide. It's too humid.
It fait bien chaud/froid pour la saison. It's very hot/cold for the season.
Il fait chaud/froid, non? It's hot/cold, isn't it?
J'ai froid aux mains/aux pieds. My hands/feet are cold.

«Voici la note...»

À L'Hôtel (Séjour et Départ)

Hotel (Stay and Departure)

Comme on fait son lit on se couche.

You've made your bed, now lie in it.

DIALOGUE

This **Dialogue** presents vocabulary useful for ensuring a pleasant hotel stay and a speedy, efficient departure. This vocabulary can also be used to talk about your own place of residence. Vocabulary blocks within this **Dialogue** offer possibilities for modification to suit a variety of real-life hotel situations.

Séjour	Hotel Stay
(Toc. Toc. La femme de chambre frappe à la porte.)	*(Knock. Knock. The hotel maid knocks on the door.)*
VOUS: Qui est-ce?	YOU: Who is it?
LA FEMME DE CHAMBRE: C'est la femme de chambre avec votre petit déjeuner.	MAID: It's the chambermaid with your breakfast.
VOUS: Un instant… Entrez!	YOU: One moment… Come in!
FEMME DE CHAMBRE: Bonjour, Monsieur / Madame.	MAID: Good morning (hello).
VOUS: Bonjour, Madame. Merci.	YOU: Good morning… Thank you.
FEMME DE CHAMBRE: Je vous en prie, Monsieur / Madame.	MAID: You're welcome.
VOUS: S'il vous plaît, Madame. Il me faut **une serviette de bain.**	YOU: Please, … I need a **bath towel.**
une ampoule pour la lampe une autre chaise une bouteille d'eau minérale des cintres *(m)* une couverture supplémentaire des draps *(m)* un autre oreiller une savonnette un tapis de bain	a light bulb for the lamp another chair a bottle of mineral water some hangers an extra blanket some sheets another pillow a bar / cake of soap a bath mat
FEMME DE CHAMBRE: Tout de suite, Monsieur / Madame.	MAID: Right away.
(Vous téléphonez à la réception.)	*(You call the front desk.)*
VOUS: La réception? Ici la chambre trente-huit. Je ne peux pas fermer / ouvrir **la fenêtre.**	YOU: Front desk? This is room 38. *(Literally: Here room 38.)* I cannot close / open the **window.**
le placard la porte le rideau le tiroir les volets *(m)*	closet / cupboard door curtain(s) drawer shutters
Et **le climatiseur** ne marche pas.	And the **air conditioner** doesn't work.
la douche la lampe le lavabo la lumière la prise de courant la télévision	shower lamp sink light electric outlet television

l'interrupteur *(m)*	(light) switch
le robinet	faucet
le téléphone	telephone
le ventilateur	fan / ventilator

L'EMPLOYÉ(E) À LA RÉCEPTION: Je vais envoyer quelqu'un.

VOUS: Ce n'est pas tout. Je n'ai pas bien dormi. Cette chambre est beaucoup trop bruyante. Je voudrais une autre chambre. Je ne suis pas content(e) du tout.

L'EMPLOYÉ: Absolument, Monsieur / Madame.

RECEPTIONIST AT THE FRONT DESK: I'll send someone.

YOU: That's not all. I did not sleep well. This room is much too noisy. I'd like another room. I'm not at all happy (about this one).

RECEPTIONIST: Certainly.

Départ

Departure

(Le lendemain matin. Vous téléphonez à la réception.)

VOUS: Je pars ce matin. Voulez-vous bien préparer la note, s'il vous plaît? Chambre trente-huit.

(À la caisse. Vous réglez la note.)

LE CAISSIER: Voici la note, Monsieur / Madame.

VOUS: Merci…Voyons. Ça, c'est la chambre. Oui, c'est bien cela. Cinq nuits. Ça, c'est les repas. Mais je crois qu'il y a une erreur. Qu'est-ce que c'est ça?

CAISSIER: C'est le service des chambres. Et ça, c'est le téléphone. Le tout fait 600 F.

VOUS: Ah, oui. Excusez-moi. C'est correct. Acceptez-vous les cartes de crédit? Les chèques de voyage?

CAISSIER: Oui, certainement, Monsieur / Madame.

VOUS: Et pouvez-vous m'appeler un taxi, s'il vous plaît? Je suis pressé(e).

(The next morning. You call the front desk.)

YOU: I'm leaving this morning. Please prepare the bill. Room 38.

(At the checkout desk. You are paying the bill.)

CASHIER: Here's your bill.

YOU: Thank you. . . Let's see. This is (for) the room. Yes, it's (really) that. Five nights. That is (for) the meals. But, I think there is a mistake. What's that (for)?

CASHIER: It's (for) room service. And that is (for) the telephone. The total is 600 francs.

YOU: Oh, yes. Excuse me. It's correct. Do you accept credit cards? Traveler's checks?

CASHIER: Yes, certainly.

YOU: And can you call me a taxi, please? I'm in a hurry.

Phrases à retenir

Memorizing these phrases from the **Dialogue** will help assure fluency in a variety of real-life hotel situations.

1. Qui est-ce?
2. Un instant… Entrez!
3. Il me faut une serviette de bain.
4. La réception? Ici la chambre trente-huit.

5. Je ne peux pas ouvrir la fenêtre.
6. Le climatiseur ne marche pas.
7. Cette chambre est trop bruyante.
8. Je voudrais une autre chambre.
9. Voulez-vous bien préparer la note, s'il vous plaît?
10. Pouvez-vous m'appeler un taxi, s'il vous plaît.

DIALOGUE EXERCISES

The following exercises provide oral and written practice in using the
vocabulary and basic sentence patterns of the **Dialogue: À L'Hôtel (Séjour et
Départ).** These exercises use *only* vocabulary and structures presented in this
Dialogue about a hotel stay and a departure, or "checking out." They do not
require familiarity with any other portions of this chapter.

Exercices d'application

A.   **Expressing a need: Il me faut...**   What do you need? You have just discovered
the following unfortunate situations in your hotel room. Use the expression **il
me faut.**

1. Il n'y a pas de serviettes dans la salle de bains.
2. Il n'y a pas de cintres dans le placard.
3. La chambre est très froide.
4. Il n'y a pas de draps sur le lit.
5. Vous voulez prendre une douche mais il n'y a pas de savon *(soap)* dans la
   salle de bains.

B.   **Classroom objects: Je ne peux pas ouvrir (fermer)...**   In the classroom, go to a
window, a door, a closet, or a desk drawer. Pretend you cannot open it: **Je ne
peux pas ouvrir la fenêtre/la porte/le placard/le tiroir.** When a classmate helps
you, then pretend you cannot get it closed again: **Je ne peux pas fermer...**

C.   **Clarification: Qu'est-ce que c'est ça?**   Point to various items in your classroom.
Pretend you do not know what the items are. Use **Qu'est-ce que c'est?** or the
more colloquial interrogation **Qu'est-ce que c'est ça?** Suggested items: **un livre,
une fenêtre, une porte, une chaise, une lumière, une prise de courant, un
climatiseur, un ventilateur, un interrupteur, un rideau.**

EXEMPLE: —*Qu'est-ce que c'est?*
    ou: —*Qu'est-ce que c'est ça?*
          —*C'est un livre.*

D.   **Qui est-ce?**   Ask classmates about other people in the class: **Qui est-ce?** When you are reminded of their names **(C'est Anne, C'est Marc, C'est Monsieur Smith),** say, **Ah, oui. Excusez-moi.**

E.   **Review.**   What do you say. . .

1. when someone knocks on your door?
2. when you need a towel?
3. when you call the main desk?
4. to indicate that your television isn't working?
5. to complain that your room is too noisy?
6. to complain that you did not sleep well?
7. to ask for another room?
8. when you want your bill prepared?

Improvisation à deux *(Exercice oral)*

F.   Use the vocabulary block options and the basic sentence structures of the **Dialogue** to improvise a dialogue with a classmate. One of you may choose to be a dissatisfied guest explaining to the hotel manager why you want to change rooms immediately. Or, you and your partner may choose to be friends traveling together and sharing a double room that is either quite satisfactory or highly unsatisfactory.

À Vous le choix *(Exercices écrits)*

G.   Write a six- to eight-line dialogue for each of the following situations, selecting appropriate phrases from the initial **Dialogue** of this chapter.

1. You are disappointed with your hotel accommodations. Express your dissatisfaction to the hotel manager.
2. You discover that your hotel bill is twice the amount you had expected to pay.
3. You have had a wonderful hotel stay.

Conversations

H.   Ask your classmates the following questions about the classroom. When two or more responses are possible, alternate answer formats are offered. Select the option that best applies to you personally. Do not limit your responses simply to those suggestions offered in these questions. Use the inclusive vocabulary options provided in the **Dialogue.**

1. Qu'est-ce qu'il y a dans la salle de classe? un climatiseur? des placards? un
   téléphone? une porte? etc.
   • Il y a un/une/des _____.
   • Il n'y a pas de _____.

2. Qu'est-ce qui ne marche pas dans la salle de classe? le ventilateur? la prise
   de courant? l'interrupteur? etc.
   • _____ ne marche pas.

3. Comment est la salle de classe? Est-elle froide? chaude? bruyante? claire?
   sombre?
   • Elle est _____.

Now ask your classmates the following questions about their homes or
dormitories. Note that **chambre** in a hotel or dormitory means *room;* **chambre** in
a house or apartment means *bedroom.*

4. Qu'est-ce qui ne marche pas chez vous? la douche? le climatiseur? le
   téléphone? etc.
   • _____ ne marche pas chez moi.

5. Qu'est-ce qu'il y a dans votre chambre? deux fenêtres? des placards? une
   prise de courant?
   • Il y a un/une/des _____.
   • Il n'y a pas de _____.

6. Comment est votre chambre? Est-elle froide? chaude? bruyante? claire?
   sombre?
   • Elle est _____.

Now ask your classmates about themselves.

7. Avez-vous bien dormi hier *(last night;* literally: *yesterday)?*
   • Oui, j'ai (très) bien dormi hier.
   • Non, je n'ai pas bien dormi hier.
   • J'ai mal dormi.

8. Êtes-vous content(e) en ce moment *(now)?*
   • Je suis (très) content(e).
   • Je ne suis pas content(e) du tout.

I.   **Review.**   What have you learned about your classmates from the preceding
Conversations?

EXEMPLES: *Marc a bien dormi hier.*
            Marie est très contente.
            La chambre de Monsieur Smith est claire.

Pensions, auberges, relais. Pensions are comparable to boardinghouses or guest homes. They generally offer a plan called **pension complète** (full room and board) or **demi-pension** (usually bed and breakfast, sometimes bed and breakfast and one other meal). Meals are generally taken together by all boarders. **Auberges** and **relais**, also called **hostelleries**, are situated in rural areas and are like American country inns. Many **châteaux** have recently been transformed into comfortable hotels on large country estates. Youth hostels, **auberges de jeunesse**, provide inexpensive room and board for young travelers. There is also an increasing number of **motels** in France.

Service charge. A service charge is generally included in the price of a hotel room. If service is not included, plan on paying 15% to 25% more for taxes **(les taxes)** and tips **(le service, les pourboires)**.

Prise de courant. French electrical appliance plugs are different from American. Adapters are available.

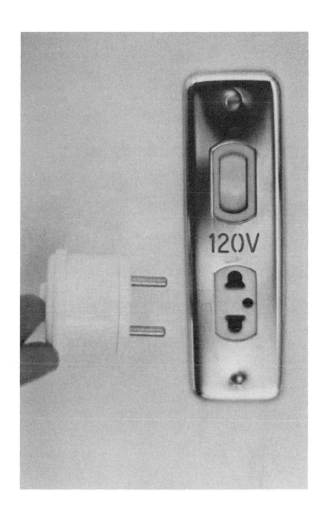

VERBES IRRÉGULIERS: connaître, dormir, faire

connaître to know		
LE PRÉSENT:	je **connais** tu **connais** il/elle/on **connaît** nous **connaissons** vous **connaissez** ils/elles **connaissent**	
LE PASSÉ COMPOSÉ:	j'**ai connu**, etc.	
LE FUTUR:	je **connaîtrai**, tu **connaîtras**, etc.	

1. **Connaître** means "to know" in the sense of "being acquainted with" a person or a thing (for example, a city, a restaurant, a book, a road) through contact or experience.

   Je connais Monsieur Duval.
   Connaissez-vous Paris?

2. **Savoir** means "to know" in the sense of "to have knowledge." (You may wish to review the irregular verb **savoir** in Chapter 2.)

3. In the **passé composé, connaître** can mean "to meet for the first time" or "to make the acquaintance of."

   J'ai connu Marc à Paris.   I met Mark (made his acquaintance) in Paris.

4. **Connaître** is never followed by **comment** (*how*), **où** (*where*), **quand** (*when*), **que** (*that*), or **si** (*if*).

Exercices d'application: connaître

A. **Je connais Monsieur...** Tell whom you know in your class by name.

EXEMPLES: *Je connais Monsieur* (indicate person by pointing).
Il s'appelle Marc Smith.
  ou: *Je connais Madame* (indicate person by pointing). *Mais je ne sais pas son nom.*

B. **Questions with *connaître*.** Answer these questions yourself. Then ask your classmates. (You may wish to use the **tu** form of address with your classmates.)
   1. Connaissez-vous (Connais-tu) les parents du professeur?
   2. Est-ce que votre (ton) professeur de français connaît vos (tes) parents?

3. Où avez-vous connu *(did you meet)* votre femme/mari/meilleur(e) ami(e)? À l'école? À Paris? À Washington? etc.[1]
4. Connaissez-vous un bon hôtel dans le quartier *(neighborhood)*? Un bon restaurant?
5. Quelles villes connaissez-vous bien? Paris? Rome? Londres? New York? etc.
6. Quelles villes ne connaissez-vous pas du tout?
7. Qui dans la classe connaissez-vous bien?

> | **dormir**   to sleep |
> | --- |
> | LE PRÉSENT: je **dors**
 tu **dors**
 il/elle/on **dort**
 nous **dormons**
 vous **dormez**
 ils/elles **dorment** |
> | LE PASSÉ COMPOSÉ: j'**ai dormi,** etc. |
> | LE FUTUR: je **dormirai,** tu **dormiras,** etc. |

Exercice d'application: **dormir**

C. **Questions with *dormir*.**   Answer these questions yourself. Then ask your classmates. (You may wish to use the **tu** form of address with your classmates.)

1. D'habitude *(usually)* dormez-vous (dors-tu) bien? Dormez-vous toujours bien?
2. Dormez-vous bien quand vous êtes fatigué(e)?
3. Avez-vous (As-tu) bien dormi hier?
4. Quand il y a du bruit *(noise)*, pouvez-vous (peux-tu) dormir?
5. D'habitude combien d'heures dormez-vous chaque *(each)* nuit?

> | **faire**   to do, to make |
> | --- |
> | LE PRÉSENT: je **fais**
 tu **fais**
 il/elle/on **fait**
 nous **faisons**
 vous **faites**
 ils/elles **font** |
> | LE PASSÉ COMPOSÉ: j'**ai fait,** etc. |
> | LE FUTUR: je **ferai,** tu **feras,** etc. |

1. For more detailed answers, you may wish to consult **Entracte 10: Places**, and **Entracte 12: Nationalities and Geographical Place Names.**

1. The verb **faire** is used to indicate that you are actually doing or making something.

   Je fais le travail.   I'm doing the work.

2. The future tense of the verb **faire** preceded by the pronoun **le** is the equivalent of the English response, "I will."

   Téléphonerez-vous?   Will you call?
   Je le ferai.   I will (do it).

3. **Ça fait combien?**   How much is that?
   Ça fait dix francs.   That comes to ten francs.

4. The verb **faire** is used in a number of common idiomatic expressions.

   faire des achats go shopping   **faire le ménage** do housework
   faire attention pay attention, be   **faire le plein (d'essence)** fill up (the
     careful   car with gas)
   faire la connaissance de   **faire une promenade** go for a walk
     quelqu'un become acquainted   **faire la queue** stand in line
     with someone   **faire du ski** ski
   faire la cuisine cook   **faire un tour en auto** go for a (car) ride
   faire mes devoirs do (my) homework   **faire la vaisselle** do the dishes
   faire mes études go to school   **faire un voyage** take a trip
   faire du français study French   **ça fait mal!** that hurts!
   faire du jogging jog   **Aïe! Vous me faites mal!** Ow! You are
   faire la lessive do the wash   hurting me!
   faire le marché grocery shop

5. Causal **faire**. The verb **faire** followed by an infinitive is used when an action is to be done by someone else. In English we use *to have* plus a past participle (I had the radio fixed) or *to make* (He makes me laugh).

   Pouvez-vous **faire réparer** le   Can you have the fan fixed?
   ventilateur?

Exercices d'application: faire

D. **J'ai fait la cuisine.**   Review the list of idiomatic expressions with **faire**. What did you do yesterday? What did you not do? (Remember that **un, une, du, de la,** and **des** become **de** when used in negative sentences.)

EXEMPLES: *Hier, j'ai fait la cuisine.*
           Je n'ai pas fait de ski.

E. **Il a fait du ski.** If the preceding exercise has been used orally in class, review what you have learned about your classmates.

EXEMPLES: *Madame Smith a fait des achats.*
Paul n'a pas fait de ski.

F. **J'aime faire du ski!** Review the list of idiomatic expressions with **faire**. What do you like to do? What do you not like to do?

EXEMPLES: *J'aime faire la cuisine.*
Je n'aime pas faire le marché.

G. **Elle aime faire du ski.** If the preceding exercise has been used orally in class, review what you have learned about your classmates.

EXEMPLES: *Monsieur Smith aime faire la vaisselle.*
Anne aime faire des promenades.

STRUCTURES

Structure 1: Conditional Tense (Regular and Irregular Verbs)

To form the conditional tense of **-er** and **-ir** verbs, add the conditional endings to the infinitive. To form the conditional tense of **-re** verbs, drop the final **e** from the infinitive and add the conditional endings to this base. The conditional endings are: **-ais, -ais, -ait, -ions, -iez, -aient.** The usual English equivalent of the conditional is *would*.

Verbes en **-er**	Verbes en **-ir**	Verbs en **-re**
donner	**remplir**	**attendre**
je donner**ais**	je rempli**rais**	j'attend**rais**
tu donner**ais**	tu rempli**rais**	tu attend**rais**
il donner**ait**	il rempli**rait**	il attend**rait**
elle donner**ait**	elle rempli**rait**	elle attend**rait**
on donner**ait**	on rempli**rait**	on attend**rait**
nous donner**ions**	nous rempli**rions**	nous attend**rions**
vous donner**iez**	vous rempli**riez**	vous attend**riez**
ils donner**aient**	ils rempli**raient**	ils attend**raient**
elles donner**aient**	elles rempli**raient**	elles attend**raient**

1. Some irregular verbs have irregular conditional bases. These bases (which are the same as the future bases) must be learned individually. The conditional endings, however, are the same as for "regular" verbs.

L'INFINITIF	LA BASE DU CONDITIONNEL
aller to go	**ir-**
avoir to have	**aur-**
être to be	**ser-**
faire to do, to make	**fer-**
pouvoir to be able, can	**pourr-**[2]
savoir to know	**saur-**
venir to come	**viendr-**
voir to see	**verr-**
vouloir to want	**voudr-**

2. Other irregular verbs follow the patterns of **-ir** and **-re** verbs.

L'INFINITIF	LA BASE DU CONDITIONNEL
apprendre to learn	**apprendr-**
boire to drink	**boir-**
comprendre to understand	**comprendr-**
connaître to know	**connaîtr-**
croire to believe	**croir-**
dire to say, to tell	**dir-**
dormir to sleep	**dormir-**
offrir to offer	**offrir-**
ouvrir to open	**ouvrir-**
prendre to take	**prendr-**
suivre to follow	**suivr-**

Exercices d'application: Conditional Tense (Regular and Irregular Verbs)

A.   **J'aimerais dormir plus.**   What would you like to do differently in your life? Use sentences with the conditional and the words **plus** (*more*) or **moins** (*less*).

---

2. The conditional of **pouvoir** means "could": **Pourriez-vous m'aider, s'il vous plait?** (*Could you help me, please?*)

You may wish to review the **-er** verbs of Chapter 2 (**Structure** 5) and the **-ir** and **-re** verbs of Chapter 4 (**Structures** 1 and 2).

EXEMPLES: *J'aimerais dormir plus.*
Je préférerais travailler moins.
Je voudrais voyager plus.

B. **À votre place, je ferais du jogging.**   Give advice based on the following statements. Use the conditional tense.

MODÈLE: Je fume beaucoup.
À votre place (If I were you), je ne fumerais pas.

1. Je vais faire du ski.
2. Je parle très rapidement.
3. Je ne vais jamais au cinéma.
4. J'arrive toujours en retard *(late)*.
5. Je ne fais pas de jogging.
6. Je ne vais pas en classe.
7. Je dors beaucoup.
8. Je viens.
9. Je bois beaucoup de café.
10. Je ne suis pas content(e) du tout.

C. **Que feriez-vous?**   What would you do if you were on vacation right now?

EXEMPLES: *J'irais à la plage.*   *Je ferais un voyage.*   *Je dormirais tard.*

D. **Il a dit qu'il irait à la plage.**   If the preceding exercise has been used orally in class, review what you have learned about your classmates. If you cannot remember, simply ask again: **Pardon. J'ai oublié...Que feriez-vous? (Que ferais-tu?)**

Structure 2: Direct and Indirect Object Pronouns

Pronouns replace nouns: I know Marc.
I know *him*.

Direct and Indirect Object Pronouns	
me, m'	me, to me
te, t'	you, to you
le, l'	him, it
la, l'	her, it
lui	to him, to her
nous	us, to us
vous	you, to you
les	them
leur	to them
en	some, some of it, some of them; of it, of them; any, any of it, any of them; about it, about them

Note: Me, te, le, and la contract to m', t', and l' before a vowel sound.

1. Object pronouns precede the verb except with positive commands (see item 5 of this section).

Je connais Marie.	I know Marie.
Je la connais.	I know her.
Je connais Marc.	I know Marc.
Je le connais.	I know him.
Je vois les valises.	I see the suitcases.
Je les vois.	I see them.

Note the placement of the object pronouns in the **passé composé**.

Il m'a parlé.	He spoke to me.
Je ne l'ai pas vu.	I did not see him (it).

2. The pronoun **en** has a number of equivalents in English. It may refer to people or to things. **J'en ai** can mean "I have some," "I have some of it," *or* "I have some of them." **Je n'en ai pas** can mean "I don't have any," "I don't have any of it," *or* "I don't have any of them."

   When a sentence ends with a number or with an expression of quantity, **en** must precede the verb. The English equivalent *(of it or of them)* is usually dropped from such sentences in English.

Avez-vous **des valises?**	Do you have any suitcases?
Oui, **j'en ai deux.**	Yes, I have two (of them).
Oui, **j'en ai beaucoup.**	Yes, I have a lot (of them).

3. When there is a conjugated verb and an infinitive, the object pronoun directly precedes the infinitive.

Je voudrais le faire.	I would like to do it.
Je vais lui parler.	I'm going to speak to him (to her).
Je ne peux pas le fermer.	I can't shut it.

4. Direct object pronouns are also used with **voici** and **voilà.**

Le voilà!	There he is! There it is!
Me voilà, enfin!	Here I am, finally!

5. With positive commands, direct and indirect object pronouns are placed after the verb. **Me** becomes **moi.** **Te** becomes **toi.**

Téléphonez-moi.	Call me.
Ouvrez-le.	Open it.
Prends-le.	Take it.

With negative commands, however, object pronouns precede the verb.

Ne me téléphonez pas.	Don't call me.
Ne le prends pas.	Don't take it.

6. Indirect object pronouns are used with the expression **il faut** *(to need)*.

Il me faut une serviette de bain.   I need a bath towel.

Il me faut... I need. . .	**Il nous faut...** We need. . .
Il te faut... You need. . .	**Il vous faut...** You need. . .
Il lui faut... He/She needs. . .	**Il leur faut...** They need. . .

7. The following verbs take **à** plus an indirect object.

Note: qqn = quelqu'un   s.o. = someone
qqch = quelque chose   s.th. = something

demander à qqn de faire qqch ask s.o. to do s.th.	**poser une question à qqn** ask s.o. a question
dire qqch à qqn tell s.o. s.th.	**répondre à qqn** answer s.o.
donner qqch à qqn give s.o. s.th.	**ressembler à qqn** resemble s.o.
montrer qqch à qqn show s.o. s.th.	**téléphoner à qqn** telephone s.o.

Exercices d'application: Direct and Indirect Object Pronouns

E.   **Je le connais. Je la connais.**   Ask classmates to confirm that they know each other. Start by asking the person on your right if he or she knows the person on your left.

EXEMPLE: —*Vous connaissez Monsieur Smith, n'est-ce pas?*
—*Oui, certainement, je **le** connais. On est dans la même classe!* (We're in the same class!)

F.   **Je lui ai téléphoné.**   Ask your classmates whom they have telephoned recently. Use the indirect object pronoun **lui** in your responses. Suggestions: **à votre père, à votre sœur, à votre frère, à votre professeur, à votre meilleur(e) ami(e), à votre mère, à votre fils, à votre fille.**

MODÈLE: votre mère
—*Avez-vous téléphoné à votre mère récemment?*
—*Oui, je lui ai téléphoné récemment.*
ou: —*Non, je ne lui ai pas téléphoné récemment.*

G.   **Le voilà! La voilà!**   Pretend that you don't know where certain of your classmates are. Ask: **Où est...?** and name a specific class member. Turn to a third classmate, who will point out the person whom you named.

EXEMPLES: —*Où est Monsieur Smith?*
—*Le voilà!*
—*Ah! Merci.*

—*Où est Marie?*
—*La voilà!*
—*Ah oui!*

H. **Montrez-moi votre (vos)...** Ask your classmates to show you their possessions. Suggested items: **votre livre de français, votre sac** *(bag)*, **vos clés** *(keys)*, **votre crayon, vos notes, votre cahier** *(notebook)*, **votre parapluie** *(umbrella)*, **votre portefeuille** *(wallet)*, **votre serviette** *(briefcase)*, **votre sac à dos** *(backpack)*, **votre dictionnaire.**

EXEMPLES: *Montrez-moi votre livre.*
Montrez-moi vos stylos.

I. **Montrez-lui votre (vos)...** Now ask classmates to show certain of their belongings to other class members. Remember that **montrez-lui** means *show (to) him* or *show (to) her.*

J. **J'en ai deux.** Answer the following questions yourself. Then ask your classmates. Use **en** in your answers to replace the noun of each question. (You may wish to use the **tu** form of address with your classmates.)

MODÈLE: —Avez-vous (As-tu) des enfants *(children)?*
—*Oui, j'en ai.*
ou: —*Oui, j'en ai deux.*
ou: —*Non, je n'en ai pas.*

1. Avez-vous des frères? Combien?
2. Avez-vous des sœurs? Combien?
3. Avez-vous un chien *(dog)?* un chat *(cat)?* des plantes?
4. Avez-vous une voiture *(car)?* deux voitures?
5. Avez-vous une bicyclette?
6. Avez-vous beaucoup d'amis?

Synthèse

À L'Hôtel. What do you think is being said in this photograph? Use vocabulary from all portions of this chapter. Offer several possibilities.

PRONONCIATION

1. Sound (Phonetic Symbol): [e]³

<table>
<tr><td>SPELLING:</td><td>é, ée, er, ez
ai in verb ending (future tense, j'ai, etc.)
conjunction et (and)
the words les, des, ces, mes, tes, ses
verb forms: je sais, tu sais, il sait, je vais</td></tr>
<tr><td>ENGLISH SOUND RESEMBLED:</td><td>Vowel sound in word day</td></tr>
<tr><td>PRONUNCIATION:</td><td>Smile. Pull the corners of the mouth back.
Slightly open lips. Do not let the sound glide
as in English. Keep it short and abrupt.</td></tr>
<tr><td>EXAMPLES FROM THIS CHAPTER:</td><td>déjeuner   télévision   supplémentaire
entrez   téléphone   réception
téléphoner   réparer   pressé</td></tr>
</table>

---

3. The [e] sound is referred to as "closed e."

2. Sound (Phonetic Symbol) [ɛ]⁴

SPELLING: **e, è, ê, et, êt, ei, ai, aî, ais, ait**

ENGLISH SOUND RESEMBLED: Vowel sound in word *set*

PRONUNCIATION: Open lips wider than for the vowel sound [e].
                                   Do not let the sound glide as in English. Keep
                                   it short and abrupt.

EXAMPLES FROM THIS CHAPTER: serviette   chaise   réception
                                   elle   fermer   bouteille
                                   savonnette   faites

Notes: 1. The word endings **ais, ait, es, est, et,** and **êt** are pronounced either [e] or
            [ɛ], depending on the speaker and the region. For example:

tu es	c'est	je voudrais	valet
il est	je fais	anglais	prêt
elle est	il fait	français	

         2. Notice these pronunciations: **nous faisons** [nufə zɔ̃]
                                         vous faites [vuf ɛ t]

«Voilà un lit...»

4. The [ɛ] sound is referred to as ''open e.''

Projet

Household objects.   *(Exercice oral ou écrit)* Using this photograph of a hotel room or one from Chapter 5, identify those objects that have been presented in this chapter. As an oral exercise, say: **Voilà un oreiller, et ça, c'est la télévision.** If written: **Dans la chambre il y a une télévision. Il y a un oreiller sur le lit**, etc. What objects from this chapter are *not* visible in the room? For example: **Dans cette chambre il n'y a pas de douche.** (Remember that **un** and **une** become **de** after **ne...pas.**)

Activités: Learning by Doing

A.   **Paying your hotel bill.**   Check out of a hotel and pay your bill. Students act as cashiers **(caissiers)** at areas designated as **la caisse.** They prepare bills for their classmates who will play the roles of departing guests. The sample bill below can serve as a model. Departing guests should examine their bills carefully. They should question the cashier on every item, including date and room number. They may acquiesce or disagree as appropriate. As many phrases and structures from this chapter as possible should be used for this activity.

GRAND HOTEL DU PALAIS ROYAL
MAISON DES UNIVERSITAIRES
SOCIÉTÉ COOPÉRATIVE · CAPITAL ET PERSONNEL VARIABLES · SIREN 38 208 75 88

4, RUE DE VALOIS
75001 PARIS

C.C.P. 16957-00 PARIS
TÉL. 261.35.51
       261.32.28

M.

DOIT

SÉJOUR DU _____ AU _____ CHAMBRE Nº _____

B.   Questionnaire: How was your stay?   Using the following questionnaire, interview a classmate on his or her hotel stay. Check off responses as they are given. When you are being interviewed you may choose to refer to a real hotel experience you have had in the recent past.

---

1. Réservations

A. Qui a effectué votre réservation dans cet hôtel:

Reservations

A. Was your reservation made through:

Une agence de voyages	☐	A travel agent
Une compagnie aérienne	☐	An airline
Le système de réservation IHC/PAN AM	☐	Inter-Continental/Pan Am reservation system
Votre bureau dans cette ville	☐	Your office in this city
Autre	☐	Other

B. A-t-on accordé à votre réservation toute l'attention voulue? .... Oui ☐ Yes   Non ☐ No

B. When you made your reservation, was it handled promptly and efficiently?

Si tel n'est pas le cas, veuillez nous indiquer vos motifs de mécontentement _____
If "NO," please tell us why you were not satisfied. _____

2. Réception et Service

A. Pourriez-vous nous donner votre opinion sur les services suivants:

Reception and Service

A. Please evaluate the service you received from:

	Bon / Good	Moyen / Average	Médiocre / Unsatisfactory	
Voiturier	☐	☐	☐	Doorman
Réceptionnaire	☐	☐	☐	Room Clerk/Receptionist
Concierge	☐	☐	☐	Concierge
Chasseur	☐	☐	☐	Bellman/Luggage Porter
Standardiste	☐	☐	☐	Telephone Operator
Femme de chambre	☐	☐	☐	Maid
Caissier	☐	☐	☐	Front Office Cashier
Service d'étage	☐	☐	☐	Room Service
Assistant de direction	☐	☐	☐	Assistant Manager
Autre	☐	☐	☐	

B. Votre arrivée et votre départ ont-ils été effectués avec l'attention voulue? .... Oui ☐ Yes   Non ☐ No

B. Were your check-in and check-out handled promptly and courteously?

Commentaires: _____
Comments: _____

3. Chambre

Votre numéro de chambre: [   ]

A. Avez vous trouvé votre chambre:

Guest Room

Guest Room number this visit: [   ]

A. Did you find this room:

Meublée avec soin et confortable .... Oui ☐ Yes Non ☐ No		Well furnished and comfortable
Y avait-il suffisamment de cintres, cendriers, etc. ..... ☐	☐	Adequately supplied with hangers, ashtrays, stationery, etc.
Propre	☐	Well cleaned

B. Avez-vous trouvé la salle de bain:

B. Did you find your bathroom:

| Suffisamment approvisionnée en serviettes et savonnettes | ☐ | ☐ | Adequately supplied with towels, soap, etc. |
| Propre | ☐ | ☐ | Well cleaned |

C. Quelles modifications pourraient être apportées à la chambre que vous avez occupée? .... ☐

C. Is there anything you would like changed or added in your guestroom?

Si "OUI," quoi? _____
If "YES," what? _____

4. Restaurants

Quelle est votre opinion sur nos restaurants:

Restaurants

How do you evaluate our restaurants:

	Excellent / Excellent	Moyen / Average	Médiocre / Unsatisfactory	
Restaurant Le Meurice	○ ☐ △	○ ☐ △	○ ☐ △	Restaurant Le Meurice
The Bar	○ ☐ △	○ ☐ △	○ ☐ △	The Bar
Room Service	○ ☐ △	○ ☐ △	○ ☐ △	Room Service

○ Qualité de la nourriture et des boissons / Quality of food and beverage   ☐ Service / Service   △ Atmosphère / Atmosphere

Faites-nous part de ce qui vous a déplu _____
Please comment specifically if you were not satisfied with the above. _____

5. Personnel

Le personnel était-il:

Staff

Was the staff:

Courtois .... Oui ☐ Yes Non ☐ No	Courteous
Aimable	☐	☐	Friendly
Efficace	☐	☐	Efficient
Soigné	☐	☐	Attentive

Merci de nous aider à vous mieux servir.

Thank you for helping us serve you better.

Nom/Name _____   Date/Date _____

Adresse/Address _____

Compagnie/Company (facultatif/optional) _____

Êtes-vous ridicule?

Adjectives:
Personal Attributes

Toute vérité n'est pas bonne à dire.   Not every truth is good to say.

Being able to describe yourself and others is useful both for matters of official record and for talking about other people.

Êtes-vous ridicule?

Réponse: • Non! Pas du tout! Au contraire, je suis _____.[1]

EXEMPLE: *Non! Pas du tout! Au contraire, je suis énergique, méthodique et sincère.*

Vocabulaire à retenir[2]   In French, adjectives agree with the nouns they describe both in gender (masculine/feminine) and in number (singular/plural). In the following list, the masculine form is given first. Substitution of the correct form of the selected adjective into the given response format will allow immediate and correct conversational self-expression.

---

adorable adorable
agréable nice, pleasant
aimable nice, kind
blagueur(-euse) a kidder
charmant(e) charming
content(e) content, happy, glad, pleased
énergique energetic
généreux(-euse) generous
gentil(le) kind

heureux(-euse) happy
intelligent(e) intelligent
méthodique methodical
modeste modest
optimiste optimistic
réaliste realistic
sincère sincere
unique unique

Springboards for Conversation

Ask your classmates these personalized questions. Answer formats are provided. Do not limit your responses simply to the suggestions offered in these questions. Use the inclusive vocabulary lists of this **Entracte** to personalize your responses.

1. Are you ridiculous? No! Not at all! To the contrary, I am _____.
2. The personality trait adjectives selected for use in the **vocabulaire à retenir** list are those most frequently chosen by students to describe themselves and their classmates. For a more inclusive listing of personal attributes, see the **Resource List** at the end of this **Entracte**. Using this longer listing will allow you to express yourself more fully and accurately in the exercises of this **Entracte**.

1. Êtes-vous ridicule?
   • Non! Pas du tout! Au contraire, je suis
     _____.

2. Êtes-vous toujours (always) _____? Souvent (often)? Parfois (sometimes)? De temps en temps (from time to time)? Rarement (rarely)? Jamais (never)?
   • Je suis toujours _____.
   • Je suis parfois _____.
   • Je suis souvent _____.
   • Je suis rarement _____.
   • Je ne suis jamais _____.

3. (Traits only you can know about yourself) Êtes-vous sincère? optimiste? équilibré(e)? perfectionniste? idéaliste? heureux(-euse)? ouvert(e)? réaliste? etc.
   • Je suis _____.
   • Je ne suis pas _____.

4. (How you appear to others) Êtes-vous agréable? courageux(-euse)? sympathique? gentil(le)? patient(e)? poli(e)? fascinant(e)? modeste? etc.
   • Je crois que je suis _____.
   • J'espère (hope) que je semble (seem) _____.
   • Je suppose que j'ai l'air (I seem to be) _____.
   • Je parais (appear) probablement _____.

Récapitulation

Recall what you have learned about your classmates and instructor. When describing classmates or instructor, keep in mind this French proverb: **Toute vérité n'est pas bonne à dire.** Use only desirable traits for these descriptions, unless a classmate has specifically selected a less desirable trait to describe himself or herself.

1. (In their own estimation:) Comment est le professeur? Et Monsieur..., comment est-il? Comment est Madame...? Comment est Mademoiselle...? (Use names of your classmates.)
   • Il/Elle est _____.
   • Il/Elle se croit _____.
   Note: If you have forgotten what they said about themselves, simply ask again. **Pardon. Je suis désolé(e), mais j'ai oublié. Êtes-vous ridicule? Ah oui. C'est ça. Vous n'êtes pas du tout** (not at all) **ridicule. Au contraire, vous êtes compétent(e).**

2. (In your estimation:) Qui dans la classe est énergique? sympathique? aimable? drôle? timide? décontracté(e)? dynamique? enthousiaste? gentil(le)? intelligent(e)? etc.
   • Le professeur est _____.
   • Moi, je suis _____.
   • Tout le monde est _____.
   • Personne n'est _____.
   • Mademoiselle... est _____.
   • Monsieur... est _____.
   • Madame... est _____.

Expansion

The **Expansion** can be used for partners or group conversation and for oral or written composition. Response options are provided.

1. Talk about your classmates and instructor "behind their backs." Say nice things about each one. Use the more desirable adjective traits of this lesson. **Qu'est-ce que vous pensez de Monsieur/Madame/Mademoiselle...?**
   • Je trouve qu'il/qu'elle est _____.
   • Il/Elle me plaît beaucoup (*I like him/her very much*) parce qu'il/qu'elle est _____.
   • Je le/la trouve _____.
   • J'aime beaucoup Monsieur/Madame/Mademoiselle...parce qu'il/qu'elle est _____.
   • Je l'adore parce qu'il/qu'elle est _____.
   • Monsieur/Madame/Mademoiselle...a l'air _____.
   • Je ne le/la connais pas très bien, mais je crois qu'il/qu'elle est _____.

2. Now select some less desirable character traits and insults and apply them in the negative to yourself, your classmates, and your instructor. In other words, say that you, your instructor, and your classmates are *not* _____. *For example:* **Le professeur n'est pas stupide!**
   • Moi, je ne suis pas _____.
   • Le professeur n'est pas _____.
   • Monsieur... n'est pas _____.
   • Madame... n'est pas _____.
   • Mademoiselle... n'est pas _____.

3. Talk about your past. How have you changed?
   • Autrefois j'étais (*I used to be*) _____. Mais, plus maintenant. *(But no longer.)* Ces jours-ci (*today*) je suis _____.

4. **Review.** If the **Expansion** questions have been used for group or partners conversation, recall what you have learned about your classmates: **Qui dans la classe est _____? Qui dans la classe se croit _____?**

Vocabulaire utile   The following adverbial modifiers for use with the adjectives of this lesson are frequently requested by students using the conversations of this **Entracte**.

très very	**pas assez** not . . . enough	**pas du tout** not at all
trop too	**plus ou moins** more or less	**si** so
assez rather	**un peu** a little	**tout à fait** entirely

Borrowed words. Some French personality trait adjectives commonly used in English: connoisseur, coquette, blasé, bon vivant, femme fatale, raconteur, nouveau riche, bourgeois, and gourmet.

Contemporary slang adjectives:
Formidable *(great)*, chouette *(great)*, chic *(great)* as in un chic type *(a great guy)*, sympa *(nice,* short for sympathique), dingue *(crazy)*.

Insults. Many of the less desirable character traits of this lesson are actually insults: idiot, imbécile, borné, etc. If you drive in France, you will probably hear these and many others. Preceded by espèce de and used in the substantive form they become even more degrading: espèce d'idiot! Others include: vaurien, crétin, animal, cochon, grosse brute, vache, and chameau.

Zodiac signs. Personality traits according to the signs of the zodiac:[3]

du bélier	Aries
du taureau	Taurus
des gémeaux	Gemini
du cancer	Cancer, Moonchild
du lion	Leo
de la vierge	Virgo
de la balance	Libra
du scorpion	Scorpio
du sagittaire	Sagittarius
du capricorne	Capricorn
du verseau	Aquarius
des poissons	Pisces

3. Definitions and translations of these personality trait adjectives may be found in the Resource Lists at the end of this **Entracte**. You may also wish to review **Entracte** 4: Dates.

BÉLIER   21 MARS—19 AVRIL

ambitieux (-euse)	enthousiaste
courageux (-euse)	optimiste
énergique	sincère

TAUREAU   20 AVRIL—20 MAI

affectueux (-euse)	persévérant(e)
généreux (-euse)	pratique
patient(e)	

LES GÉMEAUX   21 MAI—21 JUIN

changeant(e)	imaginatif (-tive)
enthousiaste	ingénieux (-euse)
habile	intelligent(e)

GÉMEAUX

(22 mai-21 juin) Mercure

SOCIALE. Votre travail vous promet de nombreuses satisfactions : faites preuve d'application. Et pas d'initiatives qui ne soient bien étudiées ! Etablissez un bon programme, ce sera votre fil d'Ariane. MON CONSEIL. Soignez vos relations

CANCER   22 JUIN—22 JUILLET

complexe	sentimental(e)
imaginatif (-tive)	timide
sensible	

LANGUAGE AND CULTURE

LION   23 JUILLET—22 AOÛT

ambitieux	fier (-ère)
énergique	généreux (-euse)
extraverti(e)	optimiste

CAPRICORNE   22 DÉCEMBRE—20 JANVIER

actif (-ive)	persévérant(e)
ambitieux (-euse)	pratique
économe	

VIERGE   23 AOÛT—23 SEPTEMBRE

économe	pratique
intellectuel(le)	travailleur (-euse)
méthodique	

VERSEAU   21 JANVIER—19 FÉVRIER

humanitaire	intelligent(e)
idéaliste	libéral(e)

BALANCE   24 SEPTEMBRE—22 OCTOBRE

affectueux (-euse)	bien équilibré(e)
charmant(e)	logique
diplomate	raisonnable

VERSEAU
(21 janvier-18 fév.) Uranus et Saturne

SOCIALE. Difficultés, heurts .. Surmontez-les avec courage, habileté et calme. Votre intuition vous permettra de mener à bonne fin les questions en instance. Finances à contrôler. MON CONSEIL. Faites preuve de fermeté et de constance, vous obtiendrez de bons résultats.

BALANCE
(24 sept.-23 oct.) Vénus

CŒUR. Très confuse la situation ; suivez votre intuition, c'est votre meilleur guide. Si absorbés soyez-vous par vos problèmes, ne négligez pas vos amis, acceptez les invitations.

POISSONS   20 FÉVRIER—20 MARS

doux (douce)	patient(e)
généreux (-euse)	romantique
mélancolique	sage

SCORPION   23 OCTOBRE—21 NOVEMBRE

courageux (-euse)	loyal(e)
énergique	passionné(e)
indépendant(e)	

SAGITTAIRE   22 NOVEMBRE—21 DÉCEMBRE

amical(e)	philosophe
impulsif (-ive)	sociable
optimiste	sportif (-ive)

POISSONS
(19 fév. - 20 mars) Jupiter et Neptune

CONSEIL. Ne soyez pas trop ambitieux et imposez-vous un peu de discipline.

Synthèse

A.   **Votre signe astrologique.**   Look at your zodiac sign in **À Propos**. Answer the following questions about yourself.

1. Sous quel signe astrologique êtes-vous né(e)?
   • Je suis né(e) sous le signe _____.
2. Quelles sont vos qualités selon votre signe du zodiaque?
   • Je suis _____.
3. Êtes-vous d'accord? *(Do you agree?)*
4. Consultez-vous votre horoscope dans le journal tous les jours? Parfois? Jamais?

B.   **Comment sont-ils?**   Describe these French people using the adjectives of this **Entracte.**

   • Il/Elle est _____.   • Il/Elle paraît *(appears)* _____.
   • Il/Elle semble *(seems)* _____.   • Il/Elle a l'air *(appears)* _____.

Madame X   Madame Y

Monsieur X

Projets

A. **Favorite people.** Using the adjectives of this **Entracte**, describe your three favorite people and your three least favorite people. These may be celebrities or people you know personally. Photographs or pictures from newspapers may be attached if desired.

B. **Superlatives.** Make awards to give to your classmates. Some category suggestions: most intelligent, kindest, most generous, most helpful, most patient, most interesting, most charming, most energetic, and most dynamic.

C. **Photographs.** Leaf through a contemporary illustrated magazine, giving your opinion of all the top personalities described. Use **trop, pas assez, si, tout à fait,** etc. as needed.

Activités: Learning by Doing

A. **Fortune-teller.** Have a fortune-telling session in class. Everyone may have a partner, or a class fortune-teller may be appointed. The partner or classmate endowed with special mystical powers tells the fortune of his or her classmates. For example: **Je regarde dans ma boule de cristal... Sous quel signe êtes-vous né(e)? Ah, oui. C'est ça... Vous êtes né(e) sous le signe de la vierge... Vous êtes économe...très économe... Alors, vous serez riche... Vous êtes travailleur (-euse)... Alors, vous serez célèbre et très heureux(-euse).**

B. **Giving and receiving compliments.** Using the vocabulary of this **Entracte,** circulate around the classroom and give compliments to each classmate you meet: **Vous êtes vraiment _____ aujourd'hui! Je trouve que vous êtes vraiment _____! (magnifique, superbe,** etc.) Help your classmates by hinting about yourself: **Dites-moi. Pourquoi m'aimez-vous? Parce que je suis si _____?** Accept compliments humbly, **à la française.**

Ah oui? Yes?	**Vous me flattez.** You flatter me.
Vraiment? Truly?	**Je suis confus(e).** I'm overwhelmed.
Vous trouvez? Do you think so?	**Vous êtes trop aimable.** You're too kind.

C.   **Billet Doux.** Using the adjectives presented in this **Entracte**, write a **billet doux** (*love letter*) to at least two other class members. These letters may be collected and delivered by an appointed **Cupidon.** *For example:* **Cher** _____/**Chère** _____. **Je vous aime (Je t'aime) parce que vous êtes (tu es)...** (*Signature*). Complete this phrase by employing as many descriptive terms as possible from this **Entracte.** (Alternatives to **Cher/Chère** _____ include: **Amour de mon cœur, Amour de ma vie, Mon ange, Chéri(e), Mon trésor, Mon amour.** Alternatives to "Signature" include: **Un admirateur anonyme, Une admiratrice anonyme,** or **Devinez qui vous écrit!**

Resource Lists of Personal Attributes

A. *Positive or Desirable Personality Traits*

actif (-ve) active
affectueux(-euse) affectionate
ambitieux(-euse) ambitious
amical(e) friendly
amusant(e) fun to be with
bon (bonne) nice
bon vivant one who enjoys life
brillant(e) brilliant
calme calm
capable capable
chaleureux(-euse) warm
compétent(e) competent
compliqué(e) complicated
consciencieux(-euse) conscientious
conservateur(-trice) conservative
courageux(-euse) courageous
décontracté(e) relaxed

discret(-ète) discreet
distingué(e) distinguished
doux(ce) sweet, mild
drôle funny
dynamique dynamic
enthousiaste enthusiastic
équilibré(e) well adjusted
extraordinaire extraordinary
fainéant(e) idler, do-nothing
fascinant(e) fascinating
fataliste fatalistic
femme fatale fascinating woman
formidable (*slang*) great
franc(-che) frank
gai(e) happy
gourmet connoisseur of food
habile skillful, clever
heureux(-euse) happy
honnête honest

humain(e) humane
idéaliste idealistic
indépendant(e) independent
individualiste individualistic
intellectuel(le) intellectual
intéressant(e) interesting
joyeux(-euse) joyous
libéral(e) liberal
loyal(e) loyal
magnifique magnificent
merveilleux(-euse) marvelous
original(e) creative
ouvert(e) open
parfait(e) perfect
passionné(e) passionate
patient(e) patient
perfectionniste a perfectionist
poli(e) polite
ponctuel(le) punctual

raconteur skilled storyteller
raffiné(e) refined
romantique romantic
sage wise, well behaved
sensible sensitive (*not* sensible)
sentimental(e) sentimental
sérieux(-euse) serious, hardworking
simple simple
sociable sociable
solide solid
souriant(e) smiling
spirituel(le) witty, clever
sportif(-ive) athletic
superbe superb
sympathique nice
tendre tender
tolérant(e) tolerant
travailleur(-euse) hardworking

B. *Less Desirable Character Traits and Insults*

agressif(-ive) aggressive
autoritaire bossy
bavard(e) talkative
bête stupid
blasé(e) world-weary
borné(e) narrow-minded
capricieux(-euse) capricious
complexé(e) withdrawn, having complexes
coquette habitual flirt
cruel(le) cruel

cynique cynical
dangereux(-euse) dangerous
désagréable disagreeable
difficile difficult to be with
dogmatique dogmatic
égoïste selfish
ennuyeux(-euse) boring
exigeant(e) demanding, unreasonable

fou (folle) crazy
gourmand(e) glutton
hypocrite hypocritical
idiot(e) idiotic
impulsif(-ive) impulsive
impatient(e) impatient
jaloux(-ouse) jealous
malheureux(-euse) unhappy, unfortunate
malhonnête dishonest

méchant(e) evil, wicked, naughty
paresseux(-euse) lazy
pessimiste pessimistic
snob snobbish
stupide stupid
superstitieux(-euse) superstitious
timide timid
triste sad
vilain(e) mean, nasty

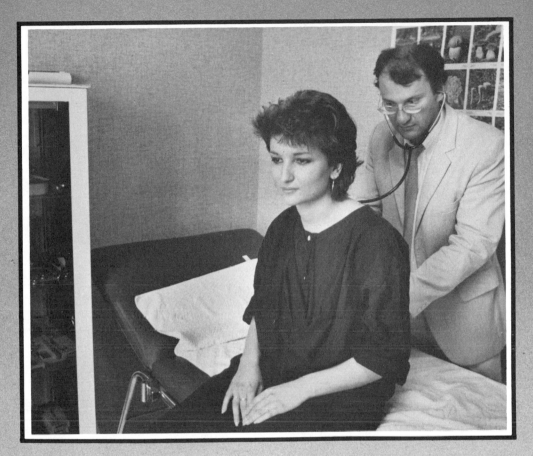

«Alors, qu'est-ce qui ne va pas?»

La Santé: Chez le Docteur

Health: At the Doctor's

Mieux vaut prévenir que guérir.

An ounce of prevention is worth a pound of cure.

DIALOGUE

This **Dialogue** presents vocabulary useful both for seeking medical assistance in an emergency and for conversing about a variety of health-related matters. Vocabulary blocks within this **Dialogue** offer options for personalization regarding your own health. They also provide possibilities for modification to suit a variety of real-life medical situations.

Chez le Docteur	At the Doctor's
LE DOCTEUR: Alors, qu'est-ce qui ne va pas?	THE DOCTOR: What's wrong?
VOUS: Eh bien, je me sens un peu **fatigué(e)** aujourd'hui.	YOU: Well, I feel a little **tired** today.
abattu(e) déprimé(e) énervé(e) épuisé(e) faible mal malade	run-down depressed on edge exhausted weak bad sick
DOCTEUR: Avez-vous de la fièvre?	DOCTOR: Do you have a fever?
VOUS: **Non.**	YOU: **No.**
Je ne crois pas. Un peu. J'ai 37 (trente-sept). J'ai 38 (trente-huit). J'ai 39 (trente-neuf). J'ai 40 (quarante).	I don't think so. A little. (My temperature is) 37 (98.6 F). 38 (100.4 F). 39 (102.2 F). 40 (104 F).
DOCTEUR: D'autres symptômes? maux de tête? diarrhée? vertiges? nausée? douleurs?	DOCTOR: Any other symptoms? Headaches? Diarrhea? Dizziness? Nausea? Aches or pains?
VOUS: J'ai mal à la **gorge.**	YOU: My **throat** hurts.
bouche cheville figure jambe droite jambe gauche joue main poitrine tête	mouth ankle face right leg left leg cheek hand chest head

1. The letter **h** in **hanche** is *aspirate*. There is, therefore, no **liaison** here. **Aux hanches** is pronounced [o·ɑ̃ ʃ]. (See Chapter 4: **Prononciation.**)

J'ai mal au **dos.**

| bras
| cou
| coude
| doigt
| front
| genou
| menton
| nez
| pied
| sein
| ventre
| visage

Et j'ai mal **ici.**

| partout
| à l'épaule (f)
| à l'estomac (m)
| à l'œil (m)
| aux dents (f)
| aux hanches (f)[1]
| aux oreilles (f)
| aux yeux (m)
| aux pieds (m)

DOCTEUR: Depuis combien de temps?
VOUS: Depuis **un jour ou deux.**

| un certain temps
| vingt minutes
| quelques jours
| une semaine
| à peu près un mois
| un an
| des années
| longtemps

DOCTEUR: Êtes-vous **allergique à la
    pénicilline?** | asthmatique
                       | cardiaque
                       | enceinte
                       | diabétique

VOUS: Non.
DOCTEUR: Je vais **vous examiner.**

| vous faire une piqûre
| prendre votre température
| prendre votre tension
| vous faire une radio
| vous vacciner contre le
    tétanos

My **back** hurts.

| arm
| neck
| elbow
| finger
| forehead
| knee
| chin
| nose
| foot
| breast
| stomach, belly
| face

And **I** hurt here.

| I hurt everywhere (I ache all over)
| my shoulder hurts
| my stomach hurts (I have a stomachache)
| my eye hurts
| my teeth hurt (I have a toothache)
| my hips hurt
| my ears hurt (I have an earache)
| my eyes hurt
| my feet hurt

DOCTOR: For how long?
YOU: For **a day or two.**

| quite a while
| twenty minutes
| a few days
| a week
| about a month
| a year
| years
| a long time

DOCTOR: **Are you allergic to penicillin?**

| Are you asthmatic?
| Do you have a heart condition?
| Are you pregnant?
| Are you (a) diabetic?

YOU: No.
DOCTOR: I am going to **examine you.**

| give you an injection
| take your temperature
| take your blood pressure
| X-ray you
| vaccinate you against
    tetanus

Déshabillez-vous. **Étendez-vous là,**

| **Ouvrez la bouche**
| **Tirez la langue**
| **Dites Ahhh... Encore**
  une fois
| **Respirez profondément**
| **Toussez**
| **Avalez**

s'il vous plaît. Ça vous fait mal?
VOUS: Non... Alors, c'est grave? Qu'est-ce que j'ai, Docteur? Faut-il m'opérer?
DOCTEUR: Non. Pas du tout. Vous avez **un gros rhume.**

| **de l'arthrite**
| **une bronchite**
| **la grippe**
| **une pneumonie**
| **des rhumatismes**

Voici une ordonnance. Prenez **deux comprimés par jour.**

| **de l'aspirine toutes les quatre heures**
| **un sédatif**
| **des vitamines**
| **ce médicament**

Et revenez me voir dans une semaine.
VOUS: Merci, Docteur... Atchoum!

Get undressed. Lie down over there,

| Open your mouth
| Stick out your tongue
| Say Ahhh . . . Again

| Breathe deeply
| Cough
| Swallow

please. Does that hurt you?
YOU: No . . . Well, is it serious? What do I have? Will I need an operation?
DOCTOR: No. Not at all. You have a bad cold.

| arthritis
| bronchitis
| the flu, influenza
| pneumonia
| rheumatism

Here is a prescription. Take two tablets every day.

| aspirin every four hours
| a sedative
| vitamins
| this medicine

And come back to see me in a week.
YOU: Thank you, Doctor . . . Achoo!

Phrases à retenir

Memorizing these phrases from the **Dialogue** will help assure fluency in a variety of real-life situations related to matters of health.

1. Alors, qu'est-ce qui ne va pas?
2. Je me sens un peu fatigué(e) aujourd'hui.
3. Avez-vous de la fièvre?
4. J'ai mal à la gorge.
5. J'ai mal ici.
6. Depuis combien de temps?
7. Êtes-vous allergique à la pénicilline?
8. Ouvrez la bouche et tirez la langue.
9. Ça vous fait mal?
10. Qu'est-ce que j'ai, Docteur?

DIALOGUE EXERCISES

The following exercises provide oral and written practice in using the vocabulary and basic sentence patterns of the **Dialogue—La Santé: Chez le Docteur.** These exercises use *only* vocabulary and structures presented in the medical **Dialogue.** They do not require familiarity with any other portions of this chapter.

Exercices d'application

A. **Ailments: Qu'est-ce qui ne va pas aujourd'hui?** What ailments do you have right now? Respond by completing some of these basic sentences from the **Dialogue.**

1. Je me sens...
2. J'ai mal à la (au, aux)...
3. Je suis...
4. J'ai...

B. **Commands: Ouvrez la bouche!** Give these commands at random to classmates who will show that they have understood you by following your instructions. If you do not wish to follow a classmate's command, say: **Absolument pas!** *(Absolutely not!),* **Je refuse!** *(I refuse!),* or **Pas moi!** *(Not I!)*

1. Ouvrez la bouche.
2. Tirez la langue.
3. Dites "Ahhh."
4. Respirez profondément.
5. Toussez.
6. Avalez.
7. Étendez-vous là.
8. Déshabillez-vous.

C. **Dialogue responses.** What could you respond to each of the following? Use sentences and phrases taken directly from the **Dialogue.**

1. Alors, qu'est-ce qui ne va pas?
2. Avez-vous de la fièvre?
3. Avez-vous mal à la gorge?
4. Êtes-vous asthmatique?
5. C'est grave?
6. Revenez me voir dans une semaine.

D. **Review.** What do you say . . .

1. when you aren't feeling well?
2. when you have a sore throat?
3. when you ache all over?
4. when you have a toothache?
5. to ask the doctor what's wrong with you?
6. when you wonder if whatever you have is serious?
7. to thank the doctor?

Improvisation à deux *(Exercice oral)*

E. Use the vocabulary block options and the basic sentence structures of the
Dialogue to improvise a dialogue with a classmate. One of you may choose to
be a doctor or nurse **(l'infirmier, l'infirmière)** and the other a patient receiving
medical assistance. Or, you and your partner may choose to be two friends
discussing your present states of health.

À Vous le choix *(Exercices écrits)*

F. Write a six- to eight-line dialogue for each of the following situations, selecting
appropriate phrases from the initial **Dialogue** of this chapter.

1. You have been feeling tired lately and have decided to see a doctor.
2. A friend of yours tells you all his or her symptoms.
3. You are consulting a new doctor, a specialist recommended to you by a
   friend.

Conversations

G. Ask your classmates these personalized questions.[2] When two or more
responses are possible, alternate answer formats are offered. Select the option
that best applies to you personally. Do not limit your responses simply to those
suggestions offered in these questions. Use the inclusive vocabulary options
provided in the **Dialogue.**

1. Comment vous sentez-vous aujourd'hui? très bien? bien? mal? abattu(e)?
   déprimé(e)? énervé(e)? épuisé(e)? malade?
   • Je me sens _____ aujourd'hui.
2. Avez-vous de la fièvre aujourd'hui?
   • Oui, j'ai _____.
   • Non, je n'ai pas de _____.
3. Avez-vous des vertiges? des maux de tête? des douleurs? des allergies?
   • Oui, j'ai _____.
   • Non, je n'ai pas de/d' _____.
4. Où avez-vous mal en ce moment? à la tête? à la gorge? à l'estomac? au dos?
   etc. Depuis combien de temps? depuis un certain temps? depuis quelques
   jours? depuis une semaine? etc.
   • J'ai mal _____ depuis _____.
   • Non. Ça va. Je n'ai pas mal _____.

---

2. There is no need to answer any question you may feel to be too personal. Learning the
vocabulary, however, can prove invaluable in a variety of real-life situations involving your health.

5. Avez-vous déjà eu *(have you ever had)* la grippe? Quand? il y a longtemps *(a long time ago)?* il y a une semaine? il y a un an? etc.
   • J'ai eu la grippe il y a _____.
   • Je n'ai jamais eu la grippe.

6. Avez-vous déjà eu une bronchite? une crise cardiaque *(heart attack)?* une pneumonie? des rhumatismes? Quand? il y a longtemps? il y a des années? il y a dix ans? etc.[3]
   • Oui, j'ai eu une/des _____ il y a _____.
   • Non, je n'ai jamais eu de _____.

7. Êtes-vous allergique à la pénicilline? à la novocaïne? aux antibiotiques? au chocolat? à la fumée *(smoke)?* à l'herbe *(grass)?* au pollen? à la pollution? à la poussière *(dust)?* À quoi êtes-vous allergique?
   • Je suis allergique _____.
   • (Je ne suis allergique) à rien.

8. Êtes-vous asthmatique? cardiaque? diabétique? enceinte?
   • Je suis _____.
   • Je ne suis pas _____.

9. Avez-vous eu un rhume récemment? Allez-vous mieux?
   • Oui, j'ai eu un rhume récemment.
   • Je vais mieux.
   • Je ne vais pas mieux.
   • Je vais beaucoup mieux.
   • Non, je n'ai pas eu de rhume récemment.

10. Prenez-vous des médicaments en ce moment? des vitamines? de l'aspirine? etc. Pourquoi?
    • Je prends _____ en ce moment parce que... (je suis malade, j'ai un rhume, j'ai des allergies, j'ai la grippe, j'ai mal au dos, etc.)
    • Je ne prends pas de _____ en ce moment.

11. Est-ce que votre tension est normale? élevée *(high)?* basse *(low)?*
    • Elle est _____.

12. Pouvez-vous me recommander un bon docteur? un bon dentiste? un bon opticien?
    • Je peux vous donner le nom et le numéro de téléphone de mon _____. Il (Elle) est excellent(e).

H.   Review. What have you learned about your classmates from these **Conversations?**

EXEMPLES: *Marc a des allergies.*
             Madame Smith a mal à la gorge.

---

3. For vocabulary relating to illnesses, refer to the **Dialogue** of this chapter. Additional illnesses which you may choose to use in your conversational exchanges include: **l'appendicite** f *(appendicitis)*, **les oreillons** m *(mumps)*, **la coqueluche** *(whooping cough)*, **la diphtérie** *(diphtheria)*, **la poliomyélite** *(polio)*, **la rougeole** *(measles)*, **la rubéole** *(German measles)*, **la scarlatine** *(scarlet fever)*, **le tétanos** *(tetanus)*, **la typhoïde** *(typhoid)*, **la varicelle** *(chicken pox)*.

Obtaining medical assistance in an emergency. In Paris, you can get emergency medical help by calling S.O.S. Médecins. To call the rescue squad (**les prompts secours**) or the fire department (**pompiers**), dial 18. The following expressions are useful in asking for emergency assistance:

Au secours!	Help!
Venez vite!	Come quickly!
Appelez un médecin, vite!	Call a doctor, quickly!
Appelez une ambulance!	Call for an ambulance!
C'est urgent!	It's urgent.

Chez le médecin. The doctor's office is referred to as **le cabinet**. This term is not to be confused with **les cabinets,** which refers to **les toilettes.** The expressions **chez le docteur** and **chez le médecin** can mean either "*at* the doctor's" or "*to* the doctor's."

La pharmacie. Pharmacies, or drugstores, in France are clearly identified by a green cross (often illuminated) displayed outside the store.

Atchoum! When someone sneezes, there are various French expressions you may use to acknowledge this action. These are equivalents for *Gesundheit* or *'Bless you.*

À vos/tes souhaits.	To your wishes.
Que Dieu vous/te bénisse.	May God bless you.

The Body: Figuratively Speaking. Parts of the body are used figuratively in a number of conversational expressions.

J'ai mal aux cheveux.	I have a hangover. (*Literally:* My hair hurts.)
Tu me casses les pieds.	You are bothering me. You annoy me. (*Literally:* You are breaking my feet.)
Il est casse-pieds.	He is annoying. He is a "pain." (*Literally:* He is a foot breaker.)
Ne te casse pas la tête.	Don't worry about it. Don't bother (doing it). (*Literally:* Don't break your head.)
Mon œil!	My eye! This is often accompanied by pulling down the lower eyelid. It is meant to refute or show disbelief in the face of a weak argument or doubtful statement.

VERBES IRRÉGULIERS: s'asseoir, se sentir

> | **s'asseoir**   to sit down |
> | --- |
> | LE PRÉSENT: je **m'assieds**
tu **t'assieds**
il **s'assied**
elle **s'assied**
nous **nous asseyons**
vous **vous asseyez**
ils **s'asseyent**
elles **s'asseyent** |
> | LE PARTICIPE PASSÉ: **assis**
LA BASE DU FUTUR ET DU CONDITIONNEL: **assiér-** |

1. **Asseyez-vous (Assieds-toi).**   Sit down.
   Voulez-vous vous asseoir?   Would you like to sit down?
2. **Assis(e),** the past participle, can be used as an adjective to mean "seated."

   Il est **assis** près de la porte.   He is seated (sitting) near the door.
   Elle est **assise** près de la porte.   She is seated (sitting) near the door.

Exercices d'application: **s'asseoir**

A. **Voulez-vous vous asseoir?**   Everyone in class stands up. Tell the person on your right side to please be seated. Treat him or her as if he or she were a guest in your home. (You may choose to use the **tu** form of address with classmates.)

EXEMPLES: *Asseyez-vous, je vous prie.*
Voulez-vous vous asseoir?

Assieds-toi, s'il te plaît.
Veux-tu t'asseoir?

B. **Asseyez-vous près de la porte.**   Repeat the preceding exercise, but this time tell your classmates where to sit. Possibilities include: **près de la fenêtre, à côté de** (next to) **Marc, entre** (between) **Marie et Anne, par terre** (on the floor), **derrière** (behind) **le bureau du professeur, devant** (in front of) **le bureau, sur les genoux de** (in the lap of) **Monsieur Smith, en face de** (opposite) **Madame Smith.**

EXEMPLE: *Asseyez-vous (Assieds-toi) près de la porte.*

C. **Il est assis. Elle est assise.**   If the preceding exercise has been done in class, describe where everyone is seated before they return to their own places.

EXEMPLES: *Marc est assis par terre.*
Marie est assise derrière Marc.

D. **Je vais m'asseoir.** Stand up. Then, using the vocabulary of this chapter's **Dialogue,** describe your present state of health. **Êtes-vous fatigué(e)? épuisé(e)? abattu(e)? faible? malade?** Indicate whether you will have to be seated in consequence.

EXEMPLES: *Je suis épuisé(e). Donc* (therefore), *je vais m'asseoir.*

Je ne suis pas fatigué(e). Donc, je ne vais pas m'asseoir. Je vais rester debout (stay standing).

➤
se sentir to feel, to be (in relation to health)	
LE PRÉSENT: je **me sens** nous **nous sentons**	
tu **te sens** vous **vous sentez**	
il **se sent** ils **se sentent**	
elle **se sent** elles **se sentent**	
LE PARTICIPE PASSÉ: **senti**	
LA BASE DU FUTUR ET DU CONDITIONNEL: **sentir-**	

Sentir *(to feel; to smell)* is conjugated like **se sentir.**

Je sens une douleur à l'épaule.	I feel a pain in my shoulder
Hmmm! **Ça sent** bon!	Mmm! That smells good!
Pouah! **Ça sent** mauvais!	Phew! That smells bad!

Exercices d'application: **se sentir** and **sentir**

E. **Comment vous sentez-vous aujourd'hui?** How are you feeling today? Ask your classmates how they are feeling. Responses will begin with **Je me sens...** Use vocabulary from the **Dialogue** of this chapter: **fatigué(e), un peu fatigué(e), très fatigué(e), abattu(e), déprimé(e), énervé, épuisé(e), faible, mal, malade, bien, en forme** *(fine, in good shape)*. If a classmate is not feeling well, assure him or her that he or she will soon be feeling much better: **Vous vous sentirez beaucoup mieux dans quelques jours.**

F. **Il se sent fatigué.** What have you learned about your classmates' health from the preceding exercise?

EXEMPLES: *Madame (Smith) se sent fatiguée.*
Paul se sent malade.
Anne se sent en forme.

G. **Ça sent bon!**   Do you like the smell of coffee? *(Hmmmmm. Ça sent bon!)* Do you dislike the smell of air pollution? **(Pouah! Ça sent mauvais!)** How do you feel about the aromas of each of the following items?

1. la pollution
2. l'herbe
3. le chocolat

4. le pain frais *(fresh)*
5. la mer
6. le rosbif

7. les cigarettes
8. les cigares
9. le fromage

STRUCTURES

Structure 1: Use of the Present Tense with **Depuis**

Depuis *(for, since)* followed by a period of time is used with the present tense to express an action or a condition that started in the past and is still going on in the present.

1. The question **Depuis combien de temps?** asks how long something has been going on.

Depuis combien de temps êtes-vous malade?	(For) how long have you been sick?

   As seen in the **Dialogue**, answers can include: **depuis vingt minutes, depuis un jour, depuis quelques jours, depuis une semaine, depuis un an, depuis longtemps,** etc.

2. The question **Depuis combien de temps?** is answered in the *present* tense in French. In English we use the present perfect tense to express this same idea.

Depuis combien de temps êtes-vous malade?	How long have you been sick?
Je suis malade **depuis** un jour.	I've been sick for one day.

3. Other constructions are used in French to express the same idea as **depuis.** These again use the present tense to express an action or a condition that started in the past and is still going on in the present. These expressions are: **ça fait... que..., voilà... que...,** and **il y a... que....** For example, to express the idea "I have been sick for three days," you can say in French:

Je suis malade **depuis** trois jours.	**Voilà** trois jours **que je suis** malade.
Ça fait trois jours **que je suis** malade.	**Il y a** trois jours **que je suis** malade.

4. The question **Depuis quand?** asks for information about a specific starting point in time. It is answered with **depuis** and the present tense.

Depuis quand êtes-vous malade?	Since when (since what point in time) have you been sick?

Je **suis** malade **depuis lundi.**	I've been sick **since Monday.**
depuis ce matin	since this morning
depuis hier soir	since yesterday evening
depuis lundi, mardi, etc.	since Monday, Tuesday, etc.
depuis deux heures	since two o'clock
depuis mon arrivée	since my arrival
depuis la semaine passée	since last week
depuis le mois passé	since last month
depuis l'année dernière	since last year
depuis janvier, février, etc.	since January, February, etc.
depuis le dix mars	since March 10
depuis 1980	since 1980
depuis mon enfance	since my childhood
depuis l'âge de cinq ans	since the age of five

Exercices d'application: **Depuis**

A. **Depuis combien de temps êtes-vous ici?** How long have you been in class? Be as precise as possible.

EXEMPLES: *Depuis cinq minutes.*
Ça fait dix-huit minutes.

B. **Il est ici depuis dix minutes.** If the preceding exercise has been used orally in class, indicate how long your classmates have been in class.

EXEMPLES: *Il est ici depuis dix minutes.*
Ça fait douze minutes qu'elle est là. (**Là** may be used to mean "here.")

C. **Depuis combien de temps...?** Answer these personalized questions yourself. Then ask your classmates. Remember to use the present tense in your responses.

MODÈLE: —Depuis combien de temps étudiez-vous le français?
—*J'étudie le français depuis deux mois.*

1. Depuis combien de temps étudiez-vous le français?
   • J'étudie…
2. Depuis combien de temps habitez-vous dans cette ville?
   • J'habite…
3. Depuis combien de temps êtes-vous étudiant(e) ici?
   • Je suis…

4. Êtes-vous marié(e)? fiancé(e)? Depuis combien de temps? Depuis combien de temps connaissez-vous votre mari? votre femme? votre fiancé(e)? votre meilleur(e) ami(e)?
   * Je suis…   * Je ne suis pas…
   * Je connais…

5. Fumez-vous? Depuis combien de temps?
   * Je fume…   * Je ne fume pas.

6. Travaillez-vous? Depuis combien de temps?
   * Je travaille…   * Je ne travaille pas.

7. Êtes-vous à la retraite *(retired)*? Depuis combien de temps?
   * Je suis…   * Je ne suis pas…

8. Savez-vous conduire *(to drive)*? Depuis combien de temps?
   * Je sais…   * Je ne sais pas…

9. Jouez-vous au tennis? au golf? Depuis combien de temps?
   * Je joue…   * Je ne joue pas…

10. Buvez-vous du café? du vin? Depuis combien de temps?
    * Je bois…   * Je ne bois pas…

11. Vous sentez-vous fatigué(e)? Depuis combien de temps?
    * Je me sens…   * Je ne me sens pas…

12. Depuis combien de temps connaissez-vous le professeur de français?
    * Je le (la) connais…

13. Depuis combien de temps travaillez-vous sur les questions de cet exercice?
    * Je travaille…

D.   **Depuis quand…?**   This exercise asks the same personalized questions as the preceding exercise. **Depuis quand,** however, is used in place of **depuis combien de temps.** Responses must give a specific starting point in time. (You may wish to review **Entracte 3:** Telling Time and **Entracte 4:** Dates.)

MODÈLE: Depuis quand étudiez-vous le français?
          J'étudie le français depuis le 3 septembre.

1. Depuis quand étudiez-vous le français?
2. Depuis quand habitez-vous dans cette ville?
3. Depuis quand êtes-vous étudiant(e) ici?
4. Êtes-vous marié(e)? fiancé(e)? Depuis quand? Depuis quand connaissez-vous votre mari? votre femme? votre fiancé(e)? votre meilleur(e) ami(e)?
5. Fumez-vous? Depuis quand?
6. Travaillez-vous? Depuis quand?
7. Êtes-vous en retraite? Depuis quand?
8. Savez-vous conduire? Depuis quand?
9. Jouez-vous au tennis? au golf? Depuis quand?
10. Buvez-vous du café? du vin? Depuis quand?

11. Vous sentez-vous fatigué(e)? Depuis quand?
12. Depuis quand connaissez-vous le professeur de français?
13. Depuis quand travaillez-vous sur les questions de cet exercice?

Structure 2: Expressions of Time—Il y a and **Pendant**

We have already seen **il y a** to mean "there is" or "there are."

Il y a can also mean "ago" when it is used with a completed action and is followed directly by an expression of time.

J'ai eu la grippe **il y a un mois.**	I had the flu a month ago.

Pendant means "for" or "during." It is used with the **passé composé** to indicate an action that endured for a period of time in the past and then ended in the past. (Remember that **depuis** indicates an action that started in the past but continues into the present.)

Pendant combien de temps **avez-vous étudié** hier soir?	(For) how long did you study last night?
J'ai étudié pendant deux heures.	I studied (for) two hours.

Exercices d'application: Il y a and **Pendant**

E. **Il y a longtemps.** Complete these statements. How long ago did you do each of the following? Use vocabulary from the **Dialogue** of this chapter.

1. Je suis allé(e) chez le docteur il y a...
2. J'ai eu un rhume il y a...
3. J'ai téléphoné à un(e) ami(e) il y a...
4. J'ai mangé il y a...
5. J'ai pris de l'aspirine il y a...
6. J'ai eu la grippe il y a...
7. J'ai vu un bon film...
8. J'ai vu mes amis il y a...

F. **Quand êtes-vous allé(e)...?** Transform the statements of the preceding exercise into questions using **quand.** Then ask your classmates. Responses should use constructions with **il y a.**

MODÈLE: Je suis allé(e) chez le docteur il y a...
—*Quand êtes-vous allé(e) chez le docteur?*
—*Je suis allé(e) chez le docteur il y a un mois.*

G. **Pendant combien de temps?** What have you done recently and for how long? You may wish to refer to the lists of verbs in Chapters 2 and 4.[4]

4. For **-er** verbs, refer to page 47. For **-ir** and **-re** verbs, refer to pages 109 and 111.

EXEMPLES: *J'ai regardé la télévision hier soir pendant trois heures.*
                   J'ai parlé avec mon ami pendant vingt minutes.
                   J'ai attendu un ami pendant deux heures.

Structure 3: Reflexive Verbs

When the subject of a verb performs an action upon itself *(he cut himself)* or
when a reciprocal action occurs *(they talk to each other/to one another)*, the reflexive
pronouns **me, te, se, nous, vous, se** are used.

Note: **Me, te, se** become m', t', and s' before vowel sounds.

1. Most verbs may be made reflexive. For example, the verb **aimer** *(to like, to love)* is nonreflexive. **Aimer,** however, can be made reflexive by having it indicate a reciprocal action.

    J'aime mon ami. Il m'aime.   I love my friend. He loves me.
    Nous nous aimons.   We love each other. (We love one
                                           another).

2. An example of a reflexive verb in English is *to enjoy oneself: I enjoy myself, you enjoy yourself, he is enjoying himself,* etc. The French equivalent of *to enjoy oneself* is also reflexive: **s'amuser.**

3. Certain verbs are reflexive in French. Their English equivalents are not necessarily reflexive. Many of the French reflexive verbs correspond to English expressions with *get: to get up* **(se lever),** *to get married* **(se marier),** and so on. The following is a list of common French reflexive verbs. Note that most of them are **-er** verbs.

s'en aller leave, go away	**se doucher** shower	**se marier (avec)** get married (to)
s'amuser (bien) have a good time	**s'énerver** get nervous, annoyed	**se peigner** comb one's hair
s'arrêter stop	**s'enrhumer** catch (a) cold	**se perdre** get lost
s'asseoir sit (down)	**s'entendre** get along	**se préparer** get ready
se brosser les cheveux brush one's hair	**se fâcher (avec)** get angry (with)	**se promener** take a walk
se brosser les dents brush one's teeth	**se fiancer** get engaged	**se rappeler** remember
se coucher go to bed, lie down	**s'habiller** get dressed	**se raser** shave
se dépêcher hurry (up)	**se laver** wash oneself	**se reposer** rest
se déshabiller get undressed	**se laver la figure (les mains, la tête,** etc.) wash one's face, hands, hair (literally: head), etc.	**se réveiller** wake up
se disputer argue, quarrel	**se lever** get up	**se sentir** feel
		se souvenir de[5] remember
		se tromper be mistaken
		se trouver be located

---

5. **Se souvenir de** is conjugated like **venir.**

Affirmative	
je **m'amuse** tu **t'amuses** il **s'amuse** elle **s'amuse** on **s'amuse**	nous **nous amusons** vous **vous amusez** ils **s'amusent** elles **s'amusent**

Negative	
je **ne m'amuse pas** tu **ne t'amuses pas** il **ne s'amuse pas** elle **ne s'amuse pas** on **ne s'amuse pas**	nous **ne nous amusons pas** vous **ne vous amusez pas** ils **ne s'amusent pas** elles **ne s'amusent pas**

Interrogative	
est-ce que je m'amuse? **t'amuses-tu?** **s'amuse-t-il?** **s'amuse-t-elle?** **s'amuse-t-on?**	**nous amusons-nous?** **vous amusez-vous?** **s'amusent-ils?** **s'amusent-elles?**

4. Reflexive pronouns precede the conjugated verb except in positive commands. (*Note:* **te** becomes **toi** in positive commands.)

> **Asseyez-vous!**
> **Assieds-toi!**

5. In reflexive constructions, parts of the body are preceded by the definite article **le, la, les** rather than by the possessive adjective **mon, ma, mes.** This usage is different from English.

Je **me** brosse **les** dents.	I'm brushing my teeth.

Note that when an action is performed by or with a part of the body, reflexive pronouns are not used. The body part, however, is still referred to by the definite article (**le, la, les**) rather than by the possessive adjective.

Levez **la** main.   Raise your hand.
Fermez **la** bouche.   Shut your mouth! Be quiet!

Exercices d'application: Reflexive Verbs

H. Vous vous asseyez!   Refer to the list of reflexive verbs. Act out selected verbs while your classmates guess what you are doing. (The informal **tu** form may be used if appropriate.)

EXEMPLES: *—Qu'est-ce que je fais?* (What am I doing?)
—Vous vous asseyez!
—Vous vous lavez les mains!

—Tu te couches!
—Tu te laves les mains!

I. Levez-vous!   Give simple commands to your classmates using reflexive verbs. (The informal **tu** form may be used.)

EXEMPLES: *Levez-vous!*
Asseyez-vous!
Réveille-toi!

J. À quelle heure vous couchez-vous?   Make questions using **D'habitude à quelle heure...?** *(Usually, at what time. . . ?).* Answer the questions yourself. Then ask your classmates. Responses use either **à** *(at)* or **vers** *(around).* (You may wish to review **Entracte 3:** Telling Time.)

MODÈLE: get up
—D'habitude à quelle heure vous levez-vous?
—Je me lève[6] vers huit heures.

1. get up
2. go to bed
3. shower
4. get dressed

5. wash
6. brush (your) teeth
7. wake up

K. Je m'amuse en classe.   Answer these questions yourself. Then ask your classmates.

MODÈLE: *—Vous amusez-vous en classe?*
—Oui, je m'amuse en classe.
ou: *—Non, je ne m'amuse pas en classe.*

6. The **je** form of the verb **se lever** (present tense) uses an **accent grave**.

1. Vous sentez-vous fatigué(e) aujourd'hui?
2. Vous disputez-vous avec vos amis? souvent? rarement? de temps en temps? et avec votre mari ou votre femme? et avec vos parents ou vos enfants?
3. Vous brossez-vous les dents après chaque repas *(after each meal)*?
4. Est-ce que votre professeur s'appelle Monsieur Duval?
5. Vous fâchez-vous facilement *(easily)*?
6. Vous énervez-vous facilement?
7. Votre meilleur(e) ami(e) se fâche-t-il (elle) facilement? et votre professeur? et votre femme ou votre mari? et votre mère ou votre père? etc.
8. D'habitude vous couchez-vous tard *(late)*?
9. D'habitude vous enrhumez-vous facilement?

L. **Il se sent fatigué aujourd'hui.**   If the preceding exercise has been used orally in class, review what you have learned about your classmates.

EXEMPLES: *Monsieur... se sent fatigué aujourd'hui.*
Madame... se couche tard.

Structure 4: Reflexive Verbs (Infinitive Form)

When the reflexive verb is in the infinitive form, the reflexive pronoun changes from **se** to **me, te, nous** or **vous** depending on the subject of the verb and comes directly before the infinitive. (Remember that **se, me, te** become **s', m', t'** before a vowel sound.)

(je/me)	**Je** vais **me reposer.**
(tu/te)	**Tu** vas **te reposer.**
(il/se)	**Il** va **se reposer.**
(elle/se)	**Elle** va **se reposer.**
(on/se)	**On** va **se reposer.**
(nous/nous)	**Nous** allons **nous reposer.**
(vous/vous)	**Vous** allez **vous reposer.**
(ils/se)	**Ils** vont **se reposer.**
(elles/se)	**Elles** vont **se reposer.**

Exercices d'application: Reflexive Verbs (Infinitive Form)

M. **Je vais me reposer.**   What are you going to do and what are you not going to do later on? Use reflexive verbs.

EXEMPLES: *Je vais me reposer.*
Je ne vais pas me promener.

N. **Il va se reposer.** If the preceding exercise has been used orally in class, review what you have learned about your classmates' plans.

EXEMPLES: *Marc va se reposer.*
Marie ne va pas se marier.

Structure 5: Reflexive Verbs (Passé Composé)

Reflexive verbs are conjugated with **être** in the **passé composé**. The past participle agrees in gender (masculine or feminine) and number (singular or plural) with the preceding reflexive pronoun when it functions as a direct object in the sentence. This is usually the case.

Affirmative	
je **me suis amusé(e)** tu **t'es amusé(e)** il **s'est amusé** elle **s'est amusée** on **s'est amusé**	nous **nous sommes amusé(e)s** vous **vous êtes amusé(e)(s)** ils **se sont amusés** elles **se sont amusées**

Negative
je **ne me suis pas amusé(e)** tu **ne t'es pas amusé(e)** Il **ne s'est pas amusé**, etc.

There are situations, however, where the reflexive pronoun is not the *direct* object of the verb, but rather the *indirect* object. In these cases, the past participle does not agree with the reflexive pronoun. This occurs, for example, in sentences where body parts are mentioned.

Elle s'est lavée.
But:
Elle s'est lavé les mains.
Ils se sont brossé les dents.

Exercices d'application: Reflexive Verbs (Passé Composé)

O. **Je me suis promené(e) hier.** What did you do yesterday? What did you not do? Select reflexive verbs from the list given in this chapter. Use the **passé composé**.

EXEMPLES: *Je me suis promené(e).*
Je ne me suis pas couché(e) tard.
Je me suis bien amusé(e).

P. **Il s'est couché tard.**   If the preceding exercise has been used orally in class, review what you have learned about your classmates.

EXEMPLES: *Marc s'est couché tard.*
Marie ne s'est pas promenée.
Madame Smith s'est promenée.

Q. **Questions using reflexive verbs.**   Answer these personalized questions yourself. Then ask your classmates.[7]

1. À quelle heure vous êtes-vous couché(e) hier soir?
2. À quelle heure est-ce que vous vous êtes réveillé(e) ce matin?
3. À quelle heure vous êtes-vous levé(e) ce matin?
4. Est-ce que vous vous êtes bien amusé(e) récemment? Avec qui?
5. Est-ce que vous vous êtes promené(e) hier soir? aujourd'hui? Avec qui?
6. Vous êtes-vous disputé(e) récemment avec un(e) ami(e)?
7. Vous êtes-vous brossé les dents aujourd'hui?

PRONONCIATION

1. Sound (Phonetic Symbol): [o][8]

SPELLING:	**o, ô, au, eau**
ENGLISH SOUND RESEMBLED:	Vowel sound in words *sn<u>ow</u>* or *g<u>o</u>*
PRONUNCIATION:	Tightly round and protrude lips. Do not let the sound glide as in English. Keep it short and abrupt.

EXAMPLES FROM THIS CHAPTER:	<u>au</u>	rep<u>os</u>	il f<u>au</u>t	be<u>au</u>coup
	<u>au</u>x	d<u>os</u>	v<u>os</u>	

2. Sound (Phonetic Symbol): [ɔ][9]

SPELLING:	**o, au**
ENGLISH SOUND RESEMBLED:	Vowel sound in words *l<u>o</u>ve* or *c<u>u</u>p*
PRONUNCIATION:	Open mouth wider than for the sound [o]. Lips are more rounded than for English sound. Do not let the sound glide as in English. Keep it short and abrupt.

---

7. For questions involving time, you may wish to review **Entracte** 3: Telling Time.
8. The [o] sound is referred to as "closed *o*."
9. the [ɔ] sound is referred to as "open *o*."

EXAMPLES FROM THIS CHAPTER:

docteur	pollution	votre
proverbe	ordonnance	professeur
opérer	bonne	normale

Notes:

1. The letter **o** is pronounced [o] when it is the final sound of a word, as in **piano, repos, vos**; when it precedes the spelling **-tion**, as in **émotion**; when it is followed by the sound [z], as in **rose, chose**. The letter **o** is pronounced [ɔ] in nearly all other positions (that is, other than in the final sound of a word), as in **docteur** [dɔktœr], **oreille** [ɔrɛj].

2. The letter **ô** (accent circonflexe) is pronounced [o] as in **hôtel, bientôt**, etc. *Exception:* **hôpital** [ɔ].

3. The spellings **eau** and **au** are pronounced [o] when they are the final pronounced sound of a word (as in **beau, il faut**) or when they end a syllable (as in **beaucoup**). In many words, however, when the spelling **au** ends a syllable, the tendency these days is to pronounce the spelling **au** as [ɔ], as in the words **mauvais, j'aurai**.

4. In syllables ending in a consonant sound, **au** is pronounced [ɔ], as in **augmenter**.

5. The nasal sound [ɔ̃] loses its nasal quality when it is followed by a double consonant or by a vowel. (See Chapter 1.) The letter **o** at this time becomes [ɔ].

bonne [bɔn]	**bon anniversaire** [bɔnaniversɛr]
comment [kɔmã]	**bon appétit** [bɔnapeti]

3. Sound (Phonetic Symbol): [ø]

SPELLING: **eu, œu, eû**

ENGLISH SOUND RESEMBLED: Vowel sound in words *put, sir, good*

PRONUNCIATION: Round and protrude lips tensely. Do not let the sound glide as in English. Make it short and abrupt. It might help first saying the French sound [e] (Chapter 6), then rounding and protruding the lips while still trying to say [e].

EXAMPLES FROM THIS CHAPTER:

deuxième	un peu	mieux
deux	yeux	pneumonie

4. Sound (Phonetic Symbol): [œ]

SPELLING: **eu, œu, œ (+il), eu (+il), ue (+il)**

ENGLISH SOUND RESEMBLED: Vowel sound in words *putt* or *cup*

PRONUNCIATION: Open your mouth wider than for the [ø] sound. Do not let the sound glide as in English. Keep it short and abrupt. It might help first saying the French sound [ɛ] (Chapter 6), then rounding and protruding the lips while still trying to say [ɛ].

EXAMPLES FROM THIS CHAPTER: peur   heure
                                docteur   œil

Notes: 1. The spelling **eu** is pronounced [ø] when it is the final sound of a syllable
                as in **peu**, **deux**, **courageux**, **deuxième**, or when it is followed by the
                consonant sounds [d], [t], [z], [ʒ], [k], as in **courageuse**.
             2. The spelling **eu** is pronounced [œ] when it occurs in a syllable ending in a
                consonant sound other than [d], [t], [z], [ʒ], [k]. Examples: **docteur**,
                heure, **acteur**
             3. The spelling **œu** is pronounced [œ] when followed by a pronounced
                consonant (as in **œuf** [œf], **hors-d'œuvre** [ɔrdœvr], **bœuf** [bœf]). It is
                pronounced [ø] when it is the final sound of a syllable (as in **des œufs**
                [ø]).

Projet

The Human Body   *(Exercice oral ou écrit).* Name the parts of the human body.
Make a rough sketch or find a photograph in a magazine (or elsewhere in this
textbook) to use as illustration. If this project is done orally, you may choose to
point to your own body, or to that of a willing classmate as you name the parts
of the body: **Voilà la tête, voilà les pieds,** etc.

Activité: Learning by Doing

Medical History.   Using vocabulary and structures from all sections of this
chapter, complete the following medical history for a classmate. Use the form
below as a model for one you will prepare on a larger sheet of paper. Ask the
questions suggested here to elicit the appropriate responses:

Nom:
Symptômes:
Maladies:
Médicaments:
Allergies:
Vaccinations:
Tension:
Groupe Sanguin:

Quel est votre nom?
Qu'est-ce qui ne va pas?
Avez-vous déjà eu les oreillons, etc.? *(Other illnesses).* **Quand?**
Prenez-vous des antibiotiques? des vitamines? etc.
À quoi êtes-vous allergique?
Êtes-vous vacciné(e) contre le tétanos? la poliomyélite? etc.
Est-ce que votre tension est normale? élevée? basse?
Quel est votre groupe sanguin? *(What is your blood type?)* Possible responses include: **O, AB, A, B, Rhésus positif** and **Rhésus négatif.**

You may wish to place your completed medical record with your passport and other identification papers, so that you will have this important information with you on any future trips to French-speaking areas.

De quelle couleur sont vos cheveux et vos yeux?

Adjectives:
Physical Traits

Il ne faut pas juger les gens sur la mine. | Do not judge people on their appearance.

Physical description vocabulary has many uses: obtaining or replacing identification papers (including lost or stolen passports), having your hair styled to your specifications at the beauty parlor or barber shop, filing a description of a possible culprit, gossiping, making small talk, and giving compliments.

De quelle couleur sont vos cheveux et vos yeux?

Réponse: • Mes cheveux sont _____ et mes yeux sont _____.[1]

EXEMPLE: *Mes cheveux sont blonds et mes yeux sont bruns.*

Direct substitution of the hair and eye color adjectives from these lists into the given response formats will allow immediate and correct conversational self-expression. No grammatical manipulation is necessary.[2]

Hair color
argentés silver
blancs white
blonds blond
bruns brown, dark brown
châtains chestnut

châtain clair *(invariable)* light brown
châtain foncé *(invariable)* dark brown
gris gray
noirs black
roux red

Eye color
bleus blue
bruns brown
brun clair *(invariable)* hazel
brun foncé *(invariable)* dark brown

gris gray
marron *(invariable)* chestnut
noirs black
verts green

Springboards for Conversation

Ask your classmates these personalized questions. Answer formats are provided.

1. De quelle couleur sont vos yeux?
   • Mes yeux sont _____.
   • J'ai les yeux _____.

2. De quelle couleur sont vos cheveux?
   • Mes cheveux sont _____.
   • J'ai les cheveux _____.

1. What color are your hair and eyes? My hair is _____ and my eyes are _____.
2. You can also say **J'ai les cheveux** _____ **et j'ai les yeux** _____. (*My hair is _____ and my eyes are _____.*) This is a more general form of self-description. We have comparable expressions in English: "My eyes are brown" and "I have brown eyes."

Récapitulation

How much can you recall about your classmates and instructor?

1. De quelle couleur sont les yeux du professeur? de Monsieur...? de Madame...? de Mademoiselle...? etc.
   • Ses yeux sont _____.
   • Il/Elle a les yeux _____.

2. De quelle couleur sont les cheveux du professeur? de Monsieur...? de Madame...? de Mademoiselle...? etc.
   • Ses cheveux sont _____.
   • Il/Elle a les cheveux _____.

3. Qui dans la classe a les yeux bleus, marron, etc.? Qui d'autre? C'est tout?
   • Monsieur/Madame/Mademoiselle... a les yeux _____.
   • Moi, j'ai les yeux _____.
   • Le professeur a les yeux _____.
   • Tout le monde a les yeux _____.
   • Personne.

4. Qui dans la classe a les cheveux blonds, bruns, etc.? Qui d'autre? C'est tout?
   • Monsieur/Madame/Mademoiselle... a les cheveux _____.
   • Moi, j'ai les cheveux _____.
   • Le professeur a les cheveux _____.
   • Tout le monde a les cheveux _____.
   • Personne.

Remarques

1. Since **les cheveux** *(hair)* is plural in French, adjectives describing hair are plural: **cheveux blonds.**
2. **Je suis chauve** means "I am bald."
3. **Je suis blond(e), brun(e)** means "I am blond, brunette." *Note:* **Je suis gris(e)** means "I'm tipsy" *(colloquial).*
4. Pronunciation:
   blonds [blɔ̃]   blancs [blɑ̃]
   cheveux [ʃ ə vø]   chevaux *(horses)* [ʃ ə vo]
5. The singular of **les yeux** is **un œil.**

Expansion

The **Expansion** can be used for partners or group conversation and for oral or written composition. Answer formats are provided. (*Note:* When using the vocabulary of this lesson to describe others, keep in mind: **Toute vérité n'est pas bonne à dire.)**

Hair qualities and styles

1. Avez-vous les cheveux _____? (Vos cheveux sont-ils _____?)

bouclés curly   **frisés** curly
courts short   **gras** oily
dépeignés tousled, uncombed, mussed up   **longs** long
   ondulés wavy
   raides straight
emmêlés tangled   **sales** dirty
en désordre mussed up   **secs** dry
fins fine

• J'ai les cheveux _____. (Mes cheveux sont _____.)

2. Avez-vous _____?

une barbe beard   **une moustache** moustache
un chignon knot
une coiffure à la mode stylish hairdo   **des nattes** braids
   des pattes sideburns
une frange bangs   **une queue de cheval** ponytail

• J'ai _____.
• Je n'ai pas de _____.[3]

3. Portez-vous _____?

une perruque wig   **la raie à gauche** part on the left
un postiche hairpiece
la raie à droite part on the right   **la raie au milieu** part in the middle

• Je porte _____.
• Je ne porte pas de _____.[3]

Eyeglasses

4. Portez-vous _____?

des lunettes (*f*) eyeglasses
des verres de contact (*m*) contact lenses
des lunettes de soleil (*f*) sunglasses

• Je porte _____.
• Je ne porte pas de _____.[3]

Height

5. Êtes-vous _____?

grand(e) tall
petit(e) short
de taille moyenne of average height
assez grand(e)/petit(e) rather tall/short

• Je suis _____.

3. **Un, une,** and **des** become **de** after **ne... pas.**

6. Êtes-vous plus grand(e) que votre
   voisin(e) de droite? que votre voisin(e) de
   gauche? que... *(your classmates)?* que le
   professeur?
   • Je suis plus grand(e) que _____.
   • Je suis moins grand(e) que _____.
   • Je suis aussi grand(e) que _____.
   • Je suis plus/moins petit(e) que _____.

Other physical traits
7. Êtes-vous _____?

adorable adorable
athlétique athletic
beau handsome
belle beautiful
bien habillé(e) well
   dressed
bien proportionné(e)
   well proportioned
(bien) soigné(e) well
   groomed
chic stylish
costaud(e) husky

distingué(e)
   distinguished looking
élégant(e) elegant
fort(e) strong, large
fragile fragile
gros(se) fat
joli(e) pretty
laid(e) ugly
magnifique magnificent
maigre thin
mignon(ne) cute

mince thin
musclé(e) having
   muscles
potelé(e) chubby
ravissant(e) ravishing
séduisant(e) seductive
sensationnel(le)
   sensational
souriant(e) smiling
superbe superb
svelte slender

• Je suis _____.

Vocabulaire utile

The following phrases are frequently requested by students using the descriptive conversations of this **Entracte**.

Oui. Yes.
C'est ça. That's right.
D'accord. I agree.
Vous avez raison. You're right.
Dans le temps j'avais... In the past I had. . .
Ah non! No!

Ce n'est pas juste. That's not accurate.
Vous avez tort. You're wrong.
J'ai les yeux _____, pas _____! I have _____ eyes, not
   _____!
J'ai les cheveux _____, pas _____! I have _____ hair, not
   _____!

You may also wish to use some of these modifiers:

plus ou moins more or less
un peu a little

assez rather
très very

trop too
pas assez not enough

Height and Weight.   In many French-speaking countries, the metric system is used. It is useful to be able to talk about height and weight using the metric system in real-life situations, such as obtaining medical care, purchasing clothes (for yourself or for others), buying food, mailing packages, and so on. Practice using metric measurements in the following conversations regarding height and weight.

> —Combien faites-vous en mètres et en centimètres? How tall are you in
> meters and centimeters?
> —Je fais ＿＿ mètre ＿＿.
> *ou:* —Je mesure ＿＿ mètre ＿＿.
>
> > EXEMPLE: *Je fais un mètre soixante.*

> —Combien pesez-vous en kilos? How much do you weigh in kilograms?
> —Je pèse à peu près *(about)* ＿＿ kilos.
>
> > EXEMPLE: *Je pèse à peu près quarante-cinq*
> > *kilos.*

To use feet and inches, pounds and ounces, say:
—Combien faites-vous en pieds et en pouces?
—Je fais ＿＿ pieds ＿＿ pouces.
—Combien pesez-vous en livres?
—Je pèse à peu près ＿＿ livres.

Some metric equivalents:	
5 pieds	= 1,50 mètres
5 pieds 3 pouces	= 1,60 mètres
5 pieds 6 pouces	= 1,68 mètres
5 pieds 9 pouces	= 1,75 mètres
6 pieds	= 1,83 mètres
6 pieds 2 pouces	= 1,88 mètres
Note: 1 inch = 2.54 centimeters.	

Some metric equivalents:
100 livres = 45 kilogrammes
120 livres = 54 kilogrammes
140 livres = 63 kilogrammes
160 livres = 73 kilogrammes
180 livres = 81 kilogrammes
200 livres = 91 kilogrammes
Note: 1 pound = .45 kilos

LANGUAGE AND CULTURE

BEAUTÉ DES CHEVEUX

Chez le coiffeur. *(At the barbershop/ beauty parlor.)* The following terms will prove useful for visits to the barbershop or beauty parlor. Simply precede any of these terms with the expression: **Je voudrais...** *(I would like).* For example: **Je voudrais une coupe, s'il vous plaît.** *(I'd like a haircut, please.)*
Je voudrais...

un shampooing		une mise en plis	set
shampoo		une décoloration	
un rinçage	tint	bleach	
un brushing	blow dry	une permanente	
une manucure	manicure	permanent	

Regarding your haircut, you may wish to specify: **Laissez-les assez longs. Ne les coupez pas trop courts.** *(Remember:* les refers to les cheveux, in the plural.)

And for the men: **Je voudrais me faire raser.** *(I'd like a shave.)* **Taillez-moi la barbe et la moustache, s'il vous plaît.** *(Trim my beard and moustache.)*

Borrowed words. English shows the influence of French styles in many borrowed words: **soigné** *(well groomed),* **magnifique, extraordinaire, élégant, distingué, chic** *(stylish),* **bouffant** *(puffed hairstyle),* and **toupée** (which is spelled **toupet** in French and means a lock of hair).

COLOREZ VOS CHEVEUX

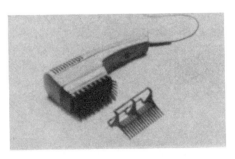

LE SECHE CHEVEUX BABYLISS

Synthèse

A. **Faites le portrait de...** Describe the people shown in these photos.

Monsieur X

Madame X

Monsieur et Madame Y

B. **Faites votre autoportrait.** *(Describe yourself.)*

• Je suis _____.   • Je n'ai pas de _____.
• Je ne suis pas _____.   • Je porte _____.
• J'ai _____.   • Je ne porte pas de _____.

(Note: **Un, une,** and **des** become **de** after **ne... pas.***)*

C. **Faites le portrait du professeur.**

• Il/Elle a _____.   • Il/Elle n'est pas _____.
• Il/Elle n'a pas de _____.   • Je le/la trouve _____. *(I find him/*
• Il/Elle porte _____.   *her to be _____.)*
• Il/Elle ne porte pas de _____.   • Je trouve qu'il/qu'elle est _____.
• Il/Elle est _____.

D. **Faites le portrait de...** Faites le portrait de votre voisin(e) de gauche *(classmate on your left)*, de votre voisin(e) de droite *(classmate on your right)*, de Madame/ Mademoiselle/Monsieur... *(classmates)*.

• Il/Elle a _____.   • Je le/la trouve _____.
• Il/Elle porte _____.   • Je trouve qu'il/qu'elle est _____.
• Il/Elle est _____.   • Il/Elle n'est pas _____.

Projet

Photographs. Use the vocabulary of this lesson to describe a picture of someone in detail. You may wish to use a magazine or newspaper photo, a snapshot you have on hand, or even a picture you have drawn.

Activités: Learning by Doing

A. **Giving and Accepting Compliments.** Circulate around the classroom and compliment your classmates and instructor using vocabulary from this lesson:

EXEMPLES: *Vous avez (Tu as) de très beaux yeux.*
Vos yeux sont très jolis.
J'aime bien votre (ta) coiffure.
Votre (ta) coiffure est très à la mode (stylish).
Je vous (te) trouve magnifique, superbe, ravissant(e), etc.

To accept a compliment you can say:

Ah oui? Really?

Vraiment? Truly?

Vous trouvez (Tu trouves)? Do you think so?

Vous êtes (Tu es) bien aimable. You're very kind.

Vous êtes (Tu es) très gentil(le). You're very kind.

Vous me flattez. You flatter me.

Je suis confus(e). I'm overwhelmed.

Je rougis! I'm blushing!

Oh là là! Oh dear!

Note cultural differences in the manner in which compliments are offered and accepted. How do they differ from your own instinctive responses?

B.   **Photographs.**   Bring to class photographs of family or friends. Describe the people shown in the photos, using the vocabulary of this **Entracte.** For example: **Voici ma mère. Elle est très belle, n'est-ce pas? Elle a les cheveux noirs et longs. Ses yeux sont bruns,** etc.

«On va au cinéma ce soir?»

On Fixe Un Rendez-vous

Making a Date

Quand le chat n'y est pas, les souris dansent.

When the cat's away, the mice will play.

DIALOGUE

This **Dialogue** presents vocabulary for making plans and for extending or accepting invitations. This vocabulary is also useful for expressing personal interests regarding a range of activities. Vocabulary blocks within this **Dialogue** offer options for personalization regarding your own preferences in entertainment. They also provide possibilities for modification to suit a variety of real-life situations involving making plans with another person.

On Fixe un Rendez-vous	Making a Date
VOTRE AMI(E): Aimeriez-vous aller	YOUR FRIEND: Would you like to go
au cinéma	to the movies
dans une boîte de nuit	to a nightclub
dans un cabaret	to a cabaret
dans une discothèque	to a discotheque
au concert	to a concert
au théâtre	to the theater
à une soirée	to a party
danser	dancing
déjeuner au restaurant	have lunch in a restaurant
dîner au restaurant	have dinner in a restaurant
voir une exposition au musée	see an exhibit at the museum
prendre un verre	have a drink (*literally:* take a glass)
ce soir?	tonight?
demain soir	tomorrow night
dimanche après-midi	Sunday afternoon
la semaine prochaine	next week
le 12 avril	April 12th
le week-end du 12	the weekend of the 12th
VOUS: **Avec plaisir.**	YOU: With pleasure.
(Bien) volontiers.	Fine. Gladly.
C'est très gentil!	You are very kind.
Oui, je veux bien.	Yes, I'd like to.
Je regrette, mais je ne peux pas.	I'm sorry, but I can't.
Je vous remercie, mais je ne suis pas libre.	Thank you, but I'm not free.
Je suis désolé(e), mais je suis occupé(e).	I'm very sorry, but I'm busy.
Malheureusement, j'ai déjà un rendez-vous.	Unfortunately, I have a date / an engagement already.
VOTRE AMI(E): Voyons... Qu'est-ce qu'on joue? Aimez-vous **les westerns?**	YOUR FRIEND: Let's see . . . What's playing? Do you like **westerns?**
les documentaires	documentaries
les films d'aventures	adventure films
les films étrangers (doublés, sous-titrés)	foreign films (dubbed, subtitled)
les films d'amour	love films

les films d'épouvante	horror films
les films d'horreur	horror films
les films policiers	detective films
les films de science-fiction	science-fiction films

VOUS: Franchement, je n'aime pas tellement les westerns. Je préfère...

VOTRE AMI(E): Aimez-vous la musique classique?

VOUS: Oui, beaucoup.

VOTRE AMI(E): Alors, nous irons à un concert ensemble. Je viendrai vous chercher vers sept heures.

VOUS: D'accord. Merci beaucoup. **À plus tard.**

À ce soir.	tonight
À demain soir.	tomorrow night
À dimanche après-midi.	Sunday afternoon
À la semaine prochaine.	next week

YOU: Frankly, I don't particularly like westerns. I prefer . . .

YOUR FRIEND: Do you like classical music?

YOU: Yes, a lot.

YOUR FRIEND: So, we will go to a concert together. I'll come pick you up around seven o'clock.

YOU: OK. Thanks a lot. (See you) later.

Phrases à retenir

Memorizing these phrases from the **Dialogue** will help assure fluency in a variety of real-life situations involving extending or accepting invitations.

1. Aimeriez-vous aller au cinéma ce soir?
2. Avec plaisir.
3. Je regrette, mais je ne peux pas.
4. Aimez-vous les films policiers?
5. Franchement, je n'aime pas tellement les westerns.
6. Oui, beaucoup.
7. Je viendrai vous chercher vers sept heures.
8. D'accord.
9. Merci beaucoup.
10. À plus tard.

DIALOGUE EXERCISES

The following exercises provide oral and written practice in using the vocabulary and basic sentence patterns of the **Dialogue: On fixe un rendez-vous.** These exercises use *only* vocabulary and structures presented in the making a date **Dialogue.** They do not require familiarity with any other portions of this chapter.

Exercices d'application

A.   **Invitations: Aimeriez-vous aller au cinéma ce soir?**   Invite a classmate to do one or more of the activities in the **Dialogue** that you would really like to do. Classmates will accept or refuse depending on their schedules. You may use **ce soir, demain soir,** or any of the other time options in the **Dialogue** vocabulary blocks. (You may wish to review **Entracte 3:** Telling Time or **Entracte 4:** Dates.)

B.   **Opinions: Aimez-vous...?**   Select two or three forms of entertainment from the **Dialogue** that appeal to you. Ask classmates whether or not they enjoy these activities. For example: **Aimez-vous le théâtre? le cinéma? Aimez-vous voir les expositions au musée? dîner au restaurant?** etc. Possible responses include: **Oui, beaucoup. Non, pas du tout. Je n'aime pas tellement... Je n'aime pas beaucoup... Je préfère...**

C.   **Dialogue responses.**   What could you respond to each of the following? Use sentences and phrases taken directly from the **Dialogue.**

1. Aimeriez-vous aller au cinéma avec moi ce soir?
2. Voulez-vous aller au théâtre ce soir?
3. Qu'est-ce qu'on joue?
4. Aimez-vous les westerns?
5. Nous irons au théâtre ensemble.
6. Je viendrai vous chercher vers sept heures.

D.   **Review.**   What do you say . . .

1. to invite someone out to dinner?
2. to invite someone to have a drink with you?
3. to accept an invitation?
4. to refuse an invitation?
5. to indicate that you have a previous engagement?
6. to ask someone if he or she likes foreign films?
7. when you really like something very much?
8. to tell someone what time you will come get him or her?

Improvisation à deux *(Exercice oral)*

E.   Use the vocabulary block options and the basic sentence structures of the **Dialogue** to improvise a dialogue with a classmate. One of you will extend an invitation, and the other will accept or refuse as appropriate.

À Vous le choix *(Exercices écrits)*

F. Write a six- to eight-line dialogue for each of the following situations, selecting appropriate phrases from the initial **Dialogue** of this chapter.

1. You make plans to do something with an old friend.
2. You make plans to do something with a new acquaintance.
3. You try to make plans with someone who does not share many of your interests.

Conversations

G. Ask your classmates these personalized questions. When two or more responses are possible, alternate answer formats are offered. Select the option that best applies to you personally. Do not limit your responses simply to those suggestions offered in these questions. Use the inclusive vocabulary options provided in the **Dialogue**.

1. Aimeriez-vous aller au cinéma ce soir? au théâtre? dans une boîte de nuit? dans une discothèque? au restaurant? au musée? à un concert?
   • Oui, ce soir j'aimerais bien aller _____.

2. Qu'est-ce que vous aimez faire? aller au cinéma? aller au théâtre? voir des expositions au musée? dîner au restaurant? déjeuner avec des amis? prendre un verre avec des amis? jouer au tennis? voir les films étrangers? écouter de la musique? inviter des amis à dîner?
   • J'aime _____.

3. Qu'est-ce que vous n'aimez pas faire? voir des expositions au musée? jouer au tennis? aller dans une boîte de nuit? etc.
   • Je n'aime pas _____.

4. Qu'est-ce que vous préférez? aller au théâtre ou au cinéma? dîner chez vous ou au restaurant? aller dans une boîte de nuit ou à une soirée? voir un film doublé ou sous-titré? la musique classique ou le jazz? les films policiers ou les films d'amour?
   • Je préfère _____.

5. Où allez-vous ce soir? dans une boîte de nuit? au cinéma? au théâtre? au musée? au restaurant? dans une discothèque? à un concert?
   • Je vais _____ ce soir.
   • Je ne sors pas ce soir.

6. Où êtes-vous allé(e) hier soir? au cinéma? au théâtre? au restaurant? etc.
   • Je suis allé(e) _____ hier soir.
   • Je ne suis pas sorti(e) hier soir.

7. Aimez-vous les films policiers? les films d'amour? les films de science-fiction? les films etrangers? les films d'epouvante? les films d'aventures? les westerns? les documentaires?
   • Oui, beaucoup.
   • Non, pas du tout.
   • Je n'aime pas tellement…
   • Je préfère…

H.   **Review.**   What have you learned about your classmates from these **Conversations?**

EXEMPLES: *Marie va au cinéma ce soir.*
            Madame Smith aime aller au théâtre.
            Paul est allé au concert hier soir.

Borrowed words.   English has borrowed the word **rendez-vous** from the French. In English, it refers to a date, often with romantic implications. In French, however, the term **rendez-vous** is very straightforward. It is used to mean an appointment of any sort, such as one with the dentist, the doctor, a client, a business associate, and so on. Another related word borrowed from the French is **tête-a-tête.** Meaning, literally, "head-to-head," it refers to an intimate conversation between (or meeting of) two people.

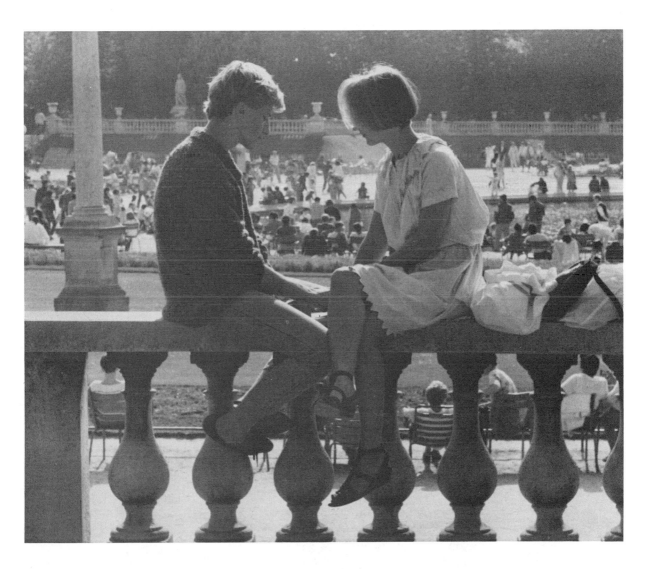

LANGUAGE AND CULTURE

VERBES IRRÉGULIERS: sortir, partir

➤
sortir to go out **partir** to depart, to leave		

LE PRÉSENT:	je **sors**	je **pars**
	tu **sors**	tu **pars**
	il/elle/on **sort**	il/elle/on **part**
	nous **sortons**	nous **partons**
	vous **sortez**	vous **partez**
	ils/elles **sortent**	ils/elles **partent**

LE PASSÉ COMPOSÉ:		
	je **suis sorti(e)**	je **suis parti(e)**

LA BASE DU FUTUR ET DU CONDITIONNEL:		
	sortir-	**partir-**

1. **Sortir** and **partir** are similarly conjugated.
2. **Sortir** and **partir** are considered verbs of "coming and going." They are conjugated with **être** in the **passé composé**.
3. When **sortir** is used transitively (that is, with a direct object), it means "to take out" and is conjugated with **avoir. Avez-vous sorti la voiture?** *(Have you taken out the car?)*
4. **Sortir** followed by **de** means "to leave" in the sense of "to go out of" or "to get out of":

Pourquoi **est-il sorti de** la classe?	Why did he leave (go out of) the class?
À quelle heure **sortez-vous du** bureau?	What time do you leave (get out of) the office?

5. The verb **quitter** is used with a direct object to mean "to leave" in the sense of "to go away from a person or place."

À quelle heure **avez-vous quitté** la maison?	What time did you leave the house?
Ne me **quittez** pas!	Don't leave me!

6. **Partir** means "to leave" in the sense of "to depart." **Partir pour** means "to leave for."

Je vais partir demain.	I'm going to leave tomorrow.
Il est parti pour le Canada hier soir.	He left for Canada last night.

7. The verb **laisser** means "to leave behind."

    J'ai laissé mon livre à la maison.   I left my book at home.

Exercice d'application: sortir and partir

Questions with *sortir* and *partir*.   Answer these questions yourself. Then, ask your classmates. (You may wish to use the **tu** form of address with your classmates.)

1. Sortez-vous (Sors-tu) souvent? Avec qui? avec des amis? avec un(e) ami(e)? avec votre (ta) femme ou (ton) mari? Où allez-vous (vas-tu)? au cinéma? au restaurant? au bar?
2. Sortez-vous le week-end prochain? Avec qui? Où irez-vous?
3. Êtes-vous (Es-tu) sorti(e) hier soir? samedi dernier? vendredi dernier? Avec qui? Où êtes-vous allé(e)?
4. Aimeriez-vous (Aimerais-tu) sortir ce soir? Avec qui? Où aimeriez-vous aller?
5. Sortez-vous ce soir?
6. Est-ce que vous partez (tu pars) pour la France demain? Est-ce que votre (ton) professeur de français part pour la France demain?

STRUCTURES

Structure 1: L'Imparfait

FORMATION

The **imparfait** of all regular and irregular verbs (except **être**) is formed by dropping the letters **-ons** from the **nous** form of the present tense and adding the appropriate endings: **-ais, -ais, -ait, -ions, -iez, -aient** (the same endings as those used for the conditional tense):

INFINITIF	LE PRÉSENT	LA BASE DE L'IMPARFAIT
aimer	nous aim**ons**	**aim-**
finir	nous finiss**ons**	**finiss-**
attendre	nous attend**ons**	**attend-**
avoir	nous av**ons**	**av-**
prendre	nous pren**ons**	**pren-**

IMPARFAIT		
Verbes en **-er**	Verbes en **-ir**	Verbes en **-re**
aimer	**finir**	**attendre**
j'aim**ais** tu aim**ais** il/elle aim**ait** nous aim**ions** vous aim**iez** ils/elles aim**aient**	je finiss**ais** tu finiss**ais** il/elle finiss**ait** nous finiss**ions** vous finiss**iez** ils/elles finiss**aient**	j'attend**ais** tu attend**ais** il/elle attend**ait** nous attend**ions** vous attend**iez** ils/elles attend**aient**

être
j'**étais** tu **étais** il/elle **était** nous **étions** vous **étiez** ils/elles **étaient**

USES

The **imparfait** *usually means was* _____*ing or used to* _____ *(I was going, we were talking, I used to like, etc.).*

1. To express an action that was going on in the past at the time when another action took place:

J'allais au cinéma quand je l'ai rencontré.	I was going to the movies when I met him.
Il faisait beau lorsque j'ai quitté la maison.	It was nice weather when I left home.

2. To express repeated or habitual actions in the past:

J'allais au cinéma chaque samedi.	I used to go to the movies every Saturday.
Je regardais beaucoup la télévision.	I used to watch/I watched (*habitual action*) television a lot.

   But:

J'ai regardé la télévision hier soir.	I watched (*not habitual action*) television last night.

3. With the verbs **avoir** and **être** in sentences that relate descriptions, age, or time:

ON FIXE UN RENDEZ-VOUS

Descriptions

J'avais soif.	I was thirsty.
J'étais malade.	I was sick.
Il était très content.	He was very happy.
Il y avait beaucoup de monde.	There were a lot of people.
J'avais de l'argent.	I had some money.
Il avait l'air fatigué.	He looked tired.

Age

Il avait vingt ans.	He was twenty (years old).
Il était jeune.	He was young.

Time

Il était trois heures.	It was 3 o'clock.
C'était en avril.	It was in April.

But:

Avoir and **être** are used in the **passé composé** to indicate what has happened in the past. For example:

J'ai eu un accident.	I had an accident.
J'ai été en France.	I've been to France.

4. With verbs expressing attitudes, feelings, or beliefs. The following verbs and expressions tend to be used in the **imparfait** rather than in the **passé composé:**

croire to believe, to think	**Je croyais** que vous étiez au cinéma.
	I thought you were at the movies.
penser to think	**Je pensais** que vous étiez en France.
	I thought that you were in France.
espérer to hope	**J'espérais** vous voir à l'exposition.
	I was hoping to see you at the exhibit.
vouloir to wish, to want	**Je voulais** aller au cinéma.
	I wanted to go to the movies.
pouvoir to be able, can	**Je ne pouvais pas** aller au théâtre.
	I wasn't able to (I couldn't) go to the theater.
savoir to know	**Je ne savais pas!**
	I didn't know!
avoir peur to be afraid	**J'avais peur** de sortir.
	I was afraid to go out.
avoir envie to feel like	**J'avais envie** de voir un bon film.
	I felt like seeing a good film.
avoir l'intention to intend	**J'avais l'intention** d'étudier un peu.
	I was intending/I intended to study a little.

These verbs and expressions are used in the **passé composé,** however, to relate what has happened in the past.

J'ai eu peur.   I became frightened.

Exercices d'application: L'Imparfait

A. **Que faisiez-vous hier soir à dix heures?** What were you doing last night at ten o'clock? Answer using **l'imparfait.** Possibilities include: **je jouais aux cartes, je regardais un film à la télévision, j'écoutais la radio, j'écoutais de la musique, je dînais avec des amis, j'étudiais, je dormais, je parlais au téléphone.**

B. **Il regardait la télévision.** If the preceding exercise has been used orally in class, review what you have learned about your classmates.

EXEMPLES: *Marc dormait.*
             Marie jouait aux cartes.
             Monsieur Smith regardait la télévision.

C. **Je regardais beaucoup la télévision.** What did you use to do a lot that you rarely do now? Possibilities include: **je sortais beaucoup, je dansais, je partais en vacances, j'écoutais de la musique, j'invitais des amis, j'allais souvent au cinéma, je regardais beaucoup la télévision,** etc.

D. **Quand vous étiez jeune...** What did you use to be like? Answer the following questions about yourself. Then, ask your classmates. Use **l'imparfait** in all responses. **Quand vous étiez jeune...**

1. qui était votre acteur préféré? qui était votre actrice préférée?
2. qui était votre chanteur préféré? qui était votre chanteuse préférée?
3. aviez-vous beaucoup d'amis?
4. comment s'appelait votre meilleur(e) ami(e)?
5. où habitiez-vous?
6. avec qui sortiez-vous?
7. quels programmes regardiez-vous à la télévision?
8. alliez-vous souvent au cinéma?
9. vouliez-vous être professeur?
10. aviez-vous une collection de disques?
11. étiez-vous timide?
12. de quoi aviez-vous peur? du noir *(of the dark)?* de vos professeurs?
13. croyiez-vous au Père Noël?
14. preniez-vous des leçons de piano? de guitare?
15. aimiez-vous étudier?
16. travailliez-vous?

E. **Je regardais la télévision.** Imagine that you were home last night watching television. Suddenly you heard a strange noise. Tell what happened, putting the following sentences into the correct verb tenses: **l'imparfait** or the **passé composé. Hier soir...**

1. Je regarde la télévision.
2. Il est neuf heures.
3. Je suis seul(e).
4. Le programme n'est pas très intéressant.
5. J'entends un bruit étrange.
6. Je vais à la porte.
7. Je vois un homme.
8. Il est jeune.
9. Il a à peu près *(about)* vingt ans.
10. Il a une moustache.
11. Il a l'air bizarre.
12. Je ferme la porte.
13. J'ai peur.
14. Je téléphone à la police.
15. L'homme part.
16. La police arrive.
17. Je n'ai plus peur.

Structure 2: L'Imparfait Used in Conditional Sentences

1. When the main clause of a sentence is in the conditional tense (would), the **si** or *if* clause must be in the **imparfait.** (See Chapter 6 to review the formation of the conditional tense.)

Si j'étais libre, **nous pourrions** aller au cinéma.	If I were free, we could go to the movies.
Si je savais bien jouer aux cartes, je jouerais avec vous.	If I really knew how to play cards, I would play with you.
Je le ferais si je pouvais.	I would do it if I could.

2. **Si** + the **imparfait** may also mean "How about...?"

| Si nous allions au cinéma ce soir? | How about going to the movies tonight? |

Exercices d'application: L'Imparfait Used in Conditional Sentences

F. **Si j'étais vous, je ne sortirais pas.** Someone is telling you his or her plans. React to each of the following statements. Say that, if it were you, you would not do it.

MODÈLE: Je sors ce soir.
Si j'étais vous (If I were you), *je ne sortirais pas ce soir.*

1. Je pars pour la France demain.
2. Je regarde la télévision.
3. Je reste à la maison.
4. J'invite mes amis au restaurant.
5. Je vais à un concert.
6. Je dîne au restaurant.

G. **Que feriez-vous si je vous donnais un coup de pied?** Ask your classmates what they would do if you were to give them a kick. Possible responses include: **je hurlerais** (yell), **je pleurerais** (cry), **je crierais «Aïe!»** (yell "Ouch!"), **je me fâcherais** (get angry), **je vous le rendrais** (kick you back), **je vous donnerais un coup de poing** (punch you), **je le dirais à ma mère** (tell my mother on you), **je vous dirais que vous êtes méchant(e)** (call you mean), **je vous donnerais une claque/une gifle** (slap you), **je vous accuserais de brutalité** (accuse you of brutality), **je vous demanderais pourquoi** (ask you why), **je serais stupéfait(e)** (be stunned), **je vous mordrais** (bite you), **je téléphonerais à la police** (call the police).

EXEMPLE: *Si vous me donniez un coup de pied, je me fâcherais.*

H. **Si je vous embrassais, que feriez-vous?** Now ask your classmates what they would do if you were to give them a kiss. Possible responses, in addition to those given in the preceding exercise, include: **je vous le rendrais** (kiss you back), **je rougirais** (blush), **je sourirais** (smile), **je serais content(e)** (be happy).

EXEMPLE: *Si vous m'embrassiez, je rougirais.*

Synthèse

L'Officiel des Spectacles.   Here are some listings from **L'Officiel des Spectacles,** a weekly magazine that provides information on what is happening in and around Paris: films, plays, concerts, exhibitions, television programs, and so on. Using vocabulary from this chapter, express reactions to these listings. You may wish to use a dialogue format for a conversation between you and a friend as you make plans based on these listings. You may wish to select some offerings of special interest to you and list them, etc.

PRONONCIATION

1. Sound (Phonetic Symbol): [a]

SPELLING:	**a, à**
ENGLISH SOUND RESEMBLED:	Halfway between the vowel sounds of *cat* and *cot*
PRONUNCIATION:	This sound is often referred to as *front a*, since it is produced toward the front of the mouth. Do not let the sound glide as in English. Keep it short and abrupt.

EXAMPLES FROM THIS CHAPTER:

l<u>a</u>   d'<u>a</u>ccord   <u>a</u>mi   ch<u>a</u>t
<u>a</u>ller   Br<u>a</u>vo!   cel<u>a</u>

Note: The spellings **oi, oî, oy** contain the vowel sound [a] along with the semi-vowel [w]. Examples from this lesson: b<u>oî</u>te [bwat], v<u>oy</u>ons [vwaj ɔ̃], joie [ʒwa], s<u>oi</u>r [swar].

2. Sound (Phonetic Symbol) [ɑ]

SPELLING:	**â, ât, as, a (+ ille), ah** (only in **Ah!**)
ENGLISH SOUND RESEMBLED:	Vowel sound in words *car* and *hot*
PRONUNCIATION:	Since this sound [ɑ] is produced farther back in the mouth than the vowel sound [a], it is often referred to as *back a*.
EXAMPLES FROM THIS CHAPTER:	th<u>é</u>âtre p<u>a</u>s je p<u>a</u>sserai

Note: Although we have distinguished here between the vowel sounds [a] and [ɑ], there is a growing tendency in contemporary French to ignore this distinction. An intermediary vowel sound is frequently employed for both cases.

Projet

What's on T.V.?   *(Exercice oral ou écrit)* Opposite is a typical French television schedule. Which broadcasts do you feel you might be interested in viewing?

Activités: Learning by Doing

A.   **Making a date.**   Use the vocabulary of the chapter **Dialogue** to make a date with a classmate to go to the theater. You will note that the **Dialogue** presents vocabulary for rather formal invitations. **Tu** and **on** are used conversationally between close friends. In this case, **on** means "we."

Informal invitations

On va au théâtre?
On sort ensemble?
Tu es libre ce soir?
Tu veux aller au théâtre avec moi?
Tu peux aller au théâtre avec moi?

Tu as envie d'aller *(feel like going)* **au théâtre?**
On peut se voir ce soir?
J'aimerais aller au théâtre ce soir. Et toi?

Informal acceptance

Ce soir? D'accord. C'est entendu *(agreed).*
C'est une bonne idée.
Ah oui!
Bon!

Pourquoi pas?
Formidable!
Fantastique!
Chic, alors!

Informal Refusal

Je n'ai pas envie.
Ça ne me dit rien. (Literally: *That says nothing to me.*)

C'est impossible.
Non, je ne peux pas.
Non, je me sens fatigué(e).

Setting the time and meeting place

On se retrouve *(we'll meet)* où et à quelle heure?

On se retrouve devant l'entrée?

Je passe te prendre? *(I'll come get you?)*

Tu passes me prendre?

B.   **Going out.**   After you have made a date to go to the theater with a classmate, buy tickets from a student ticket seller. Be seated by a student usher. Skits will be performed. (These can be based on the **Improvisations à deux** and **À Vous le choix** sections of this or any chapter covered so far in class.) In addition to the vocabulary presented above, the following phrases will prove useful for this activity.

To purchase tickets

Y a-t-il des places pour ce soir?   Are there any seats left for tonight?

Est-ce complet?   Is it full (sold out)?

Je voudrais une place à l'orchestre/au balcon.   I would like a seat in the orchestra/ balcony.

C'est combien?   How much is it?

To be seated by the usher[1]

Votre billet, s'il vous plaît.   Your ticket, please.

Par ici, s'il vous plaît.   This way, please.

After the performance

Bravo! Bis!   Hurrah! Encore!

Merci pour cette soirée.   Thank you for this evening.

C'était très agréable.   It was very pleasant.

Signs will help transform the classroom into a realistic setting for this activity. These can easily be prepared as part of the activity itself: **Théâtre, Entrée, Sortie, Orchestre, Balcon, Vestiaire** *(Coat Room),* **Locations** *(Ticket Window),* **Toilettes, Défense de fumer** *(No Smoking),* **Complet.**

---

1. In France, it is customary to tip the usher.

Qu'est-ce que vous portez aujourd'hui?

Clothing, Colors, Materials

L'habit ne fait pas le moine.

Clothes don't make the person.

Knowing the clothing, colors, accessories, and materials vocabulary of this lesson will allow you to shop for clothes, take your clothing to the cleaner's or laundry, buy gifts, give compliments, and discuss what you and others are wearing.

Qu'est-ce que vous portez aujourd'hui?

Réponse: • Je porte _____.[1]

EXEMPLE: *Je porte un tailleur, un chemisier, une ceinture, un bracelet, une montre, un collier et des lunettes.*

Direct substitution of the clothing items as they appear in these lists into the given response formats will allow immediate and correct conversational self-expression. The clothing items and accessories shown here are those most frequently worn to class by students. For additional items, such as beachwear, lingerie, evening wear, and so on, see **Vocabulaire utile,** p. 247.

Items worn above the waist
un blouson   jacket
une cape   cape
un chandail   sweater
une chemise   shirt
un chemisier   blouse
un col roulé   turtleneck
un gilet   cardigan, vest
une parka   parka
un pull   pullover
un sweat-shirt   sweatshirt
un tee-shirt   T-shirt
une veste   jacket
une veste de sport   sports jacket

Items worn below the waist
des jeans/un jean   jeans
une jupe   skirt
un pantalon   pants, slacks
des shorts/un short   shorts

Items worn on the head and neck
un chapeau   hat
une écharpe   scarf

Items worn on the hands
des gants (m)   gloves

Items worn over whole body
un complet   men's suit
un imperméable   raincoat
un jogging   jogging outfit
un manteau   coat
un pardessus   overcoat
une robe   dress
un tailleur   woman's suit

Items worn on the legs and feet
des bas (m)   stockings
des bottes (f)   boots
des chaussettes (f)   socks
des chaussures (f)/des souliers (m)   shoes
des sandales (f)   sandals

1. What are you wearing today? I'm wearing _____.

Accessories

une alliance wedding ring
une bague ring
une bague de fiançailles engagement ring
des boucles *(f)* d'oreilles earrings
un bracelet bracelet

une broche brooch
une ceinture belt
un collier necklace
une cravate tie
un foulard scarf (decorative)

des lunettes *(f)* glasses
des lunettes de soleil sunglasses
une montre watch

Colors

beige beige
blanc(he) white
bleu(e) blue
brun(e) brown
crème *(invariable)* cream
écarlate scarlet
grenat *(invariable)* garnet

gris(e) grey
jaune yellow
lie de vin *(invariable)* burgundy
marron *(invariable)* chestnut
mauve mauve
noir(e) black
orange *(invariable)* orange

pourpre purple
rose pink
rouge red
turquoise turquoise
vert(e) green
violet(te) violet

Remarques:

1. Color adjectives agree in number and gender with the nouns they describe.
   La jupe est **verte**. Les souliers sont **bruns**.

2. Color adjectives follow the nouns they describe.
   une jupe **blanche**

3. When adjectives are made compound with **foncé** *(dark)*, **clair** *(light)*, and **vif** *(bright)*, they do not agree in gender or number with the noun they describe.
   La robe est **bleu clair**.
   Note that **marron, crème, grenat, orange** and **lie de vin** are also invariable.

Springboards for Conversation

Ask your classmates these personalized questions. Answer formats are provided. Do not limit your responses simply to those suggestions offered in these questions. Use the inclusive vocabulary options provided in this **Entracte.**

1. Qu'est-ce que vous portez aujourd'hui? Quoi d'autre? C'est tout?
   • Je porte _____.

2. De quelle couleur est votre chemise? votre jupe? votre robe? etc.
   • Mon/Ma _____ est bleu(e)/jaune/orange/ etc.

3. De quelle couleur sont vos jeans? vos chaussettes? etc.
   • Mes _____ sont beiges/jaunes/rouges/etc.

ici
1er étage
chaussures
chemisiers
coordonnés sport
gym et danse
jupes
pulls
fourrures et cuirs

Récapitulation

How much can you recall about your classmates and instructor?

1. Que porte le professeur? Et Monsieur... ?
   Et Madame... ? Et Mademoiselle... ?
   • Il/Elle porte _____.

2. Qui dans la classe porte _____? Qui
   d'autre? C'est tout?
   • Monsieur/Madame/Mademoiselle... porte
     _____.
   • Moi, je porte _____.
   • Le professeur porte _____.
   • Tout le monde porte _____.
   • Personne.

3. De quelle couleur est la chemise de
   Monsieur... ? Et la jupe de Madame... ? Et
   le tailleur de Mademoiselle... ? De quelle
   couleur sont les chaussures de
   Madame...? etc.
   • Le/La _____ de Monsieur/Madame/
     Mademoiselle... est vert(e)/gris(e)/ rouge/
     etc.
   • Les _____ de Monsieur/Madame/
     Mademoiselle... sont blancs(blanches)/
     beiges/noirs(noires)/etc.

«Que porte Monsieur X?»

Clothing sizes. The French use two different terms for size: la taille (used with most articles of clothing) and la pointure (used for shoes, gloves, hats, socks, and stockings). Quelle taille faites-vous (fais-tu)? Quelle pointure faites-vous (fais-tu)? French clothing sizes differ from the American system. Here is a conversion chart, distributed by a large Parisian department store.

Laundromats. Clothing can be brought to a laundromat in France for either washing or drycleaning (nettoyage à sec).

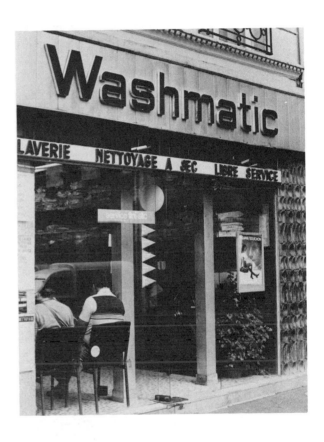

WOMEN'S DRESSES, KNITWEAR & BLOUSES							
French	36N	38N	40N	42N	44N	46N	48N
Eng.	32	34	36	38	40	42	44
Amer.	10	12	14	16	18	20	22
WOMEN'S STOCKINGS							
French	1		2		3	4	5
Eng. Amer.	8 1/2		9		9 1/2	10	10 1/2
MEN'S & WOMEN'S SHOES							
French	36	37	38	39	40	41	42	43
Eng.	3	4	5	6	7	8	9	10
Amer.	5	6	7	7 1/2	8	9	10	10 1/2
MEN'S SUITS							
French	34	36	38	40	42	44	46	48
Eng. Amer.	34	35	36	37	38	39	40	42
MEN'S SHIRTS							
French	36	37	38	39/40	41	42	43	44
Eng. Amer.	14	14 1/2	15	15 1/2	16	16 1/2	17	17 1/2

Borrowed words. The French have influenced American clothing styles, as reflected by our adoption of terms such as négligé, lingerie, and haute couture (high fashion dress design). This influence has worked in reverse, too, as the French have adopted our words for *une parka, des sneakers, un pull-over, un cardigan, un short, un smoking, un sweat-shirt, un tee-shirt, un blazer, des warm-ups* and *un jogging,* to name only a few.

Synthèse

Qu'est-ce qu'ils portent?   What are the people in these photographs wearing? Use complete sentences. You may also wish to give your opinion: **Il/Elle est... à la mode** *(stylish)*, **démodé(e)** *(out of style)*, **chic** *(stylish)*, **élégant(e)**, **ridicule. Il/Elle est bien/mal habillé(e).** *(He/She is well/poorly dressed.)*

Mademoiselle X et Monsieur X

Madame Y

Vocabulaire utile   The following vocabulary will be useful for completing the **Projets** section of this Entracte.

Additional Clothing Items

un smoking dinner jacket, tuxedo
un habit men's fancy dress suit, tails
un maillot de bain bathing suit
un bikini bikini
des shorts, un short a pair of shorts

un nœud papillon bow tie
une chemise de nuit nightgown
un négligé négligée
un peignoir housecoat
un pyjama pyjamas

une robe de chambre housecoat, bathrobe
une robe du soir evening dress
des pantoufles (f) slippers

The "Unmentionables"

une combinaison slip
une culotte underpants
une gaine girdle
une gaine-culotte pantygirdle

un gilet undershirt
un jupon half slip
des porte-jarretières garter belt

un Tee-shirt T-shirt
un slip underpants
un soutien-gorge bra

Materials and Fabrics

coton cotton
caoutchouc rubber
cuir leather
daim suède
dacron dacron
dentelle lace
feutre felt
flanelle flannel

fourrure fur
laine wool
mousseline muslin
nylon nylon
orlon orlon
polyester polyester
rayonne rayon
satin satin

soie silk
stockinet jersey
taffetas taffeta
tissu synthétique synthetic
toile linen
velours velvet
velours côtelé corduroy

Remarques: **En coton** means "made of cotton."
En laine means "made of wool."
Une jupe en laine is "a wool skirt."
Une chemise en coton is "a cotton shirt."

Other Materials

argent silver
bois wood
bronze bronze
cristal taillé cut crystal
cuir leather
cuir verni patent leather

cuivre copper
étain tin
jade jade
laiton brass
métal metal
opale opal

or gold
or blanc white gold
plastique plastic
platine platinum
verre glass

Remarques: **En or** means "made of gold."
En argent means "made of silver."
Un collier en or is "a gold necklace."

Projets

A.   **Your wardrobe.**   List and describe your entire wardrobe. Be as thorough as possible. Look through your closet and/or bureau drawers if necessary. Use color adjectives, materials, and other descriptive terms for each item. For example: **J'ai plusieurs chandails. J'ai un chandail rouge en laine et un chandail vert en orlon.**

B.   **Laundry list.**   Fill out the form below. Which of your clothes *really* need to be cleaned?

<table>
<tr><td colspan="3"></td><td colspan="3">Blanchissage, Nettoyage et Repassage</td></tr>
<tr><td colspan="6">HOTEL BAKOUA MARTINIQUE</td></tr>
<tr><td></td><td></td><td colspan="4">NOM
CHAMBRE   No_____ DATE_____ HEURES____</td></tr>
</table>

Blanchissage, Nettoyage et Repassage

NOM _____

CHAMBRE   No_____ DATE_____ HEURES_____

(Ayez l'obligeance de remplir cette liste avec précision afin que l'on puisse prendre le linge en charge)

A RENDRE

DANS LA JOURNÉE (50% majoration)	POUR DEMAIN	PAS PRESSÉ

RECOMMANDATIONS SPÉCIALES : _____

BLANCHISSAGE MESSIEURS

NOMBRE	CONTRÔLE		FRS	UN	TOTAL
		CHEMISE ORDINAIRE			
		AUTRES CHEMISES			
		CHEMISETTE			
		CHAUSSETTES			
		MAILLOT DE CORPS			
		MOUCHOIR			
		PANTALON			
		PYJAMA			
		SHORT			
		SLIP			

DAMES

NOMBRE	CONTRÔLE		FRS	UN	TOTAL
		BLOUSES			
		CHEMISE DE NUIT			
		COMBINAISON			
		CULOTTE			
		MOUCHOIR			
		PEIGNOIR			
		ROBE			
		SHORT			
		PANTALON			
		JUPE			

NETTOYAGES A SEC MESSIEURS   72 HEURES MINIMUM

NOMBRE	CONTRÔLE		FRS	UN	TOTAL
		COMPLET			
		VESTON			
		PANTALON			
		PARDESSUS			
		VESTE			
		CHANDAIL			
		CRAVATE			
		CHEMISES			

DAMES

NOMBRE	CONTRÔLE		FRS	UN	TOTAL
		ROBE			
		JUPE			
		CORSAGE			
		MANTEAU			

L'HÔTEL NE SE REND PAS RESPONSABLE DES OBJETS DE VALEUR LAISSÉS DANS LES VÊTEMENTS.

C.   **Overnight trip.**   You have to go away this week on an unexpected trip. What will you take with you? You will have to decide first where you are going and what sort of trip it will be. Be realistic. For example, it might be an unexpected business trip to California or New York, a college weekend nearby, a family gathering, and so on.

D. **Photographs.** Look through a current illustrated magazine (French if possible, but any magazine will do). Describe the clothing items worn by the people in the photographs. Include accessories, such as wristwatches, eyeglasses, earrings, etc. Specify colors and materials whenever possible. Alternative: Instead of magazine illustrations use a family photograph or pictures in this textbook.

Activité: Learning by Doing

Giving and receiving compliments. Using the vocabulary of this lesson, compliment your classmates on their apparel. Circulate around the classroom, complimenting everyone you meet on some aspect of his or her appearance. When someone compliments you, be sure to compliment him or her back. Help each other out by suggesting garments: **Comment trouvez-vous** *(what do you think of)* **cette chemise? ces chaussures? cette montre? ce bracelet? ce collier? cette bague? ces boucles d'oreilles? cette jupe? cette robe? cette cravate?** etc.

Some compliments

J'adore votre/vos _____.
J'aime bien votre/vos _____.
J'aime beaucoup votre/vos _____.
Ce/Cette _____ **vous va** *(suits you)* **à merveille!**
Quel(le) joli(e) _____!

Ce/Cette _____ **vous va à la perfection.**
Votre (Vos) _____ **est (sont) joli(e)/ exquis(e)/beau (belle)/magnifique/ adorable/ravissant(e)/élégant(e)/très chic!**

Use intensifiers with adjectives: **si, très, parfaitement, vraiment, absolument.**

Votre robe est absolument magnifique!
Votre cravate va si bien avec votre complet.
Vos chaussures vont vraiment bien avec votre tailleur.

Some typically French responses

Vous trouvez? Do you think so?
Tu trouves? Do you think so?
Vraiment? Really?
Merci. Thank you.
Ah oui, je l'aime bien aussi. I like it too.

Vous me flattez! You flatter me.
Vous êtes très gentil(le). You're very kind.
Vous êtes bien aimable. You're very kind.

Note the cultural differences in the manner in which compliments are offered and accepted. How do they differ from your own instinctive responses?

«Je voudrais louer un appartement.»

Appartement à Louer

Renting an Apartment

Petit à petit, l'oiseau fait son nid.

Rome wasn't built in a day.

DIALOGUE

This **Dialogue** presents vocabulary useful for renting or buying a house or apartment. The vocabulary blocks within this **Dialogue** offer options that will allow you to obtain a place of residence suitable to your own personal needs. They will also permit personalization in describing your current residence and places you have lived in the past. In addition, these blocks provide possibilities for modification to suit a variety of real-life situations, such as shopping for household furnishings, complimenting a French host or hostess on his or her fine taste, and so on.

À l'Agence Immobilière	At the Rental Agency
VOUS: Je voudrais louer **un appartement.**	YOU: I would like to rent an apartment.
un studio	studio
un quatre-pièces	four-room apartment
une maison de banlieue	house in the suburbs
une maison de campagne	country house
une maison particulière	single-family dwelling
une petite maison au bord de la mer	little house by the sea
une villa	villa
un pavillon	cottage
un château	château (manor)
une ferme	farm
un hôtel particulier	town house
L'AGENT: Très bien, Monsieur / Madame. J'ai un appartement à louer dans un nouvel immeuble. L'appartement se trouve au **troisième étage.**[1]	THE AGENT: Very well. I have an apartment for rent in a new building. The apartment is **on the fourth floor.** (*literally:* third floor)
sous-sol	in the basement
rez-de-chaussée	on the ground floor
quatrième étage	on the fifth (*literally:* fourth) floor
cinquième étage	on the sixth (*literally:* fifth) floor
sixième étage	on the seventh (*literally:* sixth) floor
Il n'est pas **grand**	It isn't **big**
climatisé	air-conditioned
meublé	furnished
moderne	modern
spacieux	spacious
mais il est **agréable.**	but it is **pleasant.**
clair	light, bright
charmant	charming
confortable	comfortable
ensoleillé	sunny

1. In Europe, the American first floor or ground floor is called **le rez-de-chaussée.** The American second floor is called **le premier étage.** The American third floor is **le deuxième étage,** etc.

joli
petit
tranquille (calme)

pretty
little
peaceful

VOUS: Combien de chambres y a-t-il?
L'AGENT: Il y en a deux.
VOUS: Et comment est **la cuisine?**

YOU: How many bedrooms are there?
AGENT: There are two (of them).
YOU: And what is the **kitchen** like?

la chambre d'amis
la salle de séjour (le séjour; le living)
la salle à manger
la salle de bains
la salle de jeux
le salon
le cabinet de travail

guest room
living room

dining room
bathroom
game room, rec room
parlor, living room
study, den

L'AGENT: Elle est grande.
VOUS: Y a-t-il **un lave-vaisselle?**

AGENT: It's large.
YOU: Is there a **dishwasher?**

une machine à laver
un réfrigérateur
une cuisinière
une baignoire
une douche
de la moquette partout
des placards

washing machine
refrigerator
stove
bathtub
shower
wall-to-wall carpeting
closets, cupboards

L'AGENT: Ah, oui. Et il y a aussi
un joli jardin.

AGENT: Oh, yes. And there is also a
pretty garden.

des arbres dans la propriété
un balcon
un court de tennis
une pelouse
une piscine
un potager
une terrasse
une véranda

trees on the property
balcony
tennis court
lawn
swimming pool
vegetable garden
terrace
veranda, porch

VOUS: C'est très bien. Quel est le loyer?
L'AGENT: Mille francs par mois.
VOUS: Cela me paraît raisonnable.
J'aimerais visiter l'appartement.

YOU: That's very good. What is the rent?
AGENT: One thousand francs per month.
YOU: That seems reasonable (to me). I would like to see (visit) the apartment.

Phrases à retenir

Memorizing these phrases from the **Dialogue** will help assure fluency in a variety of real-life situations involving renting or buying a place to live.

1. Je voudrais louer un appartement.
2. L'appartement se trouve au troisième étage.

3. Il n'est pas grand mais il est agréable.
4. Comment est la cuisine?
5. Y a-t-il un lave-vaisselle?
6. Il y a aussi un joli jardin.
7. Quel est le loyer?
8. J'aimerais visiter l'appartement.

DIALOGUE EXERCISES

The following exercises provide oral and written practice in using the vocabulary and basic sentence patterns of the **Dialogue: Appartement à louer.** These exercises use *only* vocabulary and structures presented in the renting an apartment **Dialogue.** They do not require familiarity with any other portions of this chapter.

Exercices d'application

A. **Descriptions: Ma chambre est grande et très claire.** Using adjectives presented in the **Dialogue,** describe your own house or apartment. Describe your bedroom, or, if applicable, your dormitory room. Use the correct form of the adjectives you select. Begin your descriptions with **Ma maison (f) est...; Mon appartement (m) est...; Ma chambre (f) est...** Here are the masculine and feminine forms of adjectives used in the **Dialogue.** Some are pronounced differently:

Masculine	Feminine
grand	grande
charmant	charmante
petit	petite
nouveau	nouvelle
spacieux	spacieuse

Others are pronounced alike:

Masculine	Feminine	Masculine	Feminine
agréable	agréable	climatisé	climatisée
calme	calme	ensoleillé	ensoleillée
confortable	confortable	meublé	meublée
moderne	moderne	clair	claire
tranquille	tranquille	joli	jolie

B. **Rooms and household objects: Il y a un réfrigérateur dans ma cuisine.** Using only the vocabulary from the last three vocabulary blocks of the **Dialogue**, talk about your place of residence. What items are found in different rooms of your house, apartment, or dormitory? What items are *not* found in these rooms?

EXEMPLES: *Il y a un réfrigérateur dans ma cuisine.*
Il n'y a pas de baignoire dans ma chambre.
(Note: **un, une** and **des** become **de** after **pas.**)

C. **Dialogue responses.** What could you respond to each of the following? Use sentences and phrases taken directly from the **Dialogue.**

1. À quel étage se trouve l'appartement?
2. Comment est l'appartement?
3. L'appartement est-il meublé?
4. La cuisine est-elle grande?
5. Y a-t-il un lave-vaisselle?
6. Quel est le loyer?

D. **Review.** What do you say . . .

1. to indicate that you wish to rent an apartment?
2. to find out on what floor of the building the apartment is located?
3. to ask if the apartment is in a new building?
4. to ask if the apartment is furnished?
5. to ask if the apartment is air-conditioned?
6. to ask how many bedrooms there are in the apartment?
7. to find out what the apartment is like?
8. to inquire about the rent?
9. when you think that the monthly rent sounds reasonable?
10. to indicate that you wish to see the apartment?

Improvisation à deux *(Exercice oral)*

E. Use the vocabulary block options and the basic sentence structures of the **Dialogue** to improvise a conversation with a classmate. One of you may choose to play the role of a rental agent while the other is a client. Or, you and your partner may choose to be two people moving to a French-speaking country, discussing in detail the sort of living accommodations you will be seeking there.

À Vous le choix *(Exercices écrits)*

F. Write a six- to eight-line dialogue for each of the following situations, selecting appropriate phrases from the initial **Dialogue** of this chapter.

1. You are renting an apartment for a short time. You will be living alone.

2. You are moving to a French-speaking country with your entire family.

3. You are dealing with a rental agent who does not understand your needs.

Conversations

G. Ask your classmates these personalized questions. When two or more responses are possible, alternate answer formats are offered. Select the option that best applies to you personally. Do not limit your responses simply to those suggestions offered in these questions. Use the inclusive vocabulary options provided in the **Dialogue.**

1. Où habitez-vous? dans une maison? dans un appartement? dans un studio? dans une chambre (dans une résidence universitaire)?
   • J'habite dans _____.[2]

2. Comment est votre maison? Est-elle grande ou petite? Comment est votre appartement? Est-il grand ou petit?
   • Il (Elle) est _____.

3. Comment est votre chambre? agréable? climatisée? confortable? grande? petite? etc.
   • Elle est _____.

4. Combien de pièces (*rooms*) y a-t-il chez vous? Quelles sont ces pièces? Nommez-les.

   EXEMPLE: *Il y a quatre pièces chez moi: la cuisine, les deux chambres à coucher, et la salle de séjour.*

5. Combien de chambres (*f*) à coucher y a-t-il chez vous? Combien de salles (*f*) de bains?

   EXEMPLES: *Il y a une chambre à coucher.*
   Il y a deux salles de bains.

6. À quel étage est votre chambre? au premier étage? au deuxième étage? etc.
   • Elle est au _____.

7. Dans quelle pièce de votre maison (de votre appartement ou de votre résidence universitaire) passez-vous le plus de temps (*spend the most time*)? Dans votre chambre à coucher? Dans la cuisine? Dans la salle de séjour? Dans la salle à manger?
   • Je passe le plus de temps dans _____.

8. Comment est la cuisine chez vous? Est-elle moderne? spacieuse? grande? petite? ensoleillée?
   • Chez moi la cuisine est _____.

---

2. **J'habite** means *I live, I live at,* or *I live in.*

9. Décrivez votre maison, votre appartement ou votre résidence. Y a-t-il des arbres? un jardin? un balcon? un court de tennis? une pelouse? une piscine? une terrasse? devant *(in front)*? derrière *(in back)*? d'un côté *(on one side)*? des deux côtés *(on both sides)*?
   • Il y a un (une) _____.
   • Il n'y a pas de _____.

10. Avez-vous déjà *(ever)* loué un appartement? Où? (À Paris? À Québec? À New York? etc.) Dans un grand immeuble? À quel étage? Combien de pièces y avait-il? Comment était l'appartement? Était-il meublé? grand? petit? charmant? etc.
    • Oui. J'ai loué un appartement. Il était _____.
    • Non. Je n'ai jamais loué d'appartement.

11. Avez-vous déjà loué une maison? Comment était-elle? grande? petite? etc.
    • Oui. J'ai loué une maison. Elle était _____.
    • Non. Je n'ai jamais loué de maison.

12. Louez-vous l'appartement, la maison ou la chambre où vous habitez en ce moment? Le loyer est-il raisonnable? cher *(high, expensive)*? bas *(low)*?
    • Oui. Je suis locataire *(a renter)*. Le loyer est _____.
    • Non. Je ne suis pas locataire. Je suis propriétaire *(owner)*.

H. **Review.** What have you learned about your classmates from these **Conversations**?

EXEMPLES: *La maison d'Anne est grande.*
La chambre de Marc est au premier étage.

I. **La Salle de classe.** Now apply this same vocabulary to the location of your French class.

1. Comment est la salle de classe? agréable? climatisée? confortable? ensoleillée? jolie? moderne? spacieuse? tranquille? claire? grande? petite? bruyante *(noisy)*? sombre *(dark)*?
   • Elle est _____.
   • Elle n'est pas _____.

2. Décrivez le bâtiment *(building)* où vous êtes en ce moment. Est-il grand? moderne? tranquille? etc.
   • Il est _____.
   • Il n'est pas _____.

Chambre, pièce, salle. In a hotel or dormitory, **une chambre** is a room. In a house or an apartment, **une chambre** is a bedroom. **Une pièce** is any room in a house or apartment. **Une salle** is used with certain fixed expressions, such as **salle de séjour, salle de bains,** and **salle de classe. Salle** can also refer to a large hall or to an auditorium.

Vivent les différences! There are a number of differences in living accommodations that invariably strike Americans visiting France for the first time.

Elevators. In many older buildings, tiny elevators have been installed in the open space that existed in the center of the winding staircase. These elevators are often used only for going up. The stairs must be used for descending. Most newer buildings, however, have modern elevators **(ascenseurs). R** on the elevator panel means **rez-de-chaussée; S/S** means **sous-sol** *(basement.)*

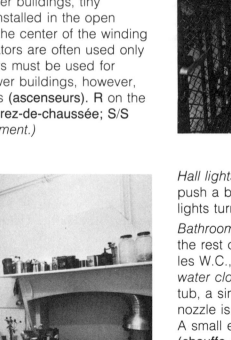

Hall lights. In many French buildings you must push a button to turn on the hall lights. These lights turn off by an automatic timer.

Bathrooms. The toilet is often separate from the rest of the bathroom and is referred to as les W.C., or **les vécés,** from the English term *water closet.* The bathroom itself contains a tub, a sink, and a **bidet.** A detachable shower nozzle is usually suspended in or near the tub. A small electric or gas-fired water heater **(chauffe-eau)** is frequently located right by the tub.

Kitchens. Another small water heater is often located by the kitchen sink.

LANGUAGE AND CULTURE

Shutters. **Volets** *(shutters)* are generally functional rather than purely decorative. At night they are pulled shut to control temperature, to reduce noise, and to increase security. Shutters are also kept closed on hot summer days, to keep the cool air inside.

Borrowed words. English has borrowed many French words related to living accommodations. **Pied-à-terre** *(literally:* foot on earth) refers to a second residence used temporarily or for convenience. **Chaise longue** *(literally:* long chair, often misspelled in English as "chaise lounge") is a reclining chair with room to put up your feet. **Concierge** refers to the person who watches over a building and its occupants. Certain personnel at better American hotels, resorts, and apartment buildings use this title. The French word **bureau** *(office* or *desk)* has been borrowed by English, where it refers to a chest of drawers. Similarly, the French word **commode** *(chest of drawers)* has been borrowed by English, where it can mean not only a chest of drawers but also a movable washstand or even a toilet!

VERBE IRRÉGULIER: vivre

> | **vivre**   to live |
> |---|
> | LE PRÉSENT: je **vis**   nous **vivons**
 tu **vis**   vous **vivez**
 il/elle **vit**   ils/elles **vivent** |
> | LE PASSÉ COMPOSÉ: j'**ai vécu,** etc. |
> | LA BASE DU FUTUR ET DU CONDITIONNEL: **vivr-** |

1. The verb **vivre** means "to live" as in "to live through," "to experience" or "to live one's life." It also can mean "to live" in the sense of "to reside."

   J'ai vécu deux ans en France. ⎫
   J'ai habité deux ans en France. ⎭   I lived two years in France.

   Il vit seul. ⎫
   Il habite seul. ⎭   He lives alone.

2. **être vivant(e)(s)** means "to be living," "to be alive."

   Sont-ils encore **vivants?**   Are they still alive?

3. English speakers use the borrowed expressions **joie de vivre** (*literally:* joy of living) to refer to people with an enthusiasm for life, and **savoir vivre** (*literally:* to know how to live) to refer to people who live with elegance and social grace.

Exercice d'application: vivre

Questions with *vivre*.   Answer these questions yourself. Then ask your classmates. (You may wish to use the **tu** form of address with your classmates.)

1. Vivez-vous (Vis-tu) seul(e) *(alone)?* avec votre (ta) famille? avec un(e) ami(e)? etc.
2. Avez-vous (As-tu) toujours vécu dans la même ville *(city)?* Dans quelles villes avez-vous (as-tu) vécu? À Paris? À Montréal? etc.[3]
3. Avez-vous vécu en France? au Canada? à l'étranger *(abroad)?* etc.[3]
4. Vos (Tes) grands-parents sont-ils encore vivants?

3. See **Entracte 12:** Geographical Place Names for more detailed answers.

STRUCTURES

Structure 1: Interrogative Adjectives

Interrogative adjectives ask the question *which?* or *what?* They agree in gender and in number with the nouns they modify.

	Singular	Plural
Masculine	quel	quels
Feminine	quelle	quelles

Quel appartement?	What (Which) apartment?
Quels appartements?	What (Which) apartments?
Quelle maison?	What (Which) house?
Quelles maisons?	What (Which) houses?

1. Interrogative adjectives may be followed directly by the noun they describe.

   Quel appartement préférez-vous?
   Quelle maison préférez-vous?

   Or, interrogative adjectives may be separated from the noun they describe by **être.**

   Quelle est votre adresse?   What is your address?

2. All forms of the interrogative adjectives are pronounced alike [kɛl].
   Exception: The letter **s** is pronounced [z] when followed by a vowel sound.

   Quels appartements? [kɛlzapartəmã]

3. The forms of **quel** are placed before nouns to mean *What a . . . !* or *What . . . s!*

   Quel appartement!   What an apartment!
   Quels appartements!   What apartments!

Exercices d'application: Interrogative Adjectives

A. **Quel appartement?** Someone is asking you for directions. Ask that person to be more specific. Use **quel** or **quelle.**

MODÈLE: Où est l'appartement?
L'appartement? Quel appartement?

Où est...
1. la maison?
2. le château?

3. la ferme?
4. le studio?

5. le quatre-pièces?   7. la piscine?
6. la cuisine?   8. le court de tennis?

B. **Quelle rue habitez-vous?** Ask your classmates where they live: **Quelle rue habitez-vous?**

EXEMPLE: —*Quelle rue habitez-vous?*
          —*J'habite 20, rue Manin.*

C. **Quelle est la date?** Formulate questions about the items listed below. Begin each question with **Quel est...** or **Quelle est....** Then ask your classmates these questions.

MODÈLE: la date   *Quelle est la date?*

1. votre nom *(m)*
2. votre numéro de téléphone *(m)*
   Exemple: C'est le sept cent soixante-cinq, quarante-trois, vingt et un. (*It's 765-4321.*)
3. la date aujourd'hui
4. votre couleur préférée *(f)*
   Exemple: C'est le bleu.[4]
5. votre cours préféré *(m)*
   Exemple: C'est le français.[5]

D. **Quel livre!** Here is an opportunity to learn or review some useful classroom vocabulary. Make a list of ten or more exclamations using **quel, quels, quelle** or **quelles** as appropriate. Use items selected from the suggestions given here. When your list is complete, point at any of these objects that actually are present in your classroom as you exclaim about them. Suggestions:

un livre   le tableau noir *(blackboard)*
un dictionnaire   une carte *(map)*
un stylo   une chaise
un crayon   la corbeille à papier *(wastebasket)*
un sac   une fenêtre
un sac à dos *(backpack)*   la porte
un journal

EXEMPLES: *Quel livre!*
           Quelle corbeille à papier!

---

4. For a list of colors, see **Entracte 8:** Clothing, Colors, Materials, page 243.
5. For additional course names, see Chapter 5 **(suivre),** p. 141 and **Appendice:** School Subjects.

Structure 2: Demonstrative Pronouns

Celui-ci and **celle-ci** *(this one)*, **celui-là** and **celle-là** *(that one)* point out a person or object. Masculine nouns are replaced by **celui-ci** and **celui-là**. Feminine nouns use **celle-ci** and **celle-là**.

Prenez le livre.	Take the book.
—**Celui-ci** ou **celui-là?**	—This one or that one?
Prenez la rue à droite.	Take the street on the right.
—**Celle-ci** ou **celle-là?**	—This one or that one?

Exercices d'application: Demonstrative Pronouns

E.   **Celui-ci ou celui-là?**   Ask a classmate for a classroom item of masculine gender. He or she will request clarification, using the phrase: **Celui-ci ou celui-là?** In response, point to the requested item, saying: **Celui-là, s'il vous (te) plaît.** Possible items of masculine gender to use: **un livre, un dictionnaire, un stylo, un crayon, un sac, un sac à dos, un journal.**

EXEMPLE: —*Je voudrais un livre.*
           —*Celui-ci ou celui-là?*
           —*Celui-là, s'il vous plaît.*

F.   **Celle-ci ou celle-là?**   Now ask a classmate for a classroom object of feminine gender. He or she will again request clarification, this time using the phrase: **Celle-ci ou celle-là?** You will now respond by pointing to the requested item, saying: **Celle-là, s'il vous (te) plaît.** Possible feminine gender classroom objects to use: **une carte, une chaise, une corbeille à papier, une feuille de papier** *(piece of paper)*, **une gomme** *(rubber eraser)*, **une serviette** *(briefcase, bookbag)*.

EXEMPLE: —*Je voudrais une feuille de papier.*
           —*Celle-ci ou celle-là?*
           —*Celle-là, s'il vous plaît.*

Structure 3: Interrogative Pronouns

The pronouns **lequel, laquelle, lesquels,** and **lesquelles** ask the question *which one?* or *which ones?* They agree in gender (masculine or feminine) and in number (singular or plural) with the nouns to which they refer. They are used to designate persons, animals, or things.

Louez l'appartement. —**Lequel?**
Fermez la fenêtre. —**Laquelle?**
Prenez les livres. —**Lesquels?**
Prenez les chaises. —**Lesquelles?**

Exercices d'application: Interrogative Pronouns

G.   **Lequel?**   Which one are you supposed to take? (This may be used as a classroom activity using the objects suggested below.

MODÈLE: le livre
—*Prenez le livre.*
—*Lequel?*

1. la chaise
2. le dictionnaire
3. le stylo
4. le crayon

5. la feuille de papier *(piece of paper)*
6. la craie
7. le sac
8. la gomme

H.   **Lequel?**   Ask for clarification, using **lequel** or **laquelle** as appropriate.

MODÈLE: J'habite le nouvel immeuble.
Lequel?

1. Je voudrais louer la maison.
2. C'est ma chambre.
3. J'ai loué l'appartement.
4. J'ai acheté la maison.

5. J'aime le jardin.
6. Fermez le placard.
7. Tu aimes le château?

Structure 4: Disjunctive or Intensive Pronouns

These pronouns are called "disjunctive" because they are separated or "disjoined" from the verb. Sometimes they are referred to as "intensive" pronouns, because they stress or "intensify" the specific person(s) involved.

moi	**nous**
toi	**vous**
lui	**eux**
elle	**elles**

Disjunctive pronouns are used:

1. after **c'est** and **ce sont.**

   Qui est-ce? C'est **toi?**   Who is it? Is it you?

2. for emphasis.

   Moi, je vais téléphoner.   *I'm* going to phone.

3. in comparisons.

   Il est plus grand que **toi.**   He is taller than you.

4. in simple statements without verbs.

Qui téléphone? **Toi** ou **moi?** Who is phoning? You or I?

5. with the expression **être à** to express ownership.

—À qui est-ce? —Whose is it?
—**C'est à moi.** —It's mine.

6. In compound subjects.

Mon mari et **moi** aimerions vous revoir. My husband and I would like to see you again.

7. After prepositions.

avec **elle** with her
chez **lui** at his place
de **moi** of/about me

Here are some common prepositions:

à cause de because of	**entre**[6] between
à côté de next to	**grâce à** thanks to
après after	**loin de** far from
au lieu de instead of	**malgré** in spite of
autour de around	**parmi** among
avant before	**pour** for
contre against	**près de** near
d'après according to	**sans** without
de la part de on behalf of, on the part of, from	**sauf** except
	selon according to
derrière behind	**sous** under
devant in front of	**sur** on
en dépit de in spite of	**vers** toward(s)
en face de opposite, facing	

Exercices d'application: Disjunctive (Intensive) Pronouns

I. **C'est à moi!** Place a personal possession (such as a book, a pen, a pencil) in a central area. All your classmates will be doing so, too. Each item will be held up one by one by the instructor, who will ask: **À qui est-ce?** (Whose is it?) Respond to each question as it pertains to you. (All class members will be responding simultaneously.) Use one of the following options:

C'est à moi! (It's mine.)
C'est à lui! (It's his.)
C'est à elle! (It's hers.)

6. English has borrowed the French expression *entre nous,* using it to mean: "between us, between you and me, in confidence."

Ce n'est pas à moi! *(It's not mine.)*
C'est à vous! *(It's yours!)*

If you feel a classmate is wrongly claiming an item that belongs to you or to another classmate, you may add:

Ce n'est pas à vous!
Ce n'est pas à toi!
Ce n'est pas à lui!
Ce n'est pas à elle!

J.   **Je suis près de lui.**   Where are you seated in relation to other students in class? Use disjunctive pronouns to refer to your classmates. Hand gestures or names can specify just who is meant by the disjunctive pronouns you select: **eux, elle, lui** or **vous.** The following prepositions of place will prove useful for this exercise: **à côté de** *(next to),* **derrière** *(behind),* **juste devant** *(right in front of),* **entre** *(between),* **en face de** *(opposite),* **loin de** *(far from),* **près de** *(near).*

EXEMPLES: *Je suis derrière elle… C'est-à-dire* (that is) *Marie.*
            Je suis près d'eux. (Point out two classmates near you.)

ST-OUEN

LOGEMENT 2 PIECES

Sortie immédiate de Paris sur quai de la Seine dans bel immeuble de 3 étages refait à neuf, ravalement escalier payé, coquet logement de 50 m² : séjour, une chambre, cuisine, salle de bains, w.c., bien ensoleillé, dernier étage sans ascenseur, chauffage électrique avec isolation laine de verre au plafond, ballon eau chaude 150 litres. Ravalement extérieur fait en 1981 payé. Affaire à saisir de suite.

PRIX : 120 000 F libre à la vente
Réf. : 22844

SOMME

PROPRIÉTÉ

Située à 30 km d'Amiens, très belle propriété construction en briques d'une superficie totale de 10 ares 94 entièrement clôturée comprenant : entrée, cuisine, séjour avec porte fenêtre, 3 chambres, salle de bains, WC, salle de jeux, grenier aménageable (possibilité de faire 2 chambres). Garage. Jardin. Toiture en tuiles de Beauvais. Plaisante affaire entièrement rénovée pouvant également convenir pour création commerce. A saisir.

PRIX : 340 000 F   **Réf. : 19543**

BRETIGNY-SUR-ORGE

A VENDRE
PAVILLON 5 PIECES

Au rez-de-chaussée, entrée cuisine, salle de séjour. Salon 1er étage. 3 chambres, penderie, salle de bains, w.c., combles aménageables. Cave + garage. Tél. après 18 h au 084.73.36 ou au 0 16.47.21.

PRIX : 550 000 F

LA SOMME

VILLA

Située dans plaisante région pêche et chasse à 10 km d'Amiens dans zone résidentielle. Bonne construction en état. Maison comprenant au rez-de-chaussée : living-room, cuisine attenante, 3 belles chambres, salle de bains, WC, chauffage central.
A l'étage possibilités d'aménagement 3 autres chambres.
L'ensemble en parfait état.
Affaire très agréable constituant excellent placement. A saisir.

PRIX : 350 000 F   **Réf. : 19577**

Synthèse

House for sale. Using vocabulary and structures from this lesson, describe the houses advertised for sale in these clippings from the real estate magazine **L'Immobilier.** Use complete sentences.

EXEMPLE: *C'est une grande maison. Elle est moderne. Au rez-de chaussée, il y a un séjour, la cuisine, et les W.C. Au premier étage il y a trois chambres, etc.*

PRONONCIATION

1. Sound (Phonetic Symbol): [j]

SPELLING:	i or y (followed by a pronounced vowel)
ENGLISH SOUND RESEMBLED:	Initial sound in word *you*
PRONUNCIATION:	This semi-vowel (or semi-consonant) is pronounced more tensely, forcefully, and rapidly than in English.
EXAMPLES FROM THIS CHAPTER:	immobil**iè**re mons**ieu**r p**ie**d
	p**iè**ce trois**iè**me lo**ye**r
	stud**io** il **y a**
	b**ie**n **y** a-t-il

Note: The sound [j] may also be spelled ill or il. Examples from this chapter: pavi**ll**on, ensolei**ll**é, trava**il**. *Exceptions:* mille, ville, tranquille are pronounced [mil], [vil], [trɑ̃kil].

2. Sounds (Phonetic Symbols): [p], [t], [k]

SPELLINGS:	p
	t, th
	qu, q, c (followed by a, o, u)
	c (+ consonant), k, que
	c (at end of word)
PRONUNCIATION:	In English, there are two pronunciations of these consonants:.
	1. With an explosion of air (as in: **p**ie, **t**ie, **k**ey)
	2. Without an explosion of air (as in: s**p**y, s**t**y, s**k**i)
	To distinguish between the two, hold your hand in front of your mouth as you say the following:
	pie—s**p**y
	tie—s**t**y
	key—s**k**i

In French, the [p], [t], and [k] sounds are
always made *without* the additional puff of air.

EXAMPLES FROM THIS CHAPTER:

[p]	[t]	[k]
petit à petit	petit	campagne
appartement	studio	quatre
pavillon	château	quatrième
pour	trouver	confortable
placards	troisième	clair
pelouse	étage	tranquille
par	travail	cuisinière
particulier	confortable	placards

Projets

A. **Floor plan** *(Exercice écrit)*. Draw a floor plan of your house or apartment. Label
all the rooms. Include cupboards, doors, windows, balconies, and other
vocabulary presented in the **Dialogue** of this chapter. Artistic ability is not
necessary for this project. (If you have a photograph of your house or
apartment, you may wish to attach it to the floor plan.)

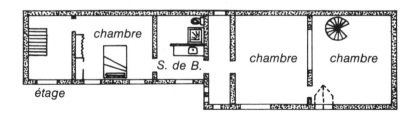

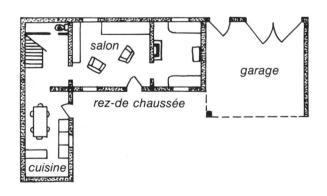

B.   **Floor plan**   *(Exercice écrit)*. Using the floor plan of the preceding project, sketch in the furnishings and other household objects of your house or apartment. To label these, you may need some of the following vocabulary in addition to that presented in the **Dialogue**.

La Cuisine

un aspirateur   vacuum cleaner
un bar   counter
une batterie de cuisine   kitchen utensils
une cafetière   coffeepot
un congélateur   freezer
un évier   sink

un four   oven
un grille-pain   toaster
une machine à laver   washing machine
une pendule   clock
des placards (de rangement)   cupboards

un plan de préparation   work area
un plan de travail   work area, counter
une poubelle   garbage pail/can
le téléphone   telephone
des tiroirs   drawers

La Salle de séjour

des bibelots   knickknacks
une bibliothèque   bookcase
un canapé   sofa, couch
une chaise   chair
une cheminée   fireplace
des coussins   cushions
un divan   couch
un élément   wall unit, room divider,

entertainment center, etc.
des étagères   shelves
un fauteuil   armchair
des lampes   lamps
un piano   piano
des plantes   plants
un radiateur   radiator
des rideaux (aux fenêtres)   curtains (on the windows)

une stéréo   stereo
une table (basse)   (coffee) table
des tableaux (aux murs)   paintings (on the walls)
un téléviseur   television
des tentures   drapes
un tourne-disque   record player

La Chambre à coucher

un bureau   desk
une commode   bureau, chest of drawers
une corbeille à papier   wastebasket
des couvertures   covers, blankets
un couvre-lit   bedspread
un édredon   quilt

une lampe de chevet   bedside lamp
un (grand) lit   (double) bed
des lits jumeaux   twin beds
des livres   books
une machine à écrire   typewriter
des oreillers   pillows

un ours en peluche   teddy bear
des photos   photos
une radio   radio
une radio réveil   radio alarm, clock radio
un réveil   alarm clock
une table de nuit   night table, bedside table

La Salle de bains

une armoire à pharmacie   medicine chest
une glace   mirror
un lavabo   sink (bathroom)

un miroir   mirror
un pèse-personne   bathroom scale
un porte-serviettes   towel rack

une prise de courant   electrical outlet
une serviette de bain   bath towel
un tapis de bain   bath mat

La Salle à manger

des assiettes plates, dishes	**des couverts** place settings	**un lustre** chandelier
des bougies candles	**des cuillères** spoons	**une nappe** tablecloth
un buffet buffet, cabinet	**des fourchettes** forks	**des tasses** cups
des couteaux knives		**des verres** glasses

C. **Household objects: Labels** *(Exercice écrit)*. Make labels for household items that you actually have in your house, apartment, or dormitory room: **le lit, la table, le réfrigérateur,** etc. Use vocabulary presented in the **Dialogue** and in **Projet B** above. Attach these labels to the respective items in your house, apartment, or dormitory room. Leaving these labels in place for a week or so will help you learn the item names in French.

Activités: Learning by Doing

A. **À Louer!** Using the vocabulary and structures of this chapter, try to rent the classroom to a classmate. Walk around the room with your prospective client, convincing him or her of the merits of your property. For example: **Quelle belle salle, n'est-ce pas? Elle est très moderne et spacieuse. Elle se trouve au deuxième étage. C'est pratique! Voici les placards; ils sont grands, n'est-ce pas? Il y a de la moquette partout.**

B. **Your room.** While a classmate describes in detail one room in his or her house or apartment (or his or her dormitory room), you will try to sketch the room. Indicate furnishings, windows, doors, and so on. (No artistic ability is necessary for this activity. A simple square can represent a table, a rectangle, a bed, and so on.) Your partner will point out in your sketch: **Il y a une table ici, juste devant la fenêtre. Le lit se trouve ici. Et il y a une porte ici,** etc. The following prepositions of place are useful for this activity:

dans le coin	in the corner
au centre/au milieu	in the center
(juste) devant le/la...	(right) in front of the. . .
au fond du/de la...	at the far end of the. . .
à côté du/de la...	next to the. . .
sur le/la...	on the. . .
à gauche (droite) du/de la...	to the left (right) of the. . .
au-dessus du/de la...	above the. . ./over the. . .
au-dessous du/de la...	under(neath) the. . .
entre...	between. . .
près du/de la...	near the. . .
derrière le/la...	behind the. . .

Combien êtes-vous dans votre famille?

The Family

Tel père, tel fils.

Like father, like son.

> Talking about one's own family and inquiring about the well-being of the families of others is a staple of conversational small talk.

Combien êtes-vous dans votre famille?

Réponse: • **Dans ma famille, nous sommes** _____. **Voyons. Il y a** _____.[1]

EXEMPLE: *Dans ma famille, nous sommes quatre.*
Voyons. Il y a mon mari, mon fils, mon chat et moi.

French possessive adjectives agree in gender and in number with the noun they modify. The family members in the following lists are each accompanied by the correct form of the possessive adjective meaning "my": **mon, ma, mes.** These vocabulary items may be substituted *directly* into the response format. No grammatical manipulation is necessary.

---

mon mari my husband	*Remember:*		
ma femme my wife	1 **un**	4 **quatre**	7 **sept**
moi I (me, myself)	2 **deux**	5 **cinq**	8 **huit**
	3 **trois**	6 **six**	9 **neuf**

Parents
ma mère my mother
mon père my father
mon beau-père my father-in-law or stepfather

ma belle-mère my mother-in-law or stepmother
mes beaux-parents my parents-in-law
mes parents *(m)* my parents or my relatives

Children
mon enfant *(m,f)* my child
mes enfants my children
ma fille[2] my daughter

mon fils[2] my son
mon beau-fils my son-in-law or stepson
ma belle-fille my daughter-in-law or
    stepdaughter

Sisters and Brothers
ma sœur my sister
mon frère my brother
ma belle-sœur my sister-in-law

mon beau-frère my brother-in-law
ma demi-sœur my half sister or stepsister
mon demi-frère my half brother or stepbrother

Grandparents and Grandchildren
mes arrière-grands-parents *(m)* my great
    grandparents

ma grand-mère my grandmother
mes petits-enfants my grandchildren

---

1. How many people are in your family? (*Literally:* How many are you in your family?) In my family, there are _____ of us. (*Literally:* We are _____.) Let's see. There's _____.
2. Pronunciation: The word **fils** is irregular, in that the final **s** is pronounced [fis]. (Remember: final **s** is usually silent.) The reason the letter **s** is pronounced in the word **fils** (which means son) is to make it sound different from the word **fille** (which means daughter). In the word **fille** [fij], the letters "l" are pronounced as the **y** in the English word *yes*.

mon arrière-grand-père my great grandfather	mon petit-fils my grandson
mon arrière-grand-mère my great grandmother	ma petite-fille my granddaughter
mes grands-parents (m) my grandparents	mes arrière-petits-enfants my great
mon grand-père my grandfather	grandchildren

Aunts, Uncles, etc.

ma tante my aunt	ma cousine my cousin (f)
mon oncle my uncle	mon neveu my nephew
mon cousin my cousin (m)	ma nièce my niece

Others

mon chat/ma chatte my cat	ma plante my plant
mon cheval my horse	mon poisson rouge my goldfish
mon chien/ma chienne my dog	mon serin my canary
mon lapin my rabbit	ma tortue my turtle
ma perruche my parakeet	

Springboards for Conversation

Ask your classmates these personalized questions. When two or more responses are possible, alternate answer formats are offered. Select the option that best applies to you personally. Do not limit your responses simply to those suggestions offered in these questions. Use the inclusive vocabulary options provided in the **Entracte.**

1. Combien êtes-vous dans votre famille?
   • Dans ma famille, nous sommes _____.
   (Indicate number of people.)
   • Il y a _____ personnes dans ma famille.
   • Ma famille est grande/petite.
   • Il y a _____. *(Name the people.)*

2. Avez-vous un/une _____? (une sœur? un frère? un fils? etc.) Avez-vous des _____? (des sœurs? des frères? des enfants? etc.)
   • Oui. J'ai un/une/des _____.
   • Non. Je n'ai pas de/d' _____.[3]

Récapitulation

How much can you recall about your classmates and instructor?

1. Combien de personnes y a-t-il dans la famille du professeur? Et de Monsieur/Madame/Mademoiselle... *(your classmates)?* Et de votre voisin(e) de gauche? Et de votre voisin(e) de droite? etc.

   EXEMPLE: *Dans la famille de Monsieur Smith il y a trois personnes. Il y a Monsieur Smith, sa femme et son fils.*[4]

(If some information has been forgotten, simply ask again. **Pardon. Je suis désolé(e), mais j'ai oublié... Combien êtes-vous dans votre famille? Ah oui. C'est ça. Merci.**)

---

3. *Remember:* **De** replaces **un/une/des** after **pas.**
4. *Remember:* **Son père** means "his or her father," **son frère** means "his or her brother," **sa mère** means "his or her mother," and so on.

2. Practice using the possessive adjectives **votre, vos, ton, ta, tes.** Verify what you remember directly with your classmates.

  EXEMPLE: *Dans votre famille il y a trois personnes, n'est-ce pas? Il y a votre frère, votre mère et vous. C'est ça?*

3. Qui dans la classe a un/une/des _____(s)? (un frère? une sœur? des enfants? etc.)
  • Monsieur/Madame/Mademoiselle... a

    _____.
  • Le professeur a _____.
  • Moi, j'ai _____.
  • Tout le monde.
  • Personne.

Expansion

The **Expansion** can be used for partners or group conversation and for oral or written composition. Answer formats are provided.

1. Combien de/d' _____ avez-vous? de cousins? de sœurs? de frères? d'enfants? de petits-enfants? etc.
  • J'ai _____.
  • Je n'ai pas de _____.
  • J'en ai _____.

  EXEMPLES: *J'ai un frère, deux sœurs et cinq cousins.*
  J'en ai deux.[5]

2. *(Masculine family members.)* Comment s'appelle votre _____? votre frère? votre père? votre oncle? votre mari? votre fils? etc.
  • Mon _____ s'appelle...

3. *(Feminine family members.)* Comment s'appelle votre _____? votre femme? votre sœur? votre tante? votre fille? votre mère? etc.
  • Ma _____ s'appelle...

4. Quel âge a votre _____? votre sœur? votre frère? votre grand-mère? votre fille? votre fils? etc.

  EXEMPLE: *Mon frère a trente ans.*[6]

5. Où habite votre _____? votre grand-mère? votre grand-père? votre sœur? votre frère? votre fils? votre fille? etc. Et qui habite chez vous?

  EXEMPLES: *Ma grand-mère habite à New York.*
  Mon fils et ma fille habitent chez nous.

6. À qui ressemblez-vous? *(Whom do you resemble?)*
  • Je ressemble à mon/ma _____.
  • Je ne ressemble à personne *(no one).*
  • Je ne sais pas.

7. Avez-vous un chien? un chat? un cheval? une perruche? etc. Comment s'appelle-t-il/elle?
  • J'ai un/une _____ qui s'appelle...
  • Non. Je n'ai pas de _____.[7]

8. **Review.** If **Expansion** questions have been used for group or partners conversation, review what you have

5. **J'en ai deux** means "I have two (of them)."
6. See **Entracte 2:** Numbers regarding numbers and age formation.
7. Remember: **Un, une,** and **des** become **de** after **pas.**

learned about your classmates: **Qui dans la classe a deux sœurs? trois enfants?** etc. **Comment s'appellent-ils/elles? Quel âge ont-ils/elles? Qui dans la classe a un chien? un chat?** etc. You may wish to conclude your classroom conversations with a friendly **Et bien des choses de ma part à votre famille!** or **Mon bon souvenir à votre famille!** *(Give my regards to your family.)*

Vocabulaire utile   The following phrases are frequently requested by students using the family-related conversations of this **Entracte**.

Je suis... I'm . . .
Il/Elle est... He/She is . . .
Vous êtes (tu es)... You are . . .
   célibataire single
   divorcé(e) divorced
   marié(e) married
   veuf/veuve widowed
   l'aîné(e) the oldest
   le cadet/la cadette the youngest
   fille unique only daughter/child
   fils unique only son/child

J'ai... I have . . .
Il/Elle a... He/She has . . .
Vous avez (tu as)... You have . . .
   une sœur aînée older sister
   un frère aîné older brother
   un frère cadet younger brother
   une sœur cadette younger sister
   beaucoup de cousins many cousins
   une grande famille large family
   une petite famille small family

French Families. A generation ago, the average French family had four or more children. The average French family today has only two children. Households generally consist of the nuclear family of parents and children, with grandparents rarely residing under the same roof.

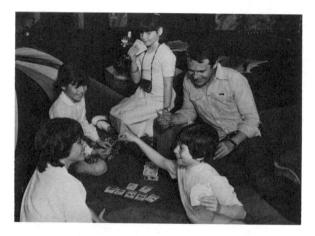

Diminutives. Here are some common diminutives and terms of endearment used with close family members: **maman** (mère); **papa** (père); **taty, tata** (tante); **tonton** (oncle); **grand-papa, bon-papa, papi** (grand-père); **grand-maman, bonne-maman, mamie, mammy, granny,** (grand-mère).

Godparents. Godparents are frequently considered part of the French Catholic family structure: **le parrain** *(godfather)*, **la marraine** *(godmother)*, **le filleul** *(godson)*, **la filleule** *(goddaughter)*.

Borrowed words. French family-related expressions commonly used in English include: **en famille** *(one of the family, informally)*, **enfant gâté** *(spoiled child, recipient of undue flattery and attention)*, and **enfant terrible** *(unruly person or child)*.

Synthèse

A. **Family photograph.** Using the vocabulary of this **Entracte,** describe this family photo. Speculate about the ages and familial relationships of the people shown. Who resembles whom? etc.

B. **Votre famille.** Tell about your own family, using the vocabulary of this **Entracte.** How many people are in your family? What are their names and ages? Where do they live? Whom do you resemble? Do you have any pets? etc. Use complete sentences.[8]

Projet

Family tree. Make a family tree (*un arbre généalogique*) for your own family. Place yourself at the center and work outward. Be as inclusive as possible. Indicate each person's name and his or her relationship to you: **ma tante Anne** or **Ma tante s'appelle Anne.** You may wish to attach photographs.

8. **Maternel(le)** means "on (my) mother's side." **Paternel(le)** means "on (my) father's side." For example: **Ma grand-mère maternelle s'appelle Dora Smith.**

Activité: Learning by Doing

Family Photograph.   Bring a photo of your family to class. Discuss this photograph with a partner or with a group. Ask your classmates questions about their photos: **Qui est ce monsieur à gauche? Qui est cette dame à droite? C'est vous? (C'est toi?) C'est votre (ta) mère? C'est votre (ton) père?** etc. You may also ask, **Comment s'appelle-t-il/elle? Où habite-t-il/elle? Quel âge a-t-il/elle?** etc.

«Je voudrais envoyer cette lettre par avion.»

À la Poste et Au Téléphone

At the Post Office and On the Telephone

Pas de nouvelles, bonnes nouvelles.

No news is good news.

DIALOGUE

This **Dialogue** presents vocabulary for dealing successfully with post office transactions, such as mailing letters, buying stamps, and picking up mail general delivery. This vocabulary may also be used when picking up personal correspondence, packages, newspapers or magazines at a hotel desk, in a dormitory, in a pension, and so on. Also introduced is vocabulary related to telephone calls. Vocabulary blocks within the **Dialogue** offer options that allow modification to suit a wide variety of real-life situations.

À La Poste	At the Post Office
(Dans la rue)	*(In the street)*
VOUS: Où se trouve le bureau de poste le plus proche, s'il vous plaît?	YOU: Where is the nearest post office, please?
UN(E) PASSANT(E): Le voilà, juste devant vous.	A PASSERBY: There it is, right in front of you.
VOUS: Ah... Merci, Monsieur / Madame / Mademoiselle.	YOU: Oh . . . Thank you.
↶	↶
(Au guichet numéro un)	*(At window number one)*
VOUS: Je voudrais envoyer **cette carte postale** par avion en Amérique. **cet aérogramme cette lettre ce gros paquet ce colis ce journal**	YOU: I would like to send this **postcard** airmail to America. **air letter letter large package parcel newspaper**
UN(E) EMPLOYÉ(E) DE LA POSTE: C'est tout?	POSTAL CLERK: Is that all?
VOUS: Je voudrais aussi des timbres, s'il vous plaît.	YOU: I'd also like some stamps, please.
L'EMPLOYÉ: Ça fait vingt francs, Monsieur / Madame / Mademoiselle.	POSTAL CLERK: That comes to (*literally:* that makes) twenty francs.
VOUS: Voilà... et pour envoyer un télégramme?	YOU: Here (they are) . . . and to send a telegram?
L'EMPLOYÉ: Adressez-vous au guichet numéro deux.	POSTAL CLERK: Go to window number two.
VOUS: Merci bien. Encore une question, s'il vous plaît. Où sont les cabines téléphoniques?	YOU: Thank you. One more question, please, Where are the phone booths?
L'EMPLOYÉ: Au sous-sol.	POSTAL CLERK: In the basement.
↶	↶
(Au guichet de la poste restante)	*(At the general-delivery window)*
VOUS: Avez-vous du courrier pour __votre nom__?	YOU: Do you have any mail for __your name__?

L'EMPLOYÉ: Votre passeport, s'il vous plaît.
VOUS: Le voilà.
L'EMPLOYÉ: Merci, Monsieur / Madame / Mademoiselle. Un instant, s'il vous plaît...Voilà. Vous avez une lettre et des cartes postales.

ᶜᵔᵓ

EMPLOYEE: Your passport, please.
YOU: Here it is.
EMPLOYEE: Thank you. One moment, please . . . Here it is. You have a letter and some postcards.

ᶜᵔᵓ

Au Téléphone

On the Telephone

UN(E) EMPLOYÉ(E) DE LA SOCIÉTÉ LAROQUE: Allô. Ici Madame / Mademoiselle / Monsieur _____.
VOUS: Bonjour, Madame / Monsieur / Mademoiselle. Je voudrais parler à Monsieur X, s'il vous plaît.
L'EMPLOYÉ: Pardon? La communication est mauvaise. J'entends très mal. Parlez plus fort, s'il vous plaît, Madame / Mademoiselle / Monsieur.
VOUS: Monsieur X, s'il vous plaît.
L'EMPLOYÈ: Ne quittez pas, je vous prie. Je vais voir s'il est là. C'est de la part de qui?
VOUS: De _votre nom_.
L'EMPLOYÉ: Monsieur X est **sorti pour le moment.**

> **en réunion**
> **absent**
> **en vacances**
> **au téléphone**
> **occupé**
> **parti déjeuner**

VOUS: Quand sera-t-il de retour?
L'EMPLOYÉ: **Je ne sais pas exactement.**

> **Dans un instant.**
> **Dans quelques minutes.**
> **Dans une heure.**
> **Avant cinq heures.**
> **Vers six heures.**
> **Pas avant sept heures.**
> **Demain.**
> **Lundi. Mardi, etc.**

Puis-je prendre un message?

VOUS: Oui, s'il vous plaît. Dites-lui de me rappeler. C'est urgent.

EMPLOYEE OF LAROQUE COMPANY: Hello. Mrs. / Miss / Mr. _____ speaking. (*Literally:* Here Mrs. / Miss / Mr. _____.)
YOU: Hello. I would like to speak to Mr. X, please.

EMPLOYEE: Excuse me? It's a bad connection. I don't hear you very well. (*Literally:* I hear very poorly.) Speak up, please.

YOU: Mr. X, please.
EMPLOYEE: Hold on, please. I'll go see if he's in. Who's calling, please?

YOU: _your name_.
EMPLOYEE: Mr. X is **out for the moment.**

> in a meeting
> away
> on vacation
> on the telephone
> busy
> out to lunch

YOU: When will he be back?
EMPLOYEE: **I don't know exactly.**

> In a moment.
> In a few minutes.
> In an hour.
> Before five o'clock.
> Around six o'clock.
> Not before seven o'clock.
> Tomorrow.
> Monday. Tuesday, etc.

Can I take a message?

YOU: Yes, please. Tell him to call me. It's important.

L'EMPLOYÉ: Certainement, Monsieur / Madame / Mademoiselle. Quel est votre numéro de téléphone, s'il vous plaît?

VOUS: C'est le 765.43.21 (sept cent soixante-cinq, quarante-trois, vingt et un).[1]

L'EMPLOYÉ: Pouvez-vous épeler votre nom, s'il vous plaît?[2]

VOUS: Bien sûr. *(Épelez votre nom.)*

L'EMPLOYÉ: Oh, ne quittez pas! Monsieur X arrive à l'instant. Je vous le passe.

MONSIEUR X: Allô, oui? Qui est à l'appareil?

VOUS: C'est ___*votre nom*___.

MONSIEUR X: Ah! Merci d'avoir téléphoné!

EMPLOYEE: Certainly. What is your phone number, please?

YOU: It's 765-4321.

EMPLOYEE: Can you spell your name, please?

YOU: Certainly. *(Spell your name.)*

EMPLOYEE: Oh, hold on! Mr. X just arrived. I'll put him on.

MR. X: Hello? Who is this? (*Literally:* Who is on the phone?)

YOU: It's ___*your name*___.

MR. X: Oh! Thank you for calling!

Phrases à retenir

Memorizing these phrases from the **Dialogue** will help assure fluency in a variety of real-life situations dealing with postal transactions and telephone conversations.

À la Poste
1. Où se trouve le bureau de poste le plus proche, s'il vous plaît?
2. Je voudrais envoyer cette carte postale par avion en Amérique.
3. Je voudrais des timbres, s'il vous plaît.
4. Où sont les cabines téléphoniques?
5. Avez-vous du courrier pour moi?

Au Téléphone
6. Bonjour, Madame. Je voudrais parler à Monsieur X, s'il vous plaît.
7. Parlez plus fort, s'il vous plaît.
8. Ne quittez pas, je vous prie.
9. C'est de la part de qui?
10. Quand sera-t-il de retour?
11. Puis-je prendre un message?
12. Dites-lui de me rappeler, s'il vous plaît.

DIALOGUE EXERCISES

The following exercises provide oral and written practice in using the vocabulary and basic sentence patterns of the **Dialogues: À La Poste** and **Au**

1. French phone numbers are given in clusters, not in a string of single digits. Written French phone numbers use periods.
2. See **Entracte 1: The Alphabet** for spelling by analogy.

Téléphone. These exercises use *only* vocabulary and structures presented in these **Dialogues.** They do not require familiarity with any other portions of this chapter.

Exercices d'application

A. **Asking directions: Où se trouve...?** Where is the nearest mailbox? the nearest hotel? etc. Use **le plus proche** with masculine nouns and **la plus proche** with feminine nouns.

MODÈLE: la boîte aux lettres *(mailbox)*
Où se trouve la boîte aux lettres la plus proche, s'il vous plaît?

1. la banque
2. la poste
3. le bureau de poste

4. l'hôpital *(m)*
5. la station de métro
6. l'hôtel *(m)*

B. **Inquiring about individuals: Je vais voir s'il est là.** Ask classmates where other class members are: **Où est Monsieur... ? Où est Marie?** etc. Responses may include: **Je vais voir s'il (si elle) est là. Oui, il (elle) est là. Non, il (elle) n'est pas là. Il (Elle) est absent(e).**

C. **Telephone numbers: Quel est votre numéro de téléphone?** What is your phone number? Give your own phone number. Then ask classmates for theirs. (You may wish to review **Entracte 2:** Numbers.)

Note: **chez moi** = where I live (my home phone); **au bureau** = at the office (my business phone)

EXEMPLE: *C'est le 765.43.21. (C'est le sept cent soixante-cinq, quarante-trois, vingt et un.)*

D. **Dialogue responses.** What could you respond to each of the following? Use sentences and vocabulary taken directly from the **Dialogue.**

1. Où se trouve le bureau de poste le plus proche, s'il vous plaît?
2. Ça fait vingt francs, Monsieur/Madame/Mademoiselle.
3. Où sont les cabines téléphoniques?
4. Votre passeport, s'il vous plaît.
5. C'est de la part de qui?
6. Puis-je prendre un message?
7. Allô, oui? Qui est à l'appareil?

E. **Review.** What do you say . . .

1. when you want to buy some stamps?
2. when you want to send a telegram from the post office?

3. when you have one more question to ask?
4. to inquire if there is any mail for you?
5. to indicate with whom you wish to speak?
6. when you cannot hear the other person clearly?
7. to tell someone not to hang up?
8. to ask who is calling?
9. to ask someone his or her phone number?
10. to thank someone for having called?

Improvisation à deux *(Exercice oral)*

F. Use the vocabulary block options and the basic sentence structures of the **Dialogue** to improvise a telephone conversation with a classmate.

À Vous le choix *(Exercices écrits)*

G. Write a six- to eight-line dialogue for each of the following situations, selecting appropriate phrases from the **Dialogue** of this chapter.

1. You are in a post office in France. You wish to mail some postcards, letters, and packages to friends back home. You are also expecting some "general delivery" mail.
2. You have a variety of transactions to complete at the post office. Unfortunately, the postal clerk is not helpful.
3. You are working for a French company. The phone rings. It is for your boss, who is out to lunch.

Conversations

H. Ask your classmates these personalized questions. When two or more responses are possible, alternate answer formats are offered. Select the option that best applies to you personally. Do not limit your responses simply to those suggestions offered in these questions. Use the inclusive vocabulary options provided in the **Dialogue**.

1. Allez-vous à la poste aujourd'hui (après la classe)? Pourquoi? pour acheter des timbres? pour envoyer une lettre? pour envoyer un paquet? pour envoyer un colis?
   • Je ne vais pas à la poste aujourd'hui.
   • Je vais à la poste acheter des timbres, etc.
2. Êtes-vous allé(e) à la poste récemment? aujourd'hui (avant la classe)? hier? la semaine passée? samedi passé? etc.
   • Je suis allé(e) à la poste _____.
   • Je ne suis pas allé(e) à la poste _____.

3. Avez-vous acheté des timbres récemment?
   - Oui, j'ai acheté _____.
   - Non, je n'ai pas acheté _____.

4. Y a-t-il un bureau de poste près d'ici?
   - Oui, il y a un _____.
   - Non, il n'y a pas de _____.

5. Quel courrier avez-vous envoyé cette semaine? une lettre? une carte postale? des lettres? des cartes postales? une carte de vœux *(greeting card)*? une invitation? À qui? à un(e) ami(e)? à votre mère? à vos parents? à votre frère? etc.
   - J'ai envoyé une _____ cette semaine.
   - Je n'ai rien envoyé.

6. Avez-vous jamais envoyé un télégramme? À qui? Avez-vous jamais reçu un télégramme? De qui? Quand? Récemment? Il y a longtemps?
   - Oui. J'ai envoyé (reçu) un _____.
   - Non. Je n'ai jamais envoyé (reçu) de _____.

7. À qui avez-vous téléphoné aujourd'hui? à un(e) ami(e)? au professeur? etc. Avez-vous téléphoné de votre chambre? de chez vous? de votre bureau? d'une cabine téléphonique? d'un téléphone public?
   - Je n'ai téléphoné à personne.
   - J'ai téléphoné à _____.
   - Je lui ai téléphoné de/d' _____. *(I called him [her] from _____.)*

8. Aimez-vous parler au téléphone? Avec qui? Avec qui n'aimez-vous pas parler au téléphone?
   - J'aime parler au téléphone avec _____.
   - Je n'aime pas parler au téléphone avec _____.
   Suggestions: avec... ma mère, mon père, mon mari, ma femme, ma sœur, mon frère, ma tante, mon oncle, ma fille, mon fils, ma grand-mère, mon ami Georges, mon amie Annette, etc.

9. Avec qui parlez-vous le plus souvent *(most often)* au téléphone?
   - Je parle le plus souvent avec mon/ma/mes _____.

10. Qui vous a téléphoné *(who phoned you)* aujourd'hui? hier soir? un(e) ami(e)? votre mère? votre sœur? un(e) collègue? Étiez-vous étonné(e) *(surprised)*?
    - Personne (ne m'a téléphoné).
    - _____ m'a téléphoné.

I.   **Review.**   What have you learned about your classmates from these **Conversations?**

EXEMPLES: *Marie a envoyé une lettre à sa mère.*
Monsieur Smith n'aime pas parler au téléphone.
Paul a téléphoné à son amie aujourd'hui.

A PROPOS

Les P.T.T. The post office in France is referred to as **le bureau de poste, la poste, les P.T.T. (Postes, Télégraphes et Téléphones)** or **P. et T. (Postes et Télécommunications)**. Postal and phone services in France are run by the **Ministère des Postes et Télécommunications**. Post offices in France are generally open weekdays from 8 A.M. to 7 P.M. and Saturday mornings until noon.

Allô. The term **allô** (hello) is used on the telephone both by the caller and by the person answering. For example, when you answer the phone, you would say "**Allô?**" or "**Allô, oui?**" If you were placing the phone call, you might begin by verifying: "**Allô, Pierre?**" In business, a switchboard operator might answer by identifying the name of the company or business: "**Société Laroque, bonjour.**" Or you, the caller, might begin a business communication by verifying: "**Allô, l'Hôtel Ritz?**" or "**Allô, le 765.43.21?**"

P.T.T.
BUREAU DE POSTE
au 1ᵉʳ étage

Stamps. Stamps may be purchased at the post office or at a **tabac** (tobacco store) in France. Stamps may also be purchased at the cigarette counter in many French cafés and restaurants.

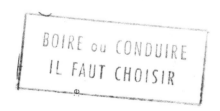

LANGUAGE AND CULTURE

Person-to-person and collect calls. To place a person-to-person call in France, say: Je voudrais téléphoner avec préavis. To call collect: Je voudrais téléphoner en P.C.V. In French-speaking Canada: Je voudrais placer un appel de personne à personne. Je voudrais placer un appel à frais renversés.

L'Écouteur. Home phones in France often have an extra listening device called l'écouteur. This can be used by a second listener or by the primary speaker as an extra earpiece.

L'Annuaire. To find out a phone number in France you can call directory assistance (Renseignements) or refer to the phone book (l'annuaire). In Paris there are separate phone books that list subscribers by name (in alphabetical order), by profession, and by street address. To find a business number, consult the yellow pages (les pages jaunes).

VERBES IRRÉGULIERS: écrire, envoyer, lire, recevoir

> | écrire   to write |
> | --- |
> | LE PRÉSENT: j'écris   nous écrivons |
> tu écris   vous écrivez |
> il/elle/on écrit   ils/elles écrivent |
> | LE PASSÉ COMPOSÉ: j'ai écrit, etc. |
> | LA BASE DU FUTUR ET DU CONDITIONNEL: écrir- |

1. **Comment est-ce que cela s'écrit?** means "How is that written?" or, by extension, "How is that spelled?"
2. **Décrire** *(to describe)* is conjugated like **écrire**.

Exercices d'application: **écrire**

  A. **Questions with *écrire*.** Answer these questions yourself. Then ask your classmates. (You may wish to use the **tu** form of address with your classmates.)

    1. Écrivez-vous (Écris-tu) à vos (tes) amis? des lettres? des cartes postales?
    2. Écrivez-vous souvent? rarement? de temps en temps?

ÉCRIRE, C'EST FAIRE DES HEUREUX

LA POSTE

3. À qui écrivez-vous souvent? À qui n'écrivez-vous jamais? À votre correspondant(e) *(pen pal)?* À votre ami(e)? À votre mari? etc.
4. Écrivez-vous avec la main droite ou avec la main gauche?
5. Avez-vous (As-tu) écrit une lettre aujourd'hui? hier soir? cette semaine? À qui?
6. À qui avez-vous écrit récemment? Qui vous a écrit récemment?

➤

envoyer to send	
LE PRÉSENT: j'**envoie** tu **envoies** il/elle/on **envoie**	nous **envoyons** vous **envoyez** ils/elles **envoient**
LE PASSÉ COMPOSÉ: j'**ai envoyé**, etc.	
LA BASE DU FUTUR ET DU CONDITIONNEL: **enverr-**	

Exercice d'application: **envoyer**

B.   **Questions with *envoyer*.**   Answer these questions yourself. Then practice using the verb **envoyer** by asking your classmates the same questions. (You may wish to use the **tu** form of address with your classmates.)

1. Envoyez-vous (Envoies-tu) des cartes postales lorsque *(when)* vous êtes (tu es) en vacances? À qui?
2. Envoyez-vous des cartes d'anniversaire *(birthday cards)* à vos (tes) amis?
3. Quel courrier avez-vous (as-tu) envoyé cette semaine? une carte de vœux *(greeting card)?* une carte postale? une lettre? À qui?

➤

lire to read	
LE PRÉSENT: je **lis** tu **lis** il/elle/on **lit**	nous **lisons** vous **lisez** ils/elles **lisent**
LE PASSÉ COMPOSÉ: j'**ai lu**, etc.	
LA BASE DU FUTUR ET DU CONDITIONNEL: **lir-**	

Exercice d'application: **lire**

C. **Questions with** *lire.* Answer these questions yourself. Then practice using the
verb **lire** by asking your classmates the same questions. (You may wish to use
the **tu** form of address with your classmates.)

1. Aimez-vous (Aimes-tu) lire?
2. Est-ce que vous lisez (tu lis) beaucoup?
3. Quels journaux lisez-vous? Quels magazines?
4. Avez-vous (As-tu) lu le journal de ce matin?
5. Lisez-vous le journal chaque jour? souvent? deux ou trois fois par semaine?
   seulement le week-end? Quel journal?
6. Avez-vous lu un roman *(novel)* récemment? Lequel?
7. Que lisez-vous en ce moment? un roman? des poèmes? un roman policier?

➤
recevoir to receive	
LE PRÉSENT: je **reçois**	nous **recevons**
tu **reçois**	vous **recevez**
il/elle/on **reçoit**	ils/elles **reçoivent**
LE PASSÉ COMPOSÉ: j'**ai reçu**, etc.	
LA BASE DU FUTUR ET DU CONDITIONNEL: **recevr-**	

Recevoir is used in some common expressions:

recevoir des amis   to have friends over, to entertain

J'aime **recevoir des amis** pendant   I like to have friends over (to entertain)
le week-end.   on weekends.

recevoir quelqu'un   to see someone (in business)

Il peut **vous recevoir** le huit à neuf   He can see you on the eighth at nine
heures.   o'clock.

recevoir un coup de téléphone   to receive a phone call

J'**ai reçu un coup de téléphone** de   I received a phone call from Marie.
Marie.

Exercice d'application: **recevoir**

D. **Questions with** *recevoir.* Answer these questions yourself. Then practice using the verb **recevoir** by asking your classmates. (You may wish to use the **tu** form of address with your classmates.)

1. Quel courrier avez-vous (as-tu) reçu cette semaine? une carte postale? une carte de vœux *(greeting card)?* une lettre? un billet doux *(love letter)?* des imprimés *(printed matter)?* une invitation? un magazine? des notes *(bills)?* un paquet? un colis? de la publicité *(advertisements, junk mail)?* un chèque? de l'argent *(money)?* De qui?
2. Qu'est-ce que vous aimez (tu aimes) recevoir? des invitations? de l'argent? des magazines? des lettres?
3. Qu'est-ce que vous n'aimez pas recevoir? de la publicité? des notes? etc.
4. Aimez-vous (Aimes-tu) recevoir des amis pendant le week-end?
5. Avez-vous reçu un cadeau *(gift)* récemment? De qui? Qu'est-ce que c'était? des fleurs *(flowers)?* des bonbons *(candy)?* etc.

STRUCTURES

Structure 1: Interrogative Pronouns

Interrogative pronouns ask questions. The following chart highlights the basic interrogative pronouns and how they are used in question sentences.

	To Designate Persons	To Designate Things
Subject	**Qui** a téléphoné? Who called?	**Qu'est-ce qui**[3] est sur la table? What is on the table?
Object	**Qui** avez-vous vu? Whom did you see?	**Que** faites-vous? **Qu'est-ce que** vous faites? What are you doing?
Object of a Preposition	**À qui** avez-vous parlé? To whom did you speak?	**De quoi** parlez-vous? What are you talking about?

1. **Qui** is used for people. **Qui est-ce?** means "Who is it?"
2. **Que** requires verb inversion: **Que faites-vous?**
3. **Qu'est-ce que** does *not* require verb inversion: **Qu'est-ce que vous faites?**
4. **Qu'est-ce que c'est?** means "What is it?" "What is that?"
5. To ask for a description or definition, use **Qu'est-ce que c'est que...?** *(What is. . . ?)*

   Qu'est-ce que c'est qu'un "annuaire"?   What is an **annuaire**?

   Qu'est-ce que c'est que cela?   What is that?
6. **À qui** can mean "to whom." It can also denote ownership.

   À qui est ce livre?   Whose book is this?
7. **Penser à** means "to think of (about)."

   À qui pensez-vous?   Whom are you thinking about?

   À quoi pensez-vous?   What are you thinking about?

Exercices d'application: Interrogative Pronouns

A. **Qui est-ce?**   Ask a classmate who another class member is. You will be told his or her name.

EXEMPLE: —*Qui est-ce?*
　　　　　　　—*C'est Madame Smith.*

B. **Qui?**   You will tell your classmates about yourself using the sentences below. They will ask **Qui?**, **À qui?**, or **De qui?** You will clarify. Fill in the blanks with the names of real people. Who actually *did* call you recently? To whom *did* you write recently? etc.

---

3. **Que** becomes **qu'** before a vowel.

MODÈLE: —J'ai téléphoné à mon ami Marc hier soir.
—*À qui?*
—*À mon ami Marc.*

1. J'ai vu _____ récemment.
2. _____ m'a téléphoné récemment.
3. J'ai envoyé une carte à _____ récemment pour son anniversaire.
4. J'ai reçu une lettre de _____ récemment.
5. J'ai écrit une lettre à _____ récemment.
6. Je pense toujours à _____.

C. **Qu'est-ce que vous avez fait?** Tell your classmates what you did last night. They will ask you to repeat this information, using the phrases **Qu'est-ce que vous avez fait?** or **Qu'est-ce que vous avez dit?** You then repeat your initial statement.

EXEMPLE: —*Je suis allé(e) au cinéma.*
—*Pardon? Qu'est-ce que vous avez fait?*
—*Je suis allé(e) au cinéma!*

D. **Qu'est-ce que c'est qu'un "journal"?** Using vocabulary items from the **Dialogue** (such as **une lettre, un timbre, un passeport, une cabine téléphonique**), quiz your classmates on the meanings of various French terms. Answers may be given in English or in French.

EXEMPLE: *Qu'est-ce que c'est qu'un "journal"?*

E. **Interrogative pronouns.** *(Personalized questions)* Answer these questions yourself. Then practice using interrogative pronouns by asking your classmates the same questions. (You may wish to use the **tu** form of address with your classmates.)

1. À qui pensez-vous (penses-tu) souvent? à vos amis? à vos parents? à vos enfants? etc.
2. De quoi rêvez-vous? d'aller en Europe? etc.
3. Que faites-vous ce soir? Allez-vous au cinéma? Téléphonez-vous à des amis? etc.
4. Qu'est-ce que vous avez fait aujourd'hui? Êtes-vous allé(e) au supermarché? Avez-vous parlé au téléphone?
5. De quoi avez-vous besoin? d'argent? de vacances? de nouveaux vêtements?
6. Chez qui allez-vous ce week-end? chez des amis? chez vos parents? chez vos enfants?
7. Avec qui avez-vous parlé aujourd'hui? avec vos amis? avec votre secrétaire? avec vos collègues? etc.
8. À qui avez-vous pensé aujourd'hui? à personne? à vos parents? à vos enfants? à votre fiancé(e)? à votre petit(e) ami(e) *(boy or girlfriend)?* etc.

9. À quoi pensez-vous? aux vacances? à vos classes? à vos problèmes?
10. Qui aimez-vous le plus? votre mari? votre femme? votre ami(e)? etc.

Structure 2: Relative Pronouns

Relative pronouns are so called because they join, or "relate," two clauses.

1. **Qui** means "who, that, which." **Qui** immediately precedes the verb of which it is the subject. It may refer to persons or things.

   C'est Paul **qui** a appelé.   Paul called.
   J'ai lu le livre **qui** est sur la table.   I read the book (that is, which is) on the table.

2. **Que (qu'** before a vowel) means "whom, which, that." It is the object of a verb. It may refer to persons or things.

   Voilà la dame **que** vous ne   There's the woman (whom) you
   connaissez pas.   don't know.
   Où est le livre **que** j'ai acheté?   Where's the book (that, which) I bought?

3. In English, relative pronouns are often omitted. They are never omitted in French.

4. **Dont** means *of whom, of which, whose, about whom,* and *about which.*

   Où est le monsieur **dont** vous   Where is the man about whom/of
   avez parlé?   whom you spoke?

5. **Où** *(where)* can also be used as a relative pronoun. When it is used in this manner it means *to which* or *in which.*

   C'est le bureau **où** je travaille.   That is the office where (in which) I work.

6. **Ce qui** and **ce que** *(what, that which)* are indefinite relative pronouns that refer to ideas that do not have number or gender.

   Ce qui is the *subject* of a clause.

   Je ne sais pas **ce qui** est arrivé.   I don't know what happened.
   Dites-moi **ce qui** vous intéresse.   Tell me what interests you.

   Ce que is used as the *object* of a clause.

   Je ne sais pas **ce que** vous voulez.   I don't know what you want.
   Dites-moi **ce que** vous voulez.   Tell me what you want.

Exercices d'application: **Relative Pronouns**

F.   **C'est lui qui a le livre.**   Give your book or pen to a classmate and declare:
C'est lui (elle) qui a le livre (le stylo)!

G. **C'est le livre que vous cherchez.** Tell a classmate that you are looking for your book: **Je cherche mon livre de français.** Your classmate will indicate a nearby book and ask, **C'est le livre *que* vous cherchez?** If it is, say, **Oui, c'est le livre *que* je cherche. Merci.** If not, continue asking until you locate the correct object. Other possible items: **mon stylo, mon crayon, mon sac, mon sac à dos, mon cahier, mon parapluie, mon journal.**

H. **Je ne sais pas ce qu'il a dit.** Indicate that you do not know the answer to each question below. Use **ce qui** or **ce que** (**ce qu'** before a vowel).

MODÈLE: Qu'est-ce qu'il a répondu?
Je ne sais pas ce qu'il a répondu.

1. Qu'est-ce qu'il a envoyé?
2. Qu'est-ce qui est dans le paquet?
3. Qu'est-ce que Paul a écrit?
4. Qu'est-ce qui est sur la table?
5. Qu'est-ce que le postier a dit?
6. Qu'est-ce qui n'est pas bon?

Synthèse

A. **Message téléphonique.** Later on today or perhaps this evening, you might find a telephone message waiting for you. Fill out the form below with the sort of message you might expect.

MESSAGE TÉLÉPHONIQUE. ☐ VISITE . . . . ☐	DATE et HEURE:
De:	Pour:
ADRESSE:	Rappelez correspondant . . . . . ☐
	Correspondant rappellera . . . . ☐
	Suite à votre appel . . . . ☐
	Demande rendez-vous . . . .
TÉLÉPHONE: POSTE:	Reçu par:
OBJET:	
Peut être rappelé le . . . entre . . . h et . . . h au numéro ci–dessus ou à	

You can use this form to practice some of the interrogative pronouns presented in the **Structures** section of this chapter. Exchange telephone messages with a classmate. Ask your partner questions about his or her telephone message. Use such inquiries as: **Qui a téléphoné? Quelle est son adresse? Quel est son numéro de téléphone? Quand a-t-il (elle) téléphoné? Et à quelle heure? Qu'est-ce qu'il (elle) a dit? À quelle heure puis-je le (la) rappeler? À quel numéro?**

B. **Répertoire adresses.** Using the vocabulary and structures of this lesson, ask your classmates for their addresses **(Quelle est votre adresse?),** for their phone numbers **(Quel est votre numéro de téléphone?),** and for the correct spelling of their names **(Quelle est l'orthographe exacte de votre nom?).** Use this illustration as a model for your own **répertoire adresses,** which you can easily make on a larger sheet of paper. Enter the information you have gathered on your **répertoire addresses.**[4]

RÉPERTOIRE ADRESSES		
NOMS	ADRESSES	NUMÉROS DE TÉLÉPHONE

PRONONCIATION

1. Sound (Phonetic Symbol): [z]

SPELLING:	**s** (between two vowels), **z**
ENGLISH SOUND RESEMBLED:	Initial sound in word *zebra*
PRONUNCIATION:	Sound is pronounced with more force and tension than in English.
EXAMPLES FROM THIS CHAPTER:	nous lisons le présent
	vous lisez composé
	ils lisent

4. You may wish to review **Entracte 1:** The Alphabet and **Entracte 2:** Numbers.

2. Sound (Phonetic Symbol): [s]

SPELLING:	**s, ss, sc** (followed by i, e, y), **c** (followed by i, e, y), **ç**
ENGLISH SOUND RESEMBLED:	Final sound in word _ki<u>ss</u>_

EXAMPLES FROM THIS CHAPTER:

<u>ç</u>a	in<u>s</u>tant	<u>c</u>'est
voi<u>c</u>i	<u>s</u>ecrétaire	je re<u>ç</u>ois
pa<u>ss</u>eport	<u>s</u>orti	pa<u>ss</u>e
adre<u>ss</u>e	ab<u>s</u>ent	
po<u>s</u>te	je <u>s</u>ais	

Notes:
1. The spelling -tion in French is pronounced [sjɔ̃]. Examples from this chapter: **applica<u>tion</u>, improvisa<u>tion</u>.**
2. Ç (c with a cedilla) only appears before **a, o,** and **u.** It is always pronounced [s].

   Contrast the voiceless consonant [s] with the voiced consonant [z], using the following words and expressions:

[s]	[z]
de<u>ss</u>ert	dé<u>s</u>ert
poi<u>ss</u>on	poi<u>s</u>on
ils <u>s</u>ont	ils‿ont

3. Sound (Phonetic Symbol): [ʃ]

SPELLING:	**ch, sch, sh**
ENGLISH SOUND RESEMBLED:	Initial sound in word _<u>sh</u>all_
PRONUNCIATION:	Avoid adding a [t] sound before it, as in the English words _cheese_ or _French._

EXAMPLES FROM THIS CHAPTER:

pro<u>ch</u>e	<u>ch</u>er
gui<u>ch</u>et	<u>ch</u>èque

Note: The spelling **ch** is pronounced [k] in some words of Greek origin, such as é<u>ch</u>o, or<u>ch</u>estre, psy<u>ch</u>ologie, ar<u>ch</u>éologie, psy<u>ch</u>iatre.

Projet

Postcards. _(Exercice écrit)_ Write and address a postcard to a classmate. (An index card will do.) Ideas for salutations, messages, and closings are suggested below. These are not literal translations of English, but actual French postcard clichés. These are used by French people the way we use such old standards as "Having a wonderful time, wish you were here."

le _____
                    (la date)

Timbre

Cher ami/Chère amie,

Mon cher Marc/Ma chère Henriette,

Cher Marc/Chère Henriette,

Vacances merveilleuses, pense à toi/vous.

  Avec toi/vous par la pensée.

  Tu me manques./Vous me manquez. [5]

  Je m'amuse bien ici.

  Il fait un temps splendide.

  Je t'aime éperdument. [6]

  Juste quelques lignes pour te/vous dire que . . .

C A R T E — P O S T A L E

_____
(nom du destinataire)

_____
(salle de classe, numéro)

_____
(ville, état, code postal)

    À bientôt de tes/vos bonnes nouvelles,
    Bien amicalement à toi/vous,
    Affectueusement,
    Amitiés,
    Je t'embrasse très fort,
    Grosses bises, [7]

_____
(Signature)

Activité: Learning by Doing

At the Post Office.   Write and address three postcards as described in the **Projet.** One card will be to the person sitting on your left in class. Another will be to the person on your right in class. The third will be to anyone else in the classroom. Once these cards are written, ask a classmate to direct you to the part of the classroom designated as **la poste: Où se trouve le bureau de poste le plus proche, s'il vous plaît?** Buy stamps from a student postal worker: **Je voudrais envoyer cette carte postale par avion. Je voudrais (acheter) des timbres,** etc. Postal workers will draw "stamps" on your cards. Now, look for the classroom mailbox: **Où se trouve la boîte aux lettres, s'il vous plaît?** Deposit your mail in this box. A student postal worker will remove these cards from the mailbox and sort them into piles, one for each class member. At the area marked **guichet de la poste restante,** claim your own mail: **Avez-vous du courrier pour...?**

5. *I miss you.*
6. *wildly/passionately*
7. *Love and kisses,*

Où êtes-vous allé(e) cette semaine?

Places

| Il vaut mieux aller au boulanger qu'au médecin. | It's better to go to the baker than to the doctor. |

Asking directions in French can be as easy as using the place name of your destination followed by **s'il vous plaît**. For example: **La banque, s'il vous plaît?** This lesson provides an opportunity to learn the names of many places you may want to go.

Où êtes-vous allé(e) cette semaine?

Réponse: • **Je suis allé(e) _____.**[1]

EXEMPLE: *Je suis allé(e) au cinéma, au supermarché, à la banque et chez le coiffeur.*

Vocabulaire à retenir	Vocabulary items listed under the heading **Vocabulaire à retenir** are each preceded by the correct prepositional form indicating "to the." Consequently, no grammatical manipulation is necessary. Simply substitute these items directly into the given response formats for immediate and correct conversational self-expression. *Note:* The items in this first list are those places most frequently requested by students. For additional places, see the Resource List at the end of this **Entracte**.

chez mon ami(e) my friend's place	**chez le coiffeur** hairdresser's (barber's)	**à l'église** (f) church	**à la pharmacie** pharmacy
à la banque bank	**chez le docteur** the doctor's	**dans un grand magasin** department store	**au restaurant** restaurant
à la bibliothèque library	**dans une discothèque** discotheque	**à la librairie** bookstore	**au supermarché** supermarket
au cinéma movies			
en classe class		**à la poste** post office	**au travail** work

Springboards for Conversation

Ask your classmates these personalized questions. Answer formats are provided.

1. Où êtes-vous allé(e) cette semaine?
   • Je suis allé(e) _____.

2. Où êtes-vous allé(e) récemment *(recently)*?
   • Je suis allé(e) _____.

---

1. Where did you go this week? I went to _____.

Récapitulation

How much can you recall about your classmates and instructor? Answer formats are provided.

1. Où Monsieur/Madame/Mademoiselle...
   est-il/elle allé(e) cette semaine? Et le
   professeur? (*Note:* If a place is forgotten,
   simply ask again: **Pardon. Je suis désolé(e),
   mais j'ai oublié. Où êtes-vous allé(e) ette
   semaine? Ah oui. C'est ça. Merci.**)
   • Il/Elle est allé(e) _____.

2. Qui dans la classe est allé _____? (chez le
   coiffeur? à la bibliothèque? à la pharmacie?
   etc.) Qui d'autre? C'est tout?
   • Monsieur/Madame/Mademoiselle... est
     allé(e) _____.
   • Le professeur est allé _____.
   • Moi, je suis allé(e) _____.

Remarques

1. The verb **aller** is conjugated with **être**. The past participle agrees in gender
   (masculine or feminine) and in number (singular or plural) with the subject of the verb.
   This does not change the pronunciation. For example: "I went" =
   Je suis allé *(m)* or **Je suis allée** *(f)*.

2. **À** + **le** contract to **au**, meaning *to the* or *at the*. For example: **Je suis allé(e) au
   supermarché** means *I went to the supermarket.* **À** + **la** remains **à la**; **à** + **l'** remains
   à l'.

3. **Chez** can be translated as *at the place of, at the office of, at the home of, to the
   place of, to the office of,* or *to the home of.* For example:
   Je suis allé(e) **chez le docteur.**   I went **to the doctor's (office).**
   Je suis allé(e) **chez mon ami(e).**   I went **to my friend's (house, place).**

4. A number of expressions use **dans** instead of **à**: **dans un grand magasin, dans une
   discothèque,** etc.

Expansion

The **Expansion** can be used for partners or group conversation and for oral or written
composition. Answer formats are provided.

1. Où devez-vous (*have to*) aller cette
   semaine?
   • Je dois aller _____.

2. Y a-t-il des absents (*absent students*)
   aujourd'hui? Qui? Où est-il/elle? Devinez
   (*guess*).
   • Il/Elle est peut-être (*perhaps*) _____.

3. Où allez-vous tous les jours (*every day*)?
   • Je vais _____.

4. Où allez-vous souvent (*often*)?
   • Je vais _____.

5. Où allez-vous de temps en temps (*from
   time to time*)?
   • Je vais _____.

6. Où allez-vous rarement *(rarely)?*
   • Je vais _____.

7. Où est-ce que vous n'allez jamais *(never)?*
   • Je ne vais jamais _____.

8. D'habitude *(usually)* où allez-vous le week-end *(on weekends)?*
   • Je vais _____.

9. Où comptez-vous *(intend)* aller ce week-end?
   • Je compte aller _____.

10. Où aimez-vous aller? au cinéma? À la bibliothèque? etc.
    • J'aime aller _____.

11. Où est-ce que vous n'aimez pas aller? chez le docteur? au travail? etc.
    • Je n'aime pas aller _____.

12. **Review.** If **Expansion** questions have been used for group or partners conversation, review what you have learned about your classmates.

EXEMPLES: *D'habitude Mme Smith va au cinéma le week-end.*
Philippe ne va jamais dans une discothèque.
Marie doit aller chez le docteur cette semaine.

Vocabulaire utile

The following phrases are frequently requested by students using the place-related conversations of this **Entracte**.

Pardon? Excuse me?
Quelle coïncidence! What a coincidence!
Moi aussi! I (did) too!
Oui. C'est ça. Yes. That's it.
Sans blague!? No kidding!?
Non. No.
Je ne suis pas allé(e)... I didn't go . . .
Dites donc! Really!

Je suis resté(e) chez moi. I stayed home.
J'ai gardé mon lit. I stayed in bed.
J'étais malade. I was sick.
Chez son ami(e). At or to his or her friend's place.
Chez ses parents. At or to his or her parents' place.
Chez lui. At or to his place.
Chez elle. At or to her place.
Nulle part. Nowhere.

Le Marché.   Although **Les Halles**, the most famous of the Parisian markets, has been moved to suburban Rungis, several local **marchés** remain in Paris. These include **le marché aux timbres** *(stamps)*, **le marché aux fleurs** *(flowers)*, **le marché aux oiseaux** *(birds)*, and several **marchés aux puces** *(flea markets)*, the best-known of these being found at the **Porte de Clignancourt**. In most French towns and cities, farmers' markets permit local farmers to sell their goods directly to the public. Some of these markets are housed in permanent facilities and are open every day of the week. Others, located under temporary canopies, conduct business only once or twice a week.

French Shops.   Large supermarkets and shopping malls (**supermarchés, hypermarchés, grandes surfaces, centres commerciaux**) are becoming common in France. Despite this new competition, however, many smaller shops still survive. Some of these typical French establishments present an interesting contrast to their American counterparts. For example, **la pharmacie** is not like the American drugstore that may sell everything from ice cream to paper supplies, but more of a medical or clinical specialty shop. **Le tabac** offers not only tobacco products, but also candy, stationery, and postage stamps. **Le kiosque à journaux** has for sale postcards, guidebooks, and tickets for the **Loterie Nationale**, in

Les bouquinistes

La crémerie

addition to the anticipated newspapers and magazines. **Les bouquinistes** are open-air stalls along the Seine River in Paris, selling new and used books, old maps, and artwork. **La boucherie-chevaline** has horse meat for sale. **La crémerie** offers dairy products, produce, and canned goods. **La charcuterie** stocks pork products, prepared salads, and a variety of cooked meats. **La pâtisserie** will occasionally have some tables where you can sit and eat pastries purchased on the premises. At the **boulangerie** you can purchase fresh-baked bread very inexpensively. Also note that **la librairie** is a bookstore, *not* a library.

Synthèse

Où allez-vous? These photographs show some typically French places you may want to visit or patronize on your next trip to France. Using these illustrations as a starting point, plan a day's worth of errands and amusement. Use complete sentences. You may use the present tense **(je vais à la banque)**, the near future **(je vais aller à la banque)** or the future **(j'irai à la banque).** Some useful vocabulary: **puis** *(then)*, **ensuite** *(next)*, **après** *(after)*, **enfin** *(finally).*

L'Opéra

Projets

A. **Mon Agenda.** Where do you have to go this week? Make your own personal agenda, using the agenda format below as a model. Include dates and times of day when possible. (You may choose to extend this project to cover two weeks or a month.)[2]

LUNDI	
MARDI	
MERCREDI	
JEUDI	
VENDREDI	
SAMEDI	
DIMANCHE	

B. **Chamber of Commerce.** List the places you would actually tell a visitor to see during a stay in your town. For example: **le musée, le zoo, le parc.** (For additional places, see the Resource List at the end of this **Entracte.**)

C. **Tourist Map.** Draw a tourist map of your town, neighborhood, or region, indicating monuments, buildings, sights, restaurants, and so on. (Artistic talent is not necessary.) Use as many of the items from this **Entracte** as possible.

2. See **Entracte 3:** Telling Time and **Entracte 4:** Dates for reference.

Activité: Learning by Doing

Asking Directions. Everyone should select three or more place names from the vocabulary list of this lesson. These are written in large print on sheets of paper and posted around the classroom with tape. Ask your classmates for directions to these places. For example: **Pardon, Madame. Le cinéma, s'il vous plaît?** A simple response will suffice: **Le voilà,**[3] **Là-bas,** or **Par là.** (*Indicate direction with a gesture.*) You may wish to use other directional phrases presented in Chapter 2.

Resource List: Additional Places

These additional places are supplied to allow greater personalization of responses. These items have all been requested by students actually using these conversations in class.

à l'aéroport airport
à l'agence de voyages travel agency
à la blanchisserie laundry
à la boucherie butcher's
à la boulangerie baker's
au bureau office
à la campagne country
au cinéma auto drive-in movies
au club country club
au commissariat de police police station
au concert concert
à la confiserie candy store
aux courses races
chez la couturière seamstress's, dressmaker's
chez le dentiste dentist's
à l'école school
chez mes enfants my children's

à l'étranger abroad
chez le fleuriste florist's
à la gare train station
chez mes grands-parents my grandparents'
à l'hôpital hospital
à la laverie (automatique) laundromat
au magasin d'antiquités antique store
au magasin d'articles de sport sporting goods store
au magasin de chaussures shoe store
au magasin de jouets toy store
au magasin de photographie photography store
au bord de la mer seashore
à la montagne mountains

au musée museum
à l'opéra opera
chez l'opticien optician's
à la papeterie stationery store
au parc park
à la piscine pool
à la plage beach
à la quincaillerie hardware store
au salon de beauté beauty parlor
à la station-service service station
dans une station de ski ski resort
à la synagogue temple
chez le tailleur tailor's
à la teinturerie dry cleaner's
au théâtre theater
à l'université university
en ville town, downtown
au zoo zoo

Note: For geographical place names, see **Entracte 12:** Nationalities and Geographical Place Names. These may be useful for clarifying such responses as **à la montagne, à la campagne, à l'étranger, chez mes grands-parents,** etc.

3. **Le voilà** becomes **La voilà** when referring to feminine nouns: **Où est la banque?—La voilà.**

«Bonnes vacances. Et bon voyage!»

En Voyage

Pierre qui roule n'amasse pas mousse.

Traveling

A rolling stone gathers no moss.

DIALOGUE

This **Dialogue** presents vocabulary useful for making travel reservations and purchasing tickets for a variety of modes of transportation. Vocabulary blocks within this **Dialogue** offer possibilities for modification to suit a wide variety of real-life travel situations. They also offer options that will allow personalization in conversations regarding your own actual travel experiences or future travel plans.

À L'Agence de Voyages	At the Travel Agency
VOUS: J'ai très envie de voir **Marseille.**[1]	YOU: I really want to see **Marseilles.**[2]
l'Amérique le Canada les États-Unis l'Europe la France la Martinique	America Canada the United States Europe France Martinique
Je pense y aller **en avion.**	I'm thinking of going (there) by plane.
en auto / en voiture en (auto)car en bateau / par bateau en train / par le train	car coach, limousine, interurban bus boat train
L'AGENT: Quand pensez-vous partir? VOUS: **Dimanche prochain,**	AGENT: When were you thinking of leaving? YOU: Next Sunday,
Aujourd'hui Ce soir Demain Bientôt Dès que possible Lundi, Mardi, etc. La semaine prochaine Dans une semaine Le mois prochain	Today Tonight Tomorrow Soon As soon as possible Monday, Tuesday, etc. Next week In a week Next month
le premier.	the first.
le deux le trois le quatre le cinq le vingt-deux	the second the third the fourth the fifth the twenty-second

1. Names of cities in French require no article. States, countries, and continents are either masculine or feminine and require the definite article. (See **Entracte 12:** Nationalities and Geographical Place Names.)
2. Note the difference in spelling: **Marseille** (French) and *Marseilles* (English).

L'AGENT: Il y a un vol direct **tous les jours**
|le lundi
|le mardi
|le mercredi
|le jeudi
|le vendredi
|le samedi
|le dimanche

à **dix heures.**[3]
|onze heures
|onze heures trente
|onze heures quarante
|douze heures
|treize heures
|treize heures quinze

VOUS: Quels sont les prix, s'il vous plaît?

L'AGENT: L'aller simple touriste fait deux cents francs. En première classe, trois cents francs.

VOUS: Alors, je voudrais un aller-retour en première classe.

L'AGENT: Un instant. Je vais vérifier... Je peux vous confirmer une place sur le vol numéro huit.

VOUS: Très bien. Merci. Mais dites-moi, comment puis-je me rendre à l'aéroport (à l'aérogare)?

L'AGENT: Vous pouvez y aller **en métro.**
|en autobus
|en taxi
|en hélicoptère
|à pied
|à bicyclette / à vélo
|à moto
|à vélomoteur

Il faut y arriver une heure à l'avance. Et n'oubliez pas de confirmer votre réservation. Bonnes vacances et bon voyage!

AGENT: There is a direct flight **every day**
|Mondays
|Tuesdays
|Wednesdays
|Thursdays
|Fridays
|Saturdays
|Sundays

at ten o'clock.
|eleven o'clock
|11:30 A.M.
|11:40 A.M.
|noon
|1:00 P.M.
|1:15 P.M.

YOU: What are the rates, please?

AGENT: One-way tourist class costs two hundred francs. First class costs three hundred francs.

YOU: Okay, I would like a round-trip ticket, first class.

AGENT: One moment, I'll check... I can confirm a space for you on flight number eight.

YOU: Fine. Thank you. But, tell me, how can I get to the airport (air terminal)?

AGENT: You can get there by **subway.**
|bus
|taxi
|helicopter
|foot
|bicycle
|
|motorcycle
|motorbike

You have to arrive there an hour ahead of time. And don't forget to confirm your reservation. (Have a) good vacation and a good trip!

---

3. The twenty-four hour clock is generally used for official purposes, such as transportation schedules.

Phrases à retenir

Memorizing these phrases based on the **Dialogue** will help assure fluency in a
variety of real-life travel situations.

1. J'ai très envie de voir la France.
2. Je pense y aller en avion.
3. Je pense partir dimanche prochain.
4. Est-ce qu'il y a un vol direct?
5. Quels sont les prix, s'il vous plaît?
6. Je voudrais un aller-retour.
7. Comment puis-je me rendre à l'aéroport?
8. Puis-je y aller en métro?
9. Bonnes vacances!
10. Bon voyage!

DIALOGUE EXERCISES

The following exercises provide oral and written practice in using the
vocabulary and basic sentence patterns of the **Dialogue: En Voyage.** These
exercises use *only* vocabulary and structures presented in the travel-related
Dialogue. They do not require familiarity with any other portions of this
chapter.

Exercices d'application

A.   Moyens de transport.   Where will you be going during the coming week? How
do you plan to get there? Use vocabulary from the **Dialogue** in your answers.
(For possible destinations, see **Entracte 10:** Places and **Entracte 12:** Nationalities
and Geographical Place Names.)

EXEMPLES: *Je vais aller à New York en avion.*
Je vais aller au supermarché en auto.
Je vais aller en classe à pied.

B.   Dates.   Where are you planning to go within the coming month? When do you
plan to go? (For departure dates, you may wish to review **Entracte 4:** Dates.)

EXEMPLES: *Je pense aller à New York, le cinq.*
Je pense aller chez mon ami, le dix.

C.   Dialogue responses.   What could you respond to each of the following? Use
sentences and vocabulary taken directly from the **Dialogue.**

1. Avez-vous envie de voir la France?
2. Comment pensez-vous y aller?
3. Quand pensez-vous partir?
4. Y a-t-il un vol direct?
5. Quels sont les prix?
6. Comment puis-je me rendre à l'aéroport?
7. Faut-il y arriver à l'avance?

D. **Review.** What do you say . . .

1. to indicate you really want to see Paris?
2. to say that you are thinking of going there by plane?
3. to find out when someone intends to leave?
4. to inquire if there is a direct flight?
5. to find out the rates?
6. when you want a round-trip ticket?
7. to find out how to get to the airport?
8. to tell someone he or she can get to a particular destination by taking the subway?
9. to wish someone a good trip?

Improvisation à deux (Exercice oral)

E. Use the vocabulary block options and the basic sentence structures of the **Dialogue** to improvise a dialogue with a classmate. One of you may choose to be a travel agent and the other a client. Or, you and your partner may be two friends discussing travel plans. A third option involves having you and your partner discuss actual past travel experiences.

À Vous le choix (Exercices écrits)

F. Write a six- to eight-line dialogue for each of the following situations, selecting appropriate phrases from the initial **Dialogue** of this chapter.

1. You have gone to a travel agent to finalize travel plans and to pick up your tickets.
2. You need a vacation but are not sure what you would like to do. You presently have a very limited budget. Discuss possibilities with a travel agent.
3. You and a friend are having a conversation about trips each of you has taken in the past.

Conversations

G. Ask your classmates these personalized questions. When two or more responses are possible, alternate answer formats are offered. Select the option that best applies to you personally. Do not limit your responses simply to those suggestions offered in these questions. Use the inclusive vocabulary options provided in the **Dialogue**.

1. Quelle(s) ville(s) avez-vous envie de voir? Paris? Québec? Genève? Londres? New York? etc.[4]
   - J'ai (très) envie de voir _____.
2. Quel(s) pays avez-vous envie de voir? La France? Le Canada? Les États-Unis? Le Mexique? La Chine? Le Japon? etc.[4]
   - J'ai (très) envie de voir le/la/les _____.
3. Comment allez-vous au supermarché? au travail? à vos cours? En voiture? en métro? en autobus? en taxi? à pied? à bicyclette? à moto? à vélomoteur? etc.
   - Je vais au supermarché _____.
   - Je vais au travail _____.
   - Je vais à mes cours _____.
4. Comment êtes-vous venu(e) en classe aujourd'hui? en voiture? en métro? en autobus? à pied? à bicyclette? à moto? à vélomoteur?
   - Je suis venu(e) en classe aujourd'hui _____.
5. Comment êtes-vous rentré(e) *(did you get home)* hier soir? en voiture? en métro? en autobus? etc.
   - Hier soir, je suis rentré(e) _____.
6. Comment voyagez-vous le plus souvent (*most often*)? en avion? en bateau? en train? en autocar? Pourquoi? Est-ce pratique? économique? rapide? agréable? etc.
   - Je voyage le plus souvent _____ parce que c'est _____.
7. Aimez-vous voyager en avion? par le train? par bateau?
   - Oui, j'aime voyager _____.
   - Non, je n'aime pas voyager _____.
   - Je n'ai jamais voyagé _____.
8. Avez-vous déjà *(ever)* voyagé en avion? Quand? Il y a une semaine? *(one week ago)?* Il y a un mois? Il y a un an? Il y a longtemps? Comment êtes-vous allé(e) à l'aéroport? en taxi? en voiture? en métro? etc.
   - Oui. J'ai voyagé en avion il y a _____.
   - Je suis allé(e) à l'aéroport _____.
   - Non. Je n'ai jamais voyagé en avion.

4. For additional cities and countries, see **Entracte** 12: Nationalities and Geographical Place Names, pages 367 and 374.

9. En avion voyagez-vous en première classe ou en classe touriste?
 • Je voyage _____.

10. Avez-vous déjà voyagé par le train? Quand? Il y a un mois? Il y a longtemps? Comment êtes-vous allé(e) à la gare? Avez-vous pris l'autobus? le métro? un taxi?
 • J'ai voyagé par le train il y a _____.
 • J'ai pris _____ pour aller à la gare.
 • Je n'ai jamais voyagé par le train.

11. Où allez-vous ce soir? chez vous? au cinéma? dans une discothèque? chez un(e) ami(e)? en ville *(downtown)?* Comment y allez-vous? en métro? en autobus? en taxi? à pied? Où allez-vous demain? Comment y allez-vous?
 • Ce soir je vais _____. J'y vais _____.
 • Demain je vais _____. J'y vais _____.

   EXEMPLE: *Ce soir je vais au cinéma. J'y vais en autobus.*

12. Pensez-vous faire un voyage? Où? en France? au Canada? en Chine? etc.[4] Quand pensez-vous partir? bientôt? la semaine prochaine? le mois prochain? dans une semaine? dès que possible? dimanche prochain?
 • Oui, je pense faire un voyage.
 • J'aimerais aller à/en/au/aux _____.
 • Je pense partir _____.
 • Non, je n'ai pas de projets de voyage *(any travel plans)*.

13. Possédez-vous (Avez-vous) une voiture? de quelle marque *(make)?* une Chevrolet? une Cadillac? une Volkswagen? Est-elle neuve *(new)?* Possédez-vous (Avez-vous) une bicyclette? une moto(cyclette)? un vélomoteur? de quelle marque?
 • Oui. Je possède (J'ai) _____. C'est une _____.
 • Non. Je ne possède pas de _____. Je n'ai pas de _____.

H. **Review.** What have you learned about your classmates from these **Conversations?**

EXEMPLES: *Marc a envie de voir Paris.*
Marie va au supermarché en voiture.
Monsieur Smith a une Toyota. Elle est neuve.

Trains in France.   In France, as in most of Europe, trains are the most popular means of public transportation. They are fast, efficient, and convenient. French trains are operated by the Société Nationale des Chemins de Fer Français (SNCF), a government regulated monopoly.

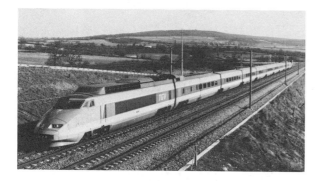

Travel Conditions.   Very high legal speed limits (75 m.p.h. on highways, 55 m.p.h. on all other roads), along with a profusion of three-lane highways (with the center lane providing a free-for-all passing lane for *both* directions), result in rather dangerous driving conditions throughout France. Pedestrians (les piétons) and bikers must exercise extreme caution.

Bicycles, Motorbikes, Motorcycles.   Les deux roues (two-wheeled vehicles) are very popular in France. These include bicycles, motorbikes, motor scooters and motorcycles. Their popularity is partly due to financial considerations. They are considerably less expensive than cars, both to purchase and to operate.

En métro.   To procure a book of tickets for the Paris métro, ask for Un carnet première/ seconde, s'il vous plaît. The first class cars are located in the center of the train. Tickets for these places are more expensive.

LANGUAGE AND CULTURE

En taxi.   To see if a taxi is free, ask the driver: Taxi! Êtes-vous libre? To say where you would like to go: À la gare, s'il vous plaît! You may wish to add: Et je suis pressé(e)! *(I am in a hurry.)*

Sur la route, en voiture.   At the gas station in France, request ordinaire, super, gas-oil (Canada: diesel), or essence sans plomb *(lead-free gasoline).* Faites le plein roughly means "Fill 'er up!"

French signs.   Here are some signs you may well encounter in your travels.

No parking. Driveway.

No pedestrians allowed.

Private way. No motor vehicles allowed.

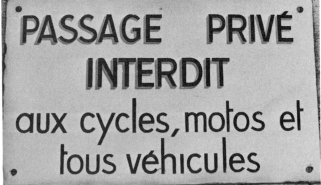

VERBES IRRÉGULIERS: conduire, mettre

➤
conduire to drive
LE PRÉSENT: je **conduis**   nous **conduisons**   tu **conduis**   vous **conduisez**   il/elle/on **conduit**   ils/elles **conduisent**
LE PASSÉ COMPOSÉ: j'**ai conduit**, etc.
LA BASE DU FUTUR ET DU CONDITIONNEL: **conduir-**

Exercice d'application: **conduire**

A.   **Questions with *conduire*.** (You may wish to use the **tu** form of address with your classmates.)

1. Savez-vous (sais-tu) conduire?
2. Aimez-vous (Aimes-tu) conduire?
3. Avez-vous (As-tu) peur de conduire *(Are you afraid of driving)* quand il y a beaucoup de circulation *(traffic)?*
4. D'habitude est-ce que vous conduisez (tu conduis) prudemment *(carefully)?* lentement? à grande vitesse *(fast)?* à toute vitesse *(at top speed)?*
5. Avez-vous un permis de conduire *(driver's license)?*
6. Avez-vous un permis de conduire international?

➤
mettre   to put, to place, to put on; to take (time)
LE PRÉSENT: je **mets**   nous **mettons**   tu **mets**   vous **mettez**   il/elle/on **met**   ils/elles **mettent**
LE PASSÉ COMPOSÉ: j'**ai mis**, etc.
LA BASE DU FUTUR ET DU CONDITIONNEL: **mettr-**

1. **Mettre** means "to put" or "to place."

Je ne sais pas où **j'ai mis** les billets.	I don't know where I put the tickets.
Mettez-le sur la table.	Put (place) it on the table.

2. **Mettre** can also mean "to put on" (referring to clothing).

Qu'est-ce que **je mets** ce soir?	What will I put on tonight?

3. **Mettre** also means "to take (time)." [5]

Combien de temps **mettez-vous** pour aller au bureau?	How long does it take you to get to the office?

Exercices d'application: **mettre**

B.   **Où avez-vous mis votre livre?**   Ask your classmates where they put certain of their possessions when they came to class. Answers will include: **Le voilà, La voilà,** and **Les voilà.** Possessions to inquire about include: **votre livre** (*m.*), **votre sac à main** (*m.*), **votre sac à dos** (*m.*), **votre stylo** (*m.*), **vos livres** (*m.*), **votre cahier** (*m.*), **votre crayon** (*m.*), **vos clés** (*f.*), **votre serviette** (*f.*) (*briefcase*). (You may wish to use the **tu** form of address with your classmates.)

EXEMPLES: —*Où avez-vous mis votre livre?*
—*Le voilà.*
—*Où as-tu mis tes clés?*
—*Les voilà.*

C.   **Questions with *mettre*.**   Answer these questions yourself. Then practice using the verb **mettre** by asking your classmates the same questions. (You may wish to use the **tu** form of address with your classmates.)

1. Combien de temps mettez-vous (mets-tu) pour venir en classe?
2. Combien de temps mettez-vous pour aller chez vous?
3. Combien de temps mettez-vous pour venir en classe quand il pleut? quand il y a beaucoup de circulation (*traffic*)?

STRUCTURES

Structure 1: Complementary Infinitives

When an infinitive follows a verb in French, in some instances a preposition (**à, de**) is used before the infinitive. In other cases, no preposition is used.

1. The following verbs commonly used in conversational French take no preposition when followed by an infinitive.

adorer to adore	**aller** to go
aimer to like	**compter** to intend, to plan
aimer mieux to prefer	**détester** to detest, to hate

5. We have a similar idiomatic expression in English: *to put in (time): How much time do you put in each day at the office? Oh, I put in eight hours or so.*

falloir to be necessary	**préférer**[6] to prefer
oser to dare	**savoir** to know how (to)
penser to intend, to think (of)	**sembler** to seem
pouvoir to be able, can	**vouloir** to wish, to want

Examples from this chapter:

Je **pense** y **aller** en avion.
Je **vais vérifier**.
Je **peux** vous **confirmer** une place.
Il **faut** y **arriver** une heure à l'avance.

2. The following verbs commonly used in conversational French take the preposition **à** when followed by an infinitive.

aider à to help	**hésiter à** to hesitate
s'amuser à to enjoy, to have fun	**s'intéresser à** to be interested in
apprendre à to learn	**inviter à** to invite
commencer à to begin	**se préparer à** to get ready
continuer à to continue	

J'apprends à faire du ski.
Je me prépare à partir en vacances.

3. The following verbs commonly used in conversational French take the preposition **de** when followed by an infinitive.

accepter de to accept	**décider de** to decide
s'arrêter de to stop	**essayer de** to try
avoir l'air de to seem	**être en train de** to be in the process of
avoir besoin de to need	**s'excuser de** to excuse, to be sorry
avoir envie de to feel like	**finir de** to finish
avoir l'intention de to intend	**oublier de** to forget
avoir peur de to be afraid	**refuser de** to refuse
cesser de to stop	**regretter de** to regret, to be sorry

Examples from this chapter:

J'**ai** très **envie de** voir Marseille.
Et n'**oubliez** pas **de** confirmer votre réservation.

Exercices d'application: Complementary Infinitives

A.   **J'ai envie de voir Paris.**   Complete each of the following sentences about yourself, using an infinitive. In addition to the verbs presented in this **Structure,** you may also wish to refer to the **-er** verbs in Chapter 2, page 47, and the **-ir** and **-re** verbs in Chapter 4, pages 109 and 111.

---

6. *Note:* **je préfère, tu préfères, il préfère, ils préfèrent.** (See **Appendice**: Spelling Changes in Certain **-er** verbs.)

1. Je sais _____.
2. Je ne sais pas _____.
3. J'adore _____.
4. Je n'aime pas _____.
5. Je pense _____.
6. Je m'amuse à _____.
7. J'hésite à _____.
8. J'ai envie de _____.
9. J'ai l'intention de _____.
10. J'ai peur de _____.

B. **Elle a envie de voir Paris.** If the preceding exercise has been used orally in class, review what you have learned about your classmates.

EXEMPLES: *Marc aime voyager.*
Madame Smith a envie de voir la France.
Marie a l'intention d'étudier ce soir.

C. **Questions with Complementary Infinitives.** Answer these questions yourself. Then practice using complementary infinitives by asking your classmates these same questions. (You may wish to use the **tu** form of address with your classmates.)

1. Avez-vous (As-tu) envie de voir la France?
2. Avez-vous envie de faire un voyage?
3. Où aimeriez-vous (aimerais-tu) aller?
4. Avez-vous l'intention de partir en voyage?
5. Quand est-ce que vous comptez (tu comptes) partir?
6. Où avez-vous l'intention d'aller?
7. Qu'est-ce que vous vous amusez (tu t'amuses) à faire pendant les voyages?

Structure 2: Infinitives after Certain Prepositions and Expressions

An infinitive is used after the following prepositions and expressions in French. (In English, the *-ing* form of the verb is used.)

avant de before	**Avant de partir,** venez me voir.
	Before leaving, come see me.
sans without	Il est parti **sans dire** au revoir.
	He left without saying good-bye.
au lieu de instead of	**Au lieu d'aller** à Paris, allez à Marseille.
	Instead of going to Paris, go to Marseilles.
passer son temps à to spend one's time	**Je passe mon temps à** voyager.
	I spend my time traveling.

Exercices d'application: Infinitives after Certain Prepositions and Expressions

D.   Moi, je passe mon temps à travailler.   Complete each of the following sentences about yourself, using infinitives.

1. Moi, je passe mon temps à _____, à _____ et à _____.
2. Ce matin j'ai quitté la maison sans _____.
3. Au lieu de/d'_____, je regarde la télévision.
4. Avant de/d'_____, j'aime regarder la télévision.

E.   Elle passe son temps à étudier.   If the preceding exercise has been used orally in class, review what you have learned about your classmates.

EXEMPLES: *Marc passe son temps à lire.*
Anne regarde la télévision au lieu d'étudier.
Monsieur Smith a quitté la maison sans lire je journal.

Structure 3: Adverbs

Adverbs modify verbs, adjectives, and other adverbs.

1. Here are some common adverbs that you have already used in this book.

à présent now	**enfin** at last, finally	**puis** then
assez enough	**ensuite** then	**si** so
aujourd'hui today	**hier** yesterday	**souvent** often
aussi also	**ici** here	**surtout** above all,
beaucoup very much, a	**jamais** ever, never	especially
lot	**là** there	**tant** so much, so many
bien well	**là-bas** over there	**tard** late
bientôt soon	**longtemps** for a long	**tôt** early
d'abord at first	time	**toujours** always
de bonne heure early	**mal** badly	**tout de suite**
déjà already	**même** even	immediately
demain tomorrow	**parfois** sometimes	**trop** too much, too
de temps en temps from	**partout** everywhere	many
time to time	**peut-être** perhaps	**vite** quickly
encore again, still	**presque** almost	

2. Some adverbs are formed by adding **-ment** to the masculine singular form of the corresponding adjective *if the adjective ends in a vowel.* This is the equivalent of the English adverbial ending *-ly.* For example, **vrai** *(true)* becomes **vraiment** *(truly).*

absolu	*absolument*	absolutely
autre	*autrement*	otherwise
facile	*facilement*	easily

probable	*probablement*	probably
rapide	*rapidement*	rapidly
vrai	*vraiment*	truly

3. Some adverbs are formed by adding **-ment** to the feminine singular form of the adjective when the masculine singular form of the adjective does *not* end in a vowel. For example, **lente** (feminine form, *slow*) becomes **lentement**.

actif, active	*activement*	actively
franc, franche	*franchement*	frankly
heureux, heureuse	*heureusement*	fortunately
lent, lente	*lentement*	slowly
naturel, naturelle	*naturellement*	naturally, of course
premier, première	*premièrement*	firstly, first of all
seul, seule	*seulement*	only
sûr, sûre	*sûrement*	surely

Note these irregularities:

| bref, brève | *brièvement* | briefly |
| gentil, gentille | *gentiment* | kindly, nicely |

With certain adverbs, the final **e** of the feminine adjective becomes **é** and is therefore pronounced:

énorme	*énormément*	enormously
précis, précise	*précisément*	precisely, exactly
profond, profonde	*profondément*	profoundly, deeply

4. Some adverbs are formed by replacing the final **-ant** of the adjective with **-amment** or by replacing the final **-ent** of the adjective with **-emment**.

constant	*constamment*	constantly
différent	*différemment*	differently
évident	*évidemment*	obviously
fréquent	*fréquemment*	frequently
indépendant	*indépendamment*	independently
intelligent	*intelligemment*	intelligently
prudent	*prudemment*	carefully
récent	*récemment*	recently

Pronunciation Note: Both the **-amment** and **-emment** endings are pronounced [amã].

5. The position of adverbs in a sentence:

a. In simple (as opposed to "compound") French tenses (the present, the **imparfait**, the future, and the conditional), an adverb never comes between the subject and the verb. It usually follows the verb directly: **Il va toujours en France.** This is unlike English, where the adverb would be placed between the subject and the verb: *He always goes to France.*

b. In compound tenses, like the **passé composé**, short adverbs usually come between the helping verb and the past participle. These include: **mal, bien, vite, même, déjà, bientôt, encore, enfin, jamais, longtemps, souvent, toujours, assez, beaucoup, trop, peu, tant,** and **peut-être.** For example: **J'ai bien dormi.** *(I slept well.)* **Je n'ai pas bien dormi.** *(I did not sleep well.)*

c. Adverbs that end in **-ment** are usually placed after the past participle in compound tenses: **Je l'ai fait lentement.** *(I did it slowly). Exceptions:* **certainement, probablement, vraiment. Il a probablement voyagé en France.**

d. Some adverbs of time (such as **hier, aujourd'hui, demain, tôt, tard**) and adverbs of place (such as **ici, là, là-bas**) usually begin or end the sentence: **Hier je suis allé au supermarché. Je suis allé au supermarché hier.**

e. **Y** *(there, to that place)* precedes the verb except with positive commands: **J'y vais.** *But:* **Allez-y!**

f. With a conjugated verb and an infinitive, the adverb generally precedes the infinitive: **Je vais beaucoup voyager.** *(I'm going to travel a lot.)*

g. In conversation, adverbs may stand alone as answers:
   Naturellement!   Moi, jamais!   Oui, probablement.

Exercices d'application: Adverbs

F.   **Je parle français assez bien.**   Describe yourself by completing each of the following sentences with an adverb presented in this chapter.

1. Je voyage _____.
2. Je travaille _____.
3. Je conduis _____.
4. Je parle français _____.
5. Je vois mes amis _____.
6. Je vais au supermarché _____.
7. J'étudie _____.
8. Je parle _____.

G.   **Il voyage beaucoup.**   If the preceding exercise has been used orally in class, review what you have learned about your classmates.

EXEMPLES: *Robert voyage beaucoup.*
            Jeanne voit ses amis de temps en temps.
            Madame Smith conduit prudemment.

H.   **Oui, toujours.**   Answer these questions yourself. Then, ask your classmates. Responses may be selected from the following adverbs: **hier, récemment, ce matin, aujourd'hui, maintenant, trop, beaucoup, constamment, probablement, malheureusement, peut-être, jamais, souvent, rarement, de temps en temps,** and **toujours.**

MODÈLE: Voyagez-vous?   *Oui, souvent.*
                    ou: *Non, jamais.*
                    ou: *Oui, toujours.*

1. Fumez-vous?
2. Allez-vous à la poste?
3. Téléphonez-vous à vos amis?
4. Téléphonez-vous à vos parents?
5. Avez-vous mangé?

6. Voyagez-vous seul(e) *(alone)*?
7. Avez-vous parlé avec le professeur?
8. Pensez-vous aller en France?
9. Avez-vous étudié?

I. **Oui, je voyage beaucoup.** Now respond again to the questions of the preceding exercise. This time, however, use complete sentences. Place the adverb correctly in the sentence.

EXEMPLES: *Oui, je voyage beaucoup.*
Oui, j'ai trop mangé.

J. **Il voyage beaucoup.** If the preceding exercise has been used orally in class, review what you have learned about your classmates.

EXEMPLES: *Monsieur Smith voyage beaucoup.*
Robert a beaucoup étudié.
Marie a trop mangé.

Synthèse

En vacances. The following questions are related to the topic of vacations. They require familiarity with all portions of this chapter. Answer these questions about yourself. Then ask your classmates. (You may wish to use the **tu** form of address with your classmates.)

1. Avez-vous (As-tu) envie de partir en vacances en ce moment?
2. Est-ce que vous partez (tu pars) en vacances? Quand comptez-vous partir? bientôt? dans une semaine? le week-end? dimanche prochain? etc. Où allez-vous? Avec qui? avec des ami(e)s? avec votre famille? seul(e)?
3. Où allez-vous (vas-tu) passer vos (tes) prochaines vacances *(next vacation)?* les vacances d'été *(summer vacation)?* de Noël? de Pâques *(Easter)?* Allez-vous passer vos vacances chez vous? chez des amis? à la campagne *(in the country)?* à la montagne? à la plage *(beach)?* dans une station de ski *(ski resort)?* à l'étranger *(abroad)?* en Europe? en Floride?[7]
4. Êtes-vous parti(e) en vacances récemment? Où êtes-vous allé(e)? Quand? Avec qui?
5. Combien de semaines de vacances avez-vous cette année? Avez-vous déjà pris vos vacances?
6. Achetez-vous des chèques de voyage avant de partir en vacances?
7. Prenez-vous beaucoup de photos lorsque vous êtes en vacances?

---

7. For additional places and geographical names, see **Entractes** 10 and 12.

A.S. = aller simple *(one way)*

A.R. = aller retour *(round trip)*

8. Achetez-vous des souvenirs lorsque vous êtes en vacances? Pour qui?
9. Qu'est-ce que vous vous amusez à faire pendant les vacances?
10. Qu'est-ce que vous refusez de faire pendant les vacances?

PRONONCIATION

1. Sound (Phonetic Symbol): [w]

SPELLING:	**ou** (followed by a vowel), **oi, oî, oy**
ENGLISH SOUND RESEMBLED:	Initial sound in word <u>w</u>et
PRONUNCIATION:	This semivowel (or semiconsonant) sound resembles the French vowel sound [u]. It is pronounced more tensely and briefly, however. It is always combined with a following vowel sound.

EXAMPLES FROM THIS CHAPTER:

v<u>oi</u>ture	v<u>oi</u>r	sav<u>oi</u>r
s<u>oi</u>r	m<u>oi</u>s	voul<u>oi</u>r
tr<u>oi</u>s	v<u>oi</u>e	bes<u>oi</u>n
v<u>oy</u>age	fall<u>oi</u>r	parf<u>oi</u>s
ch<u>oi</u>x	pouv<u>oi</u>r	l<u>oue</u>r[8]

8. Note that **louer** is pronounced as one syllable: [lwe].

2. Sound (Phonetic Symbol): [ɥ]

SPELLING:	**u** (followed by a vowel)
PRONUNCIATION:	The semivowel (or semiconsonant) sound [ɥ] resembles the French vowel sound [y]. The lips are protruded slightly further than for the [y] sound. Also, [ɥ] is said more rapidly and tensely than [y]. [ɥ] is always combined in French with a following vowel. Do not confuse this sound with the English sound [w].
EXAMPLES FROM THIS CHAPTER:	conduire aujourd'hui ensuite
	je suis puis tout de suite

3. Sound (Phonetic Symbol): [ʒ]

SPELLING:	**j, g** (followed by **i, e, y**)
ENGLISH SOUND RESEMBLED:	Middle consonant sound in the words *pleasure* and *treasure*
PRONUNCIATION:	Do not add a [d] sound before the [ʒ] sound, as in the English words *age* or *jump*.
EXAMPLES FROM THIS CHAPTER:	en voyage objets agent
	agence de voyages toujours jeudi
	bon voyage Genève je

4. Sound (Phonetic Symbol): [g]

SPELLING:	**g** (followed by **a, o, u, r**)
ENGLISH SOUND RESEMBLED:	Initial sound in English word *get*.
EXAMPLES FROM THIS CHAPTER:	aérogare regretter
	guichet gare

Notes: 1. **Second** is pronounced [səgɔ̃].
2. The spelling **e** + **x** + vowel is pronounced [ɛgz]. Examples from this chapter: exercice, par exemple.

5. Sound (Phonetic Symbol): [ɲ]

SPELLING:	**gn**
ENGLISH SOUND RESEMBLED:	Medial sound in words *onion* and *canyon*
PRONUNCIATION:	The [ɲ] sound is tenser and briefer than the English sound it resembles.
EXAMPLES FROM THIS CHAPTER:	campagne montagne signez
	consigne signature

Projet

Travel inquiries *(Exercice oral ou écrit).* You have jotted down some notes to remind yourself to ask your travel agent about an upcoming trip from Marseilles to Paris. Glancing at your brief notes, what questions will you ask?

> train? avion?
>
> direct?
>
> prix par train? avion?
>
> heures de départ? jours?
>
> prix réduits certains jours?
>
> durée du voyage..... train? avion? voiture?
>
> faut-il réserver? quand? où?
>
> hôtels?
>
> restaurants?

Activités: Learning by Doing

A. **À l'aéroport.** Turn the classroom into an airport by making and posting signs that say: **Renseignements** *(Information)*, **Comptoir de la ligne aérienne** *(Ticket Counter)*, **Porte numéro 7** *(Gate 7)*, **Consigne** *(Checkroom)*, **Objets trouvés** *(Lost and Found)*, **Salle d'attente** *(Waiting Room)*, **Guichet numéro 3** *(Ticket Window 3)*, and so on.

Comptoir: Go to the **Comptoir de la ligne aérienne** and purchase a plane ticket from the student ticket agent, who will ask you appropriate questions while filling out your ticket: **Votre nom, s'il vous plaît? Où allez-vous? Quand partirez-vous? À quelle heure? Quelle classe—économique ou première? Fumeur ou non-fumeur?** etc.

**BILLET
AIR FRANCE**

Nom de voyageur:_____

À destination de:_____

Date:_____

Départ:_____ heures

Prix:_____ francs

Air France Vol Numéro:_____

Classe ☐ touriste/économique/seconde   ☐ première

      ☐ Fumeurs   ☐ Non-fumeurs

      ☐ Aller simple   ☐ Aller-retour

Renseignements: Go to the area marked **Renseignements** and make inquiries: **Où se trouve la consigne, s'il vous plaît? Où se trouve le comptoir de la ligne aérienne? Ou est le bureau des objets trouvés? À quelle heure part l'avion pour...? Comment puis-je me rendre en ville?** etc.

Objets trouvés: Go to the **Objets trouvés** to reclaim a lost item: **J'ai perdu ma valise** (*suitcase*)/**mon passeport/mon stylo/ma serviette** (*briefcase*)/**mes bagages à main** (*carry-on luggage*)/**mon sac à main** (*purse*), etc.

Consigne: Check your coat, jacket, bookbag, etc. at the area called **La Consigne**.

Salle d'attente: In the **Salle d'attente** area, make travel-related chitchat with other travelers (your classmates) based on the vocabulary of this chapter: **Êtes-vous en vacances? Êtes-vous en voyage d'affaires? Où allez-vous? Combien de temps comptez-vous y rester? Voyagez-vous seul(e)? Avez-vous déjà voyagé en avion?** etc.

When your flight is announced, take your ticket and boarding pass. Go to **Porte numéro 7**. Board your flight. **Bon Voyage!**

B.   **À la gare.**   Turn the classroom into a train station **(la gare)** by making and posting signs that say. **Renseignements** (*Information*), **Bureau de location** (*Ticket Office*), **Accès aux quais** (*This way to the train platforms*), **Voie** (*Track*) **N° 1, Voie N° 2, Voie N° 3, Quai N° 1, Quai N° 2, Consigne** (*Checkroom*), **Objets trouvés** (*Lost and Found*), **Salle d'attente** (*Waiting Room*), and so on.

Go to the **Bureau de location de la gare** and purchase a train ticket from the student ticket agent. See the preceding **activité, À l'Aéroport,** regarding what to do at the areas designated **Renseignements, Objets trouvés, Consigne,** and **Salle d'attente.** The following vocabulary will prove useful:

Où se trouve le bureau de location de la gare/le compartiment non-fumeurs/le quai N° 1/la voie N° 5/le wagon-bar/le wagon-lit/le wagon-restaurant?	Where is the train station ticket office/no smoking compartment/train platform N° 1/track N° 5/club car/sleeping car/ restaurant car?
Un aller simple/un aller-retour première classe/deuxième classe pour le train de sept heures pour Québec, s'il vous plaît.	A one-way ticket/round-trip ticket first class/second class for the seven o'clock train to Québec, please.
Je voudrais louer une couchette.	I'd like to reserve a berth.
À quelle heure part le prochain train pour Paris?	What time does the next train for Paris leave?
C'est bien le train pour Paris?	This is the train for Paris, isn't it?
En voiture! Vos billets, s'il vous plaît.	All aboard! (Your) Tickets, please.
Pardon, est-ce que cette place est libre?	Excuse me, is this seat free?

C.   **Passport.**   By filling out a passport form for a classmate, you will review some basic question formats and some practical conversational phrases while learning some interesting biographical information about your partner. Using the illustration given here as a model, make your own passport form by folding a sheet of blank paper in half. Obtain the necessary information by asking the following questions[9]:

1. Comment vous appelez-vous? Quelle est l'orthographe exacte de votre prénom? de votre nom de famille? Pardon?
2. Quand êtes-vous né(e)?
3. Où êtes-vous né(e)?
4. Quelle est votre nationalité?
5. De quelle couleur sont vos yeux? (bleus? bruns? gris? marron? verts? noirs?)
6. De quelle couleur sont vos cheveux? (blancs? blonds? bruns? châtains? gris? noirs? roux?)
7. Où habitez-vous? Quelle est votre adresse?
8. Quelle est la date aujourd'hui? C'est le __, 19 __. Ce passeport expire donc le __, 19 __ (dans cinq ans).

To assign a passport number, ask for a telephone number or a social security number. **Quel est votre numéro de téléphone?** To secure a signature, say, **Signez ici, s'il vous plaît**. In the space marked **Photo**, sketch your partner's face.

Photo

Numéro du passeport: _____
Signature du titulaire:

_____

PASSEPORT

Nom: _____
Sexe: _____
Date de naissance: _____
Lieu de naissance: _____
Nationalité: _____
Yeux: _____
Cheveux: _____
Adresse du titulaire: _____
Date de délivrance: _____
Date d'expiration: _____

9. You may wish to review the following **Entractes** for the questions above: **1** (The Alphabet), **2** (Numbers), **4** (Dates), **7** (Adjectives: Physical Traits), **12** (Nationalities and Geographical Place Names).

Qu'est-ce que vous aimez faire?

Sports, Hobbies, and Pastimes

Heureux au jeu, malheureux en amour.

Lucky in games, unlucky in love.

Knowing the terms for a variety of pastimes will allow you to make plans, share interests, arrange dates, and make social conversation. This vocabulary is also useful in interview situations. This **Entracte** may be used as a unit or as three separate conversations: sports, hobbies, and other pastimes.

Qu'est-ce que vous aimez faire?

Réponse: • J'aime _____.[1]

EXEMPLE: *J'aime lire, parler au téléphone, faire du jogging, regarder la télévision, écouter de la musique et jouer de la guitare.*

Vocabulaire à retenir	Vocabulary items under the heading **Vocabulaire à retenir** may be substituted *directly* into the response format: **J'aime** _____. No grammatical manipulation is necessary. **J'aime lire** may be translated as *I like to read* or *I like reading. Note:* The items in the first lists are those most frequently requested by students. For additional items in each category, see the Resource List at the end of this **Entracte**.

Sports

courir run	faire des promenades walk
faire de la bicyclette bike ride	faire du ski ski
faire du cheval horseback ride	jouer au football play soccer
faire de la gymnastique exercise, do gymnastics	jouer au golf play golf
faire du jogging jog	jouer au tennis play tennis
	nager swim

Hobbies

bricoler putter	jouer du piano play piano
coudre sew	manger eat
dessiner draw	prendre des photos take pictures
faire (de) la cuisine cook	jardiner garden
faire des mots-croisés do crossword puzzles	tricoter knit
jouer de la guitare play guitar	

Entertainment and Other Pastimes

aller au cinéma go to the movies	bavarder/causer avec des amis chat with friends
aller voir des amis go see friends	
chanter sing	danser dance

1. What do you like to do? I like to _____.

dépenser de l'argent spend money	lire read
dîner au restaurant eat out	parler au téléphone talk on the phone
dormir sleep	prendre un verre avec des amis have a drink
écouter de la musique listen to music	with friends
faire des achats shop	recevoir des amis entertain, have friends over
faire un tour en auto go for a drive	regarder la télévision watch television
jouer aux cartes play cards	voyager travel

Springboards for Conversation

Ask your classmates these personalized questions. When two or more responses are possible, alternate answer formats are offered. Select the option that best applies to you personally. Do not limit your responses simply to those suggestions offered in these questions. Use the inclusive vocabulary options provided in this **Entracte**.

1. Qu'est-ce que vous aimez faire? Quoi d'autre? C'est tout?
   - J'aime _____.
   - J'aime beaucoup

2. Qu'est-ce que vous savez (know how to) faire? faire du ski? danser? nager? jouer au tennis? dessiner? tricoter? jouer au football? jouer du piano? etc.

   - Je sais _____.
   - Je sais très bien _____.
   - Je ne sais pas _____.
   - Je ne sais pas _____ du tout (at all).

Récapitulation

How much can you recall about your classmates and instructor? Answer formats are provided.

1. Qu'est-ce que le professeur aime faire? Et Madame...? Et Monsieur...? Et Mademoiselle...? Et votre voisin(e) de gauche? Et votre voisin(e) de droite? etc.
   - Il/Elle aime _____.
   Note: If a favorite activity is forgotten, simply ask again: **Pardon. Je suis désolé(e), mais j'ai oublié. Qu'est-ce que vous aimez faire? Ah oui. C'est ça. Merci bien.** To verify use **c'est ça** or **n'est-ce pas: Vous aimez faire du jogging, n'est-ce pas?**

2. Qui dans la classe aime _____? (jouer au golf, jouer au tennis, faire du jogging, écouter de la musique, lire, aller au théâtre, etc.)

   - Monsieur/Madame/Mademoiselle... aime _____.
   - Le professeur aime _____.
   - Moi, j'aime _____.
   - Tout le monde aime _____.
   - Personne n'aime _____.

3. Qui dans la classe sait _____? (nager, jouer au tennis, faire du ski, jouer au bridge, jouer du piano, jouer de la guitare, etc.)
   - Monsieur/Madame/Mademoiselle... sait _____.
   - Le professeur sait _____.
   - Moi, je sais _____, mais pas très bien.
   - Tout le monde sait _____.
   - Personne ne sait _____.

4. Quels sports pratique le professeur? Et
   Monsieur...? Et Madame...? Et
   Mademoiselle...? etc.

- Il/Elle fait du/de la _____.
- Il/Elle joue au _____.
- Il/Elle ne pratique pas de sport.

Expansion

The **Expansion** can be used for partners or group conversation and for oral or written
composition. Answer formats are provided.

1. Qu'est-ce que vous aimez faire tous les
   jours *(every day)*?
   • J'aime _____ tous les jours.

2. Qu'est-ce que vous aimez faire le week-
   end?
   • J'aime _____.

3. Qu'est-ce que vous aimez faire pendant
   les vacances?
   • J'aime _____.

4. Qu'est-ce que vous aimez faire en hiver
   (in winter)?
   • J'aime _____.

5. Qu'est-ce que vous aimez faire en été *(in
   summer)*?
   • J'aime _____.

6. Qu'est-ce que vous préférez faire le matin
   (in the morning)?
   • Je préfère _____ le matin.

7. Qu'est-ce que vous préférez faire le soir
   (in the evening)?
   • Je préfère _____ le soir.

8. Qu'est-ce que vous n'aimez pas faire?
   Pourquoi?
   • Je n'aime pas _____.
   • C'est ennuyeux *(boring)*.
   • Je suis trop *(too)* maladroit(e) *(clumsy)*,
     vieux/vieille *(old)*, occupé(e) *(busy)*, etc.
   • C'est trop dangereux, difficile, fatigant
     (tiring), etc.

9. Qu'est-ce que vous allez faire aujourd'hui?
   • Je vais _____.

10. Qu'est-ce que vous allez faire cette
    semaine *(this week)*?
    • Je vais _____.

11. Qu'est-ce que vous allez faire ce week-
    end?
    • Je vais _____.

Vocabulaire utile   The following phrases are frequently requested by students using the
conversations of this **Entracte** related to sports, hobbies, and pastimes.

Voyons... Let's see...
Euh... Umm...
Pardon? Excuse me?
Ah oui? Oh really?
Quelle coïncidence! What a
  coincidence!
Moi aussi, j'aime... I, too, like...
Vous aussi? You too?
Pourquoi pas? Why not?

Certainement. Certainly.
Oui! C'est ça. Yes. That's right.
Ça dépend. It depends.
De temps en temps, oui. From
  time to time.
Ah non. No.
Pas du tout! Not at all.
Moi non plus. I don't either.

Vous non plus? You neither?
Pas particulièrement. Not
  particularly.
Pas beaucoup. Not much.
Pas très bien. Not very well.
Qui moi? Who me?
Jamais! Never!
Dommage! That's too bad.

Sports. Until recently, bicycle riding (**le cyclisme**) was the number one sport in France, with the **Tour de France** being a well-known bicycle competition. Now **le football** *(soccer)* is the sport deemed most popular in France. Skiing is a top winter sport, especially in the French Alps and Pyrénées. **La pétanque** is a common game in France. A wooden ball about the size of an orange (**le cochonnet**) serves as the target, toward which players throw small heavy balls (**les boules**). The team or individual with the most balls nearest **le cochonnet** wins the round.

Le bricolage. "Do-it-yourself" is very popular in France, with all large department stores now catering to this new French interest.

La télévision. Over 90 percent of French households have a television set. The average French family presently spends over eighteen hours per week watching television.

Au café. Another typical French pastime is café sitting: passing an hour or so at a café table, outdoors in the nice weather, having a drink with a friend or sitting by oneself watching the world go by.

LANGUAGE AND CULTURE

Synthèse

A. **Your ideal person.** Describe your ideal mate or friend **(l'homme idéal/la femme idéale)** in terms of his or her abilities and interests. **Il/Elle aime** ____. **Il/Elle aime beaucoup** ____. **Il/Elle sait** ____. **Il/Elle sait très bien** ____. etc.

B. **Qu'est-ce qu'ils font?** Describe or name the pastimes depicted in these photographs.

Photo 1

Photo 2

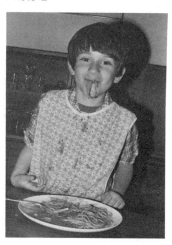

Photo 3

Photo 4

Projets

A. **Agenda.** Make a list of all the activities from this lesson that you plan to do within the next two weeks. Use agenda format. For example:

lundi dîner chez Marc, 7h.	**lundi** regarder la télé, 8h.
mardi cours du soir, 6h.	**mardi** cours du soir, 6h.
mercredi écouter de la musique et coudre de 7h à 9h.	**mercredi** aller au concert avec Marc, 8h.
jeudi cours du soir, 6h.	**jeudi** cours du soir, 6h.
vendredi aller au théâtre, 8h.	**vendredi** aller au cinéma, 6h.
samedi sortir avec Jeanne, 8h.	**samedi** aller danser dans une discothèque, 8h.
dimanche bricoler, dormir, faire la cuisine	**dimanche** bricoler, dormir.

B. **Emploi du temps.** Make a list of all the activities from this lesson that you have done in the past two weeks. You may use conversational format.

EXEMPLE: *Lundi, après la classe de français, j'ai écouté de la musique. Ensuite j'ai parlé au téléphone avec un ami. Puis j'ai regardé la télévision. Mardi, je suis allé(e) au cinéma avec Marc.*

C. **Qu'est-ce que vous aimez faire régulièrement?** What do you like to do regularly? Make a chart showing what you like to do and how often you do it.

Au moins trois fois par semaine	J'aime…
Au moins une fois par semaine	
Au moins une fois par mois	
Au moins une fois par an	

D. **Vos vacances.** Make a list of all the activities mentioned in this lesson that you did on your last vacation.

E. **Photographs.** Leaf through a magazine, describing the activities depicted in photographs, illustrations, and advertisements. (If possible, use a contemporary French magazine.)

Activité: Learning by Doing

Un Sondage. Using the chart format shown in **Projet C**, take a class poll (**un sondage**). Interview your classmates on their activities. For example: **Qu'est-ce que vous faites au moins trois fois par semaine? C'est tout? Quoi d'autre?**

Resource Lists of Additional Pastimes

These additional lists are supplied to allow greater personalization of responses. These items have all been requested by various students actually using such conversations in class.

Sports

chasser hunt
pêcher fish
faire...
  de l'alpinisme mountain climbing
  de l'athlétisme track and field
  de l'aviron rowing, crew
  du bateau boating
  de la boxe boxing
  du catch/de la lutte wrestling
  de la course automobile car racing
  du deltaplane hang gliding

de l'escrime fencing
des exercices exercising
de l'haltérophilie weight lifting
du judo judo
du karaté karate
de la marche à pied hiking
de la moto motorcycle riding
de la musculation body building
du parachutisme parachuting
du patinage sur des roulettes roller skating

du patinage sur glace ice skating
de la planche à voile windsurfing
de la plongée sous-marine scuba diving
du ski de fond/de randonnée cross-country skiing
du ski nautique waterskiing
de la spéléologie spelunking
du tir à l'arc archery
de la voile sailing
du volleyball volleyball

du yoga yoga
jouer...
  au base-ball baseball
  au basket-ball basketball
  au billard billiards
  au football américain football
  au hockey hockey
  au hockey sur glace ice hockey
  au ping-pong Ping-Pong (table tennis)
  au rugby rugby
  au squash squash

Entertainment and Other Pastimes

aller à l'opéra go to the opera
aller à un club go to a club
aller au ballet go to the ballet
aller au bar go to a bar
aller au concert go to a concert
aller au musée go to a museum
aller au théâtre go to the theater
aller aux courses go to the races
aller danser dans une boîte de nuit dance in a nightclub

aller danser dans une discothèque dance in a discotheque
assister à un match go to a game
écouter des disques listen to records
écouter la radio listen to radio
écrire des lettres write letters
faire du camping go camping
faire du lèche-vitrines window-shop

faire un somme nap
jouer au bridge play bridge
jouer aux dames play checkers
jouer aux échecs play chess
jouer au jacquet play backgammon
prendre un bain (chaud) take a (hot) bath
prendre un bain de soleil sunbathe
sortir go out
suivre des cours du soir take night classes

«À votre santé!»

Une Réception

A Social Gathering

Plus on est de fous, plus on rit.

The more, the merrier.

DIALOGUE

This **Dialogue** presents vocabulary for social gatherings: welcoming guests, making introductions, offering and accepting refreshments, and leave-taking. Additional vocabulary presented here can be used when giving and accepting gifts, making apologies, giving compliments, proposing a toast, and making small talk. Vocabulary blocks within this **Dialogue** offer options for personalization as well as possibilities for modification to suit a wide variety of real-life social situations.

Une Réception	A Social Gathering
(Accueil des invités)	*(Welcoming guests)*
L'HÔTE / L'HÔTESSE: Entrez, entrez, je vous prie. Soyez le / la bienvenu(e). Puis-je prendre votre **manteau?**	THE HOST / HOSTESS: Come in, come in, please. Welcome. Can I take your **coat?**
cape chapeau fourrure imperméable parapluie serviette	cape hat fur raincoat umbrella briefcase
VOUS: Merci… *(offrant un cadeau)* **Bon anniversaire!**	YOU: Thank you… *(offering a gift)* Happy birthday!
Bonne année! **Bonne fête!** **Bonne et heureuse retraite!** **Bon voyage!** **Joyeux Noël!** **Félicitations!**	Happy New Year! Happy Saint's Day! Happy retirement! (Have a) good trip! Merry Christmas! Congratulations!
L'HÔTE / L'HÔTESSE: C'est très gentil à vous. Mais il ne fallait pas!	HOST / HOSTESS: That's very nice of you. But you shouldn't have done it! *(Literally:* It wasn't necessary.*)*
VOUS: C'est peu de chose… un tout petit rien.	YOU: It's nothing *(Literally:* It's only a little thing… a very little something.*)*
L'HÔTE / L'HÔTESSE: Merci beaucoup! Entrez… Que puis-je vous offrir? Un whisky? Des chips?	HOST / HOSTESS: Thank you very much. Come in… What can I offer you? A whiskey? Potato chips?
VOUS: **Un verre de vin (blanc/rouge/rosé),**	YOU: **A glass of (white/red/rosé) wine,**
Du champagne **Un cognac** **De l'eau minérale** **Un gin** **Un jus de fruits** **Un porto** **Un rhum** **Un Xérès**	Champagne Cognac Mineral water Gin Fruit juice Port (wine) Rum Sherry
s'il vous plaît.[1]	please.

1. For additional food and beverage items, see Chapter 3: **Au Restaurant**.

L'HÔTE / L'HÔTESSE (*trinquant*): À votre santé!

VOUS: À la vôtre!... **C'est délicieux!**
| C'est très rafraîchissant!
| Quel parfum!

L'HÔTE / L'HÔTESSE: Encore un peu?
VOUS: **Bien volontiers.**
| Avec plaisir.
| Oui, s'il vous plaît.
| Merci, non.[2]
| Un peu.
| Un doigt. / Une goutte. / Une larme.

L'HÔTE / L'HÔTESSE (*renversant accidentellement le contenu de la bouteille sur vous*): Oh! Pardon. Comme je suis maladroit(e)!
VOUS: Il n'y a pas de mal... Je vous en prie, ce n'est pas grave...

෴

(*Conversations au salon*)
L'HÔTE / L'HÔTESSE: Je suis vraiment content(e) de vous revoir.
VOUS: Moi de même... C'est vraiment charmant chez vous.
L'HÔTE / L'HÔTESSE: Merci beaucoup. Mais dites-moi, que faites-vous ces temps-ci?
VOUS: **Pas grand-chose.**
| Rien de particulier.
| Rien de très intéressant.
| Je suis très occupé(e) ces jours-ci.
| Toujours la même chose.
| Je travaille dur comme toujours.
| Je travaille comme volontaire.
| Je suis à la retraite.
| Je suis en chômage.

L'HÔTE / L'HÔTESSE: Vous avez très bonne mine.
VOUS: Je me sens en forme. Et de toute façon, à quoi bon se plaindre?
L'HÔTE / L'HÔTESSE: C'est vrai... Venez, je voudrais vous présenter à Monsieur / Madame / Mademoiselle...
VOUS: Enchanté(e) (de faire votre connaissance). J'ai beaucoup entendu parler de vous.

HOST / HOSTESS (*proposing a toast*): To your health!
YOU: To yours!... **This is delicious!**
| This is very refreshing!
| What an aroma (taste)!

HOST / HOSTESS: A little more?
YOU: **Gladly!**
| With pleasure.
| Yes, please.
| No, thanks.
| A little.
| Just a drop. (*Literally:* A finger. / A drop. / A tear.)

HOST / HOSTESS (*accidentally spilling the contents of the bottle on you*): Oh! Excuse me. How clumsy I am!
YOU: That's OK... really. (*Literally:* There's no harm... Really, it's not serious.)

෴

(*Making small talk in the living room*)
HOST / HOSTESS: I'm really happy to see you again.
YOU: I am too... You have a lovely place here. (*Literally:* It's really charming at your place.)
HOST / HOSTESS: Thanks so much. But tell me, what are you doing these days?
YOU: **Not much.**
| Nothing in particular.
| Nothing very interesting.
| I'm very busy these days.
| Always the same thing.
| I'm working hard as always.
| I'm working as a volunteer.
| I've retired.
| I'm out of work.

HOST / HOSTESS: You look very well.

YOU: I feel fine. And in any case, what's the use of complaining?
HOST / HOSTESS: That's true... Come, I would like to introduce you to....

YOU: Delighted (to meet you). I've heard a lot about you.

---

2. You can also simply say **merci.** The implication is "No. Thank you." The **non** is understood.

ᶜ·ᵔ

(Fin d'une agréable soirée)
VOUS: Déjà **dix heures**!?! Pas possible!

| **huit heures**
| **huit heures et demie**
| **neuf heures**
| **onze heures**
| **minuit**
| **une heure**

Que le temps passe vite!

L'HÔTE / L'HÔTESSE: Vous partez déjà?
VOUS: Hélas, oui. Je dois me lever de très bonne heure demain matin.
L'HÔTE / L'HÔTESSE: Je suis désolé(e). Merci d'être venu(e)!
VOUS: J'ai passé une soirée très agréable. Merci beaucoup. Au revoir et bonsoir.

ᶜ·ᵔ

(End of a pleasant evening)
YOU: **Ten o'clock** already!?! (It's) not possible!

| eight o'clock
| eight-thirty
| nine o'clock
| eleven o'clock
| midnight
| one o'clock

How time flies! (*Literally:* How time passes quickly!)
HOST / HOSTESS: Are you leaving already?
YOU: Alas, yes. I have to get up very early tomorrow morning.
HOST / HOSTESS: I'm sorry. Thank you for coming!
YOU: I had a very pleasant evening. Thanks so much. Good-bye and good evening.

Phrases à retenir

Memorizing these phrases from the **Dialogue** will help assure fluency in a variety of real-life social situations.

1. C'est très gentil à vous.
2. Un verre de vin rouge, s'il vous plaît.
3. À votre santé! À la vôtre!
4. Bien volontiers.
5. Je suis vraiment content(e) de vous revoir.
6. C'est vraiment charmant chez vous.
7. Vous avez très bonne mine.
8. À quoi bon se plaindre?
9. Enchanté(e) de faire votre connaissance.
10. J'ai passé une soirée très agréable.

DIALOGUE EXERCISES

The following exercises provide oral and written practice in using the vocabulary and basic sentence patterns of the **Dialogue: Une Réception**. These exercises use *only* vocabulary and structures presented in the social gathering **Dialogue**. They do not require familiarity with any other portions of this chapter.

Exercices d'application

A. **Welcoming guests: Soyez le bienvenu!** Welcome the person sitting on your left side and the person on your right. Use **Soyez le bienvenu!** or **Soyez la bienvenue!** Ask if you can take the person's hat (coat, umbrella, etc): **Puis-je prendre votre chapeau (manteau, parapluie)?**

B. **Greetings: Bon anniversaire! Félicitations!** What greeting from the **Dialogue** would you use. . .

1. to wish someone a happy birthday?
2. to wish someone a good trip?
3. to wish someone a good year?
4. to wish someone a Merry Christmas?
5. to congratulate someone?

C. **Offering and accepting refreshments: Que puis-je vous offrir?** Pretend to offer refreshments to the person sitting on your left in class and to the person on your right. Select items from the **Dialogue: Puis-je vous offrir un whisky? du champagne? un verre de vin blanc?** etc. Classmates will accept or refuse, using expressions from the **Dialogue: Bien volontiers, Avec plaisir, Oui, s'il vous plaît, Merci, non,** etc.

D. **Making apologies: Oh! Pardon. Comme je suis maladroit(e)!** Gently bump the desk of the person sitting next to you and apologize for your action: **Oh! Pardon. Comme je suis maladroit(e).** Your classmate will excuse you: **Il n'y a pas de mal... Je vous en prie, ce n'est pas grave.**

E. **Introductions: Venez, je voudrais vous présenter à Monsieur Smith.** Introduce classmates to each other: **Venez, je voudrais vous présenter à Monsieur Smith.** You may wish to use the **tu** form with your classmates: **Viens, je voudrais te présenter à Monsieur Smith.** Everyone will express pleasure at meeting: **Enchanté(e). J'ai beaucoup entendu parler de vous,** etc.

F. **Leave-taking: Déjà dix heures! Pas possible!** Check the time by your watch or on the classroom clock?[3] Pretend that you must leave.

EXEMPLE: *Déjà trois heures?!? Pas possible! Que le temps passe vite! Je dois partir.*

G. **Dialogue responses.** What could you respond to each of the following? Use sentences and phrases taken directly from the **Dialogue.**

1. Puis-je prendre votre manteau?
2. Que puis-je vous offrir? Un whisky? Des chips?

---

3. You may wish to review **Entracte 3:** Telling Time.

3. À votre santé!
4. Encore un peu?
5. Je suis vraiment content(e) de vous revoir.
6. Mais dites-moi, que faites-vous ces temps-ci?
7. Vous avez très bonne mine.
8. Vous partez déjà?

H.   **Review.**   What do you say. . .

1. when someone knocks on the door, you open it, and you see that it is one of your guests?
2. when you wish to take your guest's coat?
3. when you want to introduce two people to each other?
4. when you first make someone's acquaintance?
5. when you want to offer some refreshment to your guests?
6. when you propose a toast to someone?
7. when you want to say something nice about the food or drink you are being served?
8. when you accidentally spill something on someone?
9. when someone asks you what you have been doing recently?
10. when it is time to go?

Improvisation à deux *(Exercice oral)*

I.   Use the vocabulary block options and the basic sentence structures of the **Dialogue** to improvise a dialogue with a classmate. One of you may be a host or hostess while the other is a guest at a social gathering. Or both of you may be guests making social conversation.

À Vous le choix *(Exercices écrits)*

J.   Write a six- to eight-line dialogue for each of the following situations, selecting appropriate phrases from the initial **Dialogue** of this chapter.

1. You are a gracious host or hostess making your guest feel welcome.
2. You have been hired to help host a reception at the French Embassy.
3. You are at a gathering and see a friendly looking person with whom you decide to start a conversation.

Conversations

K.   Ask your classmates these personalized questions. When two or more responses are possible, alternate answer formats are offered. Select the option that best applies to you personally. Do not limit your responses simply to those suggestions offered in these questions. Use the inclusive vocabulary options provided in the **Dialogue**.

1. C'est votre anniversaire aujourd'hui?
   - Oui, c'est mon anniversaire aujourd'hui.
   - Non, ce n'est pas mon anniversaire. C'est le _____.[4]

2. Qu'est-ce que vous aimez? le whisky? le vin rouge? le vin blanc? le champagne? le cognac? etc. Qu'est-ce que vous n'aimez pas?
   - J'aime le/la _____.
   - Je n'aime pas le/la _____.

3. Qu'est-ce que vous préférez? le vin rouge? le vin blanc? le vin rosé?
   - Je préfère _____.
   - Je n'aime pas le vin.

4. Qu'est-ce que vous n'avez jamais bu?

   EXEMPLES: *Je n'ai jamais bu de champagne.*
   Je n'ai jamais bu de cognac, etc.

5. Êtes-vous maladroit(e)? toujours? rarement? jamais?
   - Je suis _____ maladroit(e).
   - Je ne suis jamais maladroit(e).

6. Que faites-vous ces temps-ci?

   EXEMPLE: *Rien de particulier.*

7. Êtes-vous occupé(e) ces jours-ci? Très occupé(e)?
   - Je suis _____.
   - Je ne suis pas _____.

8. Vous sentez-vous en forme aujourd'hui?
   - Oui, je me sens _____.
   - Non, je ne me sens pas _____.

9. Êtes-vous allé(e) récemment à une soirée? à une réception? Avez-vous passé une soirée agréable?

   EXEMPLE: *Je suis allé(e) récemment à une soirée.*
   J'ai passé une soirée très agréable.

L. **Review.** What have you learned about your classmates from these **Conversations?**

EXEMPLES: *Paul aime le vin rouge.*
Anne est très occupée ces jours-ci.
Madame Smith se sent en forme aujourd'hui.

---

4. See **Entracte 4:** Dates.

French Celebrations. France is a Catholic country. Observance of religious holidays is important, both within the family (**les fêtes, les baptêmes, les communions, les mariages**) and nationally (**La fête des Rois, Mardi gras, Pâques, Noël**, etc.)

Birthdays (**les anniversaires**) and Saint's Days (**les fêtes**) are celebrated with greeting cards, presents, and cake.[5]

Baptisms (**les baptêmes**) are celebrated in church, with sugar-coated almonds (**les dragées**) distributed to participants.

New Year's Day (**Le Jour de l'An**) is a public holiday. Gifts (**les étrennes**) are exchanged and cards (**les cartes de nouvelle année**) are sent. On New Year's Eve, people eat a late supper called **Le Réveillon**.

Epiphany (**La fête des Rois**) is celebrated January 6, with a special cake (**la galette des rois**) with a small china figure or bean hidden in it. The person served that special portion is declared king (or queen) of the day.

Valentine's Day (**la Saint-Valentin**)—The ancient tradition of **la Fête des amoureux** was revived after World War II under the influence of Americans stationed in France.

5. To find out the date of your **fête**, see **Entracte 4:** Dates, pages 128-129.

On **Mardi gras** *(Shrove Tuesday)* the French eat thin pancakes **(les crêpes)**. There are carnivals that last several days, the largest being in Nice. French descendants in New Orleans celebrate this holiday with great enthusiasm.

Pâques *(Easter)* is celebrated by going to mass and receiving communion. Easter cards are sent. Children are given candy.

Le premier mai (May 1), people exchange lilies of the valley **(les muguets)** for good luck.

La Fête des Mères *(Mother's Day)* is celebrated in France the last Sunday in May. **(Bonne Fête, Maman!)**

La Fête des Pères *(Father's Day)* is celebrated in France the third Sunday in June. **(Bonne Fête, Papa!)**

On the French national holiday, **le 14 juillet** *(Bastille Day)*, people celebrate the storming of the Bastille by having fireworks, displaying flags, watching parades, and dancing in the streets all night long.

Noël *(Christmas)* is a religious holiday celebrated by going to midnight mass on Christmas Eve, and returning home for a large meal called **Le Réveillon**. Christmas trees in French homes often have real candles burning, and the manger is displayed nearby. Children put out shoes on Christmas Eve for **Père Noël** to fill with gifts. A chocolate cake shaped like a yule log **(bûche de Noël)** is served.

Borrowed Words. English has borrowed a number of French expressions related to the topics of this chapter, including: **R.S.V.P.** **(Répondez, s'il vous plaît)** which means "Reply, please," **clique** (an exclusive group), **début** (an initial appearance in society or a first performance), and **débutante** (a young woman making her first appearance in society).

VERBES IRRÉGULIERS: devoir, falloir

> | **devoir**   to have to; to owe | |
> |---|---|
> | LE PRÉSENT: je **dois** | nous **devons** |
> | tu **dois** | vous **devez** |
> | il/elle/on **doit** | ils/elles **doivent** |
> | LE PASSÉ COMPOSÉ: j'ai **dû**, etc. | |
> | LA BASE DU FUTUR ET DU CONDITIONNEL: **devr-** | |

1. **Devoir** means "to owe."

   Combien vous **dois-je?**   How much do I owe you?

2. **Devoir,** followed by an infinitive, has various English equivalents, depending on the tense and context.

   Présent:

Je dois partir la semaine prochaine.	I must leave next week. I have to leave next week. I am supposed to leave next week.

   Passé Composé:

J'ai dû partir de bonne heure.	I had to leave early.
J'ai dû le **perdre.**	I must have lost it.

   Imparfait:

Je devais le **faire.**	I was supposed to do it.

   Futur:

Je devrai y **aller.**	I will have to go there.

   Conditionnel:

Je devrais aller le voir.	I should go see him. I ought to go see him.

   Conditionnel Passé:

J'aurais dû vous **présenter.**	I should have introduced you. I ought to have introduced you.

Exercices d'application: devoir

A.   **Qu'est ce que vous devez faire?**   Answer these questions yourself. Then ask your classmates: **Qu'est-ce que vous devez faire? Aujourd'hui? Après cette classe? Demain? Le week-end prochain? La semaine prochaine? C'est tout? C'est urgent?** For your responses, use the present tense of **devoir** plus an infinitive. For example: **Je dois étudier.** Here are some suggestions of things you may have to do.

acheter un cadeau (pour...) buy a gift (for . . .)

aller à la banque, chez le médecin, chez le coiffeur go to the bank, doctor's, barbershop (beauty parlor)

aller au travail go to work

aller chercher mes enfants à l'école, un ami à la gare go pick up my children at school, a friend at the station

aller en classe go to class

assister à mon cours (de...) go to (my. . .) class

cirer mes chaussures shine my shoes

conduire les enfants à l'école, mon ami chez le docteur drive my children to school, my friend to the doctor's

déblayer la neige shovel snow

écrire un compte-rendu/un rapport write a report

écrire un petit mot (à...) write a note (to. . .)

envoyer une carte de vœux/un mot de remerciement (à...) send a greeting card/thank you note (to. . .)

étudier study

faire des courses run errands

faire mes devoirs do homework

faire ma gymnastique do (my) exercises

faire la lessive do laundry

faire le ménage/nettoyer la maison do housework/clean the house

faire mes provisions buy food, do marketing

faire du raccommodage do some mending

faire réparer la voiture, le lave-vaisselle, la télévision have the car, dishwasher, television fixed

faire du repassage do some ironing

faire la vaisselle do the dishes

faire un voyage d'affaires take a business trip

inviter la famille à déjeuner, à dîner invite the family over for lunch, dinner

laver/cirer le parquet wash/wax the floor

passer l'aspirateur vacuum, run the vacuum

passer chez le teinturier stop by the cleaner's

passer la tondeuse mow the lawn

payer le loyer, les impôts pay the rent, taxes

prendre des billets (d'avion, de théâtre, de concert pick up some (airplane, theater, concert) tickets

prendre ma leçon de piano take my piano lesson

préparer le dîner, les repas prepare dinner, meals

promener le chien walk the dog

rendre visite à ma grand-mère visit my grandmother

sortir la poubelle/vider les ordures take out the garbage

taper un rapport type (up) a paper

téléphoner (à...) telephone/call ...

B.   Il doit étudier.   If the preceding exercise has been used orally in class, review what you have learned about your classmates.

EXEMPLES: *Marc doit étudier.*
Anne doit aller à la banque.
Monsieur Smith doit promener le chien.

C.   Qu'est-ce que vous devriez faire?   What should you do? What are your obligations? What do you feel you ought to do at some time in the near future? Answer these questions yourself. Then, ask your classmates: **Qu'est-ce que vous devriez faire?** Use the conditional tense of **devoir** plus an infinitive in your responses. For possibilities, see the suggestions in Exercise A.

EXEMPLE: *Je devrais téléphoner à ma mère.*

D.   Il devrait inviter la famille à dîner.   If the preceding exercise has been used orally in class, review what you have learned about your classmates.

EXEMPLES: *Marc devrait téléphoner à son père.*
Anne devrait acheter un cadeau pour sa mère.
Madame Smith devrait inviter la famille à dîner.

E.   Qu'est-ce que vous auriez dû faire hier?   What should you have done yesterday that you did not do? **Qu'est-ce que vous auriez dû faire hier, et que vous n'avez pas fait?** Answer this question yourself, then ask your classmates. Use the past conditional of **devoir (j'aurais dû)** plus an infinitive in your responses. For possibilities, see the suggestions in Exercise A.

EXEMPLE: *J'aurais dû taper un rapport.*

F.   Il aurait dû assister à son cours de biologie.   If the preceding exercise has been used orally in class, review what you have learned about your classmates.

EXEMPLES: *Marc aurait dû étudier.*
Anne aurait dû assister à son cours de biologie.
Monsieur Smith aurait dû téléphoner à sa femme.

➤

falloir   to be necessary
LE PRÉSENT: il **faut** LE PASSÉ COMPOSÉ: il **a fallu** LE FUTUR: il **faudra** LE CONDITIONNEL: il **faudrait** L'IMPARFAIT: il **fallait**

1. **Falloir** is an impersonal verb whose subject is always **il.** It can be used in any tense and has a variety of English equivalents.

Il faut étudier.

> It is necessary to study.
> You/We/People must (have to) study.
> One must (has to) study.

2. **Falloir** and **devoir** are sometimes interchangeable.

Il me faut étudier. – **Je dois** étudier.   I must study.

3. **S'il le faut** means "If it is necessary./If I (you) have to./If I (you) must."

—Puis-je le faire?   —May I do it?
—Oui. S'il le faut.   —Yes. If you must.

Exercices d'application: falloir

G.   Il faut manger.   There are certain things that one has to do in life. Look at the list of activities given in Exercise A (page 349) for the verb **devoir.** Make a series of statements about what you believe people's obligations to be. Use **il faut** plus an infinitive in your statements. You may also wish to use verbs from other chapters covered in class.

EXEMPLES: *Il faut étudier.*
           Et il faut payer les impôts.

H.   Il dit qu'il faut aller en classe.   If the preceding exercise has been used orally in class, review what your classmates believe.

EXEMPLES: *Paul pense qu'il faut aller en classe.*
           Anne croit qu'il faut payer le loyer à l'avance.
           Madame Smith dit qu'il faut aller au travail tous les jours.

STRUCTURE

Structure 1: Subjunctive Mood: Formation and Use

The subjunctive is used to express possibility, feelings, and emotions. It usually occurs in dependent clauses introduced by **que.** The most commonly used subjunctive tenses are the present and past. There is no future or conditional subjunctive; the present subjunctive is used to indicate both present and future actions. The perfect subjunctive is used to indicate actions that have occurred before the action of the main verb.

1. Formation of the present subjunctive

To form the present subjunctive of regular verbs and some irregular verbs, drop the letters **-ent** from the third person plural of the present indicative (the **ils** form) and add to this base the present subjunctive endings: **-e, -es, -e, -ions, -iez, -ent.**

VERBES EN **-er**	
parler	
que je parl**e**	que nous parl**ions**
que tu parl**es**	que vous parl**iez**
qu'il/elle/on parl**e**	qu'ils/elles parl**ent**

VERBES EN **-ir**	
finir	
que je finiss**e**	que nous finiss**ions**
que tu finiss**es**	que vous finiss**iez**
qu'il/elle/on finiss**e**	qu'ils/elles finiss**ent**

VERBES EN **-re**	
répondre	
que je répond**e**	que nous répond**ions**
que tu répond**es**	que vous répond**iez**
qu'il/elle/on répond**e**	qu'ils/elles répond**ent**

The following commonly used irregular verbs have irregular subjunctive forms. These must be learned individually. The subjunctive endings, however, are the same as for regular verbs.

aller	boire	croire
to go	to drink	to believe
que j'**aille** que tu **ailles** qu'il **aille** que nous **allions** que vous **alliez** qu'ils **aillent**	que je **boive** que tu **boives** qu'il **boive** que nous **buvions** que vous **buviez** qu'ils **boivent**	que je **croie** que tu **croies** qu'il **croie** que nous **croyions** que vous **croyiez** qu'ils **croient**

faire	pouvoir	prendre
to make, to do	to be able	to take
que je **fasse** que tu **fasses** qu'il **fasse** que nous **fassions** que vous **fassiez** qu'ils **fassent**	que je **puisse** que tu **puisses** qu'il **puisse** que nous **puissions** que vous **puissiez** qu'ils **puissent**	que je **prenne** que tu **prennes** qu'il **prenne** que nous **prenions** que vous **preniez** qu'ils **prennent**

savoir	venir
to know	to come
que je **sache** que tu **saches** qu'il **sache** que nous **sachions** que vous **sachiez** qu'ils **sachent**	que je **vienne** que tu **viennes** qu'il **vienne** que nous **venions** que vous **veniez** qu'ils **viennent**

voir	vouloir
to see	to want
que je **voie** que tu **voies** qu'il **voie** que nous **voyions** que vous **voyiez** qu'ils **voient**	que je **veuille** que tu **veuilles** qu'il **veuille** que nous **voulions** que vous **vouliez** qu'ils **veuillent**

Avoir and **être** have irregular subjunctive forms, including irregular endings.

avoir	être
to have	to be
que j'**aie** que tu **aies** qu'il **ait** que nous **ayons** que vous **ayez** qu'ils **aient**	que je **sois** que tu **sois** qu'il **soit** que nous **soyons** que vous **soyez** qu'ils **soient**

2. *Formation of the past subjunctive*

The past subjunctive is made up of the present subjunctive of **avoir** or **être** and the past participle of the main verb. Remember that verbs of coming and going and reflexive verbs are conjugated with **être** as the helping verb.

VERBES EN **-er**	VERBES EN **-ir**
parler	**guérir**
que j'**aie parlé** que tu **aies parlé** qu'il **ait parlé** qu'elle **ait parlé** que nous **ayons parlé** que vous **ayez parlé** qu'ils **aient parlé** qu'elles **aient parlé**	que j'**aie guéri** que tu **aies guéri** qu'il **ait guéri** qu'elle **ait guéri** que nous **ayons guéri** que vous **ayez guéri** qu'ils **aient guéri** qu'elles **aient guéri**

VERBES EN **-re**
répondre
que j'**aie répondu** que tu **aies répondu** qu'il **ait répondu** qu'elle **ait répondu** que nous **ayons répondu** que vous **ayez répondu** qu'ils **aient répondu** qu'elles **aient répondu**

VERBS OF COMING AND GOING	REFLEXIVE VERBS
aller	**se coucher**
que je **sois allé(e)**	que je **me sois couché(e)**
que tu **sois allé(e)**	que tu **te sois couché(e)**
qu'il **soit allé**	qu'il **se soit couché**
qu'elle **soit allée**	qu'elle **se soit couchée**
que nous **soyons allé(e)s**	que nous **nous soyons couché(e)s**
que vous **soyez allé(e)(s)**	que vous **vous soyez couché(e)(s)**
qu'ils **soient allés**	qu'ils **se soient couchés**
qu'elles **soient allées**	qu'elles **se soient couchées**

3. Uses of the subjunctive

a. After impersonal expressions of necessity, doubt, emotional reaction, and possibility, the subjunctive is used in the subordinate clause and is introduced by **que.**

il est bien it is good
c'est dommage it is too bad, it is a shame
il est étonnant it is surprising
il faut it is necessary
il est important it is important

il est nécessaire it is necessary
il est possible it is possible
il semble it seems
il se peut it is possible
il est temps it is time
il vaut mieux it is better

> **Il faut que j'y aille.** I must go.
> **C'est dommage qu'il soit** déjà **parti.** It's too bad that he has left already.

b. The indicative mood is used after the following expressions of certainty in the affirmative. The subjunctive mood, however, is used when these expressions are in the negative.

il est certain it is sure
il est évident it is obvious

il est sûr it is sure
il est vrai it is true

> **Il est vrai que je suis** malade.
> **Il n'est pas vrai que je sois** malade.

c. Certain impersonal expressions that normally require the subjunctive may be followed by an infinitive to convey a general meaning, when no subject is indicated.

il est bien de
il faut
il est important de
il est nécessaire de

il est possible de
il est temps de
il vaut mieux

> **Il faut partir.**
> **Il vaut mieux étudier.**

d The subjunctive is used in clauses introduced by **que** after verbs that express
a wish, an order, a doubt, or an emotional reaction. Whenever the subject of
the main clause is different from the subject of the subordinate clause, the
subjunctive is used. When the subject of the main verb is the same as that of
the subordinate verb, the infinitive, sometimes preceded by **de** or **à,** is used
instead of the subjunctive.

aimer to like, to love	**être fâché (de)** to be angry, to be sorry
aimer mieux to prefer	**être désolé (de)** to be sorry
avoir peur (de) to be afraid	**être ravi (de)** to be delighted
douter (de) to doubt	**être triste (de)** to be sad
s'étonner (de) to be surprised	**préférer** to prefer
être content (de), être heureux (de) to be happy	**regretter (de)** to be sorry
être mécontent (de), être malheureux (de) to be unhappy	**souhaiter** to wish
	suggérer to suggest
être d'accord to agree	**vouloir** to wish, to want
être surpris (de), être étonné (de) to be surprised	

Je regrette qu'il soit en retard.	I'm sorry that he's late.
But: **Je regrette d'être** en retard.	I'm sorry that I'm late. (I'm sorry to be late.)
J'aime mieux qu'il vienne chez moi.	I prefer that he come to my house.
But: **J'aime mieux aller** chez lui.	I prefer to go to his house.
Il veut que je parte.	He wants me to leave.
But: **Il veut partir.**	He wants to leave.

e. The subjunctive is used after certain conjunctions.

afin que, pour que in order that, so that	**de peur que (ne), de crainte que (ne)** for fear that
à moins que (ne) unless	**pourvu que, à condition que** provided that
avant que (ne) before	**sans que** without
bien que, quoique although	**supposé que** supposing that
jusqu'à ce que until	
malgré que in spite of the fact that	

J'irai **pourvu que vous m'accompagniez.**	I will go provided that you accompany me.
Il va au cinéma **bien qu'il soit** très fatigué.	He's going to the movies, although he's very tired.

Ne is often used, even in conversation, in subjunctive clauses introduced by
avoir peur, de peur que, de crainte que, avant que, and **à moins que.** It does
not make the clause negative. The sentence would still be correct without **ne.**

Partez **avant qu'il (ne) soit** trop tard.	Leave before it's too late.

f. The following conjunctions, however, take the indicative mood.

après que after	**puisque** since, as long as
lorsque when	**quand** when
parce que because	**si** if, whether
pendant que while	**tandis que** whereas

Exercices d'application: Subjunctive Mood

A.   **Il faut que je fasse mes devoirs.**   *(Present Subjunctive)* What do you have to do? Refer to the list of activities given in Exercise A (page 349) for the verb **devoir**. Use the present subjunctive in your responses.

EXEMPLES: *Il faut que je téléphone à ma mère.*
Il faut que j'aille à la banque.
Il faut que je fasse mes devoirs.

B.   **Il faut qu'elle aille chez le dentiste.**   If the preceding exercise has been used orally in class, review what you learned about your classmates. This will give you some practice with the **il** and **elle** forms of the subjunctive.

EXEMPLES: *Il faut que Robert fasse ses devoirs.*
Il faut que Marie aille au travail.
Il faut que Monsieur Smith téléphone à sa mère.

C.   **Il faut que tu étudies!**   If Exercise A has been used orally in class, again review what your classmates have said about themselves. This time, however, address each classmate directly. This will give you practice using the **tu** and **vous** forms of the present subjunctive.

EXEMPLES: —*Marc, il faut que tu ailles en classe, n'est-ce pas?*
—*Oui, c'est ça. Il faut que j'aille en classe.*

—*Marie, il faut que vous alliez en classe, n'est-ce pas?*
—*Non, il faut que j'aille au travail.*

D.   **Il est bien que j'aie fait mes devoirs.**   *(Past Subjunctive)* What have you done recently? What do you think about it? Make a statement about something you have actually done (or have not done) in the very recent past. (For ideas, refer to the list of activities given in Exercise A, page 349, for the verb **devoir**.) Use the **passé composé** (indicative) in your statements. For example: **J'ai fait mes devoirs. Je n'ai pas étudié. J'ai promené le chien.** Then comment on your actions using one of these suggested phrases plus the past subjunctive: **il est bien que, c'est dommage que, il est étonnant que, il est possible que.**
Note: When doing this exercise, keep in mind that verbs conjugated with **avoir** will use **j'aie** in the past subjunctive; verbs conjugated with **être** will use **je sois.**

EXEMPLES: *Il est bien que j'aie fait mes devoirs.*
C'est dommage que je ne sois pas allé(e) en classe.

E.   **Je suis content(e) d'avoir fait sa connaissance.**   *(Infinitive Replacing Subjunctive)* Make the same statements you made in Exercise D about actions you have recently done. This time express your opinions on these actions by using **de** plus an infinitive instead of the subjunctive. The suggested expressions below will create a situation in which the subject of both clauses will be the same: **je.**

Je regrette d'avoir/d'être...   **Je suis malheureux(se) d'avoir/**
Je suis content(e) d'avoir/d'être...   **d'être...**
Je suis heureux(se) d'avoir/d'être...   **Je suis désolé(e) d'avoir/d'être...**
Je suis mécontent(e) d'avoir/d'être...   **Je suis triste d'avoir/d'être...**

EXEMPLES: *Je regrette d'avoir invité la famille à dîner.*
Je suis content(e) d'être resté(e)[6] chez moi.

F.   **Je doute qu'il ait étudié.**   *(Past Subjunctive)* If the preceding exercises have been used orally in class, review what you have learned about your classmates. This will give you some practice using the **il** and **elle** forms of the past subjunctive.

---

6. Remember that with verbs of "coming and going" the past participle agrees with the subject. (See Chapter 3, Structure 3.)

Express doubt, surprise, astonishment, happiness, anger, or even denial. Begin your reactions with:

il est bien que	il n'est pas vrai que	je suis heureux(se) que
c'est dommage que	je doute que	je suis mécontent(e) que
il se peut que	je m'étonne que	je suis triste que
il est possible que	je regrette que	je suis surpris(e) que
il n'est pas certain que	je suis content(e) que	je suis fâché(e) que

EXEMPLES: *Je doute que Marc ait étudié.*
Je m'étonne que Marie ait fait ses devoirs.
Je suis surpris(e) que Monsieur Smith soit allé chez le médecin.

G. **Je suis étonné(e) que vous n'ayez pas étudié.** If Exercises D and E have been used orally in class, again review what your classmates said about their recent activities. This time, however, address each classmate directly. Tell him or her your opinion of their action(s). This will give you practice using the **tu** and **vous** forms of the past subjunctive.

EXEMPLES: *Marc, je suis étonné(e) que vous n'ayez pas étudié.*
Marie, je doute que tu sois allée à la banque.
Monsieur Smith, je suis content(e) que vous ayez étudié.

«Il est bien que vous soyez venu me voir.»

Synthèse

Racontez votre dernière soirée.   Have you gone to a social gathering recently? Tell about it, using vocabulary and structures from the entire chapter. Answer these questions yourself. Then ask your classmates. (You may wish to use the **tu** form of address with your classmates.)

1. Êtes-vous (Es-tu) allé(e) récemment à une soirée? à une réception? Chez qui?
2. Avez-vous (As-tu) reçu une invitation?
3. Y êtes-vous allé(e) seul(e)? en groupe? avec un(e) ami(e)?
4. À quelle heure fallait-il arriver? À quelle heure êtes-vous arrivé(e)?
5. Avez-vous (As-tu) offert un cadeau? Est-ce que l'hôte ou l'hôtesse était content(e) de recevoir le cadeau? Est-ce qu'on était étonné que vous ayez (tu aies) apporté un cadeau?
6. Y avait-il beaucoup de monde? Avec qui avez-vous parlé?
7. Y avait-il de la musique? Avez-vous dansé? Avec qui?
8. Qu'est-ce qu'il y avait à boire? à manger?
9. De qui avez-vous fait la connaissance?
10. Y êtes-vous resté(e) longtemps? Jusqu'à quelle heure? Fallait-il que vous partiez de bonne heure? Étiez-vous content(e) de partir? Pourquoi avez-vous dû partir?
11. Avez-vous remercié vos hôtes en partant? Qu'est-ce que vous leur avez dit? Vos hôtes voulaient-ils que vous restiez plus longtemps?
12. Avez-vous passé une soirée agréable?

PRONONCIATION

1. Sound (Phonetic Symbol): [ə]

SPELLING:	e
ENGLISH SOUND RESEMBLED:	Vowel sound in word *push*
PRONUNCIATION:	The sound [ə] is pronounced similarly to the French vowel sound [ø] (see Chapter 7). It is often referred to as *mute E* or *unstable E*, since it may be pronounced or silent depending upon its position within a word or word group. Furthermore, a pronounced [ə] in slow speech is often silent in faster speech. (A similar dropping of sounds happens in English. Compare a slow, careful pronunciation of *good-by* with a speedy *g'by*.)

General Guidelines

Knowing just when to retain or drop the [ǝ] sound will come with practice. Here, however, are some general guidelines:

[ǝ] is pronounced in the following cases:
• In the interrogative pronoun **que (Que dit-il?)**
• In **le** after a positive command **(Ouvrez-le!)**
• When preceded by two or more pronounced consonants and followed by one **(vendredi)**
• In proper names **(Venise)**

[ǝ] is silent in the following cases:
• In final syllables **(Bon anniversairé!)** In everyday French, the final **le** and **re** are often dropped entirely, as in **tablé, quatré, livré,** etc.
• When preceded and followed by single pronounced consonants **(samédi, achéter)**
• In certain fixed groups of monosyllables: **cé que, jé te, né se, je né, je mé, ne lé**

Notes:
1. When [ǝ] occurs in successive syllables separated from each other by single pronounced consonants, every other [ǝ] is dropped. (Je lé sais. Je né le sais pas.)

2. The correct pronunciation of the spelling **e** (with no accent marks on it) is determined as follows:
   a. The spelling **e** is pronounced [ǝ] when it ends a syllable (d<u>e</u>-voir, j<u>e</u>, p<u>e</u>-tit).
   b. The spelling **e** is pronounced [ɛ] (see Chapter 6) when it is followed by a consonant sound within the same syllable (<u>e</u>lle, v<u>e</u>rt, anniv<u>e</u>rsaire).
   c. The spelling **e** followed by a double consonant may be pronounced either [e] (see Chapter 6) or [ɛ] (see Chapter 6). d<u>e</u>ssert, m<u>e</u>ssage, <u>e</u>ffort. *Exception:* Before a double r, the letter **e** must be pronounced [ɛ] (<u>e</u>rreur, t<u>e</u>rreur).

2. Intonation

In French there are two basic types of intonation: rising and falling.

1. In statements (declarative sentences) the voice rises in pitch at the end of every phrase or word group and falls at the end of the sentence. In American English, by contrast, the voice drops or remains on the same pitch after each portion of the sentence.
2. In questions that can be answered by *yes* or *no,* the voice begins on a fairly low note and rises until the end of the question, as in English.
3. In questions beginning with an interrogative pronoun (**qui, que,** etc.) or interrogative adverb (**pourquoi, où,** etc.), the voice falls at the end of the sentence.

3. Tension

In American English there is a tendency to have gliding vowels (diphthongs), prolonged consonants, mumbled final consonants, and generally relaxed delivery. In French, on the other hand, the enunciation of vowels and consonants is short, clipped, distinct. Pronounced final consonants are articulated forcefully and distinctly. There is a general tension or tightness of articulation.

Projets

A. **Cartes de vœux.** *(Exercice écrit et oral)* Using the following expressions, make several greeting cards for occasions that will soon take place—a birthday card for your sister, a get-well card for an absent class member, a Christmas card for a friend, and so on. Colored paper, crayons, and colored pens can all be used effectively.

Heureux (Bon/Joyeux) Anniversaire Happy Birthday
Heureux Anniversaire de Mariage Happy (Wedding) Anniversary
Bonne (Heureuse) Fête Happy Saint's/Name Day
Bonne Fête des Mères/des Pères Happy Mother's Day/Father's Day
Joyeux Noël Merry Christmas
Bonne (Heureuse) Année Happy New Year
Joyeuses Pâques Happy Easter
Bonne Fête à la Saint-Valentin Happy Valentine's Day
Bon Voyage (Have a) Good Trip/Bon Voyage
Vœux de prompt rétablissement Get Well

Félicitations! Congratulations!
... pour la naissance de ce beau bébé ... on your new baby
... pour votre diplôme ... on your graduation
... pour votre promotion ... on your promotion
Vœux (sincères) de Bonheur *(par exemple,* **à l'occasion de votre mariage)** Best Wishes *(for example,* on the occasion of your marriage)
Bonne (Heureuse) Retraite Happy Retirement
Meilleurs Vœux Best Wishes
Bonne Chance dans votre nouveau travail Good luck in your new job

Using the preceding list for inspiration, wish everyone in the classroom Happy Birthday, Happy Mother's Day, Have a Good Trip, Congratulations on your new baby/house/job, Get Well, etc. (Birthdays, anniversaries, upcoming holidays, saint's days, etc. may be determined by using **Entracte 4:** Dates.) Some ways to begin are: **Je te (vous) souhaite un/une...** or **Félicitations pour....**

B.   **Invitations: Written and Oral.**   You will be having an in-class party (see **Activité.**) Write an invitation to two classmates. To make sure everyone receives one, address one to the person sitting on your left in class, and the other to the person on your right. Use the models below for your invitations.

Written invitations to a social gathering

Formal

M./Mme/Mlle ___votre nom___ vous prie de lui faire l'honneur d'assister à une réception le *(date)* à *(l'heure)*. R.S.V.P. *(Votre numéro de téléphone et adresse)*.

Informal

Cher/Chère _____. Voulez-vous me faire le plaisir de venir le *(date)* à *(l'heure)*. Je réunis quelques amis et je serais très heureux(se) si vous pouviez aussi venir. Je compte sur le grand plaisir de vous revoir. ___votre nom___.[7]

You may wish to write an acceptance (or refusal) to the invitation you receive. Base your reply on whether or not you actually plan to be in class the day of the party.

Written Acceptance

Formal

M./Mme/Mlle ___votre nom___ remercie M./Mme/Mlle... de son aimable invitation et il/elle est très heureux(se) de l'accepter.

Informal

Cher/Chère _____. Merci beaucoup pour votre aimable invitation. J'accepte avec joie.[7]

Written Refusal

Formal

M./Mme/Mlle ___votre nom___ remercie M./Mme/Mlle... de son aimable invitation et il/elle regrette infiniment de ne pouvoir l'accepter en raison d'un engagement déjà pris.

Informal

Cher/Chère _____. Merci beaucoup pour votre aimable invitation. Malheureusement il m'est impossible de venir. Je suis vraiment désolé(e) de ce contretemps et vous envoie toute mon affection.[7]

These written invitations may be followed up with oral ones.[8]

Oral invitations to a social gathering

Nous donnons (Je donne) une petite réception _____ (demain soir, lundi à huit heures, etc.) Viendrez-vous? Pourriez-vous venir?

Oral Acceptance

Avec plaisir. C'est très aimable à vous. Ce serait avec plaisir. À quelle heure faut-il arriver? Puis-je amener un(e) ami(e)?

---

7. The informal **tu** form may be substituted for the **vous** form of these examples.
8. For additional oral invitations, see the **Dialogue** and **Activités** of Chapter 8.

Activité: Learning by Doing

Class Party.   Have a party in class to celebrate a coming holiday, a class member's birthday, or the end of the semester. Everyone should bring refreshments from home. Several class members will be hosts and hostesses. Mingle, making appropriate small talk from this chapter. As the class period draws to a close, guests leave, thanking hosts for a delightful party.

Many of the **Entractes** of this book include expressions that make excellent small talk. Here are some additional expressions useful for social gatherings:

Bonsoir ma chère (mon cher).
Toutes mes excuses pour mon retard.
   (formal)
Je regrette d'être en retard. *(less formal)*
J'ai été pris(e) dans un embouteillage
   (traffic jam).
La circulation *(traffic)* **était terrible.**
Que (Comme) je suis heureux(se)/
   content(e) de vous (re)voir!
Mais tout le plaisir est pour moi.
Asseyez-vous. Faites comme chez vous.
Quelle bonne surprise!
Qu'est-ce que vous faites ici?

Que le monde est petit!
Ça fait une éternité! *(It's been a long time!)*
Oui, ça fait si longtemps!
Comment va votre mari? votre femme?
Comment vont vos parents?
Et les enfants?
Il/Elle va bien.
Ils vont bien.
Mon bon souvenir à la famille. à Marie.
   à votre femme. etc.
Merci encore pour cette merveilleuse
   soirée *(marvelous evening).*

If the social gathering is in honor of the birthdays of some class members, or if Christmas or New Year's is being celebrated, everyone should bring a token (i.e., very inexpensive or homemade) gift to class. These will be given to the birthday people or else exchanged as Christmas or New Year's gifts **(les étrennes).** Use the appropriate sentences from the **Dialogue** of this chapter. You may also wish to try some of the following expressions:

J'espère que cela vous fera plaisir.   I hope that you will like this.
Vous n'auriez pas dû!   You shouldn't have (done it)!
Ouvrez-le! Regardez!   Open it! See what it is!
Oh! C'est vraiment magnifique!   Oh! It's really magnificent!
C'est précisément ce que je voulais!   It's just what I wanted!
Qu'est-ce que c'est?   What is it?
Merci mille fois!   Thanks so much! *(Literally: Thanks a thousand times!)*

De quelle
origine
êtes-vous?
Où êtes-vous
né(e)?

Nationalities and
Geographical
Place Names

Nul n'est prophète en son pays.

A prophet is without honor in his own country.

Knowing the vocabulary for nationalities and geographical place names is useful for travel. You can make conversation about your travels and inquire about the voyages of others. The typical American classroom, furthermore, lends itself to a lively discussion of ancestral background.

De quelle origine êtes-vous? Où êtes-vous né(e)?

Réponse: • Je suis d'origine _____. Je suis né(e) _____.[1]

EXEMPLE: *Je suis d'origine russe, polonaise, hongroise et anglaise. Je suis né(e) aux États-Unis.*

Vocabulaire à retenir

The following nationality adjectives are those most frequently requested by American students to describe their national origin. The feminine form of each nationality adjective is given first, followed by the masculine. Use the feminine form in your responses, because the word **origine** is feminine. Do not limit yourself simply to **américaine** unless you are pure American Indian. For additional nationality adjectives, see the Resource List at the end of this **Entracte**.

Nationality Adjectives[2]

allemande, allemand
  German
américaine, américain
  (U.S.) American
anglaise, anglais
  English
canadienne, canadien
  Canadian
chinoise, chinois Chinese

écossaise, écossais
  Scottish
espagnole, espagnol
  Spanish
française, français
  French
indienne, indien Indian
  (India)
irlandaise, irlandais Irish

italienne, italien
  Italian
japonaise, japonais
  Japanese
mexicaine, mexicain
  Mexican
polonaise, polonais
  Polish
russe Russian

Geographical place names must be preceded by the correct preposition of place. (For additional geographical place names, to make your responses more complete, see the Resource List at the end of this **Entracte**.) With feminine countries, continents, and masculine countries beginning with a vowel, **en** means "to" or "in," and **de** means "from." For example: **Je suis né(e) en Amérique.** *(I was born in America)*. Note that most countries ending in the letter **e** are feminine. *Exceptions:* **le Mexique, le Zaïre.**

---

1. What is your (national) origin? Where were you born?
I'm of _____ origin. I was born in _____.

2. Nationality adjectives are not capitalized in French.

Feminine Countries, Continents, Masculine Countries Beginning with a Vowel

Europe   Europe

Allemagne Germany	**France** France	**Roumanie** Rumania
Angleterre England	**Grèce** Greece	**Russie** Russia
Autriche Austria	**Hollande** Holland	**Suède** Sweden
Belgique Belgium	**Hongrie** Hungary	**Suisse** Switzerland
Bulgarie Bulgaria	**Irlande** Ireland	**Tchécoslovaquie**
Écosse Scotland	**Italie** Italy	Czechoslovakia
Espagne Spain	**Norvège** Norway	**Yougoslavie** Yugoslavia
Finlande Finland	**Pologne** Poland	

Amérique du Nord North America	**Asie** Asia	**Afrique** Africa
	Chine China	**Algérie** Algeria
Amérique Centrale Central America	**Inde** India	**Égypte** Egypt
	Indonésie Indonesia	**Tunisie** Tunisia
Amérique du Sud South America	**Iran** Iran	**Polynésie Française**
	Iraq Iraq	French Polynesia
Argentine Argentina	**Israël** Israel	**Australie** Australia
Bolivie Bolivia	**Mongolie** Mongolia	**Nouvelle-Zélande** New
Colombie Colombia	**Turquie** Turkey	Zealand
Guyane française French Guiana		
Uruguay Uruguay		

With masculine countries, **au** means "to" or "in," and **du** means "from." For example: **Je suis né(e) au Canada.** *(I was born in Canada.)*

Masculine Countries

Brésil Brazil	**Groenland** Greenland	**Niger** Niger	**Portugal** Portugal
Cambodge Cambodia	**Japon** Japan	**Nigéria** Nigeria	**Sénégal** Senegal
		Pakistan Pakistan	**Tchad** Chad
Canada Canada	**Luxembourg** Luxembourg		**Zaïre** Zaire
Chili Chile		**Paraguay** Paraguay	
Danemark Denmark	**Maroc** Morocco		
	Mexique Mexico	**Pérou** Peru	

With plural geographical names, **aux** means "to" or "in," and **des** means "from". For example: **Je suis né(e) aux États-Unis.** *(I was born in the United States.)*

Plural Geographical Names

Bermudes Bermuda	**Nouvelles-Hébrides** New Hebrides	**Pays-Bas** Netherlands
États-Unis U.S.		**Philippines** Philippines

Springboards for Conversation

Ask your classmates these personalized questions. Answer formats are provided.

1. De quelle origine êtes-vous? Du côté maternel *(on your mother's side)?* Du côté paternel *(father's side)?* *(Note:* Remember to use the feminine form of the adjective, even if you yourself are masculine.)
   • Je suis d'origine _____.

2. Quelle est votre nationalité? *(Note:* Use the masculine or feminine form of the adjective depending upon your own gender.)
   • Je suis _____.

3. Où êtes-vous né(e)?
   • Je suis né(e) _____.

Récapitulation

Recall what you have learned about your classmates and instructor. Answer formats are provided.

1. De quelle origine est le professeur? Et Monsieur...? Et Madame...? Et Mademoiselle...? (Your classmates). Et votre voisin(e) de gauche? Et votre voisin(e) de droite? etc. *Note:* If a national origin is forgotten, simply ask again. **Pardon. Je suis désolé(e), mais j'ai oublié. De quelle origine êtes-vous? Ah oui. C'est ça. Merci.**
   • Il/Elle est d'origine _____.

2. Qui dans la classe est d'origine _____? Qui d'autre? C'est tout?
   • Monsieur/Madame/Mademoiselle... est d'origine _____.
   • Le professeur est d'origine _____.
   • Moi, je suis d'origine _____.
   • Tout le monde est d'origine _____.
   • Personne n'est d'origine _____.

3. Où est né le professuer? Et Monsieur...? Et Madame...? Et Mademoiselle...? Et votre voisin(e) de gauche? Et votre voisin(e) de droite? etc.
   • Il/Elle est né(e) _____.

4. Qui dans la classe est né _____? Qui d'autre? C'est tout?
   • Monsieur/Madame/Mademoiselle... ɛ né(e) _____.
   • Le professeur est né _____.
   • Moi, je suis né(e) _____.
   • Tout le monde est né _____.
   • Personne.

Expansion

The **Expansion** can be used for partners or group conversation and for oral or written composition. Answer formats are provided.

1. Où habitez-vous? Dans quelle ville *(town, city)?*
   • J'habite (à) _____.
   Note: With **habiter**, the preposition is optional.

2. Où habitez-vous? Dans quel état? Dans quelle province?
   • J'habite dans l'état de _____.
   • J'habite dans le/dans la _____.

3. Où habitez-vous? Dans quel pays *(country)?*
   • J'habite en/au/aux _____.

4. D'où venez-vous? *(From where do you come?)*
   • Je viens de _____.
   Note: No article is necessary, except before masculine countries: *Je viens d'Amérique, de Rhode Island, de Montréal.* But: *Je viens du Japon.*

5. Dans quelles villes avez-vous habité? Pendant combien de temps *(for how long)?* Quand?
   • J'ai habité (à) _____.

6. Dans quels états avez-vous habité?
   • J'ai habité dans l'état de ＿＿.

7. Dans quels pays avez-vous habité?
   • J'ai habité en/au/aux ＿＿.

8. Quels pays avez-vous visités? Et quels
   états? Et quelles provinces? Et quelles
   villes?
   • J'ai visité ＿＿.
   Note: Use **le** before masculine countries, **la**
   before feminine, and **les** before plural. No
   article is needed before towns or cities unless
   included as part of their names. Use **l'état de**
   before state names.

9. Où est né votre père? Où est née votre
   mère?
   • Il/Elle est né(e) ＿＿.

10. Où est né votre grand-père maternel? Et
    votre grand-père paternel? Où est née
    votre grand-mère maternelle? Et votre
    grand-mère paternelle?
    • Il/Elle est né(e) ＿＿.
    • Je ne sais pas.

11. Où habite votre mère? Et votre père?
    Votre meilleur(e) ami(e)? Et vos grands-
    parents? Vos enfants? Vos petits enfants?
    Et le reste de votre famille?
    • Il/Elle habite ＿＿.
    • Ils/Elles habitent ＿＿.

12. Où comptez-vous *(intend)* passer vos
    prochaines *(next)* vacances?
    • Je compte passer mes prochaines
    vacances à/en/au/aux ＿＿.

13. Faites-vous des voyages d'affaires *(business
    trips)*? Où?
    • À/En/Au/Aux ＿＿.

14. **Review.** If **Expansion** questions have
    been used for group or partners
    conversation, recall what you have
    learned about your classmates.

    EXEMPLES: *Le père de Marc est né à Boston.*
    Marie compte passer ses prochaines
    vacances en France.
    Monsieur Smith vient de
    Washington, D.C.

Vocabulaire utile The following phrases are frequently requested by students using the
conversations of this **Entracte** related to nationalities and geographical place
names.

Pardon? Excuse me?
Quelle coïncidence! What a coincidence!
Moi aussi! Me, too!
Pas vrai! It's not true!
Sans blague! No kidding!
Je ne suis pas sûr(e). I'm not sure.

Je pense que... I think that. . .
Je crois que... I believe that. . .
On dit que... They say that. . .
Ah oui? Yes? Really?
Oh là là! Oh dear.
Quel mélange! What a mixture!

Francophone Countries.   French is spoken in many parts of the world. Over 130 million people consider it their first language. Besides France, it is also used in northern and western Africa, in the Caribbean, and in southeast Asia. It is one of the official languages of Switzerland, Luxembourg, Belgium, and Canada. In Canada there are over five million French speakers, mostly in or near the province of Quebec. The United States has nearly 3 million francophones, mostly living in New England and in Louisiana.

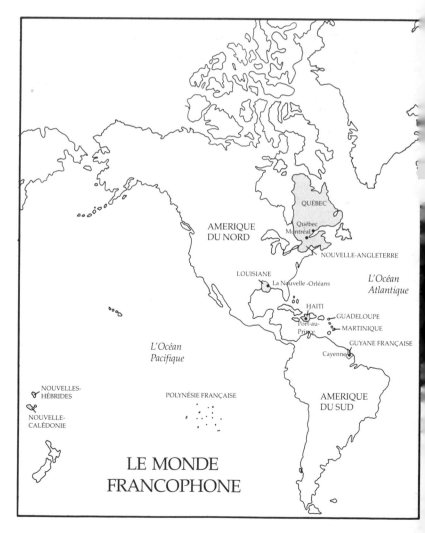

LE MONDE
FRANCOPHONE

LANGUAGE AND CULTURE

La France.   Geographically speaking, France is roughly hexagonal in shape. It is protected on the East and the South by mountains: the Alps **(Les Alpes)** and the Pyrenees **(les Pyrénées)**, respectively. It is over half a million square kilometers in size, slightly smaller than the state of Texas. It has much coastal land: the Atlantic **(l'océan Atlantique)**, the Mediterranean **(la Méditerranée)**, the English Channel **(la Manche)**, and the North Sea **(La Mer du Nord)** touch its borders. Extending from the 42nd parallel to the 51st, France is joined to the rest of Europe on its north and northeast boundaries by a flat plain. It is by way of this plain that much Franco-European commerce takes place. By this access, too, France has suffered many invasions throughout its history.

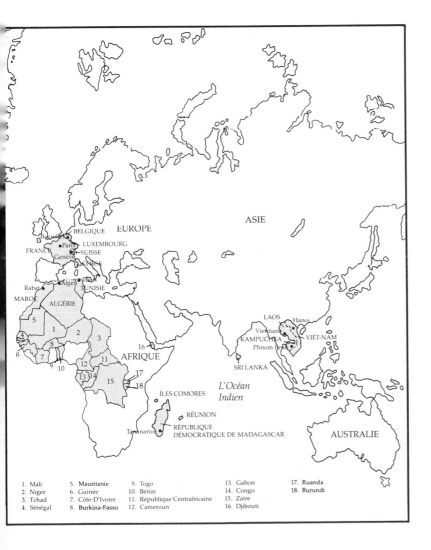

1. Mali	5. Mauritanie	9. Togo		13. Gabon	17. Ruanda
2. Niger	6. Guinée	10. Bénin		14. Congo	18. Burundi
3. Tchad	7. Côte-D'Ivoire	11. République Centrafricaine		15. Zaïre	
4. Sénégal	8. Burkina-Fasso	12. Cameroun		16. Djibouti	

The French Language. French is used as an official language by many international organizations: the United Nations, the European Common Market, and NATO, to name only a few. For many generations it has been the official language of international diplomacy.

Borrowed Words.   These French words are used in conversational English. The word **franglais** (a combination of **français** and **anglais**) refers to the use of English words in the French language, resulting in a hybrid form of speech scorned by French purists. A **coup d'état** is a violent or unconstitutional change of government, occasionally simplified to **coup** in English. An **émigré** means an emigrant or "refugee." This term was originally applied to the French aristocrats who fled France during the revolution of 1789.

Synthèse

Nations and Nationalities: Quelle est leur nationalité? You have met many interesting people at a diplomatic party. (You were invited because of your fluency in French!) Tell about these people.

MODÈLE: Monsieur Lefour (France)
Monsieur Lefour vient de France. Il est français.

1. Monsieur Smith (États-Unis)
2. Madame de Menthon (Belgique)
3. Mademoiselle Verdereau (Canada)
4. Monsieur Krisovsky (Russie)
5. Monsieur Carney (Angleterre)
6. Madame Yanagihara (Japon)
7. Mademoiselle Rodriguez (Mexique)
8. Madame Ackermann (Allemagne)
9. Monsieur Chang (Chine)
10. Madame Gopal (Inde)
11. Madame Cardillo (Italie)

Projets

A. **Mon itinéraire.** Plan a trip to some places you would really like to visit and give your itinerary. Visit as many francophone countries and regions as possible. Start and end your trip at the airport serving the city or area where you presently reside.

EXEMPLE: *Je prends l'avion à _____, pour aller à _____ en/au/aux _____. Puis je vais à _____ en/au/aux _____, etc.*

B. **National Origins.** Think of your neighbors, your close friends, your acquaintances, your relatives, and the people you deal with on a daily basis. **De quelle origine sont-ils?** Answer this question about as many of the following people as possible. When in doubt use: **Il/Elle est peut-être...** or **Je crois qu'il/elle est...** Suggestions: **votre mari, votre femme, votre mère, votre père, votre grand-mère maternelle, votre grand-père maternel, votre grand-mère paternelle, votre grand-père paternel, votre meilleur(e) ami(e), votre fiancé(e), votre camarade de chambre** (*roommate*), **votre professeur de français, votre médecin, votre dentiste.**

C. **Photographs.** Go through a current news magazine. Using the vocabulary of this lesson, discuss the people pictured. *For example:* **Il est chinois. Elle est africaine.**

D. **Where Have You Been?** Compile a list of all the cities, countries, and continents you have visited or have lived in. Give years and approximate lengths of stay whenever possible. You may wish to include photos, postcards, or magazine pictures of the places mentioned.

Resource List of Other Nationality Adjectives

Américaine, américain (*American*)
argentine, argentin Argentinean
bolivienne, bolivien Bolivian
brésilienne, brésilien Brazilian
chilienne, chilien Chilean
colombienne, colombien Colombian
guyannaise, guyannais from Guiana

nicaraguayenne, nicaraguayen Nicaraguan
paraguayenne, paraguayen Paraguayan
péruvienne, péruvien Peruvian
uruguayenne, uruguayen Uruguayan
vénézuélienne, vénézuélien Venezuelan

Européenne, europeen (*European*)
autrichienne, autrichien Austrian
belge Belgian
danoise, danois Danish
finlandaise, finlandais Finnish
grecque, grec Greek
hollandaise, hollandais Dutch
hongroise, hongrois Hungarian

norvégienne, norvégien Norwegian
portugaise, portugais Portuguese
roumaine, roumain Rumanian
suédoise, suédois Swedish
suisse Swiss
tchèque Czechoslovakian
yougoslave Yugoslavian

Africaine, africain (*African*)
algérienne, algérien Algerian
égyptienne, égyptien Egyptian
marocaine, marocain Moroccan

nigérienne, nigérien Nigerian
sénégalaise, sénégalais Senegalese
tunisienne, tunisien Tunisian

Asiatique (*Asian*)
indonésienne, indonésien Indonesian
iranienne, iranien Iranian
israélienne, israélien Israeli
pakistanaise, pakistanais Pakistani

philippine, philippin Philippine
turque, turc Turkish
vietnamienne, vietnamien Vietnamese

(*Other*)
australienne, australien Australian
cubaine, cubain Cuban
guadeloupéenne, guadeloupéen from Guadeloupe
haïtienne, haïtien Haitian

jamaïquaine, jamaïquain Jamaican
martiniquaise, martiniquais from Martinique
néo-zélandaise, néo-zélandais from New Zealand
porto-ricaine, porto-ricain Puerto Rican

Resource List of Geographical Place Names

Cities and islands
With cities and some islands, **à** means "to" or "in," and **de** means "from." For example: **Je suis né(e) à New York.** (*I was born in New York.*) Here is a list of cities and islands. Note that names of cities in French are often spelled differently from their English equivalents.

Alger Algiers
Bruxelles Brussels
Copenhague Copenhagen
Cuba Cuba
Genève Geneva
Haïti Haiti
Londres London

Marseille Marseilles
Montréal Montreal
Moscou Moscow
New York New York
Paris Paris
Port-au-Prince Port-au-Prince

Porto-Rico Puerto Rico
Québec Quebec City
Rabat Rabat
Tahiti Tahiti
Tokyo Tokyo
Tunis Tunis

U.S. states
• States ending in English with the letter **a** often end with **e** in French. These are generally considered feminine: **Floride, Pennsylvanie, Virginie, Louisiane, Californie,** and so on. With these states, use **en** to mean "to" or "in" and **de** to mean "from." For example: **Je suis né(e) en Pennsylvanie.**

• States considered masculine take **au** or **dans le** to mean "to" or "in" and **du** to mean "from." For example: **Je suis né(e) au Texas.**

• With all U.S. states, **dans l'état de** means "to" or "in": **Je suis né(e) dans l'état de Connecticut.**

Canadian provinces
• With Canadian provinces, **dans le** and **dans la** mean "to" or "in": **Je suis né(e) dans le Québec.**

Appendix A
School Subjects

The following listing of school subjects will prove useful in responding to a variety of personalized questions in this textbook.

l'algèbre	algebra	le gouvernement	government
l'allemand	German	la grammaire	grammar
l'anatomie	anatomy	le grec	Greek
l'anglais	English	l'hébreu	Hebrew
l'anthropologie	anthropology	l'histoire	history
l'archéologie	archeology	l'histoire d'art	art history
l'art	art	l'informatique	computer science
les arts ménagers	home economics	l'instruction civique	social studies
l'astronomie	astronomy	l'italien	Italian
les beaux-arts	fine arts	le japonais	Japanese
la biochimie	biochemistry	le journalisme	journalism
la biologie	biology	les langues	languages
le calcul	calculus	le latin	Latin
la chimie	chemistry	les lettres/la littérature	literature
le chinois	Chinese	les mathématiques/les maths	mathematics
le commerce	commerce, business	la médecine	medicine
la composition anglaise	English composition	la musique	music
la comptabilité	bookkeeping, accounting	l'océanographie	oceanography
		l'orthographe	spelling
la dactylographie	typing	la peinture	painting
la danse	dance	la philosophie	philosophy
le dessin	design, drawing	la physique	physics
le droit	law	la psychologie	psychology
l'écologie	ecology	la religion	religion
l'économie	economics	le russe	Russian
l'éducation	education	les sciences	science
l'éducation physique	physical education	les sciences politiques	political science
l'espagnol	Spanish	la sculpture	sculpture
le français	French	la sociologie	sociology
le génie	engineering	la sténographie	shorthand
la géographie	geography	les travaux manuels	industrial arts, "shop"
la géologie	geology	la trigonométrie	trigonometry
la géométrie	geometry	la zoologie	zoology
la gestion	management, administration		

APPENDIX B

Compound Tenses—**Les Temps composés**

Compound tenses are composed of the auxiliary verb **avoir** or **être** and the past participle.

a. Le passé composé

parler *spoke /* *have spoken /* *did speak*	arriver *arrived /* *have arrived /* *did arrive*	se lever *got up /* *have gotten up /* *did get up*
j'ai parlé tu as parlé il a parlé elle a parlé nous avons parlé vous avez parlé ils ont parlé elles ont parlé	je suis arrivé(e) tu es arrivé(e) il est arrivé elle est arrivée nous sommes arrivé(e)s vous êtes arrivé(e)(s) ils sont arrivés elles sont arrivées	je me suis levé(e) tu t'es levé(e) il s'est levé elle s'est levée nous nous sommes levé(e)s vous vous êtes levé(e)(s) ils se sont levés elles se sont levées

b. Le plus-que-parfait is composed of the imperfect tense of either **avoir** or **être** and the past participle of the verb being conjugated:

parler *had spoken*	arriver *had arrived*	se lever *had gotten up*
j'avais parlé tu avais parlé il avait parlé elle avait parlé nous avions parlé vous aviez parlé ils avaient parlé elles avaient parlé	j'étais arrivé(e) tu étais arrivé(e) il était arrivé elle était arrivée nous étions arrivé(e)s vous étiez arrivé(e)(s) ils étaient arrivés elles étaient arrivées	je m'étais levé(e) tu t'étais levé(e) il s'était levé elle s'était levée nous nous étions levé(e)s vous vous étiez levé(e)(s) ils s'étaient levés elles s'étaient levées

c. **Le futur antérieur** is composed of the future tense of either **avoir** or **être** and the past participle of the verb being conjugated:

parler *will have spoken*	**arriver** *will have arrived*	**se lever** *will have gotten up*
j'aurai parlé	je serai arrivé(e)	je me serai levé(e)
tu auras parlé	tu seras arrivé(e)	tu te seras levé(e)
il aura parlé	il sera arrivé	il se sera levé
elle aura parlé	elle sera arrivée	elle se sera levée
nous aurons parlé	nous serons arrivé(e)s	nous nous serons levé(e)s
vous aurez parlé	vous serez arrivé(e)(s)	vous vous serez levé(e)(s)
ils auront parlé	ils seront arrivés	ils se seront levés
elles auront parlé	elles seront arrivées	elles se seront levées

d. **Le conditionnel passé** is composed of the conditional tense of either **avoir** or **être** and the past participle of the verb being conjugated:

parler *would have spoken*	**arriver** *would have arrived*	**se lever** *would have gotten up*
j'aurais parlé	je serais arrivé(e)	je me serais levé(e)
tu aurais parlé	tu serais arrivé(e)	tu te serais levé(e)
il aurait parlé	il serait arrivé	il se serait levé
elle aurait parlé	elle serait arrivée	elle se serait levée
nous aurions parlé	nous serions arrivé(e)s	nous nous serions levé(e)s
vous auriez parlé	vous seriez arrivé(e)(s)	vous vous seriez levé(e)(s)
ils auraient parlé	ils seraient arrivés	ils se seraient levés
elles auraient parlé	elles seraient arrivées	elles se seraient levées

APPENDIX C

Conjugaison des Verbes

VERBES EN -er

	INFINITIF:	**parler**
	PARTICIPE PRÉSENT:	**parlant**
	PARTICIPE PASSÉ:	**parlé**

INDICATIF

	PRÉSENT	IMPARFAIT	PASSÉ SIMPLE	FUTUR
je	parle	parlais	**parlai**	parlerai
tu	parles	parlais	parlas	parleras
il	parle	parlait	parla	parlera
nous	parlons	parlions	parlâmes	parlerons
vous	parlez	parliez	parlâtes	parlerez
ils	parlent	parlaient	parlèrent	parleront

	PASSÉ COMPOSÉ	PLUS-QUE-PARFAIT	FUTUR ANTÉRIEUR
j'	ai parlé	avais parlé	aurai parlé
tu	as parlé	avais parlé	auras parlé
il	a parlé	avait parlé	aura parlé
nous	avons parlé	avions parlé	aurons parlé
vous	avez parlé	aviez parlé	aurez parlé
ils	ont parlé	avaient parlé	auront parlé

CONDITIONNEL

	PRÉSENT	PASSÉ
je	parlerais	aurais parlé
tu	parlerais	aurais parlé
il	parlerait	aurait parlé
nous	parlerions	aurions parlé
vous	parleriez	auriez parlé
ils	parleraient	auraient parlé

IMPÉRATIF

parle
parlons
parlez

SUBJONCTIF

	PRÉSENT	PASSÉ	IMPARFAIT
que je	parle	aie parlé	parlasse
que tu	parles	aies parlé	parlasses
qu'il	parle	ait parlé	parlât
que nous	parlions	ayons parlé	parlassions
que vous	parliez	ayez parlé	parlassiez
qu'ils	parlent	aient parlé	parlassent

Spelling Changes in Certain -er Verbs

Verbs ending in **-cer** change **c** to **ç** before the vowels **a** and **o** in order to keep the soft **c** sound:

> commencer: nous **commençons**
> je **commençais**
> en **commençant**, etc.

Verbs ending in **-ger** add **e** after **g** before **a** and **o** in order to keep the soft **g** sound:

> manger: nous **mangeons**
> je **mangeais**
> en **mangeant**, etc.

Verbs ending in **e** + consonant + **er** change **e** to **è** before mute **e:**

> se promener: je me **promène**
> je me **promènerai**
> je me **promènerais**, etc.

The verbs **appeler** and **jeter** double the **l** or **t** before mute **e:** je m'**appelle**, etc.

Verbs ending in **é** + consonant + **er** change **é** to **è** before mute **e** only in the present tense of the indicative and of the subjunctive:

> préférer: je **préfère**
> tu **préfères**
> qu'ils **préfèrent**, etc.

Verbs ending in **-yer** change **y** to **i** before mute **e.** Verbs ending in **-ayer** may, however, keep the **y:**

> ennuyer: j'**ennuie**
> j'**ennuierai**
> j'**ennuierais**, etc.

VERBES EN -ir

INFINITIF:	**finir**		
PARTICIPE PRÉSENT:	**finissant**		
PARTICIPE PASSÉ:	**fini**		

INDICATIF

	PRÉSENT	IMPARFAIT	PASSÉ SIMPLE	FUTUR
je	finis	finissais	finis	finirai
tu	finis	finissais	finis	finiras
il	finit	finissait	finit	finira
nous	finissons	finissions	finîmes	finirons
vous	finissez	finissiez	finîtes	finirez
ils	finissent	finissaient	finirent	finiront

	PASSÉ COMPOSÉ	PLUS-QUE-PARFAIT	FUTUR ANTÉRIEUR
j'	ai fini	avais fini	aurai fini
tu	as fini	avais fini	auras fini
il	a fini	avait fini	aura fini
nous	avons fini	avions fini	aurons fini
vous	avez fini	aviez fini	aurez fini
ils	ont fini	avaient fini	auront fini

CONDITIONNEL

	PRÉSENT	PASSÉ
je	fini**rais**	aurais fini
tu	fini**rais**	aurais fini
il	fini**rait**	aurait fini
nous	fini**rions**	aurions fini
vous	fini**riez**	auriez fini
ils	fini**raient**	auraient fini

IMPÉRATIF

fini**s**
fini**ssons**
fini**ssez**

SUBJONCTIF

	PRÉSENT	PASSÉ	IMPARFAIT
que je	fini**sse**	aie fini	fini**sse**
que tu	fini**sses**	aies fini	fini**sses**
qu'il	fini**sse**	ait fini	fin**ît**
que nous	fini**ssions**	ayons fini	fini**ssions**
que vous	fini**ssiez**	ayez fini	fini**ssiez**
qu'ils	fini**ssent**	aient fini	fini**ssent**

VERBES EN -re

INFINITIF:	**vendre**
PARTICIPE PRÉSENT:	**vendant**
PARTICIPE PASSÉ:	**vendu**

INDICATIF:

	PRÉSENT	IMPARFAIT	PASSÉ SIMPLE	FUTUR
je	vend**s**	vend**ais**	vend**is**	vend**rai**
tu	vend**s**	vend**ais**	vend**is**	vend**ras**
il	vend	vend**ait**	vend**it**	vend**ra**
nous	vend**ons**	vend**ions**	vend**îmes**	vend**rons**
vous	vend**ez**	vend**iez**	vend**îtes**	vend**rez**
ils	vend**ent**	vend**aient**	vend**irent**	vend**ront**

	PASSÉ COMPOSÉ	PLUS-QUE-PARFAIT	FUTUR ANTÉRIEUR
j'	ai vendu	avais vendu	aurai vendu
tu	as vendu	avais vendu	auras vendu
il	a vendu	avait vendu	aura vendu
nous	avons vendu	avions vendu	aurons vendu
vous	avez vendu	aviez vendu	aurez vendu
ils	ont vendu	avaient vendu	auront vendu

CONDITIONNEL

	PRÉSENT	PASSÉ
je	vend**rais**	aurais vendu
tu	vend**rais**	aurais vendu
il	vend**rait**	aurait vendu
nous	vend**rions**	aurions vendu
vous	vend**riez**	auriez vendu
ils	vend**raient**	auraient vendu

IMPÉRATIF

vend**s**
vend**ons**
vend**ez**

SUBJONCTIF

	PRÉSENT	PASSÉ	IMPARFAIT
que je	vend**e**	aie vendu	vend**isse**
que tu	vend**es**	aies vendu	vend**isses**
qu'il	vend**e**	ait vendu	vend**ît**
que nous	vend**ions**	ayons vendu	vend**issions**
que vous	vend**iez**	ayez vendu	vend**issiez**
qu'ils	vend**ent**	aient vendu	vend**issent**

VERBES IRRÉGULIERS

INFINITIF / PARTICIPES		INDICATIF			
		PRÉSENT	FUTUR	IMPARFAIT	PASSÉ SIMPLE
aller *to go* allant allé	je tu il nous vous ils	vais vas va allons allez vont	irai iras ira irons irez iront	allais allais allait allions alliez allaient	allai allas alla allâmes allâtes allèrent
asseoir *to seat* asseyant assis *or* assoyant	j' tu il nous vous ils	assieds assieds assied asseyons asseyez asseyent	assiérai assiéras assiéra assiérons assiérez assiéront	asseyais asseyais asseyait asseyions asseyiez asseyaient	assis assis assit assîmes assîtes assirent
	j' tu il nous vous ils	assois assois assoit assoyons assoyez assoient	assoirai assoiras assoira assoirons assoirez assoiront	assoyais assoyais assoyait assoyions assoyiez assoyaient	
avoir *to have* ayant eu	j' tu il nous vous ils	ai as a avons avez ont	aurai auras aura aurons aurez auront	avais avais avait avions aviez avaient	eus eus eut eûmes eûtes eurent
battre *to beat* battant battu	je tu il nous vous ils	bats bats bat battons battez battent	battrai battras battra battrons battrez battront	battais battais battait battions battiez battaient	battis battis battit battîmes battîtes battirent
boire *to drink* buvant bu	je tu il nous vous ils	bois bois boit buvons buvez boivent	boirai boiras boira boirons boirez boiront	buvais buvais buvait buvions buviez buvaient	bus bus but bûmes bûtes burent
conclure *to conclude* concluant conclu	je tu il nous vous ils	conclus conclus conclut concluons concluez concluent	conclurai concluras conclura conclurons conclurez concluront	concluais concluais concluait concluions concluiez concluaient	conclus conclus conclut conclûmes conclûtes conclurent
conduire *to drive to lead to conduct* conduisant conduit	je tu il nous vous ils	conduis conduis conduit conduisons conduisez conduisent	conduirai conduiras conduira conduirons conduirez conduiront	conduisais conduisais conduisait conduisions conduisiez conduisaient	conduisis conduisis conduisit conduisîmes conduisîtes conduisirent

CONDITIONNEL	IMPÉRATIF	SUBJONCTIF	
		PRÉSENT	IMPARFAIT
irais		aille	allasse
irais	va	ailles	allasses
irait		aille	allât
irions	allons	allions	allassions
iriez	allez	alliez	allassiez
iraient		aillent	allassent
assiérais		asseye	assisse
assiérais	assieds	asseyes	assisses
assiérait		asseye	assît
assiérions	asseyons	asseyions	assissions
assiériez	asseyez	asseyiez	assissiez
assiéraient		asseyent	assissent
or			
assoirais		assoie	
assoirais	assois	assoies	
assoirait		assoie	
assoirions	assoyons	assoyions	
assoiriez	assoyez	assoyiez	
assoiraient		assoient	
aurais		aie	eusse
aurais	aie	aies	eusses
aurait		ait	eût
aurions	ayons	ayons	eussions
auriez	ayez	ayez	eussiez
auraient		aient	eussent
battrais		batte	battise
battrais	bats	battes	battisses
battrait		batte	battît
battrions	battons	battions	battissions
battriez	battez	battiez	battissiez
battraient		battent	battissent
boirais		boive	busse
boirais	bois	boives	busses
boirait		boive	bût
boirions	buvons	buvions	bussions
boiriez	buvez	buviez	bussiez
boiraient		boivent	bussent
conclurais		conclue	conclusse
conclurais	conclus	conclues	conclusses
conclurait		conclue	conclût
conclurions	concluons	concluions	conclussions
concluriez	concluez	concluiez	conclussiez
concluraient		concluent	conclussent
conduirais		conduise	conduisisse
conduirais	conduis	conduises	conduisisses
conduirait		conduise	conduisît
conduirions	conduisons	conduisions	conduisissions
conduiriez	conduisez	conduisiez	conduisissiez
conduiraient		conduisent	conduisissent

INFINITIF PARTICIPES		INDICATIF			
		PRÉSENT	FUTUR	IMPARFAIT	PASSÉ SIMPLE
connaître *to know* connaissant connu	je tu il nous vous ils	connais connais connaît connaissons connaissez connaissent	connaîtai connaîtras connaîtra connaîtrons connaîtrez connaîtront	connaissais connaissais connaissait connaissions connaissiez connaissaient	connus connus connut connûmes connûtes connurent
coudre *to sew* cousant cousu	je tu il nous vous ils	couds couds coud cousons cousez cousent	coudrai coudras coudra coudrons coudrez coudront	cousais cousais cousait cousions cousiez cousaient	cousis cousis cousit cousîmes cousîtes cousirent
courir *to run* courant couru	je tu il nous vous ils	cours cours court courons courez courent	courrai courras courra courrons courrez courront	courais courais courait courions couriez couraient	courus courus courut courûmes courûtes coururent
craindre *to fear* craignant craint	je tu il nous vous ils	crains crains craint craignons craignez craignent	craindrai craindras craindra craindrons craindrez craindront	craignais craignais craignait craignions craigniez craignaient	craignis craignis craignit craignîmes craignîtes craignirent
croire *to believe* croyant cru	je tu il nous vous ils	crois crois croit croyons croyez croient	croirai croiras croira croirons croirez croiront	croyais croyais croyait croyions croyiez croyaient	crus crus crut crûmes crûtes crurent
devoir *to owe, must* devant dû, due	je tu il nous vous ils	dois dois doit devons devez doivent	devrai devras devra devrons devrez devront	devais devais devait devions deviez devaient	dus dus dut dûmes dûtes durent
dire *to say* disant dit	je tu il nous vous ils	dis dis dit disons dites disent	dirai diras dira dirons direz diront	disais disais disait disions disiez disaient	dis dis dit dîmes dîtes dirent
dormir *to sleep* dormant dormi	je tu il nous vous ils	dors dors dort dormons dormez dorment	dormirai dormiras dormira dormirons dormirez dormiront	dormais dormais dormait dormions dormiez dormaient	dormis dormis dormit dormîmes dormîtes dormirent

| CONDITIONNEL | IMPÉRATIF | SUBJONCTIF | |
		PRÉSENT	IMPARFAIT
connaîtrais		connaisse	connusse
connaîtrais	connais	connaisses	connusses
connaîtrait		connaisse	connût
connaîtrions	connaissons	connaissions	connussions
connaîtriez	connaissez	connaissiez	connussiez
connaîtraient		connaissent	connussent
coudrais		couse	cousisse
coudrais	couds	couses	cousisses
coudrait		couse	cousît
coudrions	cousons	cousions	cousissions
coudriez	cousez	cousiez	cousissiez
coudraient		cousent	cousissent
courrais		coure	courusse
courrais	cours	coures	courusses
courrait		coure	courût
courrions	courons	courions	courussions
courriez	courez	couriez	courussiez
courraient		courent	courussent
craindrais		craigne	craignisse
craindrais	crains	craignes	craignisses
craindrait		craigne	craignît
craindrions	craignons	craignions	craignissions
craindriez	craignez	craigniez	craignissiez
craindraient		craignent	craignissent
croirais		croie	crusse
croirais	crois	croies	crusses
croirait		croie	crût
croirions	croyons	croyions	crussions
croiriez	croyez	croyiez	crussiez
croiraient		croient	crussent
devrais		doive	dusse
devrais	dois	doives	dusses
devrait		doive	dût
devrions	devons	devions	dussions
devriez	devez	deviez	dussiez
devraient		doivent	dussent
dirais		dise	disse
dirais	dis	dises	disses
dirait		dise	dît
dirions	disons	disions	dissions
diriez	dites	disiez	dissiez
diraient		disent	dissent
dormirais		dorme	dormisse
dormirais	dors	dormes	dormisses
dormirait		dorme	dormît
dormirions	dormons	dormions	dormissions
dormiriez	dormez	dormiez	dormissiez
dormiraient		dorment	dormissent

INFINITIF PARTICIPES		INDICATIF PRÉSENT	FUTUR	IMPARFAIT	PASSÉ SIMPLE
écrire	j'	écris	écrirai	écrivais	écrivis
to write	tu	écris	écriras	écrivais	écrivis
	il	écrit	écrira	écrivait	écrivit
écrivant	nous	écrivons	écrirons	écrivions	écrivîmes
écrit	vous	écrivez	écrirez	écriviez	écrivîtes
	ils	écrivent	écriront	écrivaient	écrivirent
envoyer	j'	envoie	enverrai	envoyais	envoyai
to send	tu	envoies	enverras	envoyais	envoyas
	il	envoie	enverra	envoyait	envoya
envoyant	nous	envoyons	enverrons	envoyions	envoyâmes
envoyé	vous	envoyez	enverrez	envoyiez	envoyâtes
	ils	envoient	enverront	envoyaient	envoyèrent
être	je	suis	serai	étais	fus
to be	tu	es	seras	étais	fus
	il	est	sera	était	fut
étant	nous	sommes	serons	étions	fûmes
été	vous	êtes	serez	étiez	fûtes
	ils	sont	seront	étaient	furent
faire	je	fais	ferai	faisais	fis
to do	tu	fais	feras	faisais	fis
to make	il	fait	fera	faisait	fit
	nous	faisons	ferons	faisions	fîmes
faisant	vous	faites	ferez	faisiez	fîtes
fait	ils	font	feront	faisaient	firent
falloir	il	faut	faudra	fallait	fallut
to be necessary, must					

No present participle
Past participle: fallu
This is an impersonal verb, conjugated in the third-person singular only.

fuir	je	fuis	fuirai	fuyais	fuis
to flee	tu	fuis	fuiras	fuyais	fuis
	il	fuit	fuira	fuyait	fuit
fuyant	nous	fuyons	fuirons	fuyions	fuîmes
fui	vous	fuyez	fuirez	fuyiez	fuîtes
	ils	fuient	fuiront	fuyaient	fuirent
haïr	je	hais	haïrai	haïssais	haïs
to hate	tu	hais	haïras	haïssais	haïs
	il	hait	haïra	haïssait	haït
haïssant	nous	haïssons	haïrons	haïssions	haïmes
haï	vous	haïssez	haïrez	haïssiez	haïtes
	ils	haïssent	haïront	haïssaient	haïrent
lire	je	lis	lirai	lisais	lus
to read	tu	lis	liras	lisais	lus
	il	lit	lira	lisait	lut
lisant	nous	lisons	lirons	lisions	lûmes
lu	vous	lisez	lirez	lisiez	lûtes
	ils	lisent	liront	lisaient	lurent

CONDITIONNEL	IMPÉRATIF	SUBJONCTIF	
		PRÉSENT	IMPARFAIT
écrirais		écrive	écrivisse
écrirais	écris	écrives	écrivisses
écrirait		écrive	écrivît
écririons	écrivons	écrivions	écrivissions
écririez	écrivez	écriviez	écrivissiez
écriraient		écrivent	écrivissent
enverrais		envoie	envoyasse
enverrais	envoie	envoies	envoyasses
enverrait		envoie	envoyât
enverrions	envoyons	envoyions	cnvoyassions
enverriez	enoyez	envoyiez	envoyassiez
enverraient		envoyent	envoyassent
serais		sois	fusse
serais	sois	sois	fusses
serait		soit	fût
serions	soyons	soyons	fussions
seriez	soyez	soyez	fussiez
seraient		soient	fussent
ferais		fasse	fisse
ferais	fais	fasses	fisses
ferait		fasse	fît
ferions	faisons	fassions	fissions
feriez	faites	fassiez	fissiez
feraient		fassent	fissent
faudrait		faille	fallût
fuirais		fuie	fuisse
fuirais	fuis	fuies	fuisses
fuirait		fuie	fuît
fuirions	fuyons	fuyions	fuissions
fuiriez	fuyez	fuyiez	fuissiez
fuiraient		fuient	fuissent
haïrais		haïsse	haïsse
haïrais	hais	haïsses	haïsses
haïrait		haïsse	haït
haïrions	haïssons	haïssions	haïssions
haïriez	haïssez	haïssiez	haïssiez
haïraient		haïssent	haïssent
lirais		lise	lusse
lirais	lis	lises	lusses
lirait		lise	lût
lirions	lisons	lisions	lussions
liriez	lisez	lisiez	lussiez
liraient		lisent	lussent

| INFINITIF | | INDICATIF | | | |
PARTICIPES		PRÉSENT	FUTUR	IMPARFAIT	PASSÉ SIMPLE
mettre	je	mets	mettrai	mettais	mis
to put	tu	mets	mettras	mettais	mis
	il	met	mettra	mettait	mit
mettant	nous	mettons	mettrons	mettions	mîmes
mis	vous	mettez	mettrez	mettiez	mîtes
	ils	mettent	mettront	mettaient	mirent
mourir	je	meurs	mourrai	mourais	mourus
to die	tu	meurs	mourras	mourais	mourus
	il	meurt	mourra	mourait	mourut
mourant	nous	mourons	mourrons	mourions	mourûmes
mort	vous	mourez	mourrez	mouriez	mourûtes
	ils	meurent	mourront	mouraient	moururent
naître	je	nais	naîtrai	naissais	naquis
to be born	tu	nais	naîtras	naissais	naquis
	il	naît	naîtra	naissait	naquit
naissant	nous	naissons	naîtrons	naissions	naquîmes
né	vous	naissez	naîtrez	naissiez	naquîtes
	ils	naissent	naîtront	naissaient	naquirent
ouvrir	j'	ouvre	ouvrirai	ouvrais	ouvris
to open	tu	ouvres	ouvriras	ouvrais	ouvris
	il	ouvre	ouvrira	ouvrait	ouvrit
ouvrant	nous	ouvrons	ouvrirons	ouvrions	ouvrîmes
ouvert	vous	ouvrez	ouvrirez	ouvriez	ouvrîtes
	ils	ouvrent	ouvriront	ouvraient	ouvrirent
partir	je	pars	partirai	partais	partis
to leave	tu	pars	partiras	partais	partis
to go away	il	part	partira	partait	partit
	nous	partons	partirons	partions	partîmes
partant	vous	partez	partirez	partiez	partîtes
parti	ils	partent	partiront	partaient	partirent
peindre	je	peins	peindrai	peignais	peignis
to paint	tu	peins	peindras	peignais	peignis
	il	peint	peindra	peignait	peignit
peignant	nous	peignons	peindrons	peignions	peignîmes
peint	vous	peignez	peindrez	peigniez	peignîtes
	ils	peignent	peindront	peignaient	peignirent
plaire	je	plais	plairai	plaisais	plus
to please	tu	plais	plairas	plaisais	plus
	il	plaît	plaira	plaisait	plut
plaisant	nous	plaisons	plairons	plaisions	plûmes
plu	vous	plaisez	plairez	plaisiez	plûtes
	ils	plaisent	plairont	plaisaient	plurent
pleuvoir	il	pleut	pleuvra	pleuvait	plut
to rain					

pleuvant
plu
This is an impersonal verb, conjugated in the third-person singular only.

CONDITIONNEL	IMPÉRATIF	SUBJONCTIF	
		PRÉSENT	IMPARFAIT
mettrais		mette	misse
mettrais	mets	mettes	misses
mettrait		mette	mît
mettrions	mettons	mettions	missions
mettriez	mettez	mettiez	missiez
mettraient		mettent	missent
mourrais		meure	mourusse
mourrais	meurs	meures	mourusses
mourrait		meure	mourût
mourrions	mourons	mourions	mourussions
mourriez	mourez	mouriez	mourussiez
mourraient		meurent	mourussent
naîtrais		naisse	naquisse
naîtrais	nais	naisses	naquisses
naîtrait		naisse	naquît
naîtrions	naissons	naissions	naquissions
naîtriez	naissez	naissiez	naquissiez
naîtraient		naissent	naquissent
ouvrirais		ouvre	ouvrisse
ouvrirais	ouvre	ouvres	ouvrisses
ouvrirait		ouvre	ouvrît
ouvririons	ouvrons	ouvrions	ouvrissions
ouvririez	ouvrez	ouvriez	ouvrissiez
ouvriraient		ouvrent	ouvrissent
partirais		parte	partisse
partirais	pars	partes	partisses
partirait		parte	partît
partirions	partons	partions	partissions
partiriez	partez	partiez	partissiez
partiraient		partent	partissent
peindrais		peigne	peignisse
peindrais	peins	peignes	peignisses
peindrait		peigne	peignisse
peindrions	peignons	peignions	peignissions
peindriez	peignez	peigniez	peignissiez
peindraient		peignent	peignissent
plairais		plaise	plusse
plairais	plais	plaises	plusses
plairait		plaise	plût
plairions	plaisons	plaisions	plussions
plairiez	plaisez	plaisiez	plussiez
plairaient		plaisent	plussent
pleuvrait		pleuve	plût

INFINITIF PARTICIPES		INDICATIF			
		PRÉSENT	FUTUR	IMPARFAIT	PASSÉ SIMPLE
pouvoir	je	peux, puis	pourrai	pouvais	pus
to be able	tu	peux	pourras	pouvais	pus
can	il	peut	pourra	pouvait	put
	nous	pouvons	pourrons	pouvions	pûmes
pouvant	vous	pouvez	pourrez	pouviez	pûtes
pu	ils	peuvent	pourront	pouvaient	purent
prendre	je	prends	prendrai	prenais	pris
to take	tu	prends	prendras	prenais	pris
	il	prend	prendra	prenait	prit
prenant	nous	prenons	prendrons	prenions	prîmes
pris	vous	prenez	prendrez	preniez	prîtes
	ils	prennent	prendront	prenaient	prirent
recevoir	je	reçois	recevrai	recevais	reçus
to receive	tu	reçois	recevras	recevais	reçus
	il	reçoit	recevra	recevait	reçut
recevant	nous	recevons	recevrons	recevions	reçûmes
reçu	vous	recevez	recevrez	receviez	reçûtes
	ils	reçoivent	recevront	recevaient	reçurent
résoudre	je	résous	résoudrai	résolvais	résolus
to resolve	tu	résous	résoudras	résolvais	résolus
	il	résout	résoudra	résolvait	résolut
résolvant	nous	résolvons	résoudrons	résolvions	résolûmes
résolu	vous	résolvez	résoudrez	résolviez	résolûtes
	ils	résolvent	résoudront	résolvaient	résolurent
rire	je	ris	rirai	riais	ris
to laugh	tu	ris	riras	riais	ris
	il	rit	rira	riait	rit
riant	nous	rions	rirons	riions	rîmes
ri	vous	riez	rirez	riiez	rîtes
	ils	rient	riront	riaient	rirent
savoir	je	sais	saurai	savais	sus
to know	tu	sais	sauras	savais	sus
	il	sait	saura	savait	sut
sachant	nous	savons	saurons	savions	sûmes
su	vous	savez	saurez	saviez	sûtes
	ils	savent	sauront	savaient	surent
servir	je	sers	servirai	servais	servis
to serve	tu	sers	serviras	servais	servis
	il	sert	servira	servait	servit
servant	nous	servons	servirons	servions	servîmes
servi	vous	servez	servirez	serviez	servîtes
	ils	servent	serviront	servaient	servirent
suivre	je	suis	suivrai	suivais	suivis
to follow	tu	suis	suivras	suivais	suivis
	il	suit	suivra	suivait	suivit
suivant	nous	suivons	suivrons	suivions	suivîmes
suivi	vous	suivez	suivrez	suiviez	suivîtes
	ils	suivent	suivront	suivaient	suivirent

CONDITIONNEL	IMPÉRATIF	SUBJONCTIF	
		PRÉSENT	IMPARFAIT
pourrais		puisse	pusse
pourrais		puisses	pusses
pourrait		puisse	pût
pourrions		puissions	pussions
pourriez		puissiez	pussiez
pourraient		puissent	pussent
prendrais		prenne	prisse
prendrais	prends	prennes	prisses
prendrait		prenne	prît
prendrions	prenons	prenions	prissions
prendriez	prenez	preniez	prissiez
prendraient		prennent	prissent
recevrais		reçoive	reçusse
recevrais	reçois	reçoives	reçusses
recevrait		reçoive	reçût
recevrions	recevons	recevions	reçussions
recevriez	recevez	receviez	reçussiez
recevraient		reçoivent	reçussent
résoudrais		résolve	résolusse
résoudrais	résous	résolves	résolusses
résoudrait		résolve	résolût
résoudrions	résolvons	résolvions	résolussions
résoudriez	résolvez	résolviez	résolussiez
résoudraient		résolvent	résolussent
rirais		rie	risse
rirais	ris	ries	risses
rirait		rie	rît
ririons	rions	riions	rissions
ririez	riez	riiez	rissiez
riraient		rient	rissent
saurais		sache	susse
saurais	sache	saches	susses
saurait		sache	sût
saurions	sachons	sachions	sussions
sauriez	sachez	sachiez	sussiez
sauraient		sachent	sussent
servirais		serve	servisse
servirais	sers	serves	servisses
servirait		serve	servît
servirions	servons	servions	servissions
serviriez	servez	serviez	servissiez
serviraient		servent	servissent
suivrais		suive	suivisse
suivrais	suis	suives	suivisses
suivrait		suive	suivît
suivrions	suivons	suivions	suivissions
suivriez	suivez	suiviez	suivissiez
suivraient		suivent	suivissent

| INFINITIF | | INDICATIF | | | |
PARTICIPES		PRÉSENT	FUTUR	IMPARFAIT	PASSÉ SIMPLE
tenir	je	tiens	tiendrai	tenais	tins
to hold	tu	tiens	tiendras	tenais	tins
	il	tient	tiendra	tenait	tint
tenant	nous	tenons	tiendrons	tenions	tînmes
tenu	vous	tenez	tiendrez	teniez	tîntes
	ils	tiennent	tiendront	tenaient	tinrent
valoir	je	vaux	vaudrai	valais	valus
to be worth	tu	vaux	vaudras	valais	valus
	il	vaut	vaudra	valait	valut
valant	nous	valons	vaudrons	valions	valûmes
valu	vous	valez	vaudrez	valiez	valûtes
	ils	valent	vaudront	valaient	valurent
venir	je	viens	viendrai	venais	vins
to come	tu	viens	viendras	venais	vins
	il	vient	viendra	venait	vint
venant	nous	venons	viendrons	venions	vînmes
venu	vous	venez	viendrez	veniez	vîntes
	ils	viennent	viendront	venaient	vinrent
vivre	je	vis	vivrai	vivais	vécus
to live	tu	vis	vivras	vivais	vécus
	il	vit	vivra	vivait	vécut
vivant	nous	vivons	vivrons	vivions	vécûmes
vécu	vous	vivez	vivrez	viviez	vécûtes
	ils	vivent	vivront	vivaient	vécurent
voir	je	vois	verrai	voyais	vis
to see	tu	vois	verras	voyais	vis
	il	voit	verra	voyait	vit
voyant	nous	voyons	verrons	voyions	vîmes
vu	vous	voyez	verrez	voyiez	vîtes
	ils	voient	verront	voyaient	virent
vouloir	je	veux	voudrai	voulais	voulus
to want	tu	veux	voudras	voulais	voulus
to wish	il	veut	voudra	voulait	voulut
	nous	voulons	voudrons	voulions	voulûmes
voulant	vous	voulez	voudrez	vouliez	voulûtes
voulu	ils	veulent	voudront	voulaient	voulurent

CONDITIONNEL	IMPÉRATIF	SUBJONCTIF	
		PRÉSENT	IMPARFAIT
tiendrais		tienne	tinsse
tiendrais	tiens	tiennes	tinsses
tiendrait		tienne	tînt
tiendrions	tenons	tenions	tinssions
tiendriez	tenez	teniez	tinssiez
tiendraient		tiennent	tinssent
vaudrais		vaille	valusse
vaudrais	vaux	vailles	valusses
vaudrait		vaille	valût
vaudrions	valons	valions	valussions
vaudriez	valez	valiez	valussiez
vaudraient		vaillent	valussent
viendrais		vienne	vinsse
viendrais	viens	viennes	vinsses
viendrait		vienne	vînt
viendrions	venons	venions	vinssions
viendriez	venez	veniez	vinssiez
viendraient		viennent	vinssent
vivrais		vive	vécusse
vivrais	vis	vives	vécusses
vivrait		vive	vécût
vivrions	vivons	vivions	vécussions
vivriez	vivez	viviez	vécussiez
vivraient		vivent	vécussent
verrais		voie	visse
verrais	vois	voies	visses
verrait		voie	vît
verrions	voyons	voyions	vissions
verriez	voyez	voyiez	vissiez
verraient		voient	vissent
voudrais		veuille	voulusse
voudrais	veux(veuille)	veuilles	voulusses
voudrait		veuille	voulût
voudrions	voulons (veuillons)	voulions	voulussions
voudriez	voulez (veuillez)	vouliez	voulussiez
voudraient		veuillent	voulussent

APPENDIX D

Chansons

Here are nine popular, easy-to-learn French folksongs, along with *La Marseillaise,* the French national anthem. Folksongs are all transposed into the key of G to facilitate accompaniment by amateur musicians. These songs are recorded on a separate cassette as part of the tape program accompanying *EN FRANÇAIS.**

Frère Jacques

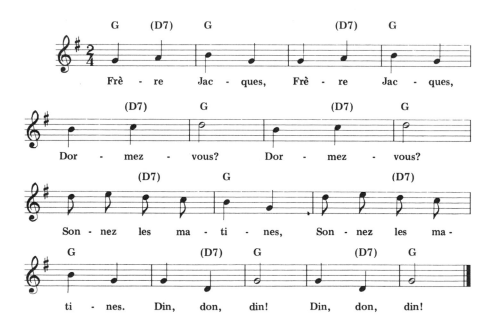

*Songs arranged by Dana Carton.

Sur le Pont d'Avignon

1. Les beaux messieurs font comme ça...   (Geste de saluer)
    Et puis encore comme ça...   (Autre salut)

2. Les belles dames font comme ça...   (Révérence)
    Et puis encore comme ça...   (Autre révérence)

3. Les officiers font comme ça...   (Salut militaire)
    Et puis encore comme ça...   (Autre salut)

Fais Dodo

Fais do - do, Co - las mon p'tit frè - re,

Fais do - do, t'au - ras du lo - lo! Ma -

man est en haut qui fait du gâ - teau, Pa -

pa est en bas qui fait du cho - co - lat.

Fais do - do, Co - las mon p'tit frè - re,

Fais do - do, t'au - ras du lo - lo!

Quand Trois
Poules Vont aux Champs

Quand trois pou - les vont aux champs,

La pre - miè - re va de - vant.

La se - conde suit la pre - miè - re,

La troi - sième vient la der - niè - re.

Quand trois pou - les vont aux champs,

La pre - miè - re va de - vant.

Alternate words to same tune:

Ah! vous dirais-je, maman!
Ce qui cause mon tourment.
Papa veut que je raisonne
Comme une grande personne
Moi, je dis que les bonbons
Valent mieux que la raison.

Alouette, Gentille Alouette

2. Je te plumerai le bec,
   Je te plumerai le bec.
   Et le bec. Et le bec.
   Et la tête. Et la tête.
   Alouette. Alouette.
   Oh!

3. Je te plumerai les pattes, etc.

4. Je te plumerai le cou, etc.

5. Je te plumerai le dos, etc.

Au Clair de la Lune

Au clair de la lu - ne, Mon a - mi Pier - rot,

Prê - te - moi ta plu - me, Pour é - crire un mot.

Ma chan - delle est mor - te, Je n'ai plus de feu.

Ou - vre - moi ta por - te, Pour l'a - mour de Dieu.

2. Au clair de la lune,
   Pierrot répondit:
   «Je n'ai pas de plume,
   Je suis dans mon lit.
   Va chez la voisine,
   Je crois qu'elle y est;
   Car dans sa cuisine,
   On bat le briquet.»

3. Au clair de la lune,
   L'aimable Lubin
   Frappe chez la brune
   Elle répond soudain:
   Qui frappe de la sorte?
   Il dit à son tour:
   Ouvrez votre porte
   Pour le Dieu d'amour!

J'ai du Bon Tabac

J'ai du bon ta - bac dans ma ta - ba -

tiè - re. J'ai du bon ta - bac, tu n'en au - ras pas.

J'en ai du fin et du bien râ - pé,
Mais ce n'est pas pour ton vi - lain nez.

Chevaliers
de la Table Ronde

Che - va - liers de la ta - ble ron - de Goû - tons

voir si le vin est bon. Che - va - bon. Goû - tons

voir, oui, oui, oui, Goû - tons voir, non, non, non, Goû - tons

voir si le vin est bon. Goû - tons bon.

2. S'il est bon, s'il est agréable
J'en boirai jusqu'à mon plaisir. (bis)
J'en boirai, oui, oui, oui, (etc.)

Savez-vous
Planter les Choux?

Sa - vez - vous plan - ter les choux? À la

mo - de, à la mo - de, Sa - vez - vous plan - ter les

choux? À la mo - de de chez nous?

Alternate tune:

2. On les plante avec le pied,
À la mode, à la mode,
On les plante avec le pied,
À la mode, de chez nous.

3. *Continue this song, each time*
substituting a different part
of the body: la main, le nez,
le coude, l'index, la tête, etc.

La Marseillaise

VOCABULAIRE

The vocabulary contains all terms included in the various exercises, improvisations, folksongs, and springboards for conversation (except for a number of the most obvious cognates). The most frequently occurring irregular verb forms, such as past participles, are listed separately and are cross-referenced. All expressions are fully cross-referenced; for example, **faire le ménage** is listed under both **faire** and **ménage**. Definitions are given *only* for the contexts in this book.

ABBREVIATIONS			
adj	adjective	*m*	masculine
adv	adverb	*n*	noun
conj	conjunction	*pp*	past participle
def art	definite article	*pl*	plural
f	feminine	*prep*	preposition
independ	independant	*pron*	pronoun
inf	infinitive	*rel*	relative

à to; at; in; toward; by
abreuver to water; to soak
absent *m* absentee
absolument absolutely
accidentellement accidentally
accompagner to accompany
accomplir to accomplish
accord *m* agreement; **être d'accord
    to agree**
achat *m* purchase
acheter to buy
acteur *m* actor
actrice *f* actress
actualités *f pl* news
addition *f* check, bill
adjectif *m* adjective
admirateur *m* admirer
admiratrice *f* admirer
adorer to love, adore
s'adresser (à) to address oneself
    (to), go (to); to apply
aérogramme *m* air letter
aéroport *m* airport
affreux (f affreuse) horrible, awful
âge *m* age; **quel âge avez-vous?**
    how old are you?
agence *f* agency; **agence de voyages**
    travel agency; **agence immobilière**
    rental agency, real estate agency
agenda *m* engagement book

agent *m* agent; policeman; **agent de
    police** policeman; **agent de
    voyage** travel agent
agréable pleasant
aider to help
aigu sharp; **accent aigu** acute
    accent
aimable kind; likeable
aimer to like; to love; **aimer mieux**
    to prefer; **où aimeriez-vous aller?**
    where would you like to go?
air *m* air; look, appearance; **avoir
    l'air de** to seem (to; to be); **avoir
    l'air inquiet** to look worried; **être
    en plein air** to be out in the fresh
    air; **mal** *m* **de l'air** airsickness
ajouter to add
Allemagne *f* Germany
aller to go; to be (*of health*); to fit; to
    suit; **s'en aller** to go way; **aller à
    la pêche** to go fishing; **aller
    chercher** to go get; to pick up;
    billet (*m*) **aller retour** round-trip
    ticket; **comment allez-vous?** how
    are you? **comment vas-tu?** how
    are you? **lui va très bien** suits
    him/her very well
allumette *f* match
alors therefore, then
alouette *f* lark

ami *m* (*f* **amie**) friend
amicalement cordially
amitié *f* friendship; **amitiés**
    sincerely, cordially (*complimentary
    close to a letter*)
amour *m* love
amusant amusing, funny
s'amuser to have a good time
an *m* year
anesthésie *f* anesthetic
ange *m* angel
animal *m* (*pl.* **animaux**) animal
année *f* year; **dans quelques années**
    in a few years, a few years from
    now
anniversaire (de naissance) *m*
    birthday; **anniversaire de mariage**
    wedding anniversary; **bon
    anniversaire** happy birthday
anonyme anonymous
antiquités *f pl* antiques; **magasin
    d'antiquités** antique store
août *m* August
apercevoir to see, to catch sight of
apéritif *m* before-dinner drink;
    cocktail
appareil *m* receiver; **qui est à
    l'appareil?** who's speaking?
appareil photo *m* camera
appartement *m* apartment

403

appel *m* call; **appel interurbain** long-distance call
appeler to call; **s'appeler** to be named; to be called
applaudir to applaud
apporter to bring
apprendre to learn
appris (*pp of* **apprendre**)
appuyer to press
après after
après-midi *m or f* afternoon
arbre *m* tree
argent *m* money; silver, **argent de poche** pocket money
argenterie *f* silverware
arpent *m* acres
arrêt *m* stop; **arrêt d'autobus** bus stop
s'arrêter to stop
arrivée *f* arrival
arriver to arrive; to happen
artichaut *m* artichoke
article *m* article; **article partitif** partitive article
ascenseur *m* elevator
Asie *f* Asia
asperge *f* asparagus; **des asperges** asparagus (*stalks and tips used as food*)
aspirateur *m* vacuum cleaner
aspirine *f* aspirin
s'asseoir to sit down
assez enough; somewhat, rather, fairly, sufficient(ly)
assis seated, sitting
assister(à) to attend
assurance *f* insurance
astigmate astigmatic
astronaute *m* astronaut
attendre to wait (for)
attente *f* wait; **salle** (*f*) **d'attente** waiting room
attention be careful, pay attention, watch out
atterrir to land
au (*prep* + *def art*) at the, to the, on the
aujourd'hui today
aussi also, too; **aussi . . . que** as . . . as
autant (de) as many, as much
auteur *m* author
auto *f* automobile, car; **faire un tour en auto** to go for a drive
autobus *m* bus, city bus
automne *m* autumn, fall; **en automne** in the fall
autoportrait *m* self-portrait, self-description; **faites votre**

autoportrait give your self-description
autorisé approved
autoroute *f* superhighway
autre another, other; **l'autre** the other (one); **quelque chose d'autre** something else; **qui d'autre?** who else?; **quoi d'autre?** what else?
autrefois formerly; of old
aux (*prep* + *pl def art*) at the, to the
avance *f* advance; **avoir de l'avance** to be early (*train, bus, plane*)
avancer to be fast; to put ahead; **ma montre avance** my watch is fast
avant (*adv, prep*) before; **avant de** before; **avant que** before
avant-hier day before yesterday
avare miserly
avec with
Avignon city in southern France
avion *m* airplane; **en avion** by plane; **par avion** airmail
avis *m* opinion; notice; notification; **changer d'avis** to change one's mind
avoir to have; **avoir besoin de** to need; **avoir bonne mine** to look healthy; **avoir chaud** to feel hot; **avoir de l'avance** to be early (*train, bus, plane*); **avoir du mal(à)** to have difficulty; **avoir du retard** to be late (*train, bus, plane*); **avoir envie de** to want (to; some of); **avoir faim** to be hungry; **avoir froid** to feel cold; **avoir l'air** to seem; **avoir lieu** to take place, to be held; **avoir mal (à)** to hurt, to have an ache; **avoir mal au cœur** to be sick to the stomach, feel nauseated; **avoir mal aux dents** to have a toothache; **avoir peur** to be afraid; **avoir soif** to be thirsty; **t'auras (tu auras)** you will have

bagages *m pl* baggage, luggage
baignade *f* bathing, swimming; **baignade interdite** no swimming
se baigner to bathe
bain *m* bath; **maillot** (*m*) **de bain** bathing suit; **salle** (*f*) **de bains** bathroom
baiser *m* kiss
baisser to lower, to put down
balcon *m* balcony
banlieue *f* suburbs
banque *f* bank

bas (*f* **basse**) low; **en bas** downstairs
bataillon *m* battalion
bateau *m* boat; **bateau à voiles** sailboat; **faire du bateau** to go boating
bâtiment *m* building
bâton *m* stick
battre to beat; **battre le briquet** to get the fire going
beau (*f* **belle**) beautiful, handsome; **faire beau** to be nice weather; **il fait beau** it is nice weather
beaucoup (de) much, a lot, a great deal, many
beauté *f* beauty; **produits** (*m pl*) **de beauté** cosmetics; **salon** (*m*) **de beauté** beauty parlor
bec *m* beak, bill
besoin *m* need; **avoir besoin de** to need
bête stupid
beurre *m* butter; **beurre de cacahuètes** peanut butter
bibliothèque *f* library
bicyclette *f* bicycle; **faire de la bicyclette** to go bicycle riding
bien well, fine; really (*intensifier*); **bien cuit** well done (*meat*)
bien que although
bientôt soon; **à bientôt** see you soon; **à bientôt de vos bonnes nouvelles** looking forward to hearing from you soon
bière *f* beer
bifteck *m* steak
billet *m* ticket; bill; **billet aller retour** round-trip ticket; **billet de seconde** second-class ticket
bis again; repeat
bise *f* kiss (*slang*); **grosses bises** hugs and kisses (*complimentary close to a letter*)
blanc (*f* **blanche**) white
blanchisserie *f* laundry
bleu blue
blond blonde
boire to drink
bois *m* wood; woods
boisson *m* drink, beverage
boîte *f* box; **boîte aux lettres** mailbox; **boîte de nuit** night club; **boîte à gants** glove compartment; **boîte à pilules** pill box
bon (*f* **bonne**) good; **bon marché** inexpensive
bonbon *m* (piece of) candy
bonjour hello

bord *m* edge; **au bord de la mer** at the sea shore, to the ocean, by the sea

botte *f* boot

bouche mouth

boucle *f* buckle; **boucle d'oreille** earring

boule *f* ball

bout *m* end

bouteille *f* bottle

bouton *m* button

bras *m* arm

bref (*f* **brève**) short, brief

briller to shine

briquet *m* lighter; **battre le briquet** to get the fire going

brosse *f* brush; **brosse à dents** toothbrush

brosser to brush

bronzer to tan; **se faire bronzer au soleil** to get a suntan

bruit *m* noise; **à grand bruit** noisily

brun brown, brunette

bruyant noisy

bureau *m* office; **bureau de location** ticket office, **bureau des objets trouvés** lost and found; **bureau de poste** post office

ça that

cabine *f* booth; **cabine téléphonique** phone booth

cacahuète *f* peanut

cadeau *m* gift, present

café *m* coffee

caisse *f* cash register

caissier *m* teller

caissière *f* teller

camarade *m f* comrade; **camarade de chambre** roommate

caméra *f* (movie, television) camera

campagne *f* country; **à la campagne** in the country

cantine *f* cafeteria, restaurant

car for, because

carnet *m* book of tickets (*subway, bus*)

carotte *f* carrot

carré square

carte *f* card; menu; map, **carte de crédit** credit card; **carte postale** postcard; **jouer aux cartes** to play cards; **carte de vœux** greeting card

cas *m* case; **cas d'urgence** emergency; **selon le cas** accordingly

case *f* square, pigeonhole, post office box

casse-croûte *m* snack

casser to break

cathédrale *f* cathedral

causer to chat

caviar *m* caviar

ce (*adj, pron*) this, that, it; **ce que** (*rel pron*) what, that which; **ce qui** (*rel pron*) what, that which; **ce sont** these are; **qui est-ce?** who is it?

ceinture *f* belt; **ceinture de sécurité** seat belt

cela that

célèbre famous

célibataire single, unmarried

cendrier *m* ashtray

cent hundred

ces these

cesser to stop

cet this, that

cette this, that

chacun *m* (*f* **chacune**) each (one)

chaîne *f* channel (*television*)

chaise *f* chair; **chaise longue** deck chair

chambre *f* bed(room); **chambre à coucher** bedroom; **femme de chambre** chambermaid

champ *m* field; **aux champs** to the fields

champignon *m* mushroom

championnat *m* championship

chandail *m* sweater

chandelle *f* candle

changer to change; to cash; to alter, modify, make a change

chanter to sing

chanteur *m* (*f* **chanteuse**) singer

chapeau *m* hat

chaque each, every

charmant charming

chasse *f* hunting; hunting season

chasseur *m* bellboy

chat *m* cat

châtain chestnut (*color*)

château *m* castle, chateau, mansion

chaud hot; **avoir chaud** to feel hot; **faire chaud** to be warm (hot) weather

chauffeur *m* driver

chaumière *f* thatched cottage

chaussette *f* sock

chaussure *f* shoe; **magasin** (*m*) **de chaussures** shoe store

chauve bald

chemin *m* track, path, way

chemise *f* shirt

chèque *m* check; **chèque de voyage** *m* travelers check; **toucher un chèque** to cash a check

cher (*f* **chère**) expensive, dear; **coûter cher** to be expensive

chercher to look for, seek; **aller chercher** to go get, pick up

cheval *m* horse; **faire du cheval** to go horseback riding

chevalier *m* knight, cavalier

cheveux *m pl* hair; **avoir les cheveux bruns** to have brown hair; **se faire couper les cheveux** to have one's hair cut

cheville *f* ankle

chez at, to, in the home of; at, to, in the office of; at the place of; **chez le coiffeur** at, to the hairdresser's; **chez lui** to his home; at his place; **chez les Smith** at, to the Smith's; **chez vous** (at) your house

chien *m* dog

chiffonné wrinkled, crumpled, rumpled

chiffre *m* figure, number

chimie *f* chemistry

chinois Chinese

chirurgien *m* surgeon

chocolat *m* chocolate; hot chocolate

choisir to choose, to select

chômage *m* unemployment; **en chômage** unemployed

chose *f* thing

chou *m* cabbage

ci-dessus above

cigare *m* cigar

cigarette *f* cigarette

cinéma *m* movies

cinq five

cinquante fifty

cintre *m* hanger

circonflexe circumflex

circulation *f* traffic

cirque *m* circus

citoyen *m* citizen

clair (*adj*) clear; light (*in color*); *n, m* light, brightness; **clair de lune** moonlight

classe *f* class; **classe de français** French class

classique classical

clé *f* key

climatisé air-conditioned

climatiseur *m* air conditioner

code *m* code; **code de la route** traffic regulations; **code postale** zip code

cœur *m* heart; **avoir le cœur gai** to be light-hearted, happy; **avoir mal**

au cœur to be sick to the stomach
coffre *m* trunk (*of car*)
se coiffer to do one's (own) hair
coiffeur *m* barber, hairdresser
coiffure *f* hairdo, hairstyle
Colas nickname for Nicolas
colis *m* parcel
collègue *m, f* colleague
combien(de) how much, how many; **combien de temps?** how long? **depuis combien de temps?** for how long? **de combien** by how much?
commander to order
comme like, as; **comme dîner** for dinner; **comme déjeuner** for lunch; **comme petit déjeuner** for breakfast
commencer(à) to begin
comment how; **comment allez-vous?** how are you? **comment ça va?** how are things?; **comment est la plage?** describe the beach; **comment est le professeur?** describe the professor; **comment est la salle de séjour?** describe the living room; **comment trouvez-vous ce bateau?** what do you think of this boat? **comment vous appelez-vous?** what is your name?
commissariat *m* **de police** police station (*urban*)
communication *f* connection
commutateur *m* switch
compagnie *f* company
compagnon *m* or *f* comrade, partner
comparaison *f* comparison
complet (*f* **complète**) full; complete
compléter to complete
compliqué complicated
composer to dial (*phone*)
comprendre to understand
compris (*pp* of **comprendre**)
compte *m* reckoning; account; **se rendre compte** to realize
compter to intend, to count (on)
comptoir *m* counter
à condition que on (the) condition that
conditionnel *m* conditional
conducteur *m* conductor, driver
conduire to drive; **permis** (*m*) **de conduire** driver's license
conduit (*pp* of **conduire**)
conduite *f* driving
confortable comfortable
congélateur *m* freezer

conjugaison *f* conjugation; **conjugaison des verbes** verb conjugations
connaissance *f* acquaintance; **faire la connaissance (de)** to meet, to make the acquaintance (of)
connaître to know
conseil *m* advice
conseiller to advise
consigne *f* checkroom, baggage room
constamment constantly
consulter to consult, look at
conte *m* tale, story
content happy
continuer to continue
contraire *m* opposite
contravention *f* traffic ticket; **avoir une contravention** to get a traffic ticket; **dresser une contravention** to write out a ticket
contre against
convenable suitable, proper, appropriate
convenir to be suitable
corps *m* body
correspondance *f* connection, change, transfer
correspondant corresponding; (*m*) caller (*telephone*)
correspondre to correspond
côté *m* side; **à côté de** next to; **de quel côté** on which side; **du côté** on the side
cou *m* neck
couchage *m* bedding; **sac de couchage** sleeping bag
se coucher to go to bed
couchette *f* berth
coude *m* elbow
couleur *f* color
coup *m* blow, knock; **coup de téléphone** phone call; **tout d'un coup** all of a sudden; **coup de pied** kick
coupe *f* cup competition
couper to cut; **couper le gazon** to cut the grass, mow the lawn; **se faire couper les cheveux** to have one's hair cut; **on nous a coupés** we've been cut off
cour *f* courtyard, square
courageux (*f* **courageuse**) courageous
courir to run
courrier *m* mail; **faire suivre le courrier** to have the mail forwarded

cours *m* course; **au cours de la semaine** during the week; **suivre un cours** to take a course
court short
cousin *m* cousin
coûter to cost; **coûter cher** to be expensive; **coûter moins cher** to be less expensive
couverture *f* cover, blanket, bedspread
crêpe *f* thin pancake
crevé flat
crier to cry out, to shout
croire to believe
croiser to cross
croisière *f* cruise; **faire une croisière** to take a cruise
cuisine *f* kitchen; cooking; cuisine; **faire la cuisine** to cook
cuisiner to cook
cuisinière *f* stove, range; **cuisinière électrique** electric stove

dame *f* lady, woman; **jouer aux dames** to play checkers
dangereux (*f* **dangereuse**) dangerous
dans in; within
danser to dance
davantage more
de of, about, from; any
déblayer to clear, to clear away
début *m* beginning; **au début** at the beginning
déchiré torn
décidé determined
décider to decide
déclarer to declare (*customs*)
décolorer to bleach; to fade; **se faire décolorer les cheveux** to have one's hair dyed
découvert (*pp* of **découvrir**)
décrire to describe
décrocher to pick up the receiver
défendre to forbid
défense *f* defense; **défense d'entrer** keep out; **défense de fumer** no smoking; **défense de stationner** no parking
degré *m* degree
dehors outside
déjà already
déjeuner *m* lunch; **petit déjeuner** breakfast; **comme déjeuner** for lunch; **comme petit déjeuner** for breakfast; **déjeuner** to have lunch
délicieux (*f* **délicieuse**) delicious
délivrance *f* delivery
demain tomorrow

demande *f* request
demander to ask
démarrer to start
dent *f* tooth; **avoir mal aux dents**
to have a toothache
dentifrice *m* toothpaste
départ *m* departure; **heures de
départ** departure times
dépasser to exceed
se dépêcher to hurry
dépenser to spend (*money*)
dépensier (*f* **dépensière**) spendthrift
déprimé depressed
depuis for, since; **depuis quand?**
since when? for how long?
dernier (*f* **dernière**) last; **la dernière**
the last (one)
des of the, from the; some
descendre to go down, descend; to
get off; to bring down; to take
down; **descendre à l'hôtel** to go
to a hotel, to stay at a hotel
descendu (*pp* of **descendre**)
se déshabiller to get undressed
désirer to want, to desire; **vous
désirez?** may I help you?
désobéir to disobey
désolé sorry
dessert *m* dessert
dessin *m* drawing, sketch; **dessin
animé** animated cartoon
dessus above
destinataire *m, f* addressee
détester to hate
dette *f* debt
deux two; **tous deux** both (of us,
of you, of them)
deuxième second
devant ahead; in front (of)
deviner to guess
devoir to owe, to have to; **devoirs**
m pl homework, assignments
Dieu *m* God
différemment differently
difficile difficult
digestif *m* after-dinner drink
dilemme *m* dilemma
dimanche *m* Sunday
din (*bell sound*)
dîner *m* dinner; **dîner** to dine, to
have dinner; **comme dîner** for
dinner
dire to say, tell; **sans rien dire**
without saying anything; **vouloir
dire** to mean
disque *m* record
se disputer to quarrel
distribuer to deliver
dit (*pp* of **dire**)
divorcer to get a divorce

dix ten
dommage *m* loss, hurt; **c'est
dommage** it's too bad, it's a pity
don (*bell sound*)
donc therefore, then; thus; now
donner to give; **donner sur** to
look out onto
dormir to sleep
dos *m* back
douanier *m* customs agent
doublé dubbed
doubler to pass
douche *f* shower
se doucher to shower
douleur *f* pain
doute *f* doubt; **sans doute**
undoubtedly
douter to doubt
doux (*f* **douce**) sweet, kind, gentle;
soft
drap *m* sheet
drapeau flag
dresser to write up, to draw up;
dresser une contravention to
write up a ticket
droit straight; right; **à droite** to or
on the right, to your right; **tout
droit** straight ahead
drôle funny
du of the, from the; some
dû (*pp* of **devoir**, *f* **due**)
dur hard

eau *f* water; **eau minérale** mineral
water
échanger to exchange
échecs *m pl* chess; **jouer aux échecs**
to play chess
éclair *m* flash of lightning; **éclairs**
lightning
école *f* school
économe economical
économique economical
écouter to listen (to)
écrire to write
écrit (*pp* of **écrire**)
écrivain *m* writer
église *f* church
égorger to cut the throat of
électrique electric
élément *m* element
éléphant *m* elephant
élève *m, f* student
élevé high
elle she, her; **c'est à elle** it's hers
elles they
emballer to wrap
embrasser to embrace; to kiss
émission *f* show (*television*)

empêcher to prevent
emploi *m* job
employé *m* employee; clerk
employer to use, employ
emporter to bring
emprunter(à) to borrow (from)
en (*prep*) in, to, by; upon, while,
when; dressed in, wearing; (*pron*)
some, any (some) of it, (some) of
them; from there; **en ce moment**
now, at this time
enceinte pregnant
encore again; still, yet
énergique energetic
s'énerver to get nervous; to be
exasperated
enfant *m* child; **être bon enfant** to
be good-natured
enfin at last, finally
ennemi *m* enemy
ennuyer to bore; **s'ennuyer** to get
bored
énorme enormous
enregistrer to check in; **faire
enregistrer mes bagages** to have
my luggage checked in
enseigner to teach
ensemble together
ensoleillé sunny
ensuite then, next; afterwards
entamer to begin; to engage in, to
start (*a conversation*)
entendre to hear; **s'entendre avec**
to get along with
entier (*f* **entière**) entire, whole
entre between, among
entrée *f* entrance
entreprendre to undertake
entrer (dans) to enter; **défense
d'entrer** keep out
envie *f* envy; desire; **avoir envie
(de)** to want (to; some of), to feel
like
envoyer to send
épais (*f* **épaisse**) thick
épeler to spell
éperdument madly, wildly
épinard *m* spinach; **des épinards**
spinach (*leaves used as food*)
épouvante *f* fright; **film
d'épouvante** horror film
équipe *f* team
erreur *f* error
escalier *m* stairs, stairway
escargot *m* snail
espagnol Spanish; *m* Spanish
language
espérer to hope
essayer to try; to try on
essence *f* gasoline

essuie-glace *m* windshield wiper
et and
établir to establish, to set up
établissement *m* establishment, place
étage *m* floor, level; **à quel étage?** on what floor?
États-Unis *m pl.* United States
été *m* summer; **en été** in summer
été (*pp* of **être**)
étendard *m* flag, banner
étendu stretched out
éternuer to sneeze
étiquette *f* label
étonné suprised
s'étonner to be surprised
étrange strange
étranger foreign; **à l'étranger** abroad
être to be; **être de retour** to be back; **être en panne** to have a breakdown; **être en plein air** to be out in the fresh air; **être en retard** to be late; **être en train de** to be in the process of; **être en vacances** to be on vacation; **être enrhumé** to have a cold; **il était** there was
étroit narrow, tight
étude *f* study; **faire ses études secondaires** to go to high school
étudiant *m* student
étudier to study
eu (*pp* of **avoir**)
événement *m* event
éventuellement eventually
exactement exactly
examen *m* examination; **examen écrit** written exam
s'excuser to excuse, to be sorry
exemple *m* example
expéditeur *m* sender
expliquer to explain

se fâcher to get angry
facile easy
facilement easily
facteur *m* mailman
facture *f* bill
faim *f* hunger; **avoir faim** to be hungry
faire to do; to make; **faire beau** to be nice weather; **se faire bronzer au soleil** to get a suntan; **faire chaud** to be warm (hot) weather; **se faire couper les cheveux** to have one's hair cut; **se faire décolorer les cheveux** to have one's hair dyed; **faire de la**

bicyclette to go bicycle riding; **faire de longues promenades à pied** to go for long walks, to hike; **faire de l'auto-stop** to hitchhike; **faire des progrès** to make progress, to progress; **faire dodo** (*slang*) to go to sleep; **faire du bateau** to go boating; **faire du camping** to go camping; **faire du cheval** to go horseback riding; **faire du gâteau** to bake a cake; **faire du lèche-vitrines** to windowshop; **faire du ski** to ski, go skiing; **faire du sport** to play sports; **faire le plein** to fill 'er up; **faire une croisière** to take a cruise; **faire la vaisselle** to wash the dishes; **faire enregistrer mes bagages** to have my luggage checked in; **faire la connaissance (de)** to meet, to make the acquaintance (of); **faire la cuisine** to cook; **faire le ménage** to do housework; **faire le tour du monde** to go around the world; **se faire mal** to hurt oneself; **faire partie de** to belong to; **se faire payer** to cash; **faire peur (à)** to frighten; **faire plaisir (à)** to please; **les faire réparer** to have them repaired; **faire ses études secondaires** to go to high school; **faire suivre le courrier** to have the mail forwarded; **faire un pique-nique** to picnic; **faire un tour en auto** to go for a drive; **faire un voyage** to take a trip, to travel; **faire une piqûre** to give an injection; **faire une promenade** to take a walk; **il fait beau** it is nice weather; **que feriez-vous si...?** what would you do if . . .?; **quelle température fait-il?** what's the temperature?
faire-part *m* announcement
fait (*pp* of **faire**)
falloir to be necessary; to need; **il faut** it is necessary; it takes (*of time*); **il me faut** I need; **il lui faut** he needs/she needs; **il nous faut** we need; **il leur faut** they need
famille *f* family; **en famille** with one's family, with your family
faner to wilt
fatigant tiring
fatigué tired
faute *f* fault; **à qui la faute?** whose fault is (was) it?
fauteuil *m* chair; armchair

faux (*f* **fausse**) false, wrong
favori (*f* **favorite**) favorite
féliciter to congratulate
femme *f* woman; wife; **femme de chambre** chambermaid
fenêtre *f* window
ferme *f* farm
fermer to close
féroce ferocious
feu *m* fire
fiancé engaged
se fiancer to get engaged
ficelle *f* string
fiche *f* form
fièvre *f* fever
fille *f* girl; daughter; **fille unique** (an) only daughter; **jeune fille** girl; **nom de jeune fille** maiden name
film *m* movie
fils *m* son; **fils unique** (an) only son
fin *adj.* fine, thin; finely (ground)
fin *f* end
finir (par) to end up (by), finish
flacon *m* flask, small bottle
fleur *f* flower
foin *m* hay; **rhume des foins** hay fever
fois *f* time; **la première fois** the first time
foncé dark
fonctionner to work, function
fontaine *f* fountain
forêt *f* forest
forme *f* form
formule *f* form; **formule de télégramme** telegram form
fort strong; **je t'embrasse fort** I send you a big hug (*complimentary close to a letter*); **parler fort** to speak loudly
foulard *m* scarf
fouler to sprain
fourrure *f* fur (coat)
français French; *m* French language
fraise *f* strawberry
franc (*f* **franche**) frank
frapper to knock; **frapper à la porte** to knock on the door
frein *m* brake
fréquemment frequently
frère *m* brother
frire to fry
froid cold; **avoir froid** to feel cold
fromage *m* cheese
fumer to smoke; **défense de fumer** no smoking
futur *m* future; **au futur** in(to) the future

gagner to earn
gai happy; **avoir le cœur gai** to be happy
galerie (f) **d'art** art gallery
gant m glove
garage m garage
garagiste m garage mechanic
garçon m boy; waiter
garder to watch over, tend; to keep
gare f train station
gâteau m cake
gauche left; **à gauche** to/on the left, to your left
gazon m lawn; **couper le gazon** to cut the grass, mow the lawn
généreux (f **généreuse**) generous
genre m type, kind
gens m pl people (in general, an undetermined number)
gentil (f **gentille**) nice; kind; agreeable
gérant (f **gérante**) hotel manager
geste m gesture
glace f ice; ice cream
gloire f glory
gonfler to inflate
gorge f throat
goûter to taste
grand big, large, tall; **à grand bruit** noisily; **de grands yeux** large eyes
grand-père m grandfather
grave serious, grave
grêler to hail (weather)
grésiller to sleet
grippe f influenza
gris grey
gros (f **grosse**) big; fat; **gros mots** curse(s)
groupe m group; **en groupe** with a group of people
guichet m window (in post office, bank, box office); counter (in bank)
guitare f guitar

habillé (de) dressed (in)
s'habiller to get dressed
habiter to live
d'habitude usually
s'habituer à to get used to
haricot m bean; **haricot vert** m string bean, green bean
haut high; **en haut** upstairs
herbe f grass
hésiter to hesitate
heure f hour; time (of day), o'clock; **heures de départ** departure times; **six heures du soir** six o'clock in the evening; **à quelle**

heure? when?, at what time?; **de bonne heure** early; **quelle heure est-il?** what time is it?; **vers huit heures** around eight o'clock; **à l'heure** on time
heureux (f **heureuse**) happy
heureusement fortunately
hier yesterday; **hier soir** last night, yesterday evening
hirondelle f swallow
histoire f story
hiver m winter; **en hiver** in winter; **sports d'hiver** winter sports
homme m man
hôpital m hospital
hors de off, outside of
hôte m host
hôtesse de l'air stewardess, flight attendant
hôtel m hotel
huile f oil
huit eight
huitième eighth

ici here; **près d'ici** near here, nearby
idée f idea
idiot idiotic
il he
ils they
il y a there is, there are; ago; **il y a deux jours** two days ago; **il y en a plusieurs** there are several of them; **y a-t-il** is there, are there
imaginer to imagine
immeuble m building
immobilier (f **immobilière**) real estate, property **agence** (f) **immobilière** rental agency, real estate agency
s'impatienter to get impatient
impensable unthinkable
imperméable m raincoat
index m index finger
indicatif m indicative; **indicatif de zone** area code
indiquer to indicate
infinitif m infinitive
infirmière f nurse
s'informer to get information
inquiet (f **inquiète**) worried; **avoir l'air inquiet** to look worried
inscrire to record; to register; to write
s'installer to move in
instant m moment, instant
interdit forbidden; **baignade interdite** no swimming

intéressant interesting
s'intéresser à to be interested in
intérêt m interest
intérieur m interior
interurbain interurban, long-distance
inutile useless
invité m guest
inviter to invite
italien (f **italienne**) Italian; m Italian language
itinéraire m itinerary

jacquet m backgammon
jambe f leg
jambon m ham
jamais never; ever
jardin m garden
jardinage m gardening
jaune yellow
je I
jeton m token
jeune young; **jeune fille** girl
joli pretty
jouer to play; **jouer aux cartes** to play cards, **jouer aux échecs** to play chess; **jouer de la guitare** to play guitar
jouir de to enjoy
jour m day; **tous les jours** every day, daily
journal m newspaper; journal, diary
journée f day; **toute la journée** all day (long)
joyeux (f. **joyeuse**) joyous; **Joyeux Noël** Merry Christmas
jupe f skirt
jus m juice; **jus d'orange** orange juice; **jus de pomme** apple juice
jusqu'à as far as, down to, up to; until
jusque even
juste exactly; sharp (time); **il est deux heures justes** it is exactly two o'clock

kilométrage m milage

la f (def art) the; (pron) her, it
là there
lac m lake
laid ugly
laine f wool
laisser to let; to leave
lait m milk
lampe f lamp

lapin *m* rabbit
laquelle which (one)
large wide; loose
latin *m* Latin
lavabo *m* sink
laver to wash; **se laver la tête** to wash one's hair
laverie automatique *f* laundromat
lave-vaisselle *m* dishwasher
le *m* (*def art*) the; (*pron*) him, it
leçon *f* lesson
léger (*f* **légère**) light (*in weight*)
légume *m* vegetable
lent slow
lentement slowly
lequel which (one)
les *pl* (*def art*) the; (*pron*) them
lessive *f* washing (*of clothes*); wash
lettre *f* letter; **boîte aux lettres** mailbox
leur (*adj*) their; (*pron*) to them
se lever to get up
librairie *f* bookstore
libre not occupied, free, unoccupied
lieu *m* place; **au lieu de** instead of; **avoir lieu** to take place, to be held; **lieu de travail** place of work
ligne *f* line; **ligne aérienne** airline
limité limited
linge *m* laundry
lire to read
lisible legible
lisiblement legibly
lit *m* bed; **lit pliant** folding bed
livre *m* book
loger to lodge
loin far
lolo (*slang*) milk
long (*f* **longue**) long
longtemps a long time; for a long time
longuement at length
lorsque when
louer to rent; to reserve
lourd heavy (*in weight*)
loyer *m* rent
lu (*pp* of **lire**)
lui he, him, to her, to him, for her, for him; **lui-même** himself; **c'est à lui** it's his
luire to glow, to shine
lumière *f* light
lundi Monday
lune *f* moon
lunettes *f pl* eyeglasses; **lunettes de soleil** sunglasses
luxueux (*f* **luxueuse**) luxurious

ma my
madame *f* Mrs., Madam
mademoiselle *f* Miss
magasin *m* store; **grand magasin** department store; **magasin d'antiquités** antique store; **magasin de chaussures** shoe store
maigrir to get thin
maillot *m* bathing suit; jersey; **maillot de bain** bathing suit
main *f* hand
maintenant now
maire *m* mayor
mais but
maison *f* house; **maison de campagne** country house; **à la maison** at home
maître *m* master; **maître nageur** lifeguard
majuscule capital
mal bad; poorly
mal *m* pain; harm; trouble; *adv* badly; **avoir du mal (à)** to have difficulty (in); **avoir mal (à)** to hurt, to have an ache; **avoir mal au cœur** to feel sick to the stomach; **avoir mal aux dents** to have a toothache; **avoir mal à la tête** to have a headache; **se faire mal** to hurt oneself; **mal de l'air** airsickness; **mal de mer** seasickness
malade sick
maladie *f* disease
maladroit clumsy
malheureux (*f.* **malheureuse**) unhappy
malheureusement unfortunately
malle *f* trunk
maman *f* mommy, mama
manche *f* sleeve
mandat *m* money order
manger to eat; **salle** (*f.*) **à manger** dining room
manquer to be missing, to be lacking; **il vous manque** you are missing; **tu me manques** I miss you; **vous me manquez** I miss you
manteau *m* coat
marché *m* market; **bon marché** inexpensive; **meilleur marché** cheaper, less expensive
marcher to walk; to march; to work (*inanimate objects*)
mardi Tuesday
mari *m* husband
marié married
se marier to get married

marque *f* make, brand
marron chestnut (*color*)
Marseille seaport city on Mediterranean coast
masculin masculine
matelas *m* mattress; **matelas pneumatique** air mattress
matière *f* material; school subject; **en quelle matière vous spécialisez-vous?** what's your major?
matin *m* morning
matines *f pl* morning bells, matins
mauvais bad
me me, to me, for me
mécanicien *m* mechanic
méconnu underestimated, misunderstood
médecin *m* doctor
médicament *m* medicine
se méfier to distrust
meilleur better; best
même very; same; **quand même** just the same; though
ménage *m* household; family; **faire le ménage** to do the housework
menton *m* chin
menu *m* menu
mer *f* sea; **mal** (*m.*) **de mer** sea-sickness
mercredi Wednesday
mère *f* mother
merveilleux (*f* **merveilleuse**) marvelous, wonderful
mes my
métier *m* occupation
métro *m* subway
mettre to put; to display; to take (*time*); to put on (*clothes*), to wear; **mettre à** to put in; **se mettre à** to begin to; **se mettre à table** to sit down at the table
meuble *m* (piece of) furniture
meublé furnished
meurtre *m* murder, manslaughter
mieux better; best; **valoir mieux** to be better
militaire military
millier *m* thousand; **par milliers** by the thousands
mince thin, slim
minéral mineral; **eau** (*f*) **minérale** mineral water
mis (*pp* of **mettre**)
mode *f* fashion, way, manner; **à la mode de chez nous** in the way we do it
modèle *m* model
moderne modern
moi me, I; **c'est à moi** it's mine
moine *m* monk

moins less; **moins de** less than; **à moins que (ne)** unless; **moins . . . que** less . . .than

mois *m* month; **par mois** per month

moment *m* moment; **en ce moment** now, at this moment

mon my

monde *m* world; people; **faire le tour du monde** to go around the world; **tout le monde** everyone

monnaie *f* change **pièce de monnaie** coin

monsieur *m (pl.* **messieurs)** Mr., sir; gentleman

montagne *f* mountain(s)

monter to go up, climb; to take up, bring up; **monter dans** to climb in, get in

montre *f* watch

montrer to show

se moquer de to make fun of

morceau *m* piece; **morceau de craie** piece of chalk

mort dead

mot *m* word; **gros mots** curse words; **petit mot** short note

moteur *m* motor

moto *f* motorcycle

mou *(f* **molle)** soft

se moucher to wipe one's nose

mouchoir *m* handkerchief

moutarde *f* mustard

mouton *m* sheep

mugir to bellow

mur *m* wall

musée *m* museum

musique *f* music

myope nearsighted

nager to swim

nageur *m* swimmer; **maître nageur** lifeguard

naissance *f* birth

naître to be born

nautique nautical; **faire du ski nautique** to go water skiing

naviguer to navigate, sail

navire *m* ship

né *(pp* of **naître)**

négatif *(f* **négative)** negative; **au négatif** in the negative

neige *f* snow

neiger to snow

n'est-ce pas doesn't he?, don't you?, isn't it?, *etc.*

nettoyer to clean; **nettoyer à sec** to dryclean

neuf *(f* **neuve)** new

nez *m* nose

ni *(conj)* **ne... ni... ni...** neither . . . nor; **ni... ni...** neither . . . nor

Noël Christmas

noir black; *m* dark

nom *m* name; noun; **nom de famille** surname; **nom de jeune fille** maiden name

nommer to name

non no

nos our

note *f* bill; grade

notre our

nous we, us

nouveau *(f* **nouvelle)** new

nouvelles *f pl* news; **à bientôt de vos bonnes nouvelles** looking forward to hearing from you soon

nuit *f* night; **par nuit** per night

numéro *m* number; **faux numéro** wrong number; **numéro de téléphone** telephone number

numérotation *f* numbering

obéir to obey

objet *m* object; **bureau** *(m)* **des objets trouvés** lost and found

obligé obliged; **être obligé** to have to

obtenir to obtain, to get

occupé busy, occupied

œuf *m* egg

offert *(pp* of **offrir)**

officier *m* (military) officer

offrir to offer, to give

oiseau *m* bird

on one, someone, people, they, we, you

oncle *m* uncle

optimiste optimistic

or *m* gold

orage *m* storm

orange *f* orange; **jus** *(m)* **d'orange** orange juice

ordinaire ordinary, regular

ordonnance *f* prescription

oreille *f* ear; **boucle** *(f)* **d'oreilles** earring

oreiller *m* pillow

oreillons *m pl* mumps

origine *f* origin; **de quelle origine êtes-vous?** what's your national origin?; **je suis d'origine...** my national origin is . . .

orthographe *f* spelling

oser to dare

ou or; **ou... ou...** either . . . or . . .

où where

oublier to forget

oui yes

ouvert open (*pp* of **ouvrir**)

ouvrir to open

paille *f* straw

pain *m* bread

paire *f* pair; **en louer une paire** to rent a pair of them

pâlir to grow pale

pamplemousse *m* grapefruit

panne *f* breakdown; **être en panne** to have a breakdown; **être en panne sèche** to run out of gas

pantalon *m* pants

pantoufle *f* slipper

papeterie *f* stationery store

papetière *f* one who sells stationery

papier *m* paper; **papier d'emballage** wrapping paper

paquet *m* package, pack

par per; by; with

parapluie *m* umbrella

parasol *m* beach umbrella, sunshade

parc *m* park

parce que because

pardon excuse me

pare-brise *m* windshield

parent *m* parent; relative

parenthèse *f* parenthesis; **entre parenthèses** in parentheses

parfait perfect

parfois sometimes

parfum *m* perfume

parking *m* parking lot

parler to speak, talk

participe *m* participle; **participe présent** present participle; **participe passé** past participle

partie *f* party; part; **faire partie de** to belong to

partir to leave; **partir en vacances** to go on vacation

partout everywhere

pas: ne... pas not; **pas du tout** not at all

passager *m (f* **passagère)** passenger

passé last; past; **l'année passée** last year; **la semaine passée** last week

passeport *m* passport

passer to pass (by, on, through); to go by; **se passer** to go by; **passer son temps à** to spend one's time; **passer une visite médicale** to have a physical examination; **passer les vacances** to spend one's vacation; **passer l'aspirateur**

to run the vacuum cleaner; **passer la tondeuse** to mow the lawn

passivement passively

pâté m pâté *(minced liver)*

patinage m skating; **patinage artistique** figure skating

patrie f country

patron m boss

patte f foot *(of bird)*; paw

pause-café f coffee break

payer to pay (for); **se faire payer** to cash

pays m country; region; town

Pays-Bas m pl Netherlands

P.C.V. (payable chez vous); téléphoner en P.C.V. to telephone collect, to call collect

pêche f fishing; peach; **aller à la pêche** to go fishing

peigne m comb

se peigner to comb one's hair

peine f pain; effort, trouble; **valoir la peine** to be worth the effort

pellicule f film

pendant during; for *(time)*; while; **pendant que** while

pénicilline f penicillin

pensée f thought; **avec toi par la pensée** thinking of you

penser (à; de) to think (of; about)

perdre to lose

se perdre to get lost

perdu *(pp of* **perdre***)*

père m father

Père Nöel Santa Claus

permettre (de) to permit

permis permitted, allowed *(pp of* **permettre***)*

permis m permit; license; **permis de conduire** driver's license; **permis d'apprenti conducteur** learner's permit *(driving)*

perruche f parakeet

perruque f wig

personnage m personage; character

personne f person; self; no one, nobody; pl people

personnel *(f* **personnelle***)* personal

peser to weigh

petit small

petit déjeuner m breakfast

peu little; **à peu près** about, around, approximately

peur f fear; **avoir peur** to be afraid; **de peur que (ne)** for fear that, lest; **faire peur à** to frighten

peut-être perhaps

pharmacie f pharmacy, drugstore

pharmacien m pharmacist

photo f photograph

phrase f sentence

piano m piano; **jouer du piano** to play piano

pièce f coin; room; **pièce de monnaie** coin

pied m foot; **à pied** on foot, by foot; **faire de longues promenades à pied** to take long walks, to hike; **coup de pied** kick

pique-nique m picnic; **faire un pique-nique** to picnic

pilule f pill; **boîte à pilules** pill box

piqûre f injection; **faire une piqûre** to give an injection

pire worse; worst

piscine f swimming pool

piste f path; ski run

placard m cupboard; closet

place f place; seat; **être à la place de** to be in the place of, to be in someone's place

plage f beach

plaindre to pity

se plaindre to complain

plaire to please; **s'il vous plaît** please

plaisir m pleasure; **faire plaisir à** to please; **jusqu'à mon plaisir** as much as I want

planche f board; plank; **planche de surf** surfboard

plancher m floor

plaque f plate; **plaque minéralogique** license plate

plein full; **être en plein air** to be out in the fresh air; **à plein temps** full-time *(job)*; **faire le plein** to fill 'er up

pleurer to cry

pleuvoir to rain; **il pleut** it's raining; **il pleut à torrents** it's pouring

plume f pen

plumer to pluck, to plume

plus (de) more; most; **ne... plus** no longer, no more; **plus... que** more . . . than

plusieurs several; **il y en a plusieurs** there are several of them

pneu m tire

pneumatique pneumatic; **matelas** *(m)* **pneumatique** air mattress

poche f pocket; **argent de poche** pocket money

poème m poem

poète m poet

point m point; **à point** medium *(cooked meat)*; **point de vue** point of view

pois m pea; **petits pois** green peas

poisson m fish; **poisson rouge** goldfish

police f police; policy

policier m detective story, police film

poliment politely

pomme f apple; **pomme de terre** potato; **pommes frites** French-fried potatoes

pompier m fireman

pont m bridge

porte f door

porte-bonheur m good-luck charm

porte-clés m key chain, key ring

portefeuille m wallet

porte-monnaie m change purse

porter to carry; to wear; **se porter** to feel *(health)*

posé asked; placed

poser to put, to place; **poser une question** to ask a question

posséder to own

possessif *(f* **possessive***)* possessive

poste f post office; **bureau** *(m)* **de poste** post office; **poste restante** general delivery **poste** m job, position; television / radio set; extension *(telephone)*; radio station

poster to mail

postiche m hairpiece

postier m *(f* **postière***)* postal clerk

potable drinkable

poule f hen

poulet m chicken

pour for

pourboire m tip

pourquoi why

pourvu que provided that

pousser to push

poussière f dust

pouvoir to be able, can; **il se peut que** perhaps; **puis-je?** may I?

pratique practical

pratiquer to play *(sports)*

préavis m advance warning; **avec préavis** person-to-person *(telephone)*

précéder to precede

précis exactly; **il est huit heures précises** it is exactly eight o'clock

préféré favorite

préférence f preference, choice; opinion

préférer to prefer

premier (*f* **première**) first; **en première** first-class
prendre to take; to pick up; to get (*some one*); to have; eat (*food*); to drink (*beverage*); to catch (*fish*); **prendre vos repas** to eat your meals
prénom *m* first name
préparer to prepare; **se préparer** to get ready
près near; **près de** near; **à peu près** about, around, approximately
presbyte far-sighted
présent present (*tense*); **au présent** in the present (*tense*)
présenter to present, introduce
président *m* president
pressé in a hurry
se presser to hurry
prêt ready
prêter to lend
prier to request; **je vous prie** please
printemps *m* spring; **au printemps** in the springtime
pris (*pp* of **prendre**)
prise de courant *f* electric outlet
prix *m* price
problème *m* problem
prochain next
proche near; **le (la) plus proche** the nearest
produit *m* product; **produits de beauté** cosmetics
professeur *m* professor, teacher; **professeur de français** French teacher
profondément deeply
progrès *m* progress; **faire des progrès** to make progress
projet *m* project; **les projets** plans
promenade *f* promenade; walk; ride; **faire de longues promenades à pied** to take long walks, to hike
se promener to go for a walk, take a walk
pronom *m* pronoun
pronominal (*pl* **pronominaux**) reflexive (*verbs*)
propre clean
propriétaire *m, f* owner
propriété *f* property, grounds
pruneau *m* prune
publicité *f* commercials (*television*)
puce *f* flea
puis then
puisque since
puissance *f* power

quai *m* wharf, pier, embankment, platform
qualité *f* quality; disposition, nature
quand when
quand même though; just the same
quarante forty
quartier *m* neighborhood; area
quatre four; **quatre-pièces** *m* four-room apartment
quatrième fourth
que that; what; **que** + *independ clause* how . . .!; **ne... que** only
quel (*f* **quelle**) which, what; what sort of; **quel** + *noun* what a . . .
quelque some, a few; **quelque chose** something; **quelque chose d'autre** something else
quelques(-uns) some; a few; several
quelqu'un someone, somebody
qu'est-ce que what; **qu'est-ce que c'est?** what is it?, what is this?
qu'est-ce qui what
qui who, whom; which; that; **qui est-ce que** whom; **à qui** to whom, whose; **à qui est-ce?** whose is this?
quincaillerie *f* hardware store
quitter to leave
quoi what; **quoi d'autre?** what else?

raccommoder to mend
raccrocher to hang up the receiver
raconter to relate, talk about, tell (about)
radiateur *m* radiator
radio *f* radio
radis *m* radish
raie *f* part (*hair*)
raison *f* reason
raisonnable reasonable
râpé grated
rappeler to call back
rarement rarely
se raser to shave
rasoir *m* razor
rassurer to reassure
ravissant ravishing
rayon *m* department (*in a store*)
réagir to react
réalisation *f* production
réaliser to realize; to come to pass
récemment recently
réception *f* reception desk (*of a hotel*)
recette *f* recipe; collection
recevoir to receive; **recevoir un coup de téléphone** to receive a phone call; **recevoir quelqu'un** to see someone
recommandé registered (*mail*)
recommander to recommend
recommencer to begin again
reçu (*pp* of **recevoir**)
réfléchir to reflect
réfrigérateur *m* refrigerator
refuser to refuse
regarder to look, to look at; **regarder par la fenêtre** to look out the window
régime *m* diet; **suivre un régime** to be on a diet
régler to adjust
regretter to be sorry
régulièrement regularly
remarquer to notice
remercier to thank
remettre to put back on
remise *f* delivery
remplacer to replace
remplir to fill (out)
remporter to carry off; to win
rencontre *f* meeting; clash
rencontrer to meet
rendez-vous *m* meeting; **avoir rendez-vous** to have a meeting; to have an appointment, a date
rendre to give back; **se rendre à** to go to, get to; **se rendre compte** to realize
renouveau *m* revival
renseignement *m* information; **bureau** (*m*) **de renseignements** information office; **service** (*m*) **des renseignements** directory assistance
se renseigner to get information
rentrer to go home
renverser to spill
réparation *f* repair
réparer to repair; **faire réparer** to have repaired
repas meal
repasser to iron; **repasser l'examen** to take the exam over
répertoire *m* repertory; **répertoire (d')adresses** address book
répéter to repeat
répliquer to respond
répondre to answer
réponse *f* answer
repos *m* rest
se reposer to rest
repousser to grow again
réserver to reserve
résidence *f* residence; **résidence universitaire** university residence, dormitory

résolu (*pp* of **résoudre**)
résoudre to resolve
respirer to breathe
ressembler (à) to resemble
ressentir to feel
rester to remain, to stay; **il me reste** I still have; **il vous reste assez de temps pour** you still have enough time to
résultat *m* result
retard *m* delay; slowness; **arriver en retard** to arrive late; **avoir du retard** to be late (*train, bus, plane*); **être en retard** to be late
retarder to be slow; **ma montre retarde** my watch is slow
retour *m* return; **billet aller retour** round-trip ticket; **être de retour** to be back
retrait *m* withdrawal; **retrait de permis de conduire** suspension of driver's license
retraite *f* retreat; retirement; **à la retraite** retired
réussir to succeed; **réussir à un examen** to pass an examination
rêve *m* dream
se réveiller to wake up
revenir to return
révérence *f* curtsy
revoir to see again; **au revoir** good-by
revue *f* magazine, review
rez-de-chaussée *m* ground floor, street level
rhume *m* cold; **rhume des foins** hay fever
rideau *m* curtain
ridicule ridiculous
rien nothing; **sans rien dire** without saying anything
rire to laugh
riz *m* rice
robe *f* dress
rocher *m* rock
roi *m* king
roman *m* novel
rond round; **tout en rond** all in a circle
rosbif *m* roastbeef
rossignol *m* nightingale
rouge red; **poisson (*m*) rouge** goldfish
rougeole *f* measles
rougir to blush
rouler to go (*speed of car*)
route *f* road; **code de la route** traffic regulations
routier (*f* **routière**) road; **carte routière** road map

roux (*f* **rousse**) red, reddish, auburn (*hair*)
rue *f* street
Russie *f* Russia

sa his, hers
sac *m* bag; **sac de couchage** sleeping bag; **sac à main** handbag, purse
saignant bleeding; rare (*cooked meat*)
saigner to bleed
saison *f* season; **pour la saison** for this time of year
sale dirty
salle *f* room; **salle à manger** dining room; **salle d'attente** waiting room; **salle de bains** bathroom; **salle de classe** classroom; **salle de séjour** living room
salon (*m*) **de beauté** beauty parlor
saluer to salute; to bow (to); to greet
salut *m* bow; greeting; salute; **salut!** Hi!; 'Bye!
sang *m* blood
sanglant bloody, cruel
sans without; **sans rien dire** without saying anything
santé *f* health; **à votre santé** to your health (*drinking toast*)
sauce *f* sauce; **sauce tomate** ketchup
saucisson *m* sausage
saumon *m* salmon; **saumon fumé** smoked salmon, lox
sauter to jump
savoir to know; to know how to; **savoir jouer** to know how to play
savon *m* soap
sec (*f* **sèche**) dry; **être en panne sèche** to run out of gas; **nettoyer à sec** to dry clean
second second; **en seconde** second-class
secondaire secondary; **faire ses études secondaires** to go to high school
secrétaire *m, f* secretary
sécurité *f* security; **ceinture de sécurité** seat belt
séjour *m* stay, visit; **salle (*f*) de séjour** living room
séjourner to stay
sel *m* salt
selon according to; **selon le cas** accordingly

semaine *f* week; **au cours de la semaine** during the week; **en semaine** during the week
sénateur *m* senator
sensible sensitive
sentir to feel; to smell; **se sentir** to feel (*health*)
séparément separately
sept seven
sérieux (*f* **sérieuse**) serious
serveuse *f* waitress
service *m* service; department; **service des renseignements** directory assistance
serviette *f* napkin; towel; briefcase; **serviette de bain** bath towel
servir to serve; **se servir de** to use; **en vous servant de** using
ses *pl* his, hers
seul alone; only
si so; as; if
signe *m* sign
signer to sign
sillon *m* furrow
simplement simply
sincère sincere
six six
ski *m* ski; skiing; **faire du ski** to go skiing; **faire du ski nautique** to go water skiing; **station de ski** ski resort
smoking *m* dinner jacket
sœur *f* sister
soif *f* thirst; **avoir soif** to be thirsty
soir *m* evening; **ce soir** this evening, tonight; **hier soir** last night; **six heures du soir** six o'clock in the evening
soirée *f* evening; party
soldat *m* soldier
solde *m* sale; **en solde** on sale
soleil *m* sun; **lunettes de soleil** sunglasses; **se faire bronzer au soleil** to get a suntan
sombre dark
somme *f* sum
son his, hers
sonner to ring
sort *m* fate, destiny, lot
sorte *f* sort, kind; **de la sorte** this way
sortie *f* exit
sortir to go out; to leave
soudain suddenly
souhaiter to wish
souligné underlined
soupe *f* soup
sous under
sous-titré subtitled

se souvenir de to remember

souvent often

soyez *(imperative of* **être**); **soyez sérieux!** be serious!

spacieux *(f* **spacieuse**) spacious

spécial special

spécialité *f* specialty

sport *m* sport, sports; **faire du sport** to play sports; **sports d'hiver** winter sports; **sports nautiques** water sports

sportif *(f* **sportive**) athletic

standardiste *m, f* switchboard operator; telephone operator

station *f* station; **station de métro** subway station; **station de ski** ski resort; **station-service** service station; **station de taxi** taxi stand

stationner to park; **défense de stationner** no parking

studio *m* studio apartment, one-room apartment

stylo *m* pen

subir to undergo

subjonctif *m* subjunctive

substantif *m* noun

succès *m* success; **avec succès** successfully

sucre *m* sugar

sucré sweet

suggérer to suggest

Suisse *f* Switzerland

suite *f* continuation; conclusion; **tout de suite** at once, immediately

suivant following

suivi (de) followed (by)

suivre to follow; **faire suivre le courrier** to have the mail forwarded; **suivre un cours** to take a course; **suivre un régime** to be on a diet

sujet *adj (f* **sujette**) subject

sujet *m* subject; **au sujet de** about; **à quel sujet?** concerning what?

supermarché *m* supermarket

super *m* high-test gasoline

sur on, upon

sympathique nice, likeable

syndicat d'initiative *m* tourist office

synthèse *f* synthesis

ta your

tabac *m* tobacco

tabatière *f* snuff box

table *f* table; **se mettre à table** to sit down at the table

tableau noir *m* blackboard

tablette *f* tablet

tache *f* spot, stain

taille *f* height, size; waist, waist-line; **de taille moyenne** of average height

tailleur *m* woman's suit

tante *f* aunt

tapis *m* rug

tard late

tarder (à) to delay (in)

teinturerie *f* dry cleaner's

téléphone *m* telephone; **coup** *(m)* **de téléphone** phone call

téléphoner to call; **téléphoner en P.C.V.** to call collect; **téléphoner avec préavis** to call person-to-person

télévision *f* television; **poste** *(m)* **de télévision** television set

tellement so much, as much

temps *m* time; tense; weather; **quel temps fait-il?** what's the weather like?; **de temps en temps** from time to time; **il vous reste assez de temps pour** you still have enough time to; **ces temps-ci** these days, recently; **à temps** on time; **à plein temps** full-time *(employment)*; **à mi-temps** (part-time *(employment)*)

tendance *f* tendency; **avoir tendance à** to tend to

tenir to hold; to keep; **tenir à** to insist upon; **tenir à ce que** to insist that

terminer to finish; **se terminer** to end

terrain *m* ground; terrain; **terrain de camping** camping ground

terrasse *f* terrace

tes your

tête *f* head; **se laver la tête** to wash one's hair

thé *m* tea

thon *m* tuna

tigre *m* tiger

timbre *m* stamp

tirer to pull; to take; to draw *(lots)*

tiroir *m* drawer

tissu *m* fabric, material; **en quel tissu est votre...?** what fabric is your . . . made of?

titulaire *m, f* holder *(of passport)*

toi you *(familiar form)*

toilettes *f pl* restroom(s), washroom(s)

tomate *f* tomato

tomber to fall; **tomber malade** to get sick; to fall ill

ton your

tondeuse *f* mower

tonner to thunder

torrent *m* torrent; **il pleut à torrents** it's pouring

tortue *f* turtle

tôt early; **il est tôt** it's early

toucher to cash *(a check)*; **toucher un chèque** to cash a check

toujours always

tour *f* tower; **la Tour Eiffel** the Eiffel Tower

tour *m* turn; tour; trick; **faire le tour du monde** to go around the world; **faire un tour en auto** to go for a drive

tousser to cough

tout *(m pl* **tous**, *f* **toute**) every, each, all; *adv* completely, entirely; *pron* all; everything; **c'est tout?** is that all? **en tout** in total; **pas du tout** not at all; **tous deux** both (of us, of you, of them); **tous les jours** every day, daily; **tout ce que** everything that, all that; **tout ce qui** everything that, all that; **tout de suite** at once, immediately, right away; **tout droit** straight ahead; **tout en rond** all in a circle; **toute la journée** all day; **tout le monde** everybody, everyone; **tout d'un coup** all of a sudden, suddenly

toux *f* cough

traduire to translate

traduit *(pp of* **traduire**)

train *m* train; **en train de** in the process of

traire to milk

trait d'union *m* hyphen

tranquille peaceful, quiet

transformer (en) to transform, change (into)

travail *m* work

travailler to work

travailleur hard-working

tremper to dunk

très very

triste sad

trois three

troisième third (one)

trop (de) too; too much, too many

trou *m* hole

trouver to find; **bureau des objets trouvés** lost and found; **comment trouvez-vous ce bateau?** what do you think of this boat?; **se trouver** to be, to be located

tu you *(familiar form)*

tyrannie *f* tyranny

un (*f* **une**) a, an; one
uniquement only
université *f* university

vacances *f pl* vacation; **en vacances** on vacation
vache *f* cow
vaisselle *f* dishes; **faire la vaisselle** to wash the dishes
valet *m* valet; **valet de chambre** valet
valise *f* suitcase
valoir to be worth; **valoir la peine** to be worth the effort; **valoir mieux** to be better
varicelle *f* chicken pox
veau *m* veal
vécu (*pp* of **vivre**)
veille *f* the evening before
vélomoteur *m* motorbike
vendeur *m* salesman
vendeuse *f* saleslady
vendre to sell
venir to come; **venir de** to (have) just
vent *m* wind
venu (*pp* of **venir**)
verbe *m* verb
vérifier to check
vérité *f* truth
verre *m* glass; **verres de contact** contact lenses
vers to, toward

verser to pour; **verser une caution** to leave a deposit, to put down a security payment
verso *m* verso; **au verso** on the back
vert green
vêtements *m pl* clothing, clothes
vexant annoying
viande *f* meat
vie *f* life; **c'est la vie!** that's life!
vieux (*f* **vieille**) old
vilain lowly, ugly, nasty
ville *f* city; **en ville** downtown, in town
vin *m* wine
vingt twenty
visage *m* face
visiter to visit, see (*a place*)
vitamine *f* vitamin
vite fast, quickly
vivre to live
vivres *m pl* provisions
vocabulaire *m* vocabulary
voici here is, here are
voilà here is, there is; here are; there are; that's
voile *f* sail, sailboat; **bateau à voiles** sailboat
voir to see
voisin *m* (*f* **voisine**) neighbor
voiture *f* car
vol *m* flight
volet *m* shutter
vos *pl* your

votre your, yours
vouloir to wish, want; **vouloir dire** to mean; **je voudrais** I would like; **veuillez** + *inf.* please; **voulez-vous** + *inf.* kindly; please
vous you; **c'est à vous** it's yours; **vous-même** yourself
voyage *m* voyage, trip; **agence** (*f*) **de voyages** travel agency; **agent** (*m*) **de voyage** travel agent; **faire un voyage** to take a trip, to travel; **en voyage** on a trip, traveling
voyager to travel
voyageur *m* traveler, passenger
vrai true
vraiment truly, really
vu (*pp* of **voir**)

wagon *m* railroad car; **wagon-restaurant** restaurant car
week-end *m* weekend
western *m* western movie, cowboy movie
whisky *m* whiskey

y there, to that place; in it; on it; **il y a** there is, there are; **y a-t-il?** is there?, are there?
yeux *m pl* eyes; **avoir les yeux bleus** to have blue eyes

GRAMMATICAL INDEX

SUBJECT INDEX

PHOTO CREDITS